WAKEUP CALL
FROM MEXICO

For Bob DiFazio —
I suspect you will
enjoy & find this
book worth your time
to represent.
all the best —

Wilson Beck

WAKEUP CALL FROM MEXICO

An Historical and Contemporary Understanding
of Mexico's Pandemic Violence, Drug War,
Kidnappings, and Illegal Immigration; How to
Safeguard America
as Mexico Spirals toward Chaos

WILSON BECK
MuchoPress
USA

Published by MuchoPress

USA

ISBN: 978-0-692-00340-4

Printed in the United States of America

Contents

Introduction

How can two 21st century cultures, two countries, two peoples who have coexisted side by side for more than two hundred years, who are separated only by an imaginary line in the desert and a shallow river which can be waded across still be so drastically dissimilar? The differences are so great that one of the two cultures has begun building walls along the desert floor in order to keep the citizens of the other culture out. One culture is recognized as one of the most vibrant, innovative, and freest places to live on planet earth. The other is teetering on the brink of becoming a failed state under the weight of ubiquitous poverty, lawlessness, population desertion, an epidemic of kidnappings, and a bloody, merciless, drug-industry induced civil war.

For more than forty years Mexico has been my second country or second home. I have travelled its country sides from the Chihuahuan and Sonoran Deserts in the north to its waterfall-fed tropical forests in Chiapas. I know its beautiful Pacific beaches from Oaxaca to Baja. After surfing the beaches at San Blas as a teenager I became enchanted with Mexico, and decided to study Pre-Columbian archaeology in school. My interests led me all over Mexico. I visited many of the fantastic ruins of the Central Valley of Mexico and the Mayan ruins in the south. I learned Spanish and became a true Mexicophile. Eventually my work led me to Mexico City, and I later retired to the quixotic state of Guanajuato in 1999. *Mexico Lindo* (Beautiful Mexico) had always been very special to me. I built a home there and began fulfilling the requirements of becoming a Mexican citizen.

In 2000 Vicente Fox was elected as president of Mexico in what were the first ever truly democratic multi-party elections in Mexican history. But was a shift towards democracy in 2000 too little, too late? Will Mexico's latest flirtation with democracy end in failure as it always has in the past? Democracy was never realized after the 1810 War of Independence from Spain. Nor was it implemented after the death of Benito Juárez, Mexico's Abraham Lincolnesque liberator, in 1867. Nor did Mexico choose the path of true democracy after paying the price of more than one million of its citizens in its bloody ten year civil war of 1910-1920. Every time Mexico has reached its hand towards democracy and social equality the sword of greed and barbarism has lopped it off. Now once again as Mexico has taken a bold step towards democracy the black hand of the drug cartels and the intolerant attitudes of the millions of impoverished are sending the country spiraling towards failure.

I watched the fabric begin to unfurl with the violent strikes in Oaxaca in 2005, and the almost disastrous national elections to seat the new president in 2006. As democracy fought for its existence prior to the turn of the century and Fox's victorious election, chaos spread across the country. Mexicans were leaving the country for the U.S. by the millions. Perhaps as many as 2 million per year were trying to exit the country. Many demographers believe that as many as 20 per cent of the total population left Mexico for the U.S. during the late nineties and early 21st century. The Mexican drug industry matured and went global. An industry which once grew and supplied marijuana to the U.S. has morphed into a global industry. Mexican drug cartels now own marijuana production, wholesale distribution, and retail sales in the U.S. They also control the majority of the marijuana operations which grow the product inside the U.S. They have usurped control of the cocaine industry from the Colombians and now own a major part of the Colombian, Peruvian, and Bolivian production of the product. They control 100 per cent of cocaine distribution to the U.S. and probably 85 per cent of the retail sales within the U.S. borders. Within in the last three years the same cartels have grabbed control of the methamphetamine industry. They have shipped production from the U.S. to Mexico and like the marijuana and cocaine industry now control wholesale distribution and retail sales within the U.S. It does not stop there. The cartels have affixed their sights on the Asian heroine market. Poppy fields have been planted in remote regions of northwest Mexico and murderous agents and investors are afield in Asia trying to reroute the heroine trade through Mexico to the U.S. It is difficult to put an exact number on the billions of dollars that is being generated on a yearly basis by the drug cartels but it probably exceeds 50 billion dollars. It most likely is larger than Mexico's petrochemical industry making it the country's largest industry.

Why was *Mexico Lindo* suddenly turning into such a violent and corrupt culture? Why had Mexico suddenly become the *Kidnapping Capital* of the world? Democracy was at hand, and yet the citizenry, fearful, jobless, and hopeless were leaving by the millions. Why had Mexico not been able to develop an equitable culture where its citizenry could enjoy a decent standard of living and a modern education? Why is eighty percent of the Mexican population still dirt poor? Why is the cultural divide between the U.S. and Mexico so great? I wanted to answer these questions.

To do so I immersed myself in the Pre-Columbian and modern Mexican history that I had studied in my university years. I wanted to marry an historical perspective with my experience of the last ten years of living in Mexico with the current disastrous downwardly spiraling direction the culture is taking. I felt that it would be important to re-investigate Mexican history in order to understand why there are so many differences in the evolution of two European-derived cultures which have come to dominate the U.S. and Mexico. The obvious starting point for understanding Mexico was at the end of Mexico's Golden Age. I reasoned that if it were possible for a people to develop into one of the world's most prolific cultures with astounding developments in architecture, mathematics, science, language, and agriculture over a six hundred year peaceful advancement surely assimilation with an equally or more advanced European culture would be not only possible but probable. But Mexico's history shows us that the people who developed the Golden Age of Mexico were not the Aztecs who collided in the 16th century with the Spaniards. The Aztecs were a brutal, barbarian race who had immigrated into the central Valley of Mexico over a two century period much the same way modern Mexicans are immigrating into the U.S. In other words, what was a small acceptable trickle sixty years ago has become an unpredictable deluge today in the U.S. the same as it was in the central Valley of Mexico one thousand years ago.

The marriage of the European and Mexican produced quite a different offspring than it did between the European and the Native North American. The biggest reason is attributable to the fact that genocide was enacted in the north and serfdom was introduced in the south. In other words, the native North Americans were either killed or sequestered to reservations while the Aztecs, Mayans, and others were bred and controlled for the value of their labor. But both the Americans and the Mexicans overthrew the domination of their European landlords and established free democracies in the turn of the 19th century right? The Americans fought their war of independence in 1776, won, and established a democracy. The Mexicans fought their war for independence in 1810, won, and instead of establishing a democracy continued with a state of serfdom where the entire country was controlled by less than five per cent of the population.

As the U.S. marched into the future after their war for independence and became one of the most vibrant of cultures in human history, Mexico stagnated under a system of corruption and inequality which produced a culture with an infrastructure comparable to third world countries around the globe. It marched forward century after century under the false guise of a democracy while it was being ruled by a one-party political machine which guaranteed riches for the wealthy and very little opportunity for anyone else. Hatred and bitterness grew over the decades between the two countries as Mexico lost more than one-third of its sovereign territory to its wily neighbors to the north. As the chasm grew between the U.S. and Mexico so did the hatred and mistrust grow between its citizenry.

Now the worst possible scenario exists between two neighbors. The two countries need each other but hate and suspect each other of treachery. For example, Mexico needs U.S. investment in its faltering energy industry but history has taught the Mexicans to be suspicious of American involvement in Mexican affairs. They have therefore legislatively outlawed foreign investment in their oil industry. The Americans need Mexican labor during various economic cycles but cannot decide on a proper administrative approach in which to manage migrant workers. The result is disastrous. Millions of untrained, uneducated, unwanted workers who do not have the proper or best qualifications to meet the employment demand are engulfing the U.S. Millions eventually end up on the welfare rolls. At the same time NAFTA is being improperly implemented and has turned into a 75 billion negative trade deficit for the U.S. The perfect symbiotic relationship can exist between Mexico and the U.S. But, both governments and respective citizenry must change their mindsets and habits in order to bring about change and to end the two hundred years of mutual disrespect that has existed between the two countries.

I have known and loved Mexico for four decades. After writing this book I have come to the conclusion that if the U.S. and Mexico do not start down a new path of cooperation Mexico will become a failed state within ten years. Democracy will fade away as it has historically, the few very wealthy Mexicans will continue to control the country, and the poor, uneducated millions will continue to seek refuge in the U.S. This will obviously be disastrous for Mexico, but it will also be disastrous for the U.S. The negative impact to the U.S. culture that will be perpetuated by the 15 or 20 million uneducated, untrained Mexicans that are already in the U.S. is almost inevitable. But if the trend of unrestricted, illegal immigration is allowed to continue the problems in crime and downward degradation of the culture in general could become the largest single detriment to the U.S. recuperating from its worst economic crisis since the Great Depression. We only need to look towards California, our nation's bellwether, to see the results of decades of unrestricted, illegal immigration of uneducated, untrained poor in order to forecast what lies ahead for the rest of the union. The last decade has seen an unprecedented spread of illegal immigration to all fifty states of the union.

As I finished writing this book and watched Barack Obama's administration take office, I was extremely disappointed to see their lack of focus on the importance of Mexican-American affairs. As this book was going through editorial scrutiny in March and April, however, the American press and eventually the Obama administration began to respond to the alarming level of violence that is occurring in Mexico. Sadly, nothing new had happened in Mexico in March and April of 2009 relative to violence. The state of chaotic behavior and large scale violence has been unabated and increasing since 2006. But suddenly in late March, the U.S. press decided to start covering the mayhem. Perhaps in response to the press coverage or perhaps to a sudden realization of the gravity of the situation, Barack Obama flew to Mexico and met with President Felipe Calderón in April. It appears that President Obama is a quick study. I am heartened to see him take the initial steps that are necessary in order to address the plethora of Mexican-American problems.

I wrote this book because I am convinced that if Mexico continues its downward spiral towards failure or even continues along its current path which is fraught with violence and corruption the outcome will be disastrous for both the U.S. and Mexico. I do not want to see this happen. I know it can be stopped. It can be changed. I love both countries. I want to see Mexico return *to Mexico Lindo*. I want to see the illegal drug industry and arms industry curtailed. I want to see an immigration policy put in place that strengthens the rights of migrating workers and insures the host country of the right to choose the type of immigrants that can eventually help contribute to the new growth of a viable U.S. economy and nation not destroy it. In reality the impact of unbridled, uncontrolled, immigration is not so different than the negative impact the U.S. experienced in 1980 after the Mariel Bay immigration from Cuba multiplied ten thousand times. I want to see a rational plan implemented which humanely addresses the 15 or 20 million illegal immigrants that are already in the U.S. The final chapter of this book is titled, 'The Best Response to a Chaotic Situation'. In it I offer reasonable solutions to many of the complex problems that exist between the U.S. and Mexico. I think now is an historic opportunity for the Mexican and American governments and citizenry to unite with 21st century ideas that can eradicate the decades and centuries old problems that continue to plague both countries.

I

America's Wakeup Call from Mexico

On the morning of September 8, 2006, I became convinced that Mexico was entering a perilous new era. In a sense it seemed to be returning to its dangerous past. It felt as if the country were slipping out of control. I was reading the morning editions of Mexico City's daily newspapers over coffee. The top story was an incredibly ugly tale of decapitated heads being rolled out of a plastic bag onto a dance floor in a discotheque in Uruapan, Michoacán, Mexico. Surprisingly the horrifying photos of five severed heads and accompanying lead stories paralleled the chapter in Bernal Díaz's book, <u>The Conquest of New Spain,</u> that I was rereading the previous night. The articles described the ongoing battle between the anti-narcotic forces of the President of Mexico, Vicente Fox, and the drug cartels in the state of Michoacán. Drug cartel mercenaries, either La Familia or Los Zetas, had captured, tortured, and decapitated, five young men. This was a continuing trend that had started in Acapulco five months earlier when two police officers were first tortured, then their heads after being hacked-off, were stuck on fence posts in front of the governor's office. Although this was a new trend, the five decapitated victims in Uruapan pushed the total to twenty-six for the year. The heads were accompanied by notes taunting the authorities and/or warning their adversaries of the danger of interfering with the cartel's drug business. These acts were brutal, defiant, and shocking. The photos of the grotesque, bloody heads on the floor of the Uruapan discotheque, Sol y Sombra, were on the front page of every major newspaper across Mexico. Suddenly, here in Mexico, heads were being lopped-off at a rate faster than they were in Iraq. The Al-Qaeda with all their online bravado of video beheadings, sharp knives, and ski-masked disguises are not half as brutal as these professionally-trained Zeta mercenaries. After twenty-six gruesome beheadings in less than five months fear was beginning to grip the country. Mexico was in the first months of what would be its continuing spiral towards chaos.

I was struck not only by the brutality of the act but by the defiant nature it exuded. The drug-cartel's intent in 2006 and today is identical to that of the Aztec's as described in Díaz's account of the Aztec's counter-attack on the Spanish conquistadors as they lay siege to Tenochtitlán (current day Mexico City) in 1521. It is total intimidation based on fear. The Spanish invaders had occupied Tenochtitlán for six months but eventually the Aztecs reclaimed their capital. Later the Spaniards lay siege to the city in their attempt to capture it a second time. There were many battles during the three-month siege of the city which followed. The Aztecs captured sixty-six of Hernán Cortés' men on one particular skirmish. After dark, the Spaniards were sacrificed on the altars of Huichilobos, the god of war. The common Aztec sacrificial method was employed. In other words, the Spaniard's hearts were literally cut from their chests while they were still alive. Afterwards they were beheaded and dismembered. Montezuma's Aztec warriors grilled some of the arms and legs over an open fire and after partially eating the flesh flung the arms, legs, and severed heads over the fortified embankments which separated them from the conquistadors. Díaz described how many of Cortés's brave explorers were overwhelmed and became sick. The Aztec warriors taunted the Spaniards throughout the night, assuring them that their flesh would soon be roasted and eaten as well. Many of the other decapitated heads were taken to the Spanish contingents whom were safeguarding each of the causeways which entered the great city of Tenochtitlán. The heads were rolled out of bags in front of the Spaniards, the same way they were thrown onto the barroom floor in Uruapan, in September 2006. As I read the article describing the brutality in Uruapan, I understood that the Aztec legacy is still alive and well in 21st century Mexico.

In effect, the drug cartels of Michoacán were communicating to President Fox and are now telling President Calderón and his federal narcotics police the same thing as was demonstrated centuries earlier in Tenochtitlán. They are demonstrating the same defiance for and brutality against opponents that has been a characteristic of their ancestry for over 1000 years. Since President Felipe Calderón took office in December 2006, more than 10,000 people have been killed in the drug wars of Mexico. Thousands more are suspected to have been killed. But, in rural Mexico and in the enormous, over-populated barrios of Mexico City, Juárez, Tijuana, Guadalajara, and Monterrey millions of Mexicans are born, live, and die without being recorded in the official census or being counted in other population statistics. Mass graves with unidentified bodies have been discovered from Chiapas to Chihuahua. In January of 2009, a drug soldier known as the 'Stew Maker' confessed after being captured by police. He claimed to have boiled more than three hundred bodies in 55-gallon drums with acid in Tijuana in 2008. He was under orders from his drug boss. It is widely believed that the actual drug related killings in the first 24 months of the Calderón presidency was probably higher than ten thousand.

In 2009, Mexico, in general, borders on being lawless. In many ways it is a country in chaos. As the economic crisis has engulfed the world, the drug industry and organized crime have engulfed Mexico. The majority of the population still lacks a high school education, 25 percent or more lack any formal education at all. Eighty-five percent of the population can be considered very poor under any reasonable definition of 21st century standards. In almost every way Mexico is a complete anomaly when compared to its neighbor to the north, the United States of America (U.S.). At this critical time in Mexico's battle to safeguard its democracy and viability as a nation against its cancer, organized crime, the disease is unabatedly spreading into the U.S. In January 2009, the FBI and Department of Justice released their study on crime and criminal gangs. It is astounding! They report that organized criminal gangs are growing in unprecedented numbers and now have more than 1.1 million members in 42 of 50 states nationwide. Both agencies are attributing 70 to 80 percent of the nation's total crime to these organized criminal gangs. The astounding part of their report, is that from state to state, they report, organized criminal gang activity has followed the migration path of illegal immigrant workers who are crossing our southern border. In other words, as illegal immigrant workers moved into new geographical areas in the last ten years they brought organized crime with them. And, the scary part of this situation is the U.S. government is looking the other way!

We *must* start asking some serious questions in the U.S. We *must* understand what is happening in Mexico. Why has *Mexico Lindo* (Beautiful Mexico) become *Mexico Peligroso* (Dangerous Mexico)? Why is there such a disparity between two cultures which are physically separated by only a river, the Rio Grande, which can often be waded across and a desert which is also easily crossed? Why does one culture lead the world, or at least successfully compete, in areas such as high-technology, education, art, standard of living, quality of life, science, math, sports, manufacturing, and so many other categories? Yet the other culture is in a quagmire of poverty, crime, and has an educational system that perennially rates near the bottom in world-wide comparisons. Why is Mexican violence so out-of-hand and illegal immigration so out-of-control that the U.S. is convinced that it must build a border fence between the two countries? Why has 15 to 20 percent of the Mexican population (15 of 110 million) illegally immigrated to the U.S., unable to survive in their own country? Why does the vast majority of the Mexican population refuse to subjugate themselves to the *rule of law*? Why does the Mexican legal system still refuse to modernize and become a system which operates under a true concept of *rule of law*? Why does a country with more than 110 million people still only have the capacity to win two medals during the 2008 Beijing Olympics? Why does one of the poorest countries on planet earth have one of the highest numbers of millionaires per capita? How can Mexico continue to accept the disproportionate distribution of wealth which produces one of the richest men in the world, Carlos Slim, on one extreme, while 85 million Mexicans live in poverty on the other? Why does Mexico garner the number one world-wide ranking in kidnappings? Why has there not been a more natural osmosis of cultural exchange between the U.S. and Mexico? Why does Mexico City continue to be one of the most dangerous, polluted, unlivable cities in the world? Why in the 21st century is democracy still struggling to succeed in Mexico? Why does Mexico have one of the highest ratios of homicides per capita in the world? Why is there so much hate and distrust between Mexicans and Americans? Why are the drug cartels severing heads in a defiant attempt to scare the government and common citizenry into submission? Why do so many basic differences exist between the Mexican and U.S. value systems? Why does Mexican popular country music glamorize and romanticize the savage, murderous lives of drug kingpins? Why has each culture evolved so differently since the arrival of the Europeans to the western hemisphere? Why are Mexicans content to live off billions of dollars of remittances sent back by family members who are illegally working in the U.S., instead of developing their own potential in Mexico? How can Mexico develop an illegal drug business, as their second or perhaps largest industry, which is destroying the lives of their citizenry and their neighbors in the U.S.? Why at the beginning of the 21st century is Mexico once again teetering on the brink of civil war and/or chaos?

How can the U.S. continue to turn a blind eye towards its closest neighbor, its third largest trade partner, its second largest supplier of energy? How can the U.S. continue to ignore a hapless population that is quickly morphing into one quarter of its own population? How can the U.S. treat a neighbor as nothing more than a source of slave-like servants? How can the U.S. be content to profit off the sales of automatic weapons that are being used to slaughter thousands of Mexicans? Why does the U.S. citizenry continue to have such a dependency on illegal drugs? Why does the U.S. government refuse to enforce immigration laws? Why do U.S. employers continue to hire illegal immigrants? Why do U.S. citizens continue to be addicted to cheap, illegal, domestic labor? When will the U.S. government wake up to the catastrophe that lies ahead if social services continue to be abused by illegal immigrants? What will the eventual cost of an unsecure border be if the U.S. government does not begin to act responsibly soon? Why does the U.S continue to permit violent criminal gangs of illegal immigrants to spread from state to state like a cancer? What will the cost be to the U.S. when the drug industry grows to 100 billion dollars a year? What will the U.S. be in fifty years if we do not wake up soon and fix the problems that are destroying Mexico now and likewise have the potential of destroying the U.S.? Why does the argument or discussion of immigration always become a liberal versus conservative confrontation in the U.S.? When will the majority of the press decide to stop labeling anyone who discusses immigration as racist nativism? When will the discussion on a national level finally recognize the vast chasm of difference between legal and illegal immigration? How do we fully understand the problems that exist between the U.S. and Mexico? How do we legitimize the symbiotic relationship that is good for both Mexico and the U.S? How do we start solving these problems that affect both countries? How does the U.S. help Mexico avoid democratic collapse and develop economic independence?

The situation needs immediate attention. Yet the Obama administration's initial foreign affairs thrust was preoccupied with the security of Israel, Iraq, and Afghanistan. Mexico seems to be completely invisible to his administration. It does not appear to be on their radar screen. Sadly, that is a mistake. At the same time, Calderón, who spoke at the World Economic Forum in Davos, Switzerland, had the audacity to challenge world leaders to face the realities of world-wide poverty and ecological problems, while 85 percent of his countrymen live in poverty in one of the most polluted landscapes on planet earth. Unfortunately, Calderón does not have the luxury or time to focus on the world's macro ecological problems. Obama focused on the Middle East while Calderón was challenging leaders to attack global warming. It is not the right focus for fixing the serious problems that exist between the U.S. and Mexico. At their pre-inauguration meeting Obama and Calderón agreed to establish a bilateral think tank to begin studying the situation. There was not much urgency in that start but we do have to start understanding the differences that exist between Mexico and the U.S. It is obvious that some of the initial answers to the questions in the previous paragraphs lie in the understanding that the U.S. and Mexican cultures are very different. The two countries do not have the obvious cultural differences that, for example, Europeans have with the tens of millions of Middle Easterners that have immigrated there in the last twenty years. But the differences are significant, revealing, and worth studying if we are to take up the task of solving the plethora of problems that exist between the two countries.

Mexico's potential failure as a democratic state, the risk seems greater than ever, can certainly be directly traced to the continual crises it has experienced over the past fifteen years beginning with the betrayal by President Carlos Salinas de Gortari in 1993. This led not only to the collapse of the Mexican economy but also to the devaluation of its monetary system. In 1994, the entire country lost two-thirds of its value and as a result, its one-party pseudo-democratic party (PRI) lost control of its tight-fisted control of the country. Since then an estimated 15 to 20 million Mexicans have emigrated to the U.S., legally or illegally, out of a population of 110 million. Democracy's debut under President Vicente Fox stumbled horribly, a mass revolt turned Oaxaca into a break-away state. The Calderón election and continued hold on a fragile democracy was only insured by a publically declared fraudulent vote count. Following the election, riots of civil disobedience paralyzed Mexico City, for months as Calderón struggled for international recognition as Mexico's legitimate leader. More than half of the population still does not recognize him as their legitimate president. The economy, unfocused, undirected, turned to a burgeoning drug-industry and remittance-industry from illegal immigrants in order to survive. The Mexican drug-cartels swiftly moved into the vacuum created by the successes of the Americans and Colombians over the Cali and **Medellín** drug-cartels grabbing complete control of the cocaine-industry. Poppy cultivation for heroine began in earnest as the infant democracy failed to exert any pressure on organized crime. American methamphetamine experts partnered with the drug cartels to solidify Mexico as the world's top producer of this super-addictive drug. Realizing the weakness of the federal government, organized crime began importing automatic weapons from the U.S. in 2004, at such a rate that Mexico has now become the most heavily armed country in Latin America. By 2006, Mexican organized criminals surpassed Colombia's gangs to become the world's most prolific kidnappers. And by the end of 2008, with more than 7000 drug-related murders and executions, Mexico had more homicides per capita than any country on the planet. As a result the peso once again tumbled in value, foreign capital continued to flee, and coupled with an ever-declining oil-industry which is quickly foundering without international investment the economy is in a disastrous shambles. Oil production is down 15 percent since 2004, and without new capital is forecast to drop another 10 percent by 2010. Unemployment and underemployment levels combined are estimated to be near or above 30 percent. The old axiom of, 'When the U.S. catches the flu, Mexico gets pneumonia.' is a current economic reality given the world financial crisis.

The bottom line, Mexico is on the threshold of a collapse. In this book I decided to examine not only Mexico's crises over the past fifteen years but also to follow historical trends in an attempt to explain many of the reasons Mexico is in its current dilemma. Being a self-proclaimed Mexicophile since my teenage years, a student of both modern and pre-Columbian Mexican history and archaeology, being bilingual and having lived in Mexico for more than a decade, travelling to 26 of its 31 states, I wanted to bring an historical perspective coupled with some of my own personal experiences together in an attempt to explain why modern Mexico is on the verge of collapse.

In order to understand the modern Mexican it is necessary to look to Mexico's past as well as the present. The first few chapters that follow in this book explain how Mexico diverged from its path of peaceful, intelligent development into a chaotic culture of sacrifice and cannibalism. The barbaric culture of the Aztec completely usurped control of what had been a 500-year period of continual advances by the Teotihuacanos and other classic Mexican cultures a little before 1000 A.D. Agriculture, architecture, science, math, and the arts had flourished. Mexico had cities of learning that rivaled the most advanced cities of Europe at the time. But the successful migration-invasion of the Aztecs, barbaric, uneducated savages from the northwest, sealed the doom of the Classic Period of Mexico. These savages, who by the time of the cultural collision with Europe 500 years later in the 16th century were sacrificing and eating more than 250,000 victims a year, would be the forbearers of the modern Mexican population. The story of their defeat, subsequent 300 years of servitude under the Spanish, fight for independence which ended in an exchange of a Spanish master for a New World master, and 200 more years of servitude are all important aspects which help explain the modern Mexican. The eventual revolution and almost 100 years of failed attempts at creating a stable democracy further define modern Mexico. I weave this story from my perspective trying to understand and explain why Mexico is the way it is in the 21st century. I dedicate one chapter to the special and enduring Mexican-American relationship that has failed to produce two respectful neighbors after 200 years of tumultuous misunderstandings.

And then I spend a number of chapters detailing Mexico's current descent into its reliance on crime and illegal immigration. Both are indicative of Mexico's failed efforts to join the modern world and provide for its citizenry. Finally, I offer an American-based approach to controlling both the drug industry and the immigration situation. This approach recognizes the rights and aspirations of the millions of illegal Mexicans that live in the U.S. It offers them a clear opportunity to eventual, legal participation and even citizenship in the U.S. I also suggest a prudent and probable method for securing the border and choking-off drug smuggling and illegal immigration. Both must be attacked without timidity.

Part of the motivation of writing this book is to give my fellow countrymen an opportunity to get current with a broad range of facts on the subject of Mexican-American relations. I believe we are out of focus as a country, as a culture with the negative impact that both the drug-industry and illegal immigration is having on the U.S. It is under-reported by the press. Their impact and the urgency of dealing with both are minimized or misunderstood by the American government. I want to urge a new awareness of this destructive and volatile situation. I do not hear many voices which are warning of the new coupling of Mexican organized crime, drugs, and illegal immigration. The FBI is one of the few voices which publicly reports on the growing relationship between overall crime in the U.S. and illegal Mexican immigration. The discussion of immigration can no longer be a passive argument between human rights advocates on one side and fanatic nativism on the other. The immigration issue has evolved way beyond the simple little concept of giving citizenship to the illegal immigrants who clean our houses and tend our yards. Bruce Bawer wrote an alarming, award-winning book, <u>While Europe Slept: How Radical Islam is Destroying the West from Within,</u> which in 2006 began opening millions of eyes to the catastrophic results Europe was facing after thirty years of unregulated immigration. His book has acted as a catalyst for many European politicians and activists who share his perspective. The American situation is similar to the European crisis with one big exception, the drug industry. The Mexican drug cartels have infiltrated the illegal immigration culture in the U.S. Illegal immigrants are now the smugglers, distributors, retailers, enforcers, money launderers, and end-users of the drug cartels total range of business.

It is not that every illegal immigrant has turned to crime but the reverse. Crime has turned to the illegal immigrant culture. It is preying upon it. The economic divide between the rich and poor in Mexico has grown so wide in the last thirty years that tens of millions of poor Mexicans are not even making it to middle school. These uneducated, unskilled, poor millions are the ones that are illegally immigrating to the U.S. Many join the ranks of organized crime on their journeys to the U.S from rural Mexico. They become smugglers or prostitute themselves in one way or another in order to pay for their illegal crossing into the U.S. Millions are already steeped in crime as they exit the inner-city barrios of Mexico City or Monterrey on their trip into the ranks of U.S. organized crime or criminal gangs which is now dominated by illegal immigrants and second generation Mexican Americans. The statistics kept by the Immigration and Customs Enforcement Agency (ICE) suggest that at least 30 percent of all the millions of illegal Mexican immigrants who are eventually caught and repatriated to Mexico from the interior of the U.S., have been convicted and spent time in prison for hard-core crime. Millions of others, hard working, well-intentioned Illegal Immigrants trying to desperately escape poverty or hoping to provide for a family back in Mexico, participate in an endless cycle of minor criminality which includes document fraud, identification theft, failure to pay income taxes, and money laundering. And many Americans not only look the other way but are complicit in the criminal activity. Americans have become addicted not only to the drugs that are smuggled into the U.S. but also the cheap, convenient, illegal laborer.

This book is about the destructive forces that are ripping the U.S. cultural fabric to shreds as a result of widespread complacency towards drug smuggling and illegal immigration. As a nation we can continue to look the other way or we can begin to sign up to that brotherhood for change that the 2008 U.S. election has so hopefully promised. The Obama administration has the capacity to tackle the situation with a modern 21st century perspective. The tide can be turned against the wave of criminality that is oozing across the southern, porous border with Mexico. We can put the plans in place and begin removing the cancerous addiction to illegal drugs that is systematically sweeping the nation. We can once again start enforcing the rule of law even if it means we must look a little harder to find someone to do our dirty jobs that we so disdain! Congress can change a fifty year-old, obsolescent immigration law that was written to address racism yet continues to be a serious impediment to the development of 21st century America. This book is a wake-up call to all Americans. Our beloved, sleepy little Mexican neighbor has changed in the last 20 years. It is time to wake up and turn our vision to the south before it is too late.

II

The Collapse of the Golden Age of Mexico

The questions we must answer as we turn our vision towards our southern neighbor concern the myriad of differences between 21st century America and 21st century Mexico. Why are there so many extreme differences?

An easy and general answer is simple. One of the most dramatic cultural collisions in the history of mankind was when Europe and America (western hemisphere) collided in the 16th century. The historical record shows that there was a significant difference between the indigenous populations of the U.S. as compared with the indigenous populations of Mexico. When Cortés and his conquistadors landed in March 1519, and claimed the land for Spain, there were between 10 and 30 million inhabitants (authorities differ in opinion) in Mexico. When the pilgrims arrived at Plymouth Rock in 1620, there were probably fewer than 5 million inhabitants in the entire region known today as the U.S. The population differences between the two regions were immense not only significantly in number but more so in terms of social, economic, and cultural development. The majority of the peoples north of the Rio Grande River as well as the northern desert regions of Mexico, were basically Hunter-Gatherers. Some rudimentary farming and architectural advances had occurred but the indigenous population had not advanced very far along the path of civilization. The Mexican civilization to the south, on the other hand, was very developed. When the Spaniards first climbed onto the slopes of the famous Popocatépetl volcano at Cholula, and gazed upon the city and floating gardens of Tenochtitlán (Mexico City), they were dumbfounded by what they saw. The greater metropolitan lake area was inhabited by more than a million people. It was planned and built in a geometric grid, with wide avenues, floating vegetable and flower gardens, and beautiful pyramids. The largest European city at that time was Seville, Spain, with a population of about 300,000 people. In other words, the pre-Columbian civilization in the U.S. was rudimentary in comparison to that of Mexico. In many ways, the cultures of central Mexico rivaled most European cultures in terms of architecture, engineering, agriculture, math, and Astronomy. Suffice it to say, the English experience and encounter to the north was very different than the Spanish experience to the south.

In general, the European response toward the indigenous populations and the ensuing results were quite different in the U.S. versus Mexico. The European immigrants, led by the English, basically annihilated and/or corralled the indigenous populations in the U.S. The vast majority of the northern tribes were either dead or on reservations by the end of the 19th century. The story in Mexico, however, was quite different. The Spaniards, who arrived and conquered the Mexicans one hundred years before the English landed at Plymouth, immediately began to intermingle with the indigenous peoples of Mexico. Hernán Cortés coupled with Doña Marina, his translator and confidant. She bore him a son but later married another Spaniard, Juan de Jaramillo, one of his officers. This did not prohibit the Spaniards from being brutal conquerors. They were brutal, dominating, and enslaved the majority of the Mexican population. They also, however, interbred with the conquered Mexicans with astounding frequency. Many of the Spaniards sired children with twenty, thirty, and even more women. The Mexicans therefore, became part of the new social system installed by the Spaniards, albeit they were second class humans (not citizens by the way). The indigenous Mexican blood and DNA were mixed with that of the Spanish conquerors, not negated as it was in the north. As a matter of fact, the vast majorities of modern day Mexicans identify and cling to their indigenous roots more than they do their European or Spanish roots. The opposite is true with the minority, 21st century Mexican whites. They value white skin and blue or green eyes obsessively. So, what is the easy, general, and simple answer to the question: Why are there so many basic differences between the Mexican and US value systems, and why has each culture evolved so differently since the arrival of the

Europeans to the western hemisphere? The indigenous peoples of the north scarcely, if at all, participated in forming the new culture, society, and country known as the U.S. The indigenous peoples of the south, however, not only participated in 500 years of mingling, marrying, evolving, and defining current day Mexico, but have also in many ways usurped cultural dominance over the Spaniards. So, the biggest difference between Mexico and the U.S., historically, is that the Spaniards interbred with the indigenous people of Mexico and the English did not.

Two very different cultures, therefore, developed over the next 500 hundred years in the U.S. and Mexico. One, a European derived culture, the other, a mixed European-Mexican culture. But who were these Mexicans? To really understand the 21st century Mexican you must go back another 500 years before the arrival of the Spanish or just prior to the turn of the first millennium. There are a number of ways to get there. I started my trip back into pre-Columbian Mexico on a train headed south from Texas.

I began to know and eventually call Mexico my second country as a teenager. Living in Texas, I had easy access to Mexico, and first travelled to the west coast for a summer vacation on the beautiful, Pacific beach at San Blas, Nayarit. I was sixteen and was enchanted with the Mexican people and culture I encountered. I had studied Spanish in school and was also happy to be finally using and integrating a second language into my life. As I began to read about Mexico, I became more and more interested in Mexican history and then in the pre-Columbian Latin American culture. I enrolled in anthropology and archaeology classes in my freshman year at college. During my first spring break in 1972, I caught a train in Austin, Texas, rode to Laredo, walked across the river bridge into Nuevo Laredo, and boarded the 'Aztec Eagle', a passenger train of the National Railways of Mexico, bound for Mexico City. My goal was to spend as much time as possible in the famous National Anthropological Museum. And, of course, I wanted to roam the streets of Mexico City, arguably one of the largest, continuously populated cities on planet earth for the past 1,000 years. The train was scheduled to leave Nuevo Laredo, at 6:00 pm and arrive in Mexico City, at 6:00 am the next morning. I took a Pullman, a sleeper, and settled in for an exciting adventure.

As the old, elegant, Aztec Eagle chugged away from Nuevo Laredo I enjoyed a beautiful sunset as the mountains of the Sierra Madre began to appear on the horizon. We stopped briefly at the station in Monterrey, which is about 3 hours south of the border. I strolled through the station, bought rice tacos, reviewed the train schedules, arrivals and destinations, and began immersing myself in Mexico. It was very exciting and so very different than the U.S. The train pulled over on a spur line about an hour south of Monterrey, and waited for a north bound train to pass. The train, instead of passing, stopped alongside the spur line. There was a lot of excitement. A train had derailed in front of us somewhere south of Saltillo. We continued to Saltillo, and there received a routing change. Instead of going south to Mexico City, we were routed due west to Torreón.

What was a tragedy for scores of Mexicans who were on the derailed train suddenly became a great adventure for me that lasted two and a half days. The train derailment which put me on this unexpected and eye-opening tour across northern and central Mexico solidified my desire to study, learn, and experience Mexico. This was my second trip into the heartland of Mexico and was pivotal on my road to becoming a Mexicophile for life. The station in Torreón was busy, the atmosphere filled with energy, although it was 3:00 am. The train wreck just south of Saltillo had killed tens of people, injured many more and disrupted the entire north to south train corridor. Trains across the entire northern grid were being rerouted. We pulled out of Torreón, around five in the morning and headed west, not south towards Mexico City, as scheduled. Our next stop was Durango, then south to Zacatecas, farther south to Aguascalientes, and then southwest to Guadalajara and eventually down to Morelia. At each city we disembarked, received the latest news on the train wreck, and had hours to browse and explore. The train was supplied with food services only for the overnight trip from Nuevo Laredo to Mexico City; therefore, at each stop I sampled the local food. It was a treat. I had my first mole sauce (a sauce blend of chocolate, chiles, and spices) enchiladas. I ate tacos, huaraches, gorditos, and pancita. I cannot remember it all. But it was Mexico. Everything was so different than what I was accustomed to in the U.S. Here was Mexico. I was just a train ride away from Texas, but the cultural differences were profound. I was so intrigued and so grateful for my good fortune of being rerouted all across Mexico. I finally arrived in Mexico City, two and half days late but extremely happy for the experience.

The trip hooked me. I spent the next ten days in the National Anthropological Museum and took three trips out to Teotihuacán, the great city of the pyramids. This is the city of the Teotihuacán culture not the Aztec culture (but I will discuss that later). I also went up to Tula to see the great monolithic statues. The anthropological museum has the best exhibit of pre-Columbian artifacts in the world. I have been many times and each time I happily anticipate the chance to see new exhibits, as the museum's warehouse of new world antiquities is immense. In my opinion, there are only two other museums in the world with comparable exhibits. They are the Egyptian Antiquities Museum of Cairo, Egypt, and the National Archaeological Museum of Athens, Greece. Although many of the regional museums throughout Mexico, which are located adjacent to various archaeological sites, have tremendous and important pre-Columbian artifacts, the museum in Mexico City has not only most of the best pieces of art and architecture but also a comprehensive collection of all of the important Mexican cultures: Olmec, Toltec, Zapotec, Teotihuacán, Mayan, Aztec, and more. If my meandering train trip had put the hook of curiosity in me, my trips to the museum and visits, to Teotihuacán and Tula, had set the hook. I was extremely affected by the diversity between the Mexico I saw on the two-day train trip from the border and the Mexico I saw at the museum, Teotihuacán, and Tula. On the one hand, was an archaeological record of a culture, of various cultures, with astonishing achievements in architecture, art, agriculture, engineering, astronomy, language, medicine, and science. On the other hand was modern day Mexico. I had just spent three days traversing 2,500 miles of Mexico, on a train. I saw a modern day Mexico, which seemed 100 years behind the technological developments of the U.S. (discounting, of course, the wealth and achievements of 5% of the Mexican population which control 95% of the country's wealth). Yet, the site of Teotihuacán was incredible, with the great Avenue of the Dead leading the way between the grand pyramids of the sun and moon.

Only the great pyramids of Cheops in Egypt, rival their grandeur. But what had happened between the time the pyramids were constructed and now? How could a culture with these capabilities and achievements marry with the Hispanic culture of Europe, and 500 years later be in such a deplorable condition?

What happened to the grandeur of the Teotihuacán culture? Why did the Spaniards and the Mexican cultures fail to forge a vibrant, viable new culture? Why was Mexico, in 1972, in such a mess? The Spaniards arrived in Mexico in 1519. The English arrived in the USA in 1620, one hundred and one years later. As I crossed the border back into Texas, and made my way back to class after Spring break, I experienced a profound and sobering culture shock. It happens to us all the first time upon returning from a third-world country. The values, the infrastructure, the wealth, the order, the respect, the materialism, all the things that we take for granted suddenly seem very odd when compared with third world poverty. I felt odd. The world looked strange. The shock, however, wore off after a few days. But I was still in a quandary. I could not understand what happened over the last five hundred years in Mexico. I made subsequent trips south over the next four years and finished my university studies in Texas. I began to realize that Teotihuacán was the key to understanding the Mexican culture. I visited many of the old and abandoned cities of the great Mexican cultures. I saw the mysterious Mayan pyramids of Tulum, and Chichén Itzá in the Yucatán Peninsula. I visited the glorious Zapotec pyramids of Mitla and Monte Albán in Oaxaca. I climbed the pyramids of the Tarascos at Tzintzuntzan, in the hills overlooking the volcanic lake of Pátzcuaro. Later, I traversed the interior maze of what remained of the Cholulan pyramid (which is the largest in the world) high on the slopes of Popocatépetl where the Spaniards first glimpsed the beauty of Tenochtitlán. And I came to one conclusion. The answer to my dilemma in understanding modern Mexico was hidden somewhere in Teotihuacán and Tenochtitlán. If I could understand what happened to the Teotihuacán culture then I could more easily understand why Mexico had not developed into the modern, vibrant culture for which it has the capacity to do. Many archaeologists and anthropologists believe the Teotihuacán culture experienced a 600 years peaceful development with virtually no warfare. This peaceful period was probably the key to the great development of civilization in the central Valley of Mexico. The story of the end of the Teotihuacán culture and the beginning of the brutal domination of the central Valley of Mexico by the Aztecs and their antecedents, the Toltecs, is where the story of understanding modern Mexico, must start. The story has to be picked up in the central Valley of Mexico, somewhere between 1000 and 1200 A.D.

The collision of cultures that began more than 1000 years ago between the Teotihuacanos (cultured, educated, peaceful) and the Toltecs (brutal, cannibalistic, militaristic) is still being played out today in the 21st century. I only need to reread the article from the Los Angeles Times of August 30, 2008, titled, "Drug war bodies are piling up in Mexico", A police officer guards the scene in the Mexican state of Yucatan where 11 headless bodies were found piled. The nearby city of Merida is normally tranquil and touristy. and "violence attributed to narcotics trafficking killed at least 136 people in Mexico from August 23 through 29. The killings took place in 18 of the 31 states and in the federal capital district."1 in order to see the face of the 21st century Aztec. Twelve decapitated bodies were found just outside the ruins of Chichén Itzá in the Yucatán. The heads of the victims were placed between their tied ankles and taunting messages were written on their backs. This type of inhuman behavior became the norm throughout Mexico, during the Aztec Epoch and continues today. As I studied Mexican prehistory my suspicions were reconfirmed. I knew there was a significant mismatch somewhere. I knew something did not fit. I could not understand how a civilization which achieved so many great things prior to the tenth century could be in such disarray in the 21st century.

Over time my reading and understanding of Mexican prehistory answered my questions. Some of the answers are quite simple and the Mesoamerican experts know it well. Some are obscure and more complicated. The Great Mexican cultures of the first millennium faded out of existence at the same time as a barbarian immigrant culture quietly crept into the Valley of Mexico from the northwest. In many ways, these barbarian cultures, which culminated with the Aztec Empire, reminds me of the millions of illegal immigrants now crossing into the U.S. each year. And I suspect that if this illegal immigration continues to go unchecked, the results may very well be the same. The advancement of a great culture not only halted but became the foundation of an aberrant, cannibalistic culture.

Archaeologists and anthropologists do not know the entire story of pre-Columbian Mexico, but they understand it well enough to know that the once great Teotihuacán culture was not advanced by the Aztecs. The modern Mexican has taken huge pride in linking himself to his Aztec ancestry since the Mexican Renaissance which followed the 1910 Revolution. What the modern Mexican does not acknowledge is that this Aztec ancestor was not responsible for the development and advancement of Mexican high culture. The Aztecs had nothing to do with the Golden Age of Mexico. Quite the contrary, under the barbaric stewardship of the Aztecs, the Mexican culture degraded and reached abysmal states of human existence.

This Toltec and eventual Aztec rise to power was not something that happened overnight. The Toltecs arrived as an invading force at the turn of the millennium but the Aztecs did not have an Attila the Hun-type, warrior-leader that ushered in their reign of barbarity. It was more like a cancer attacking a healthy human. In this case it was literally decades before the cancer took its victim. The Aztecs were Hunter-Gatherers, from the mythological island of Aztlán, who turned into migrant barbarians who then later developed a sacrificial-cannibalistic religion or belief system. They were one of the last of the nomadic immigrant groups to move into the Valley of Mexico after the demise of the Teotihuacán culture. Their nomadic cousins, the Toltec's, had preceded them and were actually responsible for burning and looting the great city of Teotihuacán three centuries earlier. The Toltecs dispersed the remnants of the once great Teotihuacán people; they usurped control of the central Valley of Mexico. They adopted agriculture and a few of the other cultural advances that the Teotihuacanos had achieved but continued to be a semi barbaric culture. After a century and a half, the Toltec culture went into decline and hundreds of Teotihuacán tribes of barbarians moved into the Valley from the northwest. They moved into the old Toltec-Teotihuacan centers and established a large network of city-state mini cultures. When the Aztecs arrived in 1250 A.D., the Valley was crowded with perhaps 5 million of Chichimec barbarians and Toltecs who had been assimilated into the new barbaric culture. The Valley was full and there was very little room for more immigrants. The way the Aztecs snuck into the Valley was analogous to the way millions of illegal Mexican immigrants are sneaking into the U.S. today. They arrived uneducated, unskilled, and poor. They were not welcomed by the Chichimecs and only found squatting rights in the most unwanted canyons and hillsides of the region. The Chichimecs, although barbaric, were civilized in comparison to the Aztecs. They had adopted the last remaining remnants of Mexico's Golden Age, most notably agriculture. Although they practiced sacrificial rituals they despised the perverse rituals and cannibalism of the Aztecs. But over time the Aztecs became useful second-class citizens who were often employed as mercenaries in city-state warfare. They were also used as laborers in the fields and in the dirtiest of jobs such as dredging the bottom of Lake Texcoco. But the perversity of the Aztec ways, especially their propensity to kidnap, rape, and flay their neighbors' wives, eventually incited the city-state leaders to unite and attack the Aztecs on the steep hillsides of Chapultepec, where they had been squatting for fifty years. Many were killed. Their leaders were executed. The Chichimec peoples wanted to rid the Valley of the scourge of the Aztec barbarians. But the survivors escaped to the reeds along Lake Texcoco where they lived a despicable existence in the insect infested mud flats. Strangely, they adapted to their new environs and flourished. They moved onto the small island in the middle of shallow Lake Texcoco, dredged the bottom to create more living area, built causeways to the mainland, and thus was the beginnings of Tenochtitlán, the island city, which eventually became Mexico City.

One thousand or perhaps twelve hundred years before the arrival of the Aztecs to the Valley, various agricultural cultures began to emerge throughout central and southern Mexico. They eventually evolved into the great cultures known as The Classical Period of Mexico. This was Mexico's Golden Age. It lasted approximately one thousand years. Its most influential center was in the Valley of Mexico where the Teotihuacanos and Cholulans shepherded the cultural advancements. To the south, the Mayans were equally prolific. Between the two, their Zapotec counterparts flourished in the mountains of Oaxaca. The people of the Valley of Mexico experienced perhaps the longest period of peaceful and quasi-peaceful human existence ever recorded. It is very likely that for six hundred years during the one thousand year Classical Period there were virtually no wars and apparently very little aggression among the various civilized regions throughout central and southern Mexico (with the exception of the Maya). As a result of this peaceful period, Mexico flourished. Discoveries and advances in math, language, science, astronomy, agriculture, engineering, construction, art, politics, religion, and trade were staggering. The Cholulans built the largest pyramid in the history of mankind of which, unfortunately, only the base still exists today. It is larger in circumference than the Egyptian pyramids at Cheops. But it was razed by the Spaniards in the 16th century who used the great stones to build their New World churches. The Mayans devised and effectively used a zero-based number system. The Teotihuacanos, of course, built the great pyramidal city just outside of present-day Mexico City. The city proper was inhabited by perhaps 100,000 Teotihuacanos and in their outlying metropolitan area were another 300,000. Most scholars believe this was one of the largest 1st millennium metropolitan areas in the world. The largest European city in A.D. 925 was Córdoba, Spain, with a population of 400,000. Quite simply, the Classical Mexicans were brilliant!

The cultures of the Classical Period of Mexico began a 1000 year odyssey which started at about the same time as the Christian (Gregorian) calendar, +/- 200 years. The development and creative process seems to have peaked after 600 or 700 years and then the cultures (for various reasons) went into decline and eventually ceased to exist entirely. As the Classical Period waned, the barbarians from the north starting with the Toltecs, were free to occupy the central Valley of Mexico. The barbarians of the north may actually have been responsible for the decline of the Classical cultures in the Valley of Mexico. We know that the Toltecs looted and burned the city of Teotihuacán around A.D. 850-900. The archaeological record, however, does not adequately show that the barbarians were responsible for the total decline of the Classical Period. It does discount their involvement in any of the cultural developments and advances of the Classical Period. It also shows that they very adeptly usurped control of the central Valley and introduced a new, violent, militaristic culture which lasted until the arrival and conquest by the Spaniards.

This 1000 year period of the Classical Mexican was extraordinary. The dominant cultures developed sequentially, communicated, shared technology and information but were quite independent from one another. The Teotihuacanos and Zapotecs were probably closer to each other than either was to the Mayan. Both were more peaceful and developed religious belief systems which consecrated rather than desecrated human life. It is now commonly believed that the Mayan belief system was much more brutal and less respectful of human life than their northern counterparts. In any regard, all three cultures flourished, developed, and expanded in basic peaceful accommodation for approximately 600 to 700 years. They defined the best and most dominant aspects of the Classical Mexican period.

The experts agree that the great Mexican cultures reached their apogee during the Classical Period. "It was the Golden Age of ancient Mexico, producing mind-stopping culture, temples, pyramids, and cities—almost all of the architectural grandeur that still lies strewn across Middle America, from great Teotihuacán in the north to Monte Albán outside Oaxaca to Palenque in Chiapas, which was the Athens of the Maya world." "Ironically, perhaps, so much of this ancient grandeur survived because all of these sites were abandoned and forgotten centuries before Cortés came".[2] The Classical period produced the so called Aztec calendar which, of course, did not originate with the Aztecs. "The Mexica or Aztecs, Tarasca, Tlaxcalteca, Mixteca, and Cempoalan peoples were all inheritors rather than creators".[3]

The concept of inheritors versus creators is very important in understanding Mexico. There was a real prehistoric digital divide for a couple of thousand years as agricultural developed. On the one hand were the Agriculturalists and on the other were the Hunter-Gatherers. The Agriculturists, of course, became the founders of the great Classical Period cultures. The millions who accepted the technology began developing at an astoundingly faster rate than their counterparts. The Hunter-Gatherers who did not adapt to agriculture became the immigrant barbarians. As history shows, unfortunately, these barbarians became the rulers of Mexico. They are the ancestors of present day Mexicans. The Creators were destroyed, the population dispersed, and their bloodlines diluted or terminated by the invading nomads from the north. More importantly, however, the Inheritors did not have the capacity or inclination to continue the upward spiraling development of the Classical Period.

The Teotihuacanos who had always acted as a buffer between the barbarians of the north and their civilized counterparts to the south were now gone. Sometime during the last century of the 1st millennium the Toltecs moved into the central Valley of Mexico. The Golden Age of ancient Mexico was at an end. "The language, race, and origin of the people who built, lived, and worshipped at Teotihuacán are all obscure. They never called their center "Teotihuacán"; this is a Nahuatl name, applied by later invaders of Mexico, which means "City of the Gods," or "The Place Where Men Became Lords."4 The ruins of Teotihuacán, as grand as they are today, barely expose the grandeur of the greatest city ever built in the western hemisphere. But for whatever reasons, the Toltec immigrants built their city of Culhuacan some 30 miles to the south on the shores of Lake Texcoco. On the island in the middle of the lake, the later arriving Aztecs built their capital Tenochtitlán which eventually became Mexico City.

The reasons are unclear as to why the Teotihuacanos left their city. It is uncertain what happened to the hundreds of thousands and perhaps millions of people who lived in Teotihuacán and the regions which constituted their empire or city-state. Many may have melded in with the invading/immigrating Toltecs. Initially many historians described the ensuing decades even centuries as a period of invasions. The Toltecs can accurately be described as invaders. The later arriving Aztecs were simply immigrants. The Toltecs first came around A.D. 850-900. There is not much of a record as to what happened. As previously noted they ransacked the capital of Teotihuacán and chose to build their new city on the shores of the lake to the south. We know that by A.D. 1350 the city of Tenochtitlán was massive and that the Aztecs had gained control from the disappearing Toltecs and earlier arriving Chichimec groups. They, as the Toltecs, were using left over Teotihuacán technology to some degree. They also had adopted some of the Teotihuacán religious beliefs. The gruesome practice of human sacrifice, however, had never been embraced by the Teotihuacanos. It is important to note that the Teotihuacanos had never been very interested in human sacrifice in order to appease their gods. The archaeological record shows that they preferred to sacrifice butterflies and moths as opposed to humans. "The leadership was dedicated to a sense of order and progress, made possible by an apparently strict adherence to regimentation".[5] Whereas the Teotihuacán leaders unified their peoples through magic, education, a shared technology of agriculture which included irrigation, and the social benefits that followed, the Toltec and Aztec leaders dominated their peoples with fear, brutality, human sacrifice, cannibalism, and strict subjugation.

With the fall of the Teotihuacán culture, strong militaristic city-states emerged in their place. The ensuing cultures became a strange mix of the remnants of an advanced, educated culture with a primitive barbaric culture. The Toltecs and ensuing waves of barbaric invaders were similar to the Apache Indians of North America at the time of western expansion in the 19th century but without horses. There is even a linguistic link between the Aztec and the Apache. Today, during many of the ritualistic-type dance festivals in the small towns of Mexico, the participants don attire which imitates both the barbarian Aztec and Apache, not the Teotihuacán culture. These dances emulate the brutal and aggressive nature of the Aztec with a focus on weaponry and the macabre. The young men are enamored with the idea of being descendents of the Aztec and the Apache. When I first encountered this perspective I thought that the modern Mexican had been watching too much television. But I was wrong. The modern Mexican is the descendent of the invading hordes of nomadic barbarians from the north to which the Apache tribes belong. Linguists have discovered that the Nahuatl or Aztec language has its roots in the northern Chihuahuan desert and along the modern Colorado-Utah border. This was the heart of the nomadic range of the Apaches. The Apaches represented the prehistoric Hunter-Gatherers or immigrant barbarians of Mexico, till almost the beginning of the 20th century. In other words, even 1000 years after the Toltecs became sedentary farmers, there were still pockets of prehistoric Hunter-Gatherers roaming the wilds of northern Mexico and the southwest U.S.

The Toltecs, Aztecs, and Apaches share a common ancestry. If not actually in DNA or blood they all descended from a wild, barbarian ancestor. The Toltecs adapted well to the sedentary, agricultural life-style they inherited from the Teotihuacanos. For a time, one of their leaders embodied the spiritual god of Quetzalcoatl who was a beneficent Teotihuacán god. The Toltec leader even took his name. His influence on the Toltec was very positive. But the savage Toltecs could not adhere for long to Quetzalcoatl's virtuous belief system. He and his followers were banished into exile. Forebodingly, his myth foretold of his return from the east. He would arrive in great ships, accompanied by harnessed monsters (horses) that would assist him in reclaiming his godship. After all, he was seen as a god by his followers. The myth persisted for centuries and was eventually played out with the arrival of Cortés.

But before Cortés' arrival, the Aztecs arrived. As I noted before, they came to the Toltec empire as another wave of immigrant barbarian. The Valley had seen successive waves of savage immigrants for 250 years prior to the Aztec's arrival. The influence of the Toltecs had been displaced by that of the Chichimecs who were more brutal, vulgar, and uncivilized than the Toltecs. Each wave was less educated and ill-prepared to participate in a civilized culture than its predecessor. This mass immigration of millions of uneducated, unskilled, barbarians is not so different than that which is happening in the 21st century in the U.S. The Toltecs were barbaric, brutal, militaristic, and savage. The Chichimecs were worse! But even the Chichimecs could not stomach the vulgar, gruesome mores of the Aztecs. The central Valley of Mexico continued a downward spiral which was characterized by war, kidnapping, enslavement, human sacrifice, and cannibalism. The Chichimecs, recognizing the Aztec for the brute he was, eventually decided to employ him as a mercenary. Initially, they paid the Aztec for his mercenary successes with bits and pieces of land. The eventual payment was their entire empire. As the Aztec mercenaries succeeded in their wars against the Chichimec rivals, they also began to acquire more and more of their land. The story is long and bloody. By A.D. 1250, the entire region which had physically defined the wondrous world of the Classical Period of Mexico was now in chaos. The Aztecs became the dominant influence as they were the most brutal. But the brutality, barbarism, kidnapping, slavery, gruesome human sacrificial habit, cannibalism, and general cultural decay were rampant throughout the region. The beneficent gods of the Teotihuacanos had been exchanged for the blood-thirsty gods of the Aztecs and Chichimecs. A common sacrificial rite was the extraction and consumption of the human heart while the human still gasped his last precious breaths of air. Human heads were severed by the tens of thousands atop alters which were constructed on the Aztec temples. The inner religious sanctuaries were plastered with coat after coat of human blood. It was a 300 year blood fest.

This became the Mexican nature! This was the Aztec legacy! Human sacrifice was not an Aztec invention. Records depict the brutality of the Maya and others. But the Aztec, instead of embracing and advancing the incredible achievements of the Classical Period, did the unthinkable. The Aztec turned mankind to the dark force, to the dark side. The depths of which this interminable slide reached is hard to imagine. The economic gain most prized by the Aztec became the heart and head of a captured foe. The victims were slated for torture, decapitation, and consumption. The Aztecs became cannibalistic, eating the arms and thighs of their sacrificed foes. The temples ran red with blood. The majority of the Mexican cultures fell sway to their dominating ways and became similarly savage and blood-thirsty. The cultures that were not directly controlled by the Aztecs or in strategic alliances with them were fighting for their survival.

It was an amazing period. The Aztecs and others continued to benefit from the ongoing use of advanced agricultural, engineering, and construction techniques. They used the calendar and astronomical savvy to determine planting cycles. Advances in math, science, and even art, however, seemed to have practically stopped. The entire reason for existence under their belief system became blood. It was all about blood and human sacrifice. Their stock market was the head count of their foes. All strategies, all decisions, all endeavors were about capturing, torturing, and beheading human beings. These are the ancestors of the modern-day Mexicans, who are still decapitating the heads of their enemies in the state of Michoacán, Guerrero, Chihuahua, the Yucatán, and others.

These ancestors, these Aztecs, these inheritors of the Golden Age of Mexico had either conquered, made alliances, or were at war with every other city-state in Mexico. This was the state of affairs when the Spaniards arrived in the early 16th century. It took the Agriculturists more than 2500 years to reach their apogee in the Classical Period. Now in less than 500 years the Toltec, Chichimec, and Aztec barbarians had completely perverted the Golden Age of Mexico.

This was a collision of different cultures. This was not an evolution of the Classical Mexican culture. The Golden Age of Mexico and its peoples (even if they were in a cycle of decline) collided with the nomadic, barbarians of the north. The barbarians usurped control of this Classic culture, embraced whatever achievements suited their taste and intellectual capacity, merged the religious belief system with their own into a perverted manifestation of blood-thirsty savagery, and discarded the rest. As Mexico struggles to maintain its democracy in the 21st century this collision continues to be ongoing. In many ways the digital divide still exists between the barbarians and those that are more civilized.

The first major collision in Mexico was, in essence, between Classical Mexican Culture and the barbarians. The Toltecs, Chichimecs, and eventually the Aztecs transformed the Golden Age of Mexico into the Dark Ages. The disparity between the two cultures was technology in the form of agriculture which, of course, led to the other technological differences. The second major collision was between the Aztecs, the other Dark Age cultures, and the Spaniards in the 16th century. The disparity between these two cultures was also technology. The progression of Mexican history after the Aztecs took control of the central Valley around 1400 A.D. illustrates two important things. One, the indigenous Mexicans encountered by the Spaniards in 1519, was the descendants of the barbarian Toltecs, Chichimecs, and Aztecs not the Teotihuacanos of the Golden Age of Mexico. And two, the cultural collisions that started around A.D. 900, when the northern nomads invaded the central Valley persist into the 21st century. There has been an ongoing and violent collision of peoples who are on different sides of the technological-type divide. The subsequent collisions reached crescendos with the arrival of the Spanish, then during the ten year struggle for independence from Spain, again during the civil Revolution of 1910-1920, then with the upheaval of the one-party political system, PRI, which started in 1994. The manifestation of the next crescendo will somehow be played out over the relationship between Mexico and the U.S., over the question of drug smuggling and illegal immigration.

I think it is important to analyze the Mexican character as well as their cultural psyche after each one of these so-called crescendos. When the Aztecs entered the civilized world of Mexico, they were uncivilized barbarians without a culture. "And the Mexica (Aztec) understanding of the past was not too clear; they were inheritors of a culture whose origins and values they only dimly understood."6 Two hundred years later they had usurped control of the entire Toltec empire. In the next one hundred years they had tripled the size of their empire and quadrupled the sphere of their influence to include the majority of what is modern day Mexico. They were masters of their fate. They subjugated the entire region by employing legions of fierce, pitiless, murdering, warriors who terrorized their entire Aztec realm. Their character reflected their ruthless, blood-thirsty scheme. There was no trust, no honesty, no harmony, no respect, and no aspirations to reach higher goals. Their mythology and religion supported no grand ideals but quite the contrary. It was a religion based on appeasement. The heads were severed, the blood was spilled, and the sacrifices were made to appease a blood-thirsty pantheon of gods. Men reflect their gods. Gods reflect the men who create them. The Aztec character was that of a blood-thirsty, ruthless savage but now he had a culture.

Imagine the cultural psyche of the Aztecs. This culture bred fear, nurtured relentless aggression, and placed pride in the fierce, strong warrior-kidnapper. The most honored were the merciless warriors, the savage priests who ripped the pounding hearts from their captive's chests and swilled their blood even as they drew their last breaths. Imagine the psyche that supported this evil savagery. It was a strange dichotomy of fear and strength. This was the Aztec world that collided with the 16th century Spaniards in 1519, when Hernán Cortés and his 600 men landed on the east coast near the present-day port city of Veracruz, Mexico.

Mexico's Collision with Europe

I refer to the Spanish arrival in Mexico, as the second cultural collision of the Mexicans. The first was the collision between the sophisticated culture of the Teotihuacanos and the barbarian Aztecs. Christopher Columbus arrived in the New World in 1492. His first landfall was on one of the many Bahamian Cays. He visited the Caribbean islands of Cuba, and Haiti, before eventually returning to Spain. Over the next 25 years the Spanish explored, conquered, and settled many of the Caribbean islands. As the Spanish acquired the local languages they became aware of the existence of the mainland of Mexico. They heard fantastic stories about the culture and peoples that lived there. They hoped the stories were true and that the Mexican culture was as rich as the stories indicated. Cuba became the departure point for exploring and seeking out the mainland. Prior to Hernán Cortés's historic conquest of Mexico, two expeditions explored and made landfalls at various points along the Yucatán Peninsula and northward along the coast.

In 1517, the expedition of Francisco Hernández de Córdoba explored the beaches of the Yucatán Peninsula and made contact with the indigenous population. These peoples were the inheritors of the once great Mayan culture. Their attitude was very aggressive and threatening towards Hernández and his men. The Spaniard's first landing was just north of the popular tourist beaches of Cancún and Cozumel. They sailed westward along the northern Yucatán coast. They then followed the western peninsular coast as far south as Campeche, before returning to Cuba. At each landfall they were ferociously attacked and lost approximately 60 men. On each occasion they were tricked into entering the coastal towns under the guise of peace and were then ambushed. At Cape Catoche (north of modern day Cancún), the Spaniards initially routed their attackers and got a quick glimpse of the small town. The central religious structure contained a sacrificial stone slab which was dripping with fresh human blood. The walls were plastered with blood and Hernández believed the human sacrifices had only just taken place prior to the attack. In any event, the survivors were thankful to return to Cuba, with their lives. They now had an idea of the dark force that was controlling the cultures of Mexico.

The second expeditionary force was captained by Juan de Grijalva. This force of four ships and 250 men retraced the route of the first expedition. They continued along the coast as far as Veracruz, before returning to Cuba. Along the way they learned some startling things. First thing they learned was that the language spoken by the peoples of the Yucatán was completely different than the language spoken farther along the coast. This language was that of the Mexicans and of the dominant culture of the mainland. They suspected that the Mexican influence was prevalent throughout the mainland. The leader was named Montezuma and he was very much aware of not only their movements, landfalls, and activity but also knew of the exploits of Francisco Hernández's first expedition. Second, the Spanish began to uncover and understand the true depths to which this sacrificial culture had plunged. Bernal Díaz, one of the explorers, described, "Here we found five Indians who had been sacrificed to them that very night. Their chests had been struck open and their arms and thighs cut off, and the walls of these buildings covered with their blood. All this amazed us greatly, and we called this island the Isla de Sacrificios (Island of Sacrifices), as it is named on the charts."1 And third, the mainland seemed to be rich with gold. They traded green beads, cut glass, and mirrors for approximately 20,000 pieces of gold. When the expedition returned to Cuba, with the gold, a third expedition was quickly planned.

The third expedition was, of course, that of Hernán Cortés and is legendary. His expedition became the Spanish conquest of Mexico. It is one of the most extraordinary tales of all time. It is as fantastic as the imaginary tales of J.R.R. Tolkien's trilogy, The Lord of the Rings. Cortés's small band of men reminds me of the Fellowship of the Ring marching into Mount Doom.

But this is not fiction. Hernán Cortés with 600 men and sixteen horses sailed in eleven ships from Cuba, on February 10, 1519. Cuauhtémoc, the last Aztec tyrant, was captured on the 13th of August, 1521, two and a half years later and suddenly 500 years of Aztec tyranny was at an end. Cortés defeated an empire with his original 600 men who were joined by an additional 600 hundred reinforcements halfway through the campaign. Twelve hundred Spaniards defeated 10 million Aztecs! It is incomprehensible! It is mind-boggling! It could not happen. But it did. To understand how this happened is to truly understand the nature, the psyche of the Aztec culture, and the ancestors of modern Mexico.

The Cortés expedition arrived at the current port of Veracruz, in March of 1519, after a number of forays along the coast. The local population spoke Náhuatl. This is the language of the Aztec. It still exists today. Mexican Spanish is peppered with its words and influences. By good fortune, communication was possible through two translators. It was a little complicated but here is how it worked. Jerónimo de Aguilar, a Spanish Franciscan friar and sailor, had been held captive in the Yucatán for ten years after a disastrous shipwreck left he and a few others stranded. He was repatriated during the Grijalva, second mainland expedition of which I have already written. He learned the Mayan (or Tabascan) language during his captivity. He did not, however, speak Náhuatl, the Aztec language. Fortunately, Cortés had been given a female slave after the expedition defeated the fierce warriors at Champotón. She, later named Doña Marina, was Aztec and spoke both Aztec and Mayan. Thus the communication between Cortés and the Aztecs was possible. Cortés spoke Spanish to Jerónimo de Aguilar who then translated to Doña Marina in Mayan. She then translated the communications into Aztec. And then it all happened in reverse. As a result of this, Doña Marina played an important role in the ensuing conquest. Her place in history is portrayed in various ways. The European historians portray her as a heroine while the Mexican historians portray her as a traitor.

Cortés, with the help of Doña Marina, discovered that the peoples of the coastal region around Veracruz, the Cempoalans, were under the control of the Aztecs of Tenochtitlán. They were servants of the Aztecs. The Aztecs ruthlessly dominated them.

They sent their tax collectors on a routine basis to extract their wealth of gold and precious stones. They sent their warriors to rape and acquire their young daughters. But, worst of all, they demanded a routine bounty of young boys and girls which were eventually sacrificed and eaten at the temples in Tenochtitlán. As a matter of ensuing discovery Cortés found this to be true in many of the regions of Mexico. The Cempoalans were terrified of the Aztecs and succumbed to their demands. So did most of the other populations of the city-states throughout Mexico. By the 15th century, with few exceptions, the Aztecs dominated all of the inheritor cultures which now controlled the regions of the extinct cultures of the Classical Period of Mexico. These inheritor cultures had become the subcultures of the Aztecs.

Cortés grasped the situation very quickly. He saw the perversity of the Aztec culture and how it had turned the entire region into a living hell. He realized that if he could convert the outlying city-states into allies he could defeat the Aztecs. He believed that he must turn the dark savage psyche back towards the light. He ordered the Cempoalans to, "give up sodomy, for they had boys dressed as women who practiced that accursed vice for profit. Moreover everyday they sacrificed before our eyes three, four, or five Indians, whose hearts were offered to their idols and whose blood were plastered on the walls. The feet, arms, and legs of their victims were cut off and eaten, just as we eat beef from the butchers in our country. I believe they even sold it in the tianguez or markets."2 The decadence was so complete and compelling that all of the Aztec subcultures had adopted the barbaric and cannibalistic practices, and belief systems, of the Aztec. It was a great sickness that spread from Tenochtitlán, and affected tens of millions. These millions were Cempoalans, Tabascans, Cholulans, Talascalans, etc.; all were afflicted with the disease. It is a valid claim that virtually every modern Mexican is descended from this horrific Aztec culture. It does not matter if the blood or DNA can be traced back to a Cempoalans or Talascalan lineage. The common cultural denominator of all Mexicans is the Aztec. The Aztec dominated the other cultures so completely that they were in essence Aztec subcultures which embraced an immoral, degrading belief system. This belief system would eventually fail the entire culture and aid in its demise. The exact populations of the Aztec Empire and the central Valley of Mexico at this time are uncertain. It was certainly larger than 10 million and probably close to 25 million. The odds that Cortés faced were staggering.

It is easy to draw parallels between the city-states of 16th century Mexico, and the drug cartels of 21st century Mexico. The odds that the current president of Mexico, Felipe Calderón, faces are staggering. The drug gangs of Sinaloa, Juárez, Nayarit, and Mexico City, coupled with the corrupt police forces remind me so much of the Aztec city-states. The Aztec commerce was all about human sacrifice and gold. The cartels' commerce is all about drugs and gold. The brutal and savage force used by each is very similar. The way they both participate in a brutal belief system is similar. Human life means little to either culture. In many ways, the challenges of Calderón are not so different than those faced by Cortés.

Cortés discovered, from his encounters on the eastern coast with the Cempoalans, that the city-states which emulated and were a part of the Aztec culture actually hated and despised the Aztecs. He convinced the Cempoalans to arrest the Aztec tax collectors and make an alliance with the Spaniards against the Aztecs. It was a coup de grâce. He convinced the Cempoalans to give him 2,000 soldiers to accompany him on the road to Tenochtitlán, and his eventual encounter with Montezuma. The trip from the coast at Veracruz to Tenochtitlán is about 250 miles. Cortés knew, after conferring with the Cempoalans, that this would be a dangerous and treacherous undertaking. All of the city-states between the coast and Tenochtitlán were under the influence of the Aztecs. They practiced human sacrifice, were cannibalistic, and were allies of Montezuma. If not, they were under his constant attack. As Cortés left the coast he was besieged by a group of his soldiers who wanted to take three of the ships and return to Cuba. After counseling with his stalwart supporters he decided to scuttle the ships and force his entire expedition onward to the capital of Montezuma and the Aztecs. The road from the Cempoalan city soon reached the outskirts of the Tlaxcalans' city. Here Cortés began to learn of the depths of the Mexican treachery.

The Cempoalans, Cortés' allies, characterized the Tlaxcalans as peace-loving haters of the Aztecs and Montezuma. So naturally Cortés approached Tlaxcala hoping to find additional allies for his march to Tenochtitlán. Instead he encountered ferocious warriors. The expedition was attacked three times and barely was able to avoid complete defeat and annihilation. The Spaniards persevered as a result of their superior war technology, i.e., muskets, crossbows, canons, cavalry, armor and the ability to use them. The Tlaxcalans, in contrast, had wooden swords which were fixed with sharpened or flaked, flint knives. They were still using the spear-hurling atlatls which had been mastered 10,000 years before the turn of the millennia. And their rock-throwing sling-shots were right out of the Old Testament. Their arrows were also fitted with stone tips. The New World man had not yet mastered metallurgy to any great extent. And, of course, they had never laid eyes on a horse. They initially thought that a mounted cavalryman was some sort of monster or ferocious god, thinking that the man and horse was the same creature. The Tlaxcalans finally decided to make peace with Cortés after they suffered heavy casualties and could not defeat these odd-appearing Spaniards. In each encounter along the coast including the one with the Cempoalans, the Spaniards had encountered attacks. None of the prior attacks compared to the Tlaxcalans' onslaught. Nevertheless, the Tlaxcalans were massacred by the hundreds, eventually sued for peace, and invited the expedition to move into their city. They had been fearful that Cortés and his men were a new Aztec trick; that, they were in league with the Aztecs. But Cortés convinced them otherwise and spent a month gaining their confidence, allegiance, and eventual alliance. He had done the same with the Cempoalans.

The month-long stay in Tlaxcala gave the Spaniards a close look at this savage Mexican culture. Bernal Díaz writes, "I must now tell how in this town of Talascala we found wooden cages made of lattice-work in which men and women were imprisoned and fed until they were fat enough to be sacrificed and eaten." "When Cortés saw such great cruelty he showed the Caciques (leaders) of Talascala how indignant he was and scolded them so furiously that they promised not to kill and eat any more Indians that way. But I wondered what use all these promises were, for as soon as we turned our heads they would resume their old cruelties."[3] Humans were sacrificed on a daily basis on the blood encrusted alters. In many areas human skulls had been neatly stacked and were easy to count. One stack contained more than one hundred thousand skulls. The Spaniards were getting closer and closer to Mount Doom and the evidence of evil was everywhere. It was like Joseph Conrad's Heart of Darkness. Cortés was being drawn upstream towards Montezuma and the source of all this evil. It also reminds me of the scene in the movie Apocalypse Now where the boat crosses into Cambodia from Vietnam and the bodies are hanging everywhere. The young Captain Willard realizes that Kurtz and the evil that he represents are very close. Cortés realized the same.

Another interesting thing happened in Tlaxcala. The leaders of Tlaxcala revealed to Cortés a part of their mythology. In their religion, there was the prophecy of the arrival of fair-skinned, blued-eyed gods from the East. These gods, it was prophesized, would become their new leaders. Cortés had sensed this earlier. In Champotón, he had called his captains together and advised them of his intuitions on this subject. Doña Marina had told him that they were using the local word for god to describe the Spaniards. The Cempoalans leaders had also told Cortés that they believed he and his Spaniards were invincible and were some type of gods. But now, the Tlaxcalans were going even further. They were declaring the Spaniards the returning gods of the Quetzalcoatl mythology. They had every right to be in Mexico. It was destiny. Their arrival was the manifestation of religious prophecy. At the same time, Montezuma and many of the other city-state leaders were concluding the same thing. They were not, however, planning to facilitate the return of Quetzalcoatl.

The Spaniards spent a month in Tlaxcala recovering from their wounds. They learned that the rewards of military victory included human beings. The Tlaxcalan leaders offered their daughters and most beautiful women to the Spaniards. Xicotenga, the Tlaxcalan leader, wanted Cortés to couple with his daughter. So, he simply gave her to Cortés. It became quite customary for the Spanish conquistadors, married or not, to receive Mexican women as their concubines. It is an odd thing. The Spanish were Catholic and did not believe in polygamy. The conquistadors, however, accepted the Mexican women as their concubines and immediately began to impregnate them. This practice continued for centuries and eventually became one of the most despised subjects in Mexican history.

Montezuma began to send emissaries to Cortés in Tlaxcala. He sent presents of gold and precious stones. He entreated Cortés to accept and recognize his obedience to King Carlos V of Spain, whom by now he was very well aware. Cortés had explained to all of the conquered city-state leaders that all of his endeavors were in the name of King Carlos V. At first Montezuma did not want Cortés to continue his march to Tenochtitlán. Montezuma later schemed with the Cholulans and invited Cortés to come quickly to Tenochtitlán via the road through Cholula. Montezuma and the Cholulans were planning an ambush with 50,000 warriors. His emissaries eventually brought Cortés a treaty to Tlaxcala which guaranteed his safety. The Tlaxcalans warned him of the treacherous Mexicans, and pleaded with him to stay. Díaz recorded the insightful response of Xicotenga, "a treaty was useless, since enmity was always deeply rooted in their hearts, and such was the Mexican character that under cover of peace they would only practice greater treachery, for they never kept their word, whatever they promised. He begged Cortés to say no more about a treaty, and implored him once more to be on his guard against falling into the hands of this wicked race."4 Cortés was further advised, "neither to embark on the expedition nor to put the least trust in Montezuma or any Mexican."5

This concept of the "wicked race" and treacherous, deceitful Mexican character was first explained to me when I was living in Mexico City, in the early nineties. I had read Bernal Díaz's book many years before and had discounted his description of the Mexican character. Anyway, one of my associates in Mexico, who was a native of the state of Michoacán, explained it to me. His ancestors, the Tarascans, were never completely conquered by the Toltecs or Aztecs although they were attacked on many occasions. According to the local legends of Michoacán via my good friend, the Aztecs actually distinguished themselves as valiant mercenaries for the Toltecs in the last great battle between the Toltecs, Aztecs and the Tarascans. The Toltecs, according to this hand-me-down story, had attacked the Tarascans on many occasions. The Tarascans were very skillful at luring their attackers into the precipitous gorges and canyons of their homeland, Michoacán. They would do this by first attacking their intruders with an obviously inferior force and then would feign a retreat into the gorges and ravines. Of course, it was a trap and their warriors were waiting to descend on the intruders. Their strategy worked again and again and they were consistently able to avoid falling under the tyranny of the Toltecs. With the arrival of the devious Aztec mercenary, however, things changed. Being aware of the disastrous past that their Toltec bosses had with the Tarascans, the Aztecs decided to implement a new strategy. And it worked, to some extent anyway. The Aztecs invaded Michoacán, and then played along when the Tarascans setup their proverbial trap but sent a larger force of warriors behind the Tarascan flank. When the hidden Tarascan army descended on their foe they were suddenly outflanked and surrounded by the Aztecs. The ensuing battle was fierce and although neither side won, the Tarascans agreed to begin paying tribute to Tenochtitlán. But according to my friend the tribute was paid directly to the Aztecs and not the Toltecs. The Tarascans still cling to the claim that they never fell under the influence of the barbarism and savagery of the Aztec. This semi-victory, he claimed, was the end of the Toltec's reign and the beginning of the Aztec's. To this day, supposedly, the people of Michoacán despise the so-called Chilangos of Mexico City. This story is undocumented, of course, but the reputation of the treacherous, deceitful, and savage Aztec or Mexican is still alive today.

Cortés knew that his destiny lay ahead in Tenochtitlán. He had lost approximately 75 soldiers since he left Cuba, and had been advised by the Tlaxcalans not to proceed to Tenochtitlán. Instead of returning to Veracruz, he asked his new allies for 2,000 more warriors to accompany his expedition to Cholula, and eventually Tenochtitlán. Cholula became the key for Cortés. It could open the gates and drawbridges of Tenochtitlán. Cortés and his grizzly band of 400 Spaniards, 12 remaining horses, a combined force of 6,000 Cempoalans and Tlaxcalans were coaxed into the very heart of Cholula, some 60 miles to the southeast of the infamous

Tenochtitlán. Cholula is on the slopes of the twin volcanoes, Popo and Izta. They rise to 17,887 and 17,342 feet above sea level, respectively, and are always covered with snow. They are called the twin sisters. They are magnificent! Only the Pico de Orizaba volcano which rises to the heavens at 18,405 feet is higher. The Gallegos, the Spaniards, had never seen anything like the twin sisters. As they arrived in Cholula from Tlaxcala, the great Popo was spewing ash and lava from its crater and the valiant Diego de Ordáz with a group of Tlaxcalans scaled the summit and looked into the mighty crater. The site they beheld was something no western European had beheld. This was out-of-this world stuff for the Spaniards. They were in a space out of time.

As they ascended the foothills of the great volcanoes on the approach to Cholula, they caught their first glimpse of Tenochtitlán, some 60 miles away. It lay in the middle of a great lake and was connected to the mainland in 3 places by large causeways. The city itself was huge by European standards. It was an engineering masterpiece. It had sluice gates for controlling the level of the lake. The causeways had numerous draw-bridges. There were two great aqueducts which connected it to the fresh-water springs in the mountains. It was surrounded by floating gardens of flowers and vegetables. The geometric grids of streets were visible even from the slopes of Popo and Izta. Magnificent pyramids rose in the center and surveyed the entire layout. And along the shore of the lake were another 10 or 12 large cities with similar grandiose features. Farther inland the Gallegos or Spaniards could see even more cities. The total population of the immediate area probably approached 2 million. In comparison, the largest European city in 1519 was Paris, France. Its population was somewhere near 200,000. There were probably 300,000 people living in the center of Tenochtitlán. Perhaps the only larger city in the early 16th century was Beijing, China, with a population of 600,000. Including the entire Lake Texcoco population, Tenochtitlán was probably four times the size of Beijing. At this moment in time, this first glimpse of Tenochtitlán from Cholula was truly the pinnacle of first contact between the European and the American. And, here was **Cortés** with 400 soldiers and approximately 6,000 indigenous warriors' intent on conquering Tenochtitlán. It was incredible! It was seemingly impossible! How could the indefatigable **Cortés** pull it off this time?

Cholula, Cholula. Just the sound of Cholula gives me the goose bumps! Cholula was the spiritual city of the Teotihuacanos before the Toltecs and then the Aztecs usurped their authority and culture. It was founded on the slopes of the twin sisters because it is a magical place. The eastern and western Sierra Madre Mountains which traverse the whole of Mexico, from north to south begin to come together here. They finally merge into one glorious mountain range in Oaxaca. And not surprisingly Oaxaca is where **Cortés** chose to build his hacienda after the conquests. But here as the ranges merge the twin volcanoes rise to the heavens. The presence of these snow-covered giants dominates the entire region. When I was living in Bosque de La Herradura in Mexico City, in the early nineties, I could see them from my garden after a big storm. The rest of the time they were obscured by the pollution. In 1519, when **Cortés,** arrived they were spectacular. Cholula, Cholula. It sits almost between the twin sisters as you approach from the east. Cholula was sacred to the Teotihuacanos. The original Cholulans were peaceful and avoided all conflicts. They were spiritual. Cholula was the spiritual center of the Golden Age of Mexico. The Cholulans and Teotihuacanos built the largest pyramid in the world here on the slopes of Popo and Izta. Today, after it was raised by the Spaniards and their allies, only the base remains. This base is 20% again larger than the great pyramid base of Cheops. By good fortune and a bribe I was able to climb the great Cheops pyramid in 1982, just at sunset. I watched the sun set over the Nile river valley and remember thinking about the extraordinary pyramids at Cholula and Teotihuacán.

I was in my mid twenties when I began to have a recurring dream about a great maze. In the first dreams I remember entering the maze with a torch. I would try to find my way through the maze and the torch would falter so I would return to the entrance. The entrance was massive and made of stone. At the same time in my conscious life I was maturing and considering whether to continue with a young love affair, whether to continue studying archaeology, whether to continue, etc. I was maturing and making the normal decisions of early adulthood. With each recurring dream

I would advance farther into the maze. As I advanced consciously in my decision making in my day to day life I seemed to advance farther in the maze in my dreams. I had this recurring dream for approximately 3 years. When I was 29 I decided to make a big change in my life. I headed to Europe for a 6 month trip. It turned into an 18 month journey that included most of Europe and North Africa. It was the right thing for me to do at that time in my life. At about the same time I finally found my way through the maze in my dreams. There seemed to be a correlation between my decision to go to Europe and my successful traversing of the maze. As I had been meandering through the maze for almost 3 years I no longer needed a torch. I knew all of the tunnels in the maze. I knew the wrong turns as well as the correct turns. During my final dream I emerged at the far side of the maze. I entered the sunlight and overhead was a brilliant blue sky. I was overlooking a broad plain. Directly in front of me was an old Spanish-style church. I surveyed the area and saw a great number of Spanish-style churches. I felt happy and content. I was at the end of a long journey. I stopped having that series of recurring dreams. It was over, or so I thought. A few years later my fiancé and I planned a trip to Cholula, as I wanted to see this magnificent site of which I had read but never seen. We stayed in the nearby city of Puebla, and drove out to Cholula by car. I had a strange feeling of familiarity as we arrived at the base of the old pyramid. I parked and we walked to the entrance and paid the fee to enter the narrow passageways which are still passable inside the great base. I declined to take a guide at the entrance because it felt so familiar. I followed my instinct and entered the dark chasm of the maze. My fiancé grasped my hand and followed. At each turn, in the dark, I knew to go left or right. I had visited this maze many, many times. I knew the smooth feel of the large hewn boulders. I knew where to duck low so as not to bump my head. We passed through the maze very rapidly. I was almost running as we came to the first glimpse of light at the far exit. I stopped. It felt as though I were back in my dreams. I told my fiancé that when we came to the exit we would see a large old Spanish church and incredibly blue skies. As we slowly approached the exit I could see the brilliant blue sky above Popo and Izta once again. As we walked clear of the pyramid we were directly opposite an old Spanish church. She was startled and thought it must be a joke. I was reconfirmed that there are things that happen in the world which are unexplainable. I was wowed by what had happened. I could not explain it. I still cannot explain it. I was wowed at Cholula and so were **Cortés** and his men.

Bernal Díaz wrote of the first sight of Tenochtitlán from Cholula, "When we saw so many cities built out on the water, and so many great towns on the dry land, and those straight, long causeways that led toward Tenochtitlán, we were amazed and said that this was like the enchantments..."6 The Spaniards were amazed at the site of both Cholula and Tenochtitlán in the distance. The interesting thing, however, is that these peoples were the inheritors of this culture. The great pyramid at Cholula had been built 1000 years before by the true Cholulan culture which was, of course, a sister culture of the Teotihuacanos. The technology and engineering that was applied in the construction at Tenochtitlán was that of the Teotihuacanos. "The Mexica (Aztecs) lordlings and bureaucrats had learned all the old skills and traditions. They planned, built, and used splendid houses, temples, causeways, bridges, roads, and dikes. They carried on all the ancient arts and crafts, though without the charm and elegance of the Classical civilization..." "There is no evidence that the Mexic civilization was making any progress, especially when measured against what had preceded it."7 But even as **Cortés** and his men entered the beautiful city of Cholula, Montezuma planned his treachery.

Word of the conquistador's arrival and subsequent successes with both the Cempoalans and Tlaxcalans had spread throughout the Aztec Empire. Montezuma was perplexed. On the one hand, he was ready to kill, sacrifice, and eat the Spaniards as was the custom of the Aztecs. On the other hand, many people were becoming convinced that Cortés was actually the reincarnation of the god Quetzalcoatl and was fulfilling the ancient prophecy of his return. Montezuma decided to set a trap with the aid of the Cholulans to kill and capture the Spaniards. He promised to give the Cholulans 20 of the Spaniards to be sacrificed and eaten at Cholula. The remaining Spaniards who were not killed in the attack would be taken to Tenochtitlán to suffer the same fate. The plan was simple. Montezuma sent 30,000 warriors to Cholula.

They were hidden in the ravines and canyons on the outskirts of the city. The Cholulans had 8,000 warriors in the city who would act as a personal security force for Cortés as they marched the 60 miles to Tenochtitlán. The conquistadors would be trapped between the Cholulan warriors and Aztec warriors once they were outside the city. Montezuma sent his lying emissaries to Cortés with more presents of gold in order to entice him to Tenochtitlán. Doña Marina, however, learned of the plot and notified Cortés in advance.

Cortés and his captains devised a brilliant counter strategy. On the proposed morning of departure for Tenochtitlán, the Spanish secretly encircled the Cholulans inside the city. Without warning they viciously attacked. Thousands of warriors were caught in the crossfire of musket and canon and all the exits for retreat were closed and fortified. Within 3 hours more than 6,000 Cholulan warriors lay dead in the main plaza. Thousands of women and children were also killed. The remaining Cholulans fled the city. Surprisingly, the 30,000 Aztec warriors did not come to the aid of their comrades. These Cholulans were their comrades-in-arms. The Cholulans and Aztecs were neighbors, cousins, brothers, sisters, brother-in-laws, sister-in-laws, and friends. They were not strangers. They were not enemies. The superior force of 40,000 Cholulans and Aztecs could have easily overcome **Cortés** and his allies. But the Aztecs watched the massacre from outside the city and then returned to Tenochtitlán. This cowardliness seemed to be an Aztec character trait and **Cortés** had seen it in their other battles. They had witnessed something quite similar in each of the many attacks they had endured over the past six months. Once the battle tide slightly began to turn in favor of the Spaniards, the Mexicans would lose all courage and flee. **Cortés** was glad to see the cowardly Aztecs fleeing towards Tenochtitlán. He and his men dropped to their knees to give thanks. Montezuma with his huge armies could have attacked and annihilated the handful of Spaniards at any strategic point along the 250 mile road from the coast to the capital. The Aztec garrisons throughout the empire totaled more than a million warriors. Yet, **Cortés** and his 400 soldiers had taken the prestigious city of Cholula on the outskirts of the grand capital.

This ferocious, savage, cannibalistic culture seems to have bred an army of cowards. In reality it was a culture of cowards. They were brutal, yes, horrendous, murderous, liver-eating cannibals. But they were also cowards. This cowardly propensity in many ways explains their system of accommodation. The wars that were fought were typically not wars on a grand scale. Wars were fought between the various city-states of Mexico, but not on a grand scale. The battles (with some exceptions such as the Tarascan battles) were kidnapping skirmishes. They were people-obtaining skirmishes, grand-scale kidnappings. Montezuma would, for example, send an army of 50,000 warriors against a city-state such as Cempoala. The Cempoalans would field perhaps 30,000 warriors in defense. After a small but bloody encounter the Cempoalans would agree to exchange a large number of people in order to make the peace. This was the Mexican system of accommodation. The Cempoalans had this same relationship with various city-state neighbors as well. The Cempoalans would accommodate the larger, more powerful Aztecs, and then in turn be accommodated by some other weaker city-state. The commerce was humanity. Many of the people given to the Aztecs would have been slaves, kidnapped neighbors, people that had been captured in similar battles by the Cempoalans. Many of the defeated ranks of warriors were captured, put in cages to be fattened, sacrificed, dismembered, and then eaten. Unfortunately, the Aztecs also took the prized sons and daughters of their subservient neighbors. And so this commerce was practiced via war throughout the empire. The entire empire of city-states had embraced this bloody scheme. It was not a political confederacy which was ruled by the Aztecs. It was a system of accommodation built around fear, survival, and cowardice.

This system, in itself, explains why the Aztecs did not rush to the rescue of their neighbors. They were not accustomed to supporting their neighbors. They comingled, coexisted, banded together to send warriors in pursuit of bloody bounty in order to sacrifice to their gods. But they did not support each other in any political confederation based on common good or a common value system. The Mexicans had evolved or degraded to the status of slaves throughout the empire. They were slaves to this system of accommodation and sacrifice. In reality they had even accepted the bondages of slavery but without chains. They were not slaves in the more traditional European-African-type relationship. It was a cultural enslavement. "The habit of deference and subordination was engrained in the Mexic soul, and the Conquest hardly affected it".[8] No person was permitted to appear in front of Montezuma unless he was dressed in rags. Even great captains, warriors, and other city-state leaders were accustomed to dressing in rags when in the audience of Montezuma. They were not allowed to look at Montezuma eye-to-eye. These great leaders, in turn, demanded the same of their underlings. Everyone had become subservient. Everyone had become a slave. This attitude is still prevalent in 21st century Mexican relationships. The attitude of the subservient man still exists in Mexico. Every worker has his Patron and treats him as if he is his super-father or superior. It had evolved for 500 years under the Toltecs and Aztecs. And Montezuma was the head slave. He was driven to perpetuate this 500 year-old system of accommodation, subservience, and sacrifice. The altar was his master. This altar demanded the hearts and blood of victim after victim. He had only to maintain a superior force of warriors in order to perpetuate his position, his family, his culture, his city-state, his enslaved empire. But now he was being invaded by a force which he did not understand. The Spaniards were not interested in captives. They were not sacrificing human beings to the gods. They were spreading the rumors of a merciful, loving, caring god. And they were successfully conquering one city-state after the next. They were encamped in the city of Cholula, a mere 60 miles from his capital. His plan to annihilate them had failed. Montezuma began to wonder if **Cortés** was the reincarnation of Quetzalcoatl, the ancient god of Tula. The ancient, blue-eyed, bearded Quetzalcoatl who had sailed to the east with promises to one day return may have returned as **Cortés**.

Quetzalcoatl's rule was in the early days of the Toltec regime. The Toltecs, antecedents of the Aztecs, had usurped control of the Classical, Golden Age of Mexico from the Teotihuacanos. They were nomadic invaders from the northwestern part of Mexico. They were uneducated and barbarous. But, they were initially influenced in a positive way by the remnants of the once great Teotihuacán culture. "At the beginning of the tenth century they swept into the central valley by Mixcoatl (Cloud Serpent), a Mexican Genghis Khan, who swiftly scattered his demoralized opponents."9 Oddly, Mixcoatl's son was educated in the tradition of the ancient Teotihuacán god, Quetzalcoatl, and eventually took his name. He assumed leadership of the Toltecs and began to embrace the ancient ideas of education, culture, architecture, agriculture, and peace. The barbarous Toltecs, however, were unable to assimilate on a large scale. After twenty years of enlightened rule, Quetzalcoatl and his followers were forced into exile. They supposedly sailed across the Gulf to the Yucatán Peninsula with promises to one day return and once again enlighten the brutes from the north.

Montezuma was a descendent of these brutes from the north. He knew the legend of Quetzalcoatl. He had seen the painted codices which depicted Cortes' 11 ships which had sailed into the harbor at Veracruz from the east. He had seen the painted portraits of the blue-eyed, bearded conquistador. **Cortés** and his men appeared to be invincible. **Cortés** preached of a single god, a peaceful god, who did not demand sacrifices. Was **Cortés** the returning Quetzalcoatl? Was he fulfilling the promises of Quetzalcoatl?

Montezuma contemplated his next move while **Cortés** did the same. Their belief systems, their values guided them. **Cortés** was confident. He had the loyalty of his men and the allegiance of 8,000 indigenous warriors. Although a forceful leader, **Cortés** empowered his captains and sought their counsel. He was known as an ingenious peace maker among his captains. His will was indefatigable, driven by his devout religious beliefs. He believed that his god was directing this entire melodrama of the conquest of Mexico. His skills at preaching to the conquered Mexicans were well honed as he routinely convinced his vanquished enemies to become his allies. The values of the 16th century Christian faith were the values of **Cortés**. He believed that he had the responsibility to be the keeper of his brother, his friend, and his neighbor. He believed in a higher purpose for mankind and the rewards of immortality in paradise. This reward was only achievable through a life of service both to mankind and god. It was based on a concept of good deeds and true hearts. The soldiers had complete trust in his battlefield strategies. His enemies had come to believe in the rumors he spread of their invincibility and godliness. His mission included many things, but among them were the intent to rid the indigenous population of the savage system of human sacrifice and cannibalism.

Montezuma, in contrast, had a completely different value and belief system. He was educated to be a priest but the untimely death of his militaristic brother changed his destiny. Montezuma's name means, *The Angry Lord*. His father's name translates as, *The Scourge*. Montezuma was accustomed to the sound of shrieking warriors as they had their hearts snatched from their breasts. He was famous for routinely ordering the brutal death of any potential opponent or advisor that fell from his grace. He would order not only their deaths but that of their entire families. He would have the brains of their children smashed upon the altars or sides of their homes before they would be completed destroyed. With Montezuma vengeance gained a new meaning. He was feared throughout the empire. Fear and brutality were the glue that bound his empire together. But from his religious training there was a mystical side to his nature. He, like **Cortés,** believed in his divine destiny that was both foretold and watched over by his gods. His gods, however, were merciless. They demanded sacrifices. The pantheon of gods that he worshipped had translated names such as: *Lover of Hearts, Drinker of Blood, God of Coyotes, god of the Monsters, Lord of the Phantoms, Snake Mother, Feeder of the Beasts, and Lord of the Dark*. His mission was to satisfy the blood-thirst of the gods.

On the surface this was a classical collision of good versus evil, light versus dark. The Spaniards spent two weeks in Cholula, after the victorious massacre of 6,000 Cholulans. **Cortés** with the assistance of Doña Marina, once again, made the peace and formed an alliance with another conquered city-state. As the conquistadors searched the city of Cholula in the ensuing days after the battle they discovered hundreds of large wooden cages. The cages were filled with young men and boys who were being fattened for the butcher. They had encountered this in every village and town on the march from the sea. But the quantity of cages and number of captives was a bit mind-boggling to the Spaniards. They were feeling the deep, dark hand that was upon the land and as they were drawn closer to the epicenter of the dark force and the horrendous evidence of its wickedness were more and more appalling. Archaeologists and population experts believe the Aztec culture was responsible for the sacrifice of "20,000 to 50,000 people a year in the 15th and early 16th centuries".[10] In other words, they were sacrificing between 2 and 5 million people a century. Imagine, 50 to 150 people being brutally sacrificed and eaten every single day in the central Valley of Mexico. The hundreds of thousands of skulls that the conquistadors found in village after village evidenced this gruesome behavior. Cortés instructed his men to break open the cages and set the captives free. He vowed to do the same thing in Tenochtitlán, and throughout the New World.

Once again, the treacherous Montezuma sent mixed signals to Cortés. After the defeat at Cholula, Montezuma once again sent his emissaries with presents of gold. He disclaimed all responsibility for the Cholulan's plan to attack and kill his men. This is such a Mexican thing. This has persisted and is pervasive throughout the culture. This inability to accept responsibility for any mistake is a dominant Mexican characteristic. No matter how insignificant or how serious the misdeed, Mexicans are taught from an early age to discount personal responsibility. The idea of apologizing does not exist in the Mexican belief system. I can count, on one hand, the number of times I have heard a Mexican take responsibility and apologize for poor behavior or any inappropriate action in the last 35 years. They just do not take personal responsibility for mistakes. It is just not part of the culture. This behavior existed 500 years ago and still exists today. He entreated **Cortés** to march to Tenochtitlán, and embrace him as his true friend. He, of course, was not responsible for the plan to ambush, kill, capture, sacrifice, and eat the Spaniards. It was a Cholulan plan. After all, his emissaries explained, the Cholulans were a deceitful and treacherous people. As before, he swore allegiance to the great Emperor of Europe and invited Cortés to enter Tenochtitlán, as a friend.

Cortés counseled with his captains and allies. They decided to march into Tenochtitlán. As they marched through the many towns and villages between Cholula and the Aztec capital they were greeted by the inhabitants with hospitality, presents, and stories of hatred for Montezuma. They were told stories of the tax collectors whose favorite insult was to violate the attractive, young, women of the villages in front of their fathers and husbands. Violate, of course, means rape. Imagine the scene of a group of Aztec tax collectors entering a small town to excise the tribute, collect the taxes. There was no money or bartering system. They came for humans. They took gold too. But they came for the live bodies. And while the captives were being taken out of the cages and harnessed by rope for the trip to Tenochtitlán, the tax collectors were raping the young women in the town square. Imagine the scene. My culture is so different that I have a hard time even getting a visual image of that scene. The fathers and husbands stood there and watched as their daughters and wives were raped. How can that actually happen? How can a father choose life over the accepted rape of his young daughter? How can a husband watch as his wife is brutalized by a stranger? But they themselves knew that their time would soon come to repeat this scene in another weaker village. They knew that they would soon be perpetuating the same violence on some other victim. This also, was part of the great system of accommodation. It was a broad, accepted scheme of violent interaction. It was not only accepted but was practiced at all levels. The Spaniards listened to the complaints and were appalled. They promised to rid the land of tyranny, sodomy, rape, robbery, sacrifice, and cannibalism. They once again set their sights for the center of this hellish place, Tenochtitlán.

The scholars still argue over the improbable outcome of **Cortés'** encounter with Montezuma. It is still almost impossible to believe that **Cortés** and his troops, now less than 400 men strong could conquer the Aztecs. It was 9 months earlier when more than 600 stalwart soldiers had left Cuba, in search of the riches of the mainland. And now they were crossing the great Itztapalapa causeway and straight into the belly of the beast. Montezuma held his hundreds of thousands of warriors at bay. He did not order a massacre of which the outcome would have been certain. On the contrary, he and his ghastly group of blood-thirty god worshippers coaxed **Cortés** into the city. They housed the entire entourage in great halls which were connected to beautiful gardens that were fed by the waters of the great lake Texcoco. Montezuma wanted to be reassured that the Spaniards were real men and not the reincarnation of Quetzalcoatl. He had no intention of incurring the wrath of the god, Huichilobos, the Drinker of Blood, by making the mistake of killing the returning god Quetzalcoatl. Montezuma was brutal, savage, murderous, and vengeful, but he was also very fearful, superstitious, and cowardly. He met **Cortés** face-to-face and then began an almost endless sacrificial offering to Huichilobos in order to ascertain his instructions. When **Cortés** and a few captains were taken by Montezuma to one of his religious temples they found, "smoking braziers", "in which they were burning the hearts of three Indians whom they had sacrificed that day; and all the walls and shrines of that shrine were so splashed and caked with blood that they and the floor too were black. Indeed, the whole place stank abominably. We then looked to the left and saw another great image of the same height as Huichilobos, with a face like a bear and eyes that glittered." "This Tezcatlipoca, the god of hell, had charge of the Mexicans' souls, and his body was surrounded by figures of little devils with snakes' tails."11 Montezuma was imploring his gods to give him direction. He contemplated the annihilation of the invaders. But a combination of indecision and powerful intimidation from **Cortés** prevented Montezuma from ordering an immediate massacre or capture.

This was no baby diapers, oops, wrong place, wrong time scenario. The conquistadors were not only inside the gates of hell on earth they were in the very belly of the beast. They had been sucked into the temple of death inside Mount Doom. They could not have been in a more dangerous situation. Montezuma could have had them for dinner at any time he or the gods wished.

Soon enough he realized that the Spaniards were not gods. But the wiley Cortés with the articulate arguing of Doña Marina convinced Montezuma that the legends, myths, prophecies were being fulfilled. No, the Spaniards were not gods. But they were the embodiment of the prophecies. These Spaniards were the blue-eyed, bearded ones who arrived over the great sea from the east. Montezuma called his great captains together and told them, "to reflect how for many years past they had known for certain from their ancestral tradition, set down in their books of records, that men would come from the direction of the sunrise to rule these lands, and that the rule and domination of Mexico would then come to an end. He believed that from what his gods had told him that we were these men." 12 There could be no doubt, Doña Marina argued, that these were the men who would end the 500 year reign of the Toltec-Aztec culture in central Mexico. Just as Montezuma began to accept his inevitable defeat as fate, many of his chieftains began to plot against him and the Spaniards. Sensing the possibility of an attack, Cortés captains advised an immediate sequestering of Montezuma.

It is almost unexplainable (from a European perspective) but Montezuma agreed to accept house arrest under the watchful eye of the Spaniards. But it was not entirely beyond understanding. In reality it was predictable, true to course. It is what should be expected from the Mexican culture. This impeccable sense of irresponsibility and indecision were part of the Aztec psyche. Montezuma could not save his culture for fear of somehow being held responsible by his evil gods. He did not want the responsibility of interfering with destiny. Furthermore, he had no desire to save his culture. This was not a culture of heroes. The Aztec story was not a story of good prevailing over evil. It was the reverse. There were no individual heroes who were slaying dragons in order to save mankind. This was a warrior society, a kidnapping society. The goal was to capture human beings not slay dragons or save the women and children from the invading hordes. The Aztecs were the hordes. It was a 500 year history of evil prevailing over good. The noble concepts of the Teotihuacanos had been subverted centuries ago. Those sentiments were no longer part of the 15th century Aztec world. The gods were no longer being entreated to produce a good crop and provide for the well being of society. The sacrifices were an ever increasing habit of brutal human sacrifice and cannibalism. This culture had degenerated to such a perverse nature that the concept of a hero (Montezuma) saving his culture was impossible. He could have killed and sacrificed the conquistadors. But he was not driven to save his culture. Montezuma was preoccupied with destiny and was the consummate Mexican. His own well being, his own personal interaction with Cortés, and this fantastic cultural collision is what drove his actions. He ordered his generals, his leaders from

Tacuba, Texcoco, Cholula, from all his regions to bring gifts of gold to Cortés and his men.

Cortés and his men were in Tenochtitlán for approximately 6 months before the situation started to deteriorate. Montezuma, who was under house arrest, was watched closely. On a routine basis he and Cortés met. The silver-tongued Cortés convinced him to bring all the gold in the storage vaults of his various city-states to Tenochtitlán. During these six months more than 600,000 pounds of gold and precious jewels were collected and turned over to the Spaniards. Montezuma placated his leaders with words the same way as Cortés placated Montezuma. But the Aztecs were malcontented. Many looked for an opportunity to oust Montezuma and attack the Spaniards. The opportunity came with the sudden arrival on the coast of a 19-ship armada from Cuba. Unfortunately, for Cortés, the armada had not been sent to reinforce his expedition. Its leader, Pánfilo de Narváez, was sent to replace Cortés and assume control of the Spanish conquest of New Spain (Mexico). On learning of the situation Cortés took half of his men and marched back to Cempoala and ambushed Narváez's exploratory landing party. He captured Narváez and eventually convinced his men to switch allegiances to him.

What a seemingly good stroke of luck for Cortés. Narváez's force included 900 men, 90 cavalry, 80 crossbowmen, and the same number of musketeers. All totaled Cortés now had almost 1300 men. Just as he was relishing his good luck he received news from his men that the Aztecs had launched a viscous attack in Tenochtitlán. With his new army he made a forced march back in a week's time. The Aztecs commenced an all-out attack as soon as he had entered the city. For five days and nights the fighting never ended. Montezuma tried to negotiate a peace but was killed by his own warriors. In desperation Cortés and his men abandoned the great capital on the 5th night after their return. They were pursued and trapped on the many bridges along the causeways. Hundreds were killed as they made their escape to Otumba, where they stopped to regroup. The Aztecs again attacked relentlessly and hundreds more were killed. The retreat continued to Tlaxcala. Fortunately, the Tlaxcalans were reliable allies as they hated Montezuma and his warriors. They came to Cortés' rescue and summoned a force of 30,000 men and halted the Aztec attack. It had been disastrous for the conquistadors. Nearly 900 brave men were dead or captured. Eighty percent of their cavalry was lost. Their powder and canons were lost. Ninety percent of the gold was lost. Every single survivor was wounded. Montezuma, who had been in their sequestered protection, was dead. Cortés had to make a serious decision. He had two choices. They could return to Veracruz, and then to Cuba on the ships of Narváez. Or, they could recuperate under the protection of the Tlaxcalans and make plans for the re-conquest of mighty Tenochtitlán. Cortés, of course, chose the latter.

Surprisingly, to Cortés, the Aztecs did not attack the Tlaxcalans. He had seen their strength in his defeat in Tenochtitlán, and Otumba. With allies, their combined forces were in the hundreds of thousands or perhaps more. He could not understand why Cuauhtémoc, the new leader, chose to return to Tenochtitlán. Cortés did not realize the true relationship between Tlaxcala (and other semi-independent city-states) and the Aztecs. He was accustomed to the European template for societal and political interactions. These templates did not exist in the New World. The entire setup was different. The Aztecs were not interested in administering political control over the other city-states. They were interested in dominating them, controlling them. They wanted their closest allies to be part of their inner circle. They wanted the other city-states to be their breeding grounds and warehouses for human flesh. They needed large pools of human victims. It was a unique situation that anthropologists have not encountered anywhere else in the world. The entire societal/political system was driven by the need to sacrifice and then cannibalize human beings. The world has never seen anything that compares to this!

The Tlaxcalans were permitted to exist as a powerful city-state. The Aztecs wanted the Tlaxcalans to be successful in their endeavors to perpetuate this cannibalistic culture. But they did not want them to be in their inner circle of city-states such as Cholula or Texcoco. They did not want to eat the members of their inner circle, their closest neighbors, and relatives. But they did want large pools of human victims in a close proximity. Therefore, city-states like Tlaxcala were not conquered and administered politically. They were dominated and controlled. But, the Aztecs encouraged the Tlaxcalans to emulate their template, their model. And the Tlaxcalans, the Cempoalans, and the other city-states did just that. Each city-state had its inner circle of allies. Each had its arch enemies. They all worshipped the same pantheon of gods. They all sacrificed their captured victims and ate their flesh.

For various reasons, many of the 20th century historians gloss over the importance of cannibalism in the Aztec or Mexican culture. Few anthropologists or archaeologists offer reasons as to why this culture became so dependent on human flesh. There is also no consensus on the numbers of sacrificial deaths that were taking place throughout central Mexico. Most experts believe the number was between 20,000 and 50,000 on an average year in the 15th century. Others, however, believe it was much higher. "Recently, Woodrow Borah, possibly the leading authority on the demography of Mexico at the time of the conquest, has also revised the estimated number of persons sacrificed in central Mexico in the 15th century to 250,000 per year, equivalent to 1 percent of the total population. According to Borah, this figure is consistent with the sacrifice of an estimated 1,000 to 3,000 persons yearly at the largest of the thousands of temples scattered throughout the Aztec Triple Alliance". [13] There are more than 11,000 known archaeological sites of cities, towns and villages from this era. The 90 or so that have been scientifically excavated verify levels of sacrificial and cannibalistic behavior which support Borah's calculations.

Whatever the actual number, it was very, very large. In 1487, for example, the great pyramid at Tenochtitlán was dedicated to Huichilobos, god of war. Numerous Aztec codices (fig-bark painted books of the Aztecs) and later recorded Aztec histories describe the mass sacrifices that took place during that short period of a few days or perhaps a month. One puts the number at 20,000 while another states the sacrificial deaths at 72,344. Three other sources agree that the number was precisely 80,400. This enormous slaughter ranks as one of the worst single-event atrocities that were ever perpetrated by man against man in history. The total number of sacrificial deaths during the reign of the Aztecs was probably 35 million or more persons. This ranking would put the

Aztecs in fifth place for all-time atrocities only behind, "World War II - 55 million; Mao Zedong - 40 million; the Mongolian Conquests – 40 million; and the Lushan Revolt – 36 million".[14] It is incredible to realize that it took place during the 14th and 15th centuries. If Borah's estimates are accurate, we can calculate that 4,250,000 persons were sacrificed during Montezuma's 17 year reign alone. This system was killing people almost as fast as their European and Asian successors: Stalin, Mao Zedong, and Adolf Hitler in the 20th century.

Cuauhtémoc and his warriors returned to Tenochtitlán, because Cortés was no longer a threat to their system. They had killed and captured many of his men. The captured Spanish soldiers along with hundreds of Tlaxcalan warriors were now in cages being fattened on corn cakes and beans. Cuauhtémoc and his allies were having huge sacrificial ceremonies honoring their gods. The palpitating hearts of the Tlaxcalans were being cut from their chests with sharp obsidian blades. Their blood was being plastered on the walls of the Huichilobos shrines. The Aztecs, Cholulans, and Texcocos were feasting on their arms and legs. Their torsos were fed to the Aztec's captured jaguars and pumas. Upon the conquistadors' return to Tenochtitlán, they would witness the live sacrifice and consumption of their own former companions and brothers-in-arms. No modern Europeans had witnessed this atrocity before the Spaniards.

Fortunately for the Spaniards, the Tlaxcalans believed in their mythology. They believed that they would be delivered from the dark hand that covered the land. Or maybe they were just fearful of the dark, evil system that made murderous, cannibals out of otherwise decent human beings. They wanted to believe in the prophetic return of the peaceful god, Quetzalcoatl. They put their faith in Cortés and his men. They swore an allegiance to help him recover from his defeat and once again march against the Aztecs in Tenochtitlán.

The Spaniards regained their strength, recovered from their wounds and made their plans as the final months of 1520 waned. The news of Mexican gold had spread to the islands of the Caribbean and to Spain. Ships with much needed supplies arrived and Cortés rebuilt his army. He also devised a new strategy for conquering the Aztecs. Tenochtitlán was an island city in the middle of Lake Texcoco which was 30 miles long and 15 miles wide. The city was connected to the mainland by three causeways and two aqueducts. Cortés planned to blockade the causeways, cut the aqueducts which supplied fresh water, and gain control of the lake. He needed an armada of strong boats in order to dominate the lake. As Cortés and his Tlaxcalan and Cempoalan allies controlled all the land west from Tlaxcala to the coast; he decided to send his carpenters with Tlaxcalan aid into the tropical forest near Veracruz to cut wood and fashion 13 sailing boats. His plan was bold. He would lay siege to the great Aztec city and force them to surrender.

While his carpenters cut trees, Cortés took his army to Texcoco, which was on the Tlaxcalan side of the lake. Once again he was able to make allies with a hostile enemy. The Mexicans were extremely fickled. Their pattern of behavior was one that Cortés now knew very well. The leaders of the various city-states surrounding the lake were allies with the Aztecs of Tenochtitlán. Their warriors were at the disposal of the brave but young Aztec leader, Cuauhtémoc, who had assumed control shortly after the defeat of the Spaniards when they were driven from the city. But these subservient leaders and warriors were not stalwarts. Knowing this, Cortés decided to circumambulate the lake and defeat or win over the alliance of each of the various city-states that supported Cuauhtémoc. The Mexican behavior was predictable. Cortés and his men would be taunted by the Mexicans as they entered each region or city-state. The Mexicans would yell insults and whistle. They would threaten them with sacrifice; remind them that very soon they would be feasting on their arms and legs. Their heads, they screamed, would be added to the skull racks. Once the real fighting began it usually was over in a matter of thirty minutes or an hour. These so called allies of the Aztecs were quick to make the peace, declare defeat, change allegiances, give up slaves, forfeit warriors, and surrender daughters and wives to be raped. It was the Mexican system of accommodation.

Cortés's march around the lake took him as far south as Cuernavaca, and as far north as Tepotzotlán. In some cases the fighting was viscous and Iztapalapa, the gateway city to the southern causeway, was razed. Many of these warriors and some others took their canoes and joined the Aztecs in Tenochtitlán. In any event, they reconnoitered the entrances to the three causeways, neutralized most of the outlying city-states, and finalized their strategy of laying siege to the city.

News arrived, as they returned to Texcoco, on the eastern shore, that 8,000 Tlaxcalans and the Spanish carpenters were on the road from Veracruz, with the unassembled but manufactured components for the 13-ship armada. Cortés' scheme   was grandiose. The line of Tlaxcalan workers who carried the beams and planks stretched for six miles. Riggings of sails, oars, canons, and various armaments were supplied from the newly arriving Spanish ships at the coast. Each launch would carry twelve oarsmen, a canon, twelve crossbowmen and musketeers, and a captain. They would support Cortés's new army of which there were almost a thousand Spaniards and an assembly of more than 30,000 Tlaxcalans, Cempoalans, and others. As Cortés completed his circumambulation of the lake, his allied support grew to 50,000 warriors. The scope of this endeavor was now enormous.

The launches were assembled, a division of soldiers with allies was sent to capture and control each of the three causeways, and Cortés took personal control of the armada. The siege of Tenochtitlán began on May 13, 1521. The Aztecs were not indecisive or weak like their subserviant city-state neighbors. They were not accustomed to defeat. They were not planning to lose their empire. The war was on! It was brutal, fierce. Books have been filled with chapters of the heroic, gruesome fighting on both sides. The advantage and apparent victory went back and forth from Aztec to Spaniard many times. On one occasion a daring raid by Cortés faltered and 65 men were captured by Cuauhtémoc's warriors. For the ensuing 10 days, Cortés, Bernal Díaz, Pedro de Alvarado, and the rest, "saw our comrades who had been captured in Cortés's defeat being dragged up the steps to be sacrificed. When they had hauled them up to a small platform in front of the shrine where they kept their accursed idols...", "...laid them down on their backs on some narrow stones of sacrifice and, cutting open their chests, drew out their palpitating hearts which they offered to the idols before them. Then they kicked the bodies down the steps, and the Indian butchers who were waiting below cut off their arms and legs and flayed their faces,", "then they ate their flesh with a sauce of peppers and tomatoes."15 This went on for ten days and nights. The fighting had been continual for almost two months and seemed to intensify with each day. Now, not surprisingly, ninety percent of the Spaniard's allies forsook their allegiance and oath of support and returned to their homes. Cortés was left with a small, battered, severely wounded army and only 2,000 of the most stalwart Tlaxcalan and Texcoco braves.

His bold attack was disastrous and almost sealed their defeat. His Texcoco allies advised him to be patient and give the siege more time to work. He took their advice. The Aztecs were denied easy access to fresh water and their food convoys via canoe were not adequate to supply their needs. They were beginning to die of thirst and hunger. Another curious thing had happened as well. The previous year at least one of the soldiers of Narváez's battalion who accompanied Cortés back to Tenochtitlán had smallpox. When the Aztecs exorcised their city of the Spaniards the year before, unfortunately for them, they did not exorcise this virus. The New World Man was not prepared for this virus as was the European. It had devastating effects. The combination of the smallpox virus, lack of fresh water and insufficient food, and the resumed attacks of the Spaniards finally took its toll. Ninety-three days after the siege began it was over. Cuauhtémoc was in custody, the Aztec peoples were dead, dying, or fleeing in all directions. As was stated by George W. Bush, "Mission Accomplished".

The 500-year reign of the Toltec-Aztec Empire was at an end. The dark side of the force was defeated, not destroyed but defeated. Tenochtitlán was razed. The city was completely destroyed. Afterwards the Spaniards were in a state of shock. Many soldiers later reported the sensation of going deaf as the battle abruptly ended. They had become accustomed to a 24-hour bombardment of yells, screams, whistles, drums, horns, and the constant sound of battle. It was a surrealistic scene. It was quiet. The bodies were lying everywhere. Decapitated heads were stacked in rows and rotting. The walled area where they kept their wild animals was strewn with hundreds of partially eaten human torsos. It was like a hellish dream. But this was no dream! This was the evidence of what happens to humanity gone afoul. This was like Auschwitz. Later, Bernal Díaz counted one stack of skulls which contained more than 136,000 skulls. It was only one stack of many. The walls of the shrines were dripping with fresh sacrificial blood. They had finally reached the Heart of Darkness. The stench of death and human decay were so strong that the Spaniards had to retreat from the island city.

Cortés called for Mass and the weary Spaniards dropped to their knees and gave thanks. It was over!

Many historians characterize this as a great conflict between two religions. But, the Aztecs had no religion. This was a culture which had gone the wrong way. The sacrificing and cannibalizing of 25 or 35 million human beings was not fashion. It was not religion. It was not a symbolic bread-eating or wine-drinking metaphor. It was the real thing. It was not symbolic. This was a culture, a society, an entire sub-continent which had evolved without human spirit. There were no gods. There were only idols. The offering of the blood to the idols was a sham. Everyone came for the meat, the arms, and the legs. There was no love of humanity, only love of human flesh. When the Aztec warrior left his home to do battle he was going off to a big barbeque. The idols were an excuse. They were used as a scapegoat for the Mexican deviant and grotesque culture. This culture accommodated 500 years of human cannibalism.

As I read the daily newspaper from Mexico City, I see the same dominant, Aztec characteristics continuing to emerge again and again throughout the history of Mexico. The propensity to revert to the system of accommodation and barbarity seems to be as much genetic as it is learned behavior. The city of Tijuana is besieged by the same barbarous element that controlled Tenochtitlán, in the 16th century. This element has no value for humanity. Human life means nothing. On September 10, 2008, the vice president and director of medical services for Tijuana sent a plea to the President of Mexico, Felipe Calderón, "S.O.S. FROM TIJUANA: Organized crime has kidnapped our city with fear, intimidation, and murder. Here we have 20 kidnappings which result in murder every day. Would be victims are shot dead in front of their homes and schools if they refuse to go with the kidnappers. People are murdered for their cell phones. The city has become the kidnapping capital of the world. Everyone is afraid to walk down the street to take in the sunshine. The city has become a paradise for criminals. Everyday there are hundreds of armed robberies, any woman driving alone is subject to attack and rape. The police and businessmen are part of the criminal system. The criminals kidnap the children of the wealthy class. They rob the homes of the poor. And the middle class are like a sandwich in between the two. Their children are kidnapped, their homes burglarized, and they are assaulted in the streets. The local and federal government does nothing because of their fear or complicity. The entire population is terrorized. When President Calderón are you going to fulfill your promises and restore order to our city of chaos?"16 Are there any doubts that the descendents of the Aztecs live on?

The bleeding hearts, historians, politicians, poets, or writers who want to marginalize the destructive, horrendous nature of the Aztec culture are not looking at the facts. Volumes have been written which criticize the negative impact the European culture had on the Mesoamerican cultures. Viruses introduced by the Europeans killed millions. That was inevitable. The Spanish enslaved, in one way or another, millions of indigenous peoples. Slavery was not a new concept to the Americas. The English, French, and others annihilated the less developed cultures to the north. That could have been avoided. What happened in Mexico, however, was not only inevitable but from a humanistic perspective imperative. Cortés, the beloved peace-maker, as he was known by many of his men, was not a war-mongeror. He tried at every encounter to peacefully assimilate the indigenous peoples of Mexico. The Aztecs were not interested in peaceful assimilation and suffered defeat. This Aztec culture which succeeded the Toltecs, who had usurped the glory, prestige, accomplishments, and infrastructure of the Classical Mexican, was now defeated. This was the second great collision of the Mexican cultures. The first saw a disappearance of a grand and glorious reign of mankind. Six hundred years of peace had produced a culture that excelled in every direction from math and astronomy to architecture and agriculture. This second culture excelled only at destroying and desecrating humanity. It lived on the cooked flesh of humanity. And now it was defeated; Mexico began a transition into a new era.

IV

The New Mexican-European Hybrid

Anew order was created after the Spanish conquest of Mexico. A new Mexican emerged as well. The destruction of the Pre-Columbian culture also destroyed the old Aztec man. For the next 350 years Mexico would struggle to define itself. After its first 300 years it would fight to gain independence from Spain only to subsequently submit to the wealthy new Mexican-Spaniard. Its newly gained independence would then be lost after 50 years of mismanagement, corruption, greed, and ineptitude. The destiny and character of a people formed by the marriage of the European and the Mexican began to emerge. In one way the start to this new union was spectacular. The Dark Ages of Mexico were finished. But the Mexican soul was tainted with the guilt of more than 200 years of brutal sacrifice and cannibalism. The Spaniards had no respect for a people they considered inferior and almost subhuman by any measure. The two cultures coupled. The resultant new Mexican became one of the most extraordinarily misfits, incapable, maladjusted, human beings imaginable.

Tenochtitlán was razed. The city was looted. Many inhabitants were killed while others were dispersed throughout the Valley. The leader, Cuauhtémoc, was captured, tortured and later hanged. The Spaniards built their new capital of New Spain on the foundations of the pyramids of Tenochtitlán. The 332 city-states which were under the influence of the Aztecs were divided among the conquistadors. The inhabitants became vassals to the Spaniards. The once savage, warring, brutal, Aztec, who was dominated by Montezuma and driven by engrained cannibalistic culture, was now no more than a real slave, a piece of property of a Spanish owner.

The Spanish administration of New Spain, as Mexico became

known for the next 300 years, was not enlightened. Carlos V, who was the King of Spain, was also the Emperor of the Holy Roman Empire. His successive governmental appointments in New Spain perpetuated the idea of ruthless domination over the indigenous populations. The conquistadors were allowed to collect tributes from their vassals. They were also given control over their labor. In other words, the Mexicans were required to pay their owners one-third of any product or wealth they produced and were also required to work without pay. The conquistadors were required, theoretically, to provide for the well-being and protection of their vassals. Cortés was awarded 22 city-states (the richest in all of Mexico), 46,000 vassals, and given the title of Marqués del Valle de Oaxaca.

The impact of the Spaniard on the Mexican culture was diametric. On the one hand he was liberating the Mexican from a barbarous, inhuman past. On the other he was enslaving the culture in order to exploit the continent of its riches. Which was worse? The answer to this depends on the perspective of the historian. It is hard to imagine what would have happened in Mexico if it had not collided with the European cultures. The Aztec or Mexican culture was spiraling downward. It had been declining for more than 500 hundred years. The rate of descent had increased during the last 200 years under the influence of the Aztec. The historians that so easily overlook the barbarous nature of what Mexico had become so often want to characterize the Aztec culture as a continuation of the great cultures which had preceded it, but that is not the case. The anthropologists give the Toltec and Aztec cultures very little credit for advancing Mexican civilization at all. Many of these same historians characterize the Spanish conquest of Mexico, in a negative light. Many of the post-revolutionary (1920) philosophies state, for example, that "...his (Cortés') memory has been vilified."1 And it was replaced with anti-foreign and exalted native values. "Thus, Cortés, the fair invader, has become the perpetrator of the Cholula massacre, the exterminator of Mexican civilizations, the destroyer of Indian civilizations, the destroyer of Tenochtitlán, and the executioner of Cuauhtémoc, and is viewed in Mexico in dark terms."2 That perspective, however, is not universally accepted.

Today the argument continues among academics and scholars: Was the destruction caused by the invading Spaniards worse than if they had not invaded? Should Cortés be considered a liberator or a dark destroyer and enslaver? Would the modern Mexicans be better off if the Aztecs had defeated the Europeans? Would the Mexicans of the 21st century be better equipped to assimilate into modern reality if the Aztec culture of brutality and aggression had been allowed to evolve? Does a 16th culture which was dependent on widespread kidnapping, sacrifice, and cannibalism have the capacity to evolve into a modern nation? Or does the 21st century reemergence of widespread kidnapping, beheadings, and violence suggest otherwise? These questions will continue to be debated in academia and perhaps played out on the streets of Tijuana and Juárez, the barrios of Mexico City, and the killing fields of the marijuana growing zones. Can this culture which is now 110 million strong find a new direction? Or will Mexico become a failed state, a cultural backwater where daily accounts like the report of September 14, 2008, in The Los Angeles Times continue to describe a culture gone array? "According to a tally kept by the Reforma newspaper, 3,148 people have been killed in drug-related violence in 2008, with Friday the single most deadly day of the year; 17 other people in addition to the 24 bodies piled outside Mexico City, were killed elsewhere in Mexico in shootings and attacks. Many victims turn up headless, including 12 bodies discovered on Aug. 28 on the Yucatan peninsula. The pace of the bloodletting far outstrips that of the previous year. Kidnappings are also at epidemic levels".[3] This report was in mid-September of 2008. By year-end the deaths had reached 6,000.

In 1521 the Spaniards were victorious and the Aztecs were defeated. The conquest, of course, is seen as the correct inevitability in the eyes of the Spanish and the Spanish immigrants. Mexico became New Spain. The Spanish immigrants first arrived by the thousands then by the tens of thousands. Mexico became an extension of the Spanish Empire. Everything Spanish was in and everything indigenous was out! The language became Spanish and Catholicism became the religion. Sacrificing was out and communion was in! New proteins like beef and pork were introduced in place of human flesh. The Mexicans became the laborers, the slaves for all the Spanish projects. The Spaniards were on an insatiable quest for gold and silver. The Mexicans became their excavators and miners. The Catholic Church was tasked with converting the cannibals into Christians. They needed cathedrals and built them by the hundreds. The Mexicans became the masons, carpenters, and laborers. The vast arable lands were put under the plow and the Mexicans became the agricultural slaves of the Spanish. In all the Spanish endeavors, the Mexican became the laborer, the slave, the human ox. They died by the millions. In many, very real terms, the Mexican is still the same type of slave today in 21st century Mexico that he was in the 16th century. The outcome of the New World-New Spain social and economic order was disastrous for the Mexican.

There is a lot of disagreement among the demographic experts as to the level of population in Mexico prior to the Spanish arrival. There is a large argument as to what the negative impact was as well. However, it is widely agreed that the impact of the conquest (death due to battle), death from smallpox and typhus, and attrition caused by brutal treatment from the Spaniards was initially paramount to extinction. The report of demographer, Robert McCaa, which he presented at the Reunion of National Investigations of Mexican Demographics in 1995, probably states the most widely accepted range of both the population prior to 1521, and the impact seen by 1595, towards the end of the century. To take the most extreme case, a population of somewhere between 18 and 30 million people was reduced to a population of as few as 1.4 million. That is a depopulation of somewhere between 78 and 95 percent of the total. All of the demographers agree that by 1595, the Mexican population had been reduced to somewhere between 1.1 and 3.5 million people. They still out numbered the Spaniards more than 100 to 1.

But as the Mexican population declined, the new Mexican man emerged. The new Mexican was the product of the Spanish conquistador male and the indigenous Mexican woman. The social class that arose in Mexico was simple and categorical. Spaniards born in Spain were at the top of the social order. They had all of the opportunities that go hand in hand with the upper class. The children of Spaniards, who were born in Mexico, were called Criollos. They were white, of course, (by Spanish-Mexican standards) but did not have the same rights or privileges as their Spanish-born equivalents. They could not obtain the highest positions in government, religion, or in the military. They could advance in all three but could not attain the upper-echelon positions in either of the three. The mixed offspring of the Spanish and Criollos with the Mexican were called Mestizos. With few exceptions the Mestizos did not advance in society in any category. There were very few Spanish women in Mexico, for the first 50 years after the conquest so the Spanish men took Mexican concubines, very few married. Another interesting point, the vast majority of the Spanish men was already married and therefore was committing bigamy or polygamy in many cases. This was illegal under Spanish law but permitted in Mexico. The 16th century Spanish just like 21st century foreigners today were very willing to check their morality at the Mexican border upon arrival. The Aztecs had practiced polygamy so the Spaniards quickly followed suit. Although illegal in 21st century Mexico, the custom of males having a legal wife and a number of illegal wives prevails.

It is also interesting to note the typical makeup of the family unit that results from the co-mingling of illegal Mexican immigrants in the U.S. in the 21st century and draw a parallel to the 16th century. Most of the illegal arrivals from Mexico, to the U.S., are men between the ages of eighteen and thirty. The statistical information on illegal immigrants is sketchy at best but interviews made through various service organizations suggest that the vast majority of these young men have left families behind in Mexico. They are married and have children or they have an unmarried partner and one or more children back in Guanajuato or Michoacán, wherever home is in Mexico. The typical illegal immigrant stays an average of five years on the first trip across the border. During this stay he typically looks for and finds a female partner who is a US citizen. The goal of most illegal male immigrants is to find a legal US female in order to marry and acquire legal citizenship. The matchup is normally with poor, uneducated, and problematic US females. In other words, the illegal immigrants are successful at coupling with the US females who are having a difficult time marrying US males. In many cases the new couples begin having children in the US. The result is very similar to the situation that existed in New Spain in the 16th century. The Spanish conquistadors and subsequent Spanish immigrants were establishing families in two different countries. The Spanish immigrants were not illegal immigrants. But, the polygamous activity was illegal and the results were similar to those seen today in the U.S. It was acceptable for the 16th century Spanish immigrant to father and then shirk the familial responsibility of fatherhood. The parallel between the 16th century Spaniard and the 21st century Mexican is easy to make. This became normal for the Mestizo. It became normal and acceptable for the New World Spaniard. It is normal for the 21st century illegal Mexican immigrant in the U.S.

This problem of illegitimate children and single-mother families among illegal immigrants and the co-mingling of illegal immigrants in the U.S. with U.S. citizens are creating a subculture of Americans who are, unfortunately, not adequately assimilating into the mainstream culture. The influx of illegal Mexican immigrants is having a stunning impact on the basic family unit in which they are involved. In 1980, researchers and sociologists in the U.S. were shocked to discover that approximately 25% of all families in which one parent was an illegal immigrant were single-mother families. In other words, unwed or divorced mothers were raising children without the support of a father in one out of four of these families. The same researchers discovered that by 2005, three out of four of these families were single-mother families. That is 75%. There are 10 to 15 million illegal Mexican immigrants in the US. An estimated eight-five percent of them are men. How many millions of illegitimate, unattended, unwanted, neglected children are they propagating? No one knows but the negative impact to society is obvious.

The point is simple. The initial familial structures that were established between the co-mingling of the Spaniard and the Mexican were not conducive to producing a stable, healthy society. The coupling was typically illegal (not sanctioned by the church or the legal system). The offspring produced were generally considered illegitimate. The mothers usually had the entire responsibility of providing for the offspring. The fathers typically denounced the legality of the children and refused to support them as anything other than another vassal. The majority of the 16th century Mestizos were abandoned by their Spanish fathers and reared by their Mexican mothers. The Mestizo child became part of the Mexican society and not part of the Spanish society. They were raised speaking the Náhuatl language and not Spanish. Half of his blood was Spanish but on all other counts he was Mexican.

This Illegitimacy became an accepted norm among the Spaniards and Mexicans. In practice, the Mexican culture completely accepts the concept of illegitimacy. It is a normal mode of life in Mexico. The Catholic Church discourages unwed pregnancies on the one hand but its refusal to promote birth control perpetuates it on the other hand. Not only is it common and popular to impregnate unwed partners in 21st century Mexico, but it is extremely common for the man to leave the pregnant woman and child without financial support. It is a tradition that stems from the initial family structures that were established between the 16th century Spaniards and Mexicans. It has also become very common for the child to be reared by the maternal grandmother. Large percentages of Mexican men and women seem to have no problem at all with walking away from the responsibility of raising their children. Fortunately, the grandmothers find pleasure in supporting their grandchildren. Polygamy has become so popular in Mexico that it has even achieved mythical proportions. In middle-class Mexico, the truck driver is romanticized in much the same way as the European or American sailor has been for centuries. He is called a trailero and is rumored to have a family in every town between home and the border of the U.S. It is romanticized to the point that many young men enter this profession, as if a sailor is going off to sea, in their teens and early twenties before eventually settling into another field. It is akin to a badge of honor. The Mexican male who can proudly boast of being a trailero for three or four years and spreading his seeds from Mexico City to Laredo is revered among his comrades.

Unfortunately, the word Mestizo was almost synonymous with the word bastard. These 16th century children were raised in a single-parent home by their mothers and grandmothers. They were generally not given the name or any advantage of their father's position or wealth. It is much easier to produce a bastard than to be born one and live and die as one. These Mestizos, their offspring, and the pureblood, non-hybrid Mexicans became the new Mexican. Their interaction with the Spanish-born immigrants and the Mexican-born Criollos became the third cultural collision of the Mexican culture spawning the 1810 war of independence from Spain

By 1570, or so, the marital needs of the Spanish men were met by sufficient arrivals of Spanish women. The Spanish men were never very interested in marrying the Mexican women anyway. They considered the Mexicans to be a lower class of humanity. "All too many Spaniards, however, considered the Indians (Mexicans) simply pagans, cannibals, and sodomites. Natives were frequently described as lazy, disposed to vices, and backward. Their capacities became such a subject of dispute that in 1537 the Pope issued a writ (Sublimis Deus) declaring that the Mexicans were indeed men and capable of reason!"4

"The Mestizos were, by and large, poor, uneducated, and in a distinctly inferior socioeconomic class. For every Mestizo who gained a comfortable place in society (actually claimed by the father), there were a hundred others who remained culturally adrift, living in miserable circumstances and scorned by the upper class."5 Although only a small percentage of Spanish men had actually married Mexican women, the practice was almost completely abandoned with the arrival of sufficient quantities of Spanish women in the later part of the 16th century.

By 1570 or so, the new Mexican man was emerging from the smoldering ashes of the Aztec defeat of 1521. He was a defeated creature in all aspects. The population of the entire subcontinent was reduced from 25 million to 3 million (Mexican and Mestizo). They were without land, without assets, virtual slaves. The millions of dollars worth of gold, silver, and precious stones which had been the legacy of their ancestors were gone. They were treated like animals barely capable of cognizant thought. The women were bred like bitches (by the Spanish men) in order to reproduce more workers, more vassals. Needless to say, they developed a serious attitude! They began to refer to the conquest as La Chingada. This was like the Big Bang theory in reverse. This was not the beginning of their universe but the dismal destruction of their universe. The Chingada was the supreme rape, pillage, and desecration of the Mexican culture. The Mexican became the children of the Chingada or the children of the big cluster-fuck! They had been fucked over with a capital 'F' and going forward all Mexicans, men and women, were nothing more than the children of this inglorious rape. The Mestizos were literally the children of the Chingada, but all Mexicans came to view themselves as children of the great violation. This concept is still so prevalent that each year on Independence Day tens of millions of Mexicans repeat the traditional shout, 'Viva Mexico, children of the Chingada!' They still have the same attitude! They have not abandoned their feelings of being the victims of the Spanish violation of Mexico.

In layman's terms the modern Mexican's psyche continues to feel fucked over. No one has ever explained it better than the Mexican Nobel Prize winning author Octavio Paz in his book, The Labyrinth of Solitude. "When we shout, 'Viva Mexico, hijos de la chingada', we express our desire to live closed off from the outside world, and above all, from the past. In this shout we condemn our origins and deny our hybridism."6 "The Mexican condemns all his traditions at once..." "The Mexican does not want to be an Indian or a Spaniard. Nor does he want to be descended from them. He denies them. And he does not affirm himself as a mixture, but rather as an abstraction: he is a man. He becomes the son of Nothingness. His beginnings are in his own self." 7

The new Mexican, in traditional Aztec form, looked for someone to blame. He found La Malinche, Doña Marina, Cortés's interpreter and mistress. She became the definitive traitor. After all, she also bore him the first Mestizo child of the New World. She allowed the rape. She participated in the Chingada. She was the ally of Cortés. She became the mother of the Chingada. And all women became victims of the Chingada. All men now became perpetrators, violators, rapists, thus the word chingón. All the Mestizo and Spanish men became perpetrators. This is where the concept of the Mexican macho started. This is where the Mexican man supposedly lost his respect for the Mexican woman. I do not think the Aztec man ever had respect for women or very many men for that matter but from the time of the conquest the new Mexican man developed an attitude of being the chingón. He wanted to be the actuator of the violence. As Paz describes it, "To the Mexican there are only two possibilities in life: either he inflicts the action implied by chingar on others, or else he suffers them himself at the hands of others."8 "The only thing of value is manliness, personal strength, a capacity for imposing oneself on others."9 "The macho is the gran chingón. One word sums up the aggressiveness, insensitivity, invulnerability and other attributes of the macho power."10 "…the fact is that the essential attribute of the macho -- power -- almost always reveals itself as a capacity for wounding, humiliating, and annihilating. Nothing is more natural, therefore, than his indifference to the offspring he engenders."11

The dichotomy of the Mexican character is well documented. After the conquest he developed, "traits of a subjected people who tremble and disguise themselves in the presence of the master." "All their relationships are poisoned by fear and suspicion: fear of the master and suspicion of their equals. Each keeps a watch over the other because every companion could also be a traitor."12 This is an engrained Mexican characteristic, this inability to trust anyone is omnipresent. To illustrate this point here is a trite but 21st century example. I remember the first week I began playing golf after joining a club when I moved to Mexico in 1998. I was playing in a foursome and we had bet 50 pesos (5 US dollars) on the outcome. At the turn, I went to the bathroom and was a little tardy in arriving to the tenth tee box. The two opposing golfers had already teed-off and were walking down the fairway. My partner was anxiously telling me to hurry and tee-off as we needed to catch up with our opponents. After I teed-off he practically jogged down the fairway in order to arrive in the vicinity of our opponent's balls as quickly as possible. I was not sure why he was so concerned, so I asked. He explained that all Mexicans cheat each other. I was incredulous. But, some are more adept at it than others, he explained, but they all cheat. Every Mexican views all other Mexicans with suspicion as they expect to be cheated. It is the normal thing. It is what everybody does. The concept of cheating is accepted. It is universal in Mexico. It is a holdover from the Aztec system of accommodation. The Mexicans do not despise each other for not respecting the rule of law but quite the contrary. They are constantly on the alert for the opportunity to take advantage of any situation. They have been disenfranchised for centuries and therefore have become responsive opportunists. It is acceptable to take any advantage in all situations for personal gain even if it is illegal. When Mexicans do abide by the rule of law it is not for conceptual or moral reasons. They abide by the rule of law only in order not to get apprehended by the police. Friends, neighbors, or strangers will always look the other way so long as they are not the ones getting swindled. This is the reason for the famous Mexican philosophy of no te metes or do not get involved, or in other words, please look the other way whilst I screw this unaware bystander. The opportunity to take advantage of a situation, person, company, or government agency is seen as good fortune. Everyone is ready to take their turn when the opportunity is availed. That is the reason there is so much corruption in Mexican government, business, and yes, personal relationships. It is difficult to write this without being racist but it is a Mexican reality.

A month or so later I played in a club sponsored golf scramble. By this time I had met a number of fellow golfers and was invited to be part of a foursome in the tournament. When I arrived at nine to tee-off I was surprised to find eight golfers, not four. The Mexicans are so accustomed to this pervasive habit of cheating that they schedule two foursomes to play together in order to watch each other. This is so absurd and also very funny! The game of golf is based on personal integrity. There are no referees. There are no judges. The integrity of the individual golfer is of the utmost importance. Each individual golfer has the responsibility, under the rules, of recording his score, assessing the appropriate penalties and adhering to the rules during play. But in Mexico, and I have played at courses all over the country, east coast and west coast, north and south, the golfers have absolutely no trust in each other. They spend an inordinate amount of time following each other from rough to rough to make sure that no one is moving a ball inappropriately. They each independently keep score of everyone else's score. And it does not matter if the bet is 5 pesos or 5000 pesos or no bet at all. It matters not whether the companion golfer is a friend or a stranger. There is absolutely no trust. The scramble took an agonizing six and a half hours to play.

On the way home from the tournament I stopped for gasoline at the nearby PEMEX station. I asked the attendant to fill the tank with premium grade gasoline as I pondered this idea of trust. He asked me to look at the pump and verify that he had reset the pump to zeroes since filling the last car. Okay, I verified it. I commented that I was not expecting him to cheat me. He was not concerned about that. He was concerned about the reverse. He wanted to make sure that after he filled the tank I would not try to cheat him by accusing him of cheating me. What a system! That was in 1999. Ten years later the gas attendants are still asking their customers to verify the zeroes on the pump. I habitually ask them the same question. Are you insuring me that you are not going to cheat me, or are you protecting yourself from being cheated by me? The response has always been the later. The pump attendant assumes that I will try to cheat him so he does his best to prevent it. This attitude is pervasive throughout the Republic.

I can remember a million occasions over the past 35 years that illustrate this day to day reality. It is not a fanciful concept. It is part of the fabric of Mexico, and the Mexican. And guess what? The illegal immigrant brings this attitude with him when he swims the Rio Grande River or crosses the Sonora Desert on his way to Tucson, or San Antonio. In business it is the same. I was working in Mexico City, for example, in 1992 and 1993. My company had leased a very lovely home for my family and me in the Bosque de la Herradura section of town. The lease agreement included a hefty damage deposit as it was an expensive home. The owner of our home lived two blocks away and we became friends. We spent many hours together and I appreciated his warmness. I considered him a friend. When we left Mexico in 1993, he kept the deposit. I think the amount was 5000 US dollars. It was his opportunity to take advantage of a situation and he did it. My company had the option of making a legal demand in order to recover the money but did not. The last thing you want to do in Mexico, is get embroiled in a legal dispute. The Mexicans refer to their legal system as a revolving door. Once you enter it becomes very hard to find the exit. Anyway, the landlord, who I thought was my friend, was very happy to swindle my company out of $5000. He participates in a system which encourages and accepts this type of behavior.

The concept of cheating is not the same in Mexico as it is in the U.S. Sure, on one level, cheating or disavowing the rule of law in general is the same concept. But in the Mexican system of accommodation it is not the same. In theory, Octavio Paz got it right. The Mexican has become accustomed to only two paths of action. He is either the fuckee or the fuckor. And nobody wants to be the victim. Remember, prior to 1521 the victim did not get a chair at the dinner table. He was the main course. There is deception, trickery, fraud, bilking, duping and bamboozling everywhere in Mexico. It is ubiquitous, but the suspicion of it is even more insidious.

Octavio Paz so correctly wrote "The Mexican is always a problem, both for other Mexicans and himself. There is nothing simpler, therefore, than to reduce the whole complex group of attitudes that characterize us, -- especially the problem that we constitute for ourselves (e.g. constant suspicion) -- to what may be called the "servant mentality"13 "The character of the Mexican is a product of the social circumstances that prevail in our country, and the history of Mexico". "The situation that prevailed during the colonial period would thus be the source of our unstable attitude."14 Paz stated it perfectly correct, with one exception. He makes the mistake of crediting the inheritor cultures, Toltec and Aztec, as being a logical continuance of the Classical Period. He neglected to investigate the true nature of the Aztec culture. Unfortunately, his timeline for analyzing the sociological and psychological state of the Mexican started in 1521, after the conquest. He inappropriately assumed that the Aztec culture was civilized just because they had usurped the clothing of the Teotihuacanos. The Colonial period did not introduce the Mexican man to a world of deception and treachery. That system had existed for 500 years during the Toltec-Aztec dominated centuries. The common new Mexican continued his life as a slave the same as it had been for centuries. The big difference is that now he had a new master, the Spaniard. A system of human exploitation continued to dominate in Mexico.

This is the dichotomy of the new Mexican character. On one side, the Mexican is closed, weak, fearful, suspicious, and trembling. He harbors all the characteristics which derive from the slave mentality. On the other, he has developed an aggressive, undisciplined, undirected posture which is intent on taking advantage of anyone and everyone, friend and foe alike, before the same happens to him. This posture derives from bitter resentment of his situation. He considers himself a child of the Chingada (nothing more than a disinherited, illegitimate offspring of the Spanish conquest). These conceptual definitions of the Mexican character make it easier to understand the plethora of problems that exist in Mexico. Not surprisingly, these same problems are being exported to the U.S. with the daily arrival of every illegal immigrant from Mexico.

The new Mexican was basically a slave. Their Aztec leadership had been annihilated. None of the old social structure fit into the new Spanish state. There was no Aztec middle-class which could have emerged after the conquest. There were no Aztec merchants who could have assimilated into the new culture. The old culture was a bartering system. The Aztecs had no monetary system. The local products were traded at the daily or weekly markets called tianguez. Not surprisingly, these still exist in Mexico but the bartering system has died away. The weekly markets or tianguez are still a vibrant part of 21st century Mexican life. The Aztec agricultural system was based on production in small plots that were individually maintained. There was no agribusiness in 16th century Mexico. Thus, there was no transition for the Aztec agronomist in the new culture. The only place in society for the new Mexican was that of laborer. The Spanish managed all aspects of the economy, society, government, religion, education, and the military. The only probable career path an Aztec may have had, sadly, was the military. And the Aztec, Cholulan, and Tlaxcalan warriors were employed in the further expansion and conquest of southern Mexico, northern Mexico, and Central America. But, of course, the Mexican warrior was an old-world, old-technology warrior. His importance to the conquistador was his role as a porter more than that of a warrior.

So, the new Mexican existed apart from the Spaniard. The

two cultures continued to be in collision. The Aztec and Spaniard had mixed their blood and there were some cultural sharing and overlapping. But, for the most part, there were still two distinct peoples. The Spanish masters and the Mexican vassals. For the foreseeable future, "self-serving Spaniards justified keeping them in bondage, in line with Aristotelian philosophy that some men were the "natural slaves" of those "superior" to them."15

Thus Mexico developed for the next 200 or so years. After 1570, the Spaniards basically stopped intermarrying with the Mexicans. So, society was very structured, very brown and white so to speak. The Mexicans were at the bottom of the social ladder along with the Mestizos who continued to be born out of wedlock. The Criollos or Mexican-born Spanish and the Spanish-born Spanish were the real citizens of Mexico. By the end of the 18th century the Mexican population had recovered from the disastrous 16th century plagues and the initial conquest. The population had reached a level of approximately six million. Perhaps, 25,000 to 50,000 were Spanish-born immigrants as this part of the population was somewhat transient. The Criollos numbered more than one million. The remaining population was a mix of indigenous Mexican, probably four million, and another one million of mixed blood. The Mexicans and Mestizos were, "Illiterate, inhibited, and conditioned by their fate, the colored masses were generally ignorant of, and little affected by, imperial political and economic decisions. But they nursed a deep resentment against all whites, Spanish or criollos."16   After 250 years had passed Aztec descendents, nearly 5 million strong, were still disenfranchised children of the Chingada.

The late 18th century was a time for social change around the world. The American colonists gained independence from England. The French overthrew the monarchists and established a democracy. Free republics were springing up everywhere. Just off the Mexican shores, the Haitians established an independent nation. The Mexicans followed suit. In 1810, a group of Criollos led by a Catholic priest and a few high-ranking military officers declared independence from Spain. They formed a militia of Criollo officers and a rabble of indigenous Mexican and Mestizo troops. The battle for independence lasted for eleven years. It took many shapes, many forms. The original organizers were captured and beheaded. Afterwards their heads were displayed on the main square of Guanajuato for years. It was reminiscent of the old Aztec days. Both sides took to the habit of decapitating and then displaying the heads of captured soldiers. In the end a prominent Spanish colonel, Agustín de Iturbide, brokered a peace with the Criollos. Instead of establishing an independent, democratic nation as was envisioned by many of the early participants, he established a monarchy. On July 21, 1822, he had himself crowned Emperor Agustín of Mexico.

It was such an interesting turn of events. Emperor Agustín looked to the colonial past in order to fashion his new nation. He was unduly influenced by the colonial period. He saw how easily the Mexicans had been dominated and used as farm animals for the past 300 years. He was more than content to establish a free nation for the Criollos and leave the Mexicans in virtual bondage. And therefore, modern Mexico was created. The name of New Spain would no longer be used. Also, the Spanish fifth (20% percent tax) would no longer be paid by the colonials. There would no longer be any differences in civil or economic rights between Mexican-born or Spanish-born whites. The Criollos and the Spaniards in Mexico would all have the same rights. The Mexicans, five-sixths of the population, however, would have no rights whatsoever. So, contrary to the wonderful birthing of democratic nations around the world, Mexico was born an independent monarchy where five out of six people were without rights and open to continued exploitation by the white minority.

This is the history that the Mexican so proudly celebrates every 16th of September with such enthusiasm. The famous Grito or shout for freedom is reenacted in every town and city square throughout Mexico every September the 16th (midnight on the 15th). The enthusiasm is more exaggerated than that seen on the 4th of July in the U.S. The large square in Mexico City is crowded with more than one million people. The president of Mexico recites the original Grito just as Father Hidalgo did in 1810. And it is all a sham! It is one big lie! The Mexicans did not gain freedom. The Mexicans did not gain independence. The Criollos did! The upper-class, Mexican-born Spaniard gained his independence from Spain. Spain lost the crown jewel of the colonial period. The upper-class, Mexican-born Spaniard was now in charge of his own destiny. He had the right, among many others, to continue to charge 20% of anything owned, made, or acquired by any Mexican living on his land. And all of the Mexicans and Mestizos lived on Criollo land. They did not have the right to own land. The size of some of the properties owned by the Criollos and Spaniards is staggering. One family, for example, owned a ranch almost the size of the country of Portugal. Another family owned a ranch with more than fourteen million registered acres. And yet eighty-five percent of the population was completely disenfranchised! Is it any wonder that events like the one of September the 16th, 2008, still happen?

On Independence Day 2008, in Morelia, the capital of Michoacán, the citizenry were brutalized by terrorist bombers as the governor of the state enthusiastically reenacted the Grito. Morelia is the home-city of President Felipe Calderón. Three hundred thousand Mexicans had gathered in the square to yell, Viva Mexico. As the fireworks were exploding and the crowd was yelling, three bombs were detonated in the crowd. They were probably grenades. Seven people were killed immediately, fifteen were seriously maimed, and more than one hundred and twenty others were hospitalized with injuries. The police claimed drug cartel involvement. The federal and local governments claimed the same and are using the popular word terrorism. Is it drug-trafficking terrorism? That is a new twist. We know that the middle-eastern terrorists often finance their endeavors and attacks with the money which comes from the sale of opium and heroin. But, the authorities in Mexico are saying that the drug cartels are using terrorism in Mexico as a negotiating tool. They want the government of Felipe Calderón to call off the federal troops. They want to continue to operate in a corrupt environment. They want to share their illegal profits with the police, legislators, governors, and presidents as they always have. And if Calderón thinks he can change Mexico, well, he better be ready for a gruesome realization. The Mexican drug cartels are as brutal and ruthless as their Aztec ancestors. They have no qualms about killing innocent women and children. Ten of the wounded civilians in Morelia were under twelve years old. Many of the adults were women. These so-called terrorists are blind to age, sex, and innocence. "Calderon condemned the incident as cowardly and called on Mexicans to unite against what he described as criminal deeds." "These are abominable acts that were clearly attacking our national security, committed by real traitors who have no respect for others or the nation," Calderon said during a wreath-laying ceremony in Mexico City that was part of the Independence Day celebration."17

The vast majority of Mexicans do not feel like traitors. They feel disenfranchised. They are disenfranchised. They know enough about their history to understand that there is not much difference between today's distribution of wealth and that of the early 19th century when the Criollos achieved independence from Spain. The rich get richer and the poor get kids. The opportunities are so limited in Mexico, that millions turn to crime, drugs, or illegal immigration. This attack in Morelia is not the first time that innocents have been indiscriminately attacked and killed. It was, however, such a blatant and open attack on innocent civilians that many Mexicans are comparing it with the cowardly attacks in New York on 9/11/2001. Many people are saying that Mexican National holidays and celebrations will never again be the same. Mexicans believe their culture may be spinning out of control and headed towards a class war. The President, Calderón, is right. There is a large element of Mexicans who do not have respect for the rule of law, the nation, or others. Unfortunately, they respect America and Americans even less.

Americans, French, and others created real democracies in the late eighteenth century. These democracies were built on documents and proclamations that espoused, if not insured, the ideals of freedom, independence, equality, and justice. These movements motivated the original organizers of the Mexican independence movement. The rank and file of the army for independence was comprised of Mexicans who had been fed the propaganda of freedom and equality. The War for Independence in Mexico, however, accomplished only one thing. Mexico became independent from Spain. The same exploitive, racist, and elitist system continued. The Criollos and left-over Spanish-born immigrants were still the winners. The poor, illiterate masses were no better off in 1821, after the war than they were before it started in 1810. The cultural collision continued. The resentment of the masses became more acute, more hateful. The disenfranchised became even more loathing than before of the rich.

Mexico is still in the midst of serious civil strife. The battle between the disenfranchised and the corrupt government can no better be illustrated than in the story of the siege of Oaxaca in 2006. What began as a perennial teacher's strike became a civil rebellion which lasted for seven months. Oaxaca City is the capital of the state of Oaxaca which is in south-central Mexico. It is a fantastically beautiful, mountainous area where the eastern and western mountains converge. It was home to the culture that built the beautiful city of Monte Albán which was later sacked by the barbarous Mixtecs a thousand years ago. Cortés was so struck by its natural beauty that he chose to make his home there for many years after the conquest. Today, it is a city of 300,000 people with a fantastic climate and a European-Mexican flavor. Prior to 2006 it was a favorite vacation and expatriate spot for Europeans and Americans. But now, after the explosive rebellion of 2006, no one knows what will happen. The once tranquil capital is a powder keg ready to explode.

In May, 2006 a group of striking teachers marched to demand higher wages. They have been doing this for thirty-five years in Oaxaca. Teacher wages in Mexico are some of the lowest in the hemisphere. Seizing on the political atmosphere that existed due to the upcoming presidential elections a whole cast of players got involved. The teachers were soon joined by political malcontents, down-trodden agricultural workers, left-wing university students, underpaid miners, Hugo Chavez-paid activists, and more. The situation turned violent and twenty people were killed, including an American photo journalist. The people of Oaxaca basically declared independence from Mexico, and established a state of civil rebellion. This was in June of 2006. Seven months later federal troops finally regained control of the city and outlying provinces. I cringed as I watched the wanton destruction of Oaxaca City that was being reported on the evening newscasts. The public library was destroyed. The university was in flames. Twenty percent or more of the 16th and 17th century buildings in the historic center were looted and damaged almost beyond repair. I first visited Oaxaca in the summer of 1973 and was enchanted with its beauty and tranquility. Oaxaca is colonial city which had escaped the ravages of the war for independence and later the civil war. I have enjoyed the tranquility of the central square beneath the canopy of the 150 foot tall banyan trees many times. Oaxaca has always been a magical place for me and thousands of others. To witness the government siege and destruction was terrible. We may eventually become accustomed to this type of activity in the new Mexico of the 21st century. The rebellion was eventually smashed and order was reinstated by federal troops but many Mexicans agree that, "The struggle in Oaxaca is, in many respects, a precursor of other struggles yet to come," says Luis Hernandez Navarro, an early member of the teachers' movement and now the opinion pages editor of the national newspaper, La Jornada." "Oaxaca contains the core contradictions in Mexican society and anticipates conflicts that will surge in other states." 18

The 2006 conflict in Oaxaca demonstrates the continued possibility of a new civil war in Mexico. The situation in Mexico is super-volatile. A teacher's strike turned into a civil rebellion because, in many ways, Mexico continues to be the same country it was in 1821. The disparity between 10% of the population who control 90% of the means and the other 90% of the population is very similar in 2009, to the situation that existed in 1821. Mexico, one of the poorest countries in the world, is home to billionaire Carlos Slim Helú who is the, "Second-richest man in the world this year; even richer than Microsoft's Bill Gates, at least for now, thanks to strong Mexican equities market and the performance of his wireless telephone company, America Movil. The son of a Lebanese immigrant, Slim made his first fortune in 1990 when he bought fixed line operator Telefonos de Mexico (Telmex) in a privatization. In December, America Movil struck a deal with Yahoo to provide mobile Web services to 16 countries in Latin America and the Caribbean. A widower and father of six, Slim is a baseball fan and art collector. He keeps his art collection in Mexico City's Museo Soumaya, which he named after his late wife. "19 He was ranked number one by Forbes in 2007. Tens of millions of Mexicans are struggling to buy corn tortillas and yet Carlos Slim

Helú is worth 60 billion dollars. He vacillates between being the richest and third richest man in the world depending on the price of his stock investments on any given day. Billionaires, Warren Buffet, Bill Gates, and Michael Dell are admired in the U.S., for their business and investment savvy. Americans know that intelligence, investment, timing, and hard work define American billionaires. Mexicans loath Carlos Slim Helú because they know the system in Mexico is corrupt. They believe that Carlos Slim made his billions the old-fashioned, Mexican way. They do not admire the man or the system. They want change.

Emperor Agustín of Mexico, like Carlos Slim Helú, tried to consolidate and expand his wealth. The new Mexican Empire was enormous. It stretched from Panama in the south to California and Colorado in the north. It included the present U.S. states of California, Arizona, New Mexico, Colorado, Utah, Nevada, and Texas. The emperor sent his minister to Washington, and a long, arduous relationship that still exists began in December of 1822. The Americans recognized Mexico as a sovereign country with nineteen states and four territories. It agreed to recognize the Sabine River (the current border between Texas and Louisiana) as the eastern border of the Mexican territory of Texas. Unfortunately, for the new emperor, it was easier to get foreign cooperation than it was domestic support. His empire collapsed within months and Mexico began a one hundred year cycle of failed governments, constitutions, and disastrous wars.

In 1824, a constitution established a government very similar to what had been established in the U.S. earlier. It would be run by an executive branch, have a bicameral legislature, and a judicial branch. It was initially established along federalist lines. The states, in lieu of a popular vote, even elected the president and vice-president. Interestingly, one provision in the new constitution provided the government, military, and the clergy complete immunity to prosecution in civil courts. This was the first constitutional act which basically legalized corruption in Mexico. The first ten years of constitutional rule established many of the modern era political characteristics that persist today. For example, the government established import and sales taxes but, the local officials were the leaders of the smuggling organizations which circumvented tax collection. The establishment of the two-book accounting system which is still prevalent institutionalized income tax avoidance.   Political corruption, not unknown during the colonial period, now reached new heights."20 The new Republic was off to a terrible start.

The first five presidents were all military heroes from the War of Independence. None finished their terms in office. Three out of the first five vice-presidents lead revolts which overthrew their own president. After the first ten years of Criollo management the country was in disastrous shape. The presidency had changed hands ten times in as many years. The Criollo government finally expelled the remaining Spaniards and Mexico really became a country for Mexicans not Europeans. The Criollos and mixed-blood Mestizos began to intermingle again. Slavery was abolished in 1829, and Mestizos could become land owners and participate in business, government, and the military. However, it was essential to be white in order to succeed in business. A white-skinned Mestizo had a much better chance of realizing his dreams than a prieto (very dark-skinned) or moreno (brown skinned) Mestizo. The Criollos were no better at managing the country than their Spanish predecessors. Sensing the disunity in the new Republic, Spain launched a feeble attempt to recapture Mexico, but was soundly defeated in late 1829. This victory for Mexico would be its last positive achievement for many years.

What happened over the next 20 years was sad as well as incomprehensible. The politicians refused to agree on any coherent plan for managing the country. Santa Ana was the military general who had defeated the last Spanish invasion in 1829. On June 8, 1833, twenty days after being elected the 10th leader since the War of Independence, Santa Ana promptly retired. He decided that the presidency was not exciting enough for his tastes. He wanted to be doing something more scintillating than crafting a new nation. Can you imagine if Thomas Jefferson had decided three weeks after being elected president that he was suddenly too bored to do the job! That was basically Santa Ana's perspective. This, unfortunately for Mexico, was a precedent which continued for the next 22 years. Thirty-six presidents took office from 1833 to 1855. Santa Ana gave it a try ten more times. He never finished a single term but left office with more wealth than he had when he entered on each occasion. As a matter of fact none of the elected presidents finished their terms. These Mexican politicians just did not have any stamina or desire to manage the country. They were only interested in personal gain. Think of the absurdity of an institution, the national government in this case, that cannot persevere long enough to complete one presidential term in its first 30 years of existence. Between 1824 and 1855, during its first 30 years as a free nation 50 presidents were sworn into office. That is an average of one president every seven months for thirty years. There is no wonder that the Mexican population has never had any confidence in Mexican political institutions. I can be sympathetic in dismay! But most Americans probably do not understand the depths of Mexican political incompetence and corruption.

The presidents who were coming and going were laughing all the way to the bank. As the country sank economically the various presidents walked away with millions. At one point, in 1845, Santa Ana had accumulated more than 483,000 acres of land with 40,000 head of cattle and untold millions of dollars. "He presided over a brazenly corrupt regime. Bribery was the calling card for those seeking concessions." "Because local officials studied well the lessons of their superiors, graft and corruption soon penetrated all levels of government. Contraband was rampant, indeed, was encouraged by venal port officials." 21 "Often clever but never wise, he (Santa Ana) set an example of dishonesty, deception, and complete failure to adhere to any set of principles."22 He was a master extortionist. He defined the political climate of accommodation in the new Mexican republic. In retrospect, it was not very different than the historical system of accommodation of the Aztecs had been. In other words, his fellow politicians were content to look the other way as he extorted millions from the national coffers. They were patiently waiting to take their turn to do the same thing. He brokered his way in and out of the presidential office eleven times in eighteen years. The results were devastating each time for the Republic. But even worse, for the country and the future of Mexico, were, by far, his squandering away of Texas, in 1836 and the other territories, including California, in 1845.

Unfortunately, Santa Ana and the majority of the other

presidents whom misguided Mexico, were poorly educated military Criollos. They were ill-equipped to govern the new Republic. The presidents themselves had no faith in the founding constitutions of the nation. The history of the Constitution was as comical as the parade of presidents coming and going from the capital building. The first Constitution of Apatzingán which united the insurgents of the War for Independence was written in 1812. Later that year it was scrapped for the Constitution of 1812. The new Federal Constitution replaced it in 1824. It was soon abandoned for the Constitution of 1836. In turn, the Constitution of 1857 replaced it. Again, in 1917, the revolutionaries implemented yet another Constitution. The Mexicans experimented with five different Constitutions during its first thirty-five years of existence. These poorly educated, military leaders were unable and unwilling to create a true democratic nation. The presidential office was used as a mechanism for personal gain and the needs and requirements of a burgeoning nation were never prioritized.

I discovered that the situation had not changed very much when I moved to Mexico City, in the early nineties. Carlos Salinas de Gortari was president of Mexico. He was in the early years of his six-year term. Many business professionals were in love with his words, programs to strengthen the business environment, overture to foreign investors, and dedication to run a transparent, honest administration which was focused on ending corruption in government. It was an exciting time to be in Mexico City. It was obvious that the opening of credit markets in Mexico would finally broaden the small middle class of Mexico and solve many of the problems of poverty. Salinas de Gortari had established strong relationships with George H.W. Bush and later with Bill Clinton. Salinas negotiated the repayment of Mexican foreign debt. His economists helped craft and negotiate NAFTA. He arranged for the privatization of Telmex (the Mexican phone monopoly), Banamex (the national bank of Mexico), and TV Azteca (the Mexican television monopoly). The atmosphere around evening cocktails when discussing the new possibilities for Mexico was electric. Everyone wanted to forget the reality of the history of the office of presidency that had existed for the past one hundred and sixty years. Salinas was going to demonstrate to the world that

Mexico had changed, that Mexico was ready to become a modern, respectable nation. Many financial reporters predicted Mexico's emergence as a new first-world economy. According to Salinas, the corruption in Los Pinos (the Mexican White House) would soon be a thing of the past.

What a huge disappointment for me and my Mexican friends! Salinas turned out to be perhaps the biggest crook in Mexican presidential history. By the time he left office, he and his family had squirreled away hundreds of millions of dollars in Swiss and foreign bank accounts. His sister-in-law was arrested trying to withdraw eighty-four million dollars from a Geneva bank account in 1995. The account was in the name of an alias for her husband, Raul Salinas de Gortari, Carlos' older brother. The facts soon emerged of Raul's Mexican Mafia involvement and presumably that of the President's as well. Raul was convicted of murder and spent four years in prison but was later acquitted after a successful appeal in 2005. He walked free after posting a nonrefundable three million dollar bond. He was acquitted and could not be retried for the same crime, but he paid a three million dollar bond anyway. What is the saying in the U.S.? 'Go figure'. Furthermore, Salina's privatization of Telmex, TV Azteca, Banamex, and four hundred other government controlled monopolies had robbed the Republic of untold billions. The benefactors, as in the days of the early republic, were the President's personal friends, confidants, business associates, as well as the President and his family, of course. Carlos Slim Helú leveraged his good luck into a sixty billion dollar empire. He is now recognized as being one of the world's richest men. Ricardo Salinas Pliego, who was given the special privilege of acquiring TV Azteca, has also become a multi-billionaire. Roberto Hernández and his partner Alfredo Harp Helú, cousin of Carlos Slim Helú, sold Banamex to Citibank for 12.5 billion dollars. Carlos Salinas facilitated these privatizations and no doubt continues to benefit monetarily. But, swindling the country out of billions was not the only thing Carlos Salinas de Gortari and Santa Ana had in common.

Salinas' manipulation of the monetary system, embezzlement, privatization improprieties, and misrepresentation of the true value of the Mexican peso caused a national disaster only twenty-two days after he left office. The peso devalued from 3.3 pesos to 7.3 pesos to the dollar in one week. In a matter of five days the pesos was worth about 40% of what it was before the devaluation. Foreign investment fled the country by the billions. It was commonly referred to as the Mexican Peso Crisis. It was so severe and world-reaching that Bill Clinton and the International Monetary Fund guaranteed 50 billion dollars in loans to Mexico. Many U.S. and European banks were at risk of collapsing due to the Mexican government's default on its loans. Fortunately, the bailout worked and Mexico's economic hemorrhaging stopped. By the time Mexico repaid the loans, however, another 500 million dollars of tax payers money in interests was lost. And all thanks to Carlos Salinas de Gortari. The negative impact his presidency had on the country was immeasurable. In scope, it was similar to Santa Ana's debacle when he lost Texas, New Mexico, Arizona, and California in the middle of the 19th century. Very little seems to have changed in Mexican politics in almost 200 years. The office of presidency continued to be used for the personal enrichment of the upper-class citizenry.

The presidential impunity which is guaranteed by the constitution perpetuates and safeguards the status quo. Historically, starting with Emperor Agustín, the Mexican presidents have taken their millions and gone into exile in Europe. Salinas de Gortari was no exception. While his brother Raul was under investigation for murder and embezzlement, Carlos went underground in Europe. He would occasionally surface in France, Spain, or elsewhere and vehemently defend his innocence. He would then disappear again. The entire affair was somewhat reminiscent of Emperor Agustín's period of exile. Salinas had his glitzy paparazzi. The press chased him down with their cameras whenever they received news of his whereabouts. Fortunately for Salinas, the country was in a more forgiving mood when he returned to Mexico in 2001. Agustín did not encounter the same forgiveness. Upon his return the ex-Emperor was put in front of a firing squad and summarily executed. Many people believe Salinas should suffer the same fate!

This revolving door presidency changed with the arrival of Benito Juárez in 1858. Mexican society had begun to change after the final expulsion of the Spaniards in 1829. The Mestizos, who were of mixed-blood, were defining lower-class society. But the pure-blood Mexicans, almost 50% of the population, were still living in small villages, existing almost like animals. Their huts were thatched with mud or built of adobe and, "inside the hut, upon a floor of earth as nature formed it, burns day and night the sacred fire of the domestic hearth. Near it stands the metate and metapile, a flat and cylindrical stone for crushing the maize (corn), and the few earthen pots and dishes, a pitcher for water with a gourd shell dipper, constitute the whole wealth of the Indian's cottage. Neither table nor benches cumber the room within, mats of rushes or palm leaves answer for both seat and table. These serve as beds and as a final resting mat for the grave as well."23 Half of the population, approximately three or four million Mexicans, had virtually nothing. These pure-blood Mexicans were basically outside of the two-class system of Mexican society. Another forty percent of the population, Mestizos, poor Criollos, and Mexicans who had accepted the Spanish language and culture made up the lower class of society. In reality this 40 percent of the population was little more than beasts of burden. The remaining ten percent were white, Criollo, and very wealthy.

Benito Juárez was neither white nor wealthy but was an anomaly in Mexican society. Educated as an attorney, he was also a pureblooded Zapotec who was born in Oaxaca. His ascent to the presidency would not be through peaceful elections but through all-out civil war. The civil war of 1858 to 1861 is called the Reform War. It did eventually bring many of the disenfranchised Mexicans more into the mainstream but it was certainly not a class war in the traditional sense. The liberals and conservatives had been fighting over the presidency and the direction of the country for thirty-five years. They could not decide upon leadership or a constitution which defined the new Mexican culture. Finally, the conservatives aligned with the clergy and opposed the liberals. Both sides claimed control of the Republic. Both sides claimed valid presidents and passed legislation which denounced the other side. A viscous three-year war ensued. This was not as long or bloody as the War for Independence had been. It lasted more than ten years and claimed 500,000 lives. This war was costly nonetheless with more than 70,000 casualties. But the largest casualty was the

Mexican Republic. The civil war so discombobulated the country that within months Mexico lost its sovereignty to France.

Once again, as in the years of the Spanish conquest, the Mexicans would be defeated because of their own internal strife. The inability of the Mexicans to agree on how best to structure their young nation cost them their sovereignty. The four year civil war left the country destroyed and many people destitute. The countryside was ravaged. The mines had been flooded and the agricultural zones burned and destroyed. The Mexican government owed Britain, France, and Spain millions of pesos. Benito Juárez, a Zapotec from Oaxaca and President, decided to suspend all foreign debt-payments. This had become a recurring theme of the Mexican government and would continue for decades. As a result foreign governments have developed a strong suspicion against lending money to Mexico. Governments and international financial institutions have very little faith in any agreements or contracts consummated with Mexico or Mexicans. Historically, Mexicans have not met their financial obligations to foreign governments or financial institutions. The three European creditors decided the only response to this continued and proclaimed delinquency was war. They attacked and occupied Veracruz in 1861. By 1863, reinforced by 50,000 French troops, Maximilian, Archduke of Austria, was proclaimed Emperor of Mexico by Napoleon III, and Mexico lost its sovereignty.

Less than fifty years after it began Mexico's first experiment in nationhood was at an end. It had been a disastrous endeavor. More than fifty presidents were seated. Not a single president finished his term in office. Numerous constitutions were written, approved, and then rejected. The latest of the constitutions which was written in 1857 was suspended. A number of civil wars had been fought, the largest being that of 1857. Hundreds of thousands of Mexicans had been killed, perhaps a million. Two wars (one with Texas, one with the U.S.) resulted in the loss of more than fifty percent of the motherland. The federal coffers were empty and large debts were owed abroad. And now the government was dissolved, the country was occupied by French troops, and a foreign monarch was seated on the throne in Mexico City. The atmosphere was chaotic and desperate. In short, Mexico had failed to define itself as a nation or a people, had lost half of its territory, and was incapable of securing its remaining borders.

V

How Mexico Got to the 21st Century

Modern Mexican history begins with the Liberal political victory of 1867. In a very real sense the Republic finally became a nation.[1] But at what cost? During the previous sixty years Mexico had experimented with independence and nationhood. The experiment ended disastrously for the Mexicans as they lost their sovereignty from 1863 to 1867. Liberals, democrats, and nationalists then united and expelled the French monarchists. Afterwards, the Reformists, beginning with Benito Juárez, ushered in ten years of positive change. The Reformists introduced Mexico to the concepts of democracy, human rights, capitalism, separation of church and state, privatization of property, reduction of military, mass education, free elections, and the orderly, systematic transition of government. These are, of course, the normal modus operandi of a democracy. But unfortunately it was more than the culture could sustain. The Mexicans were not ready for freedom or democracy. This new experiment in democracy was short-lived and was replaced by a brutal dictatorship which lasted for forty years. This forty-year regime solidified Mexico's commitment to the concept of the paternal state and established the foundation for the one party political atmosphere which dominated Mexico throughout the 20th century. It also radically redistributed land and wealth to such an extent that a ten year civil war which killed more than one million citizens ensued in 1910. Mexico emerged from this revolution (civil war) wearing a mask of democracy which, however, did not permit a real democratic election until the year 2000. Now in the 21st century, once again Mexico is experimenting with democracy, but again, at what cost? Mexico's first march to modernization and democracy in the 21st century began with Benito Juárez being elected president in 1867.

When I think of Benito Juárez, I think of Abraham Lincoln. He is one of the good guys with a capital G. He led the Reformist movement and expelled the monarchists from Mexico. Although he was very sympathetic towards the politicos who had supported Maximilian's empire, he showed no mercy for Maximilian. He wanted to prove that there would be no going back so he stood him in front of a firing squad. Poor Maximilian, he was a liberal who was put on the throne by conservatives (and Napoleon III), only to be defeated and shot by the liberals. His liberal policies actually alienated his political support. Anyway, Juárez led the Reformists and the nation into a new era of political and social reform. Abraham Lincoln did the same in the U.S. I remember standing in front of Lincoln's statue in the Abraham Lincoln Park in the Polanco section of Mexico City in 1992. I was thinking about the similarities between Juárez and Lincoln. Both were secularists, humanists, and suffragists among other things. They are widely considered to be modern day liberators. A little Mexican boy standing beside me asked his mother who was the man in the statue. She replied that he was Abraham Lincoln, a famous American inventor. Lincoln was as equally successful with his inventions as Juárez was with introducing a lasting democracy in Mexico.

It is difficult for me to believe that Juárez accomplished everything he did. He was born in rural Oaxaca, not the beautiful capital of Oaxaca City. When he was twelve years old he left his adobe hut and walked 45 miles to the capital to live with an uncle. He had been orphaned by his parents and was living with his grandmother in traditional Mexican style. He was a full-blooded Zapotec Indian who only learned to speak Spanish after he arrived in Oaxaca. In many ways his story is like Lincoln's but with significant differences. Can you imagine if Lincoln would have been black? Well, think of Juárez as being black. In early 19th century Mexico, brown was black. I was born in rural Mississippi. I know all about racism. I never thought bigotry, discrimination, and hateful racism could ever have a more dreadful face than rural, southern Mississippi. I was wrong. The racism that was practiced in Mexico was worse, in many ways, than the racism I had seen in

Mississippi. Of course, the times were different. But in 1858, when Juárez first took the presidency, the brown-skinned Mexican was still not considered a decent human being by the white Criollos. "The white is the proprietor; the brown the worker. The white is rich; the brown poor and miserable. The pure descendants of the Spanish have within their reach all of the knowledge of the century and all of the scientific discoveries; the brown is completely unaware of it. The white dresses like a Parisian fashion plate and uses the richest of fabrics; the brown runs around almost naked. The white lives in the cities in magnificent houses; the brown is isolated in the country or outskirts of the cities, his house a miserable hut. They are two different peoples in the same land; but worse, they are enemies."2 But the irony is that the Criollos, despite their haughtiness and protestations were mixed-blood Mexicans. After three hundred and fifty years of intermingling there were very few truly pureblood Spaniards in Mexico. Therefore, color was very important. If you were white, you were Spanish. The rich Criollo men who had brown characteristics married as white as possible to enhance the possibility of white offspring. The Mexican denied his indigenous blood and roots but they were there. The Mexican was Spanish but he was also Aztec, Maya, and Zapotec. Once the revolutionary war was fought, the Mexican would clamber to boast of his Mexican blood, but not in 1858. And incredibly, Benito Juárez, a very dark-skinned, Zapotec, became president of Mexico! By the way, Juárez married white also. He may have been a liberal but he was not color blind.

Colorism, the social importance of the shade of skin, in Mexico is quite different than in many other lands. Skin color is very important in Mexico. White is at the top and black is at the bottom. Black is so reviled that it almost does not exist. Blacks from around the world know this and basically do not immigrate to Mexico. First, I want to explain the color scale in Mexico. White is preferential. It has its special names as do the other variations of skin color. These names are used in public quite openly. For example, when I walk through a market in Mexico, I am entreated by the vendors to buy their goods. They call out to me, güero (whitey), without shame or without intended discrimination. Skin pigmentation is a big deal. Race or place of origin is not so important. Light brown skin has various names as does moderately brown skin, and then a little bit darker skin has its own names, even darker shaded skins have more names until you reach black. The black or very dark-skinned man in the market will be hailed just as openly as the whitey but with the name of negrito or prieto (blacky). This awareness of skin pigmentation is incredible. Kids are given the nickname of whitey, browny, creamy, or blacky and it sticks for life. The downside, of course, of this astute recognition of skin color is that it was used as a prerequisite for success in Mexico. For that reason it is all the more remarkable that Juárez actually became president in the 19th century. The Americans, of course, did not follow suit until the 21st century. Racism and colorism are different concepts but variations on the same scheme. The scheme is discrimination.

The poor, wretched, brown Mexicans who did not stay on the haciendas in the countryside lived in the sprawling ghettos of the cities. The discrimination was as evident in the city as it was in the countryside. Mexico City became infamous among the travelling elite of Europe as having the most deplorable, filthy, disgusting beggars on planet earth. In Mexico City, the destitute congregated in Nezahualcóyotl, the sprawling slum which is home to more than a million poor Mexicans today. Nezahualcóyotl is a neighborhood inside of Mexico City. It is a city inside a city. The poverty, crime, lawlessness, and degenerative humanness are so exaggerated as to be beyond belief. The police keep their distance and seldom enter the large barrio as organized criminals rule the streets. In the 1990's, the mafia (organized crime) leaders of Nezahualcóyotl took control of the distribution of electricity within the barrio. I am not sure how they manipulated the control of meters, electrical leads etc., but they took control of the distribution of electricity and subsequently began charging the citizens inside the slum. A day- to-day fight resulted between the criminals and the electrical power department of Mexico City. First the fight was between the thugs and the technicians of the electric department. The technicians would go into Nezahualcóyotl to set meters or reroute wiring and would never return. Then the battle began between the thugs and the police. The result was just as disastrous for the police as it was for the electricians. Finally, the CFE (Federal

Electric Commission) and the city, after losing more than twenty employees and number of policemen decided to give the electricity distribution rights to the thugs.

The Mexico that Juárez inherited was lawless as well. It was very chaotic, extremely underdeveloped. As in the past, the effort to expel a foreign force, the French, left the Republic in a dangerous state of affairs. Juárez' approach to the lawlessness and corruption he found within the police and military ranks was very similar to Calderón's approach in 2006. He reduced the standing army from sixty to twenty thousand and created a new independent force of seven thousand five hundred, mounted, federal police. He named them the Rurales. They were assigned the responsibility of guarding the gold and silver shipments from the mines to the capital as well as sorting out disputes and injustices in the rural countryside. Most of the Rurales were pureblood Mexicans like himself: Zapotecs, Yaquis, or Mestizos (mixed-bloods). The Rurales were created in response to the lawlessness that Juárez inherited. They would continue to grow in numbers and importance in the coming years of the Porfirio dictatorship. Being a Zapotec, Juárez placed his confidence in these Rurales.

I had met Zapotecs at Mitla and Monte Albán when I was exploring Oaxacan archaeological ruins in the early seventies. These modern Zapotecs, although better dressed than their counterparts of 1858, are still living in abject poverty in the Mexican countryside. Thousands of these rural Zapotecs and millions of others illegally cross the U.S. border each year looking for work. Thousands more cultivate marijuana in the mountains of Oaxaca for export to the U.S. cities. It is interesting how the screw turns. Juárez, the champion of reform, a world renowned liberator from Oaxaca, is considered the Lincoln of Mexico, yet his home state is a cultural backwater where poverty, racism, illiteracy, marijuana cultivation, and corruption prevail. I still have a hard time imagining Juárez as president of Mexico in 1858.

Juárez fought to change Mexico. He fought with his intelligence, leadership, and diplomacy, but sadly was able to accomplish very few lasting social reforms that benefitted Mexico. His successes and opportunities were hampered by disunity among the liberal ranks and the rebellious nature of Mexican politics.

After he was first elected in 1858, the conservatives rebelled and invited Maximilian to be emperor during Juarez's first term of office. Most of the first decade of his leadership was spent fighting the illegitimate but parallel government of the conservatives and then in expelling Maximilian and the French. He finally was able to focus on reforming the country starting in 1867. He energized the education system, privatized the millions of acres of land that were owned by the Catholic Church, separated church from state affairs, and demilitarized the government. Had it not been for Porfirio Díaz's continued rebellion and an early heart attack his legacy may have really been important. However, par for the course, Porfirio Díaz mounted yet another armed revolt late in Juarez's last administration and as a result many of his reform programs were poorly enacted or completely stifled.

The odd thing about Díaz was his reason for opposing Juárez. Both Díaz and Juárez were liberals when it came to education, religion, and philosophy. But Díaz opposed Juárez on terms of governmental transition. Juárez was the most popular president that ever led Mexico. He won reelection easily. But Díaz, ironically, did not want to see an abuse of power by any single president. He, therefore, under the guise of the Constitution of 1857, opposed Juárez' continued stewardship of Mexico. His rebellion faltered and Juárez, fortunately, continued at the helm until his heart attack in 1872.

Although it was short-lived, the impact that Juárez and the liberal movement had on Mexico was very interesting. "Despite all the predictions of the clearest thinkers, the liberal revolution did not bring about the birth of that strong bourgeoisie (middle class) which everyone saw as the only hope for Mexico. On the contrary, the sale of church properties and the disappearance of communal indigenous landholdings (which had precariously survived three and a half centuries of abuses and seizures by land agents and hacienda owners) accentuated the feudal character of our country. Those who benefitted were a group of speculators, who made up the aristocracy of the new regime."3 "The republic, with no enemy to face now that the conservatives and imperialists had been defeated suddenly found itself without a social basis" "Power could belong to whoever dared reach out his hand for it.

And Porfirio Díaz dared."4 So, more than anything else, Juárez and the liberal revolution destroyed the historical fabric of Mexico, on the one hand, and created an opportunity for an even more exaggerated abuse of the same-type of system, on the other. Mexican history shows us that for every step forward Mexico takes it very quickly takes two or three in reverse.

Education is a perfect example. Juárez and the liberals had succeeded in building approximately seven thousand new schools during the Juárez years. But during the succeeding Porfirio years, access to the schools was basically limited to Criollo, white, males. Unfortunately, this set a precedent which continues today. In 2008, for example, Mexico had more than eleven thousand public schools which still did not have internet connections. In the 21st century that is the same as having a school without a library.

But on a larger scale, the freeing-up of Church and ejido (communal) property did not positively affect the average, Mexican citizen as the liberals had envisioned. It did avail the opportunity for the rich to get even richer. The liberals, led by a pureblooded Zapotec, Benito Juárez, ended up robbing the other pureblooded Mexicans out of the majority of their property. It was not their intention but here is how it worked. Liberal laws were passed which recognized the ownership of property for all individuals. Everyone was afforded the right to own property. The Catholic Church was the largest single property owner in Mexico. Juárez stripped the Catholic Church of all the property it owned which did not relate specifically to its religious charter. Of course, the wealthy Mexican upper class quickly procured this land. It was not distributed or made available for purchase in a just manner. The pureblood Mexicans lived predominantly on ejidos or communal land. The liberal government attempted to distribute this land to individual owners. Adequate titles, surveys, etc. however, did not exist and ownership of millions of acres went, not to indigenous Mexicans but to the corrupt Criollo officials or to wealthy Criollos who could buy it from corrupt government officials. Most of these large land transfers from the poor to the rich took place during the Porfirio years which followed the liberal reform movement. But the reformers paved the way for what was to follow. Díaz and the liberals had ushered in democracy (although it was short-lived), freedom, and secularism, but the corrupt Mexican elite once again rose to the occasion and subverted these advances.

Now, after three hundred and fifty years of being disenfranchised, a flirtation with democracy and freedom made life for eighty percent of the population even worse. "Within five years after the land law became operative, land companies had obtained possession of over 68 million acres of rural land and by 1894 one-fifth of the total land mass of Mexico. Not yet completely satisfied, the companies received a favorable modification of the law in 1894, and by the early 20th century most of the villages in rural Mexico had lost their ejidos and some 134 million acres of the best land in Mexico had passed into the hands of a few hundred fantastically rich families. Over one-half of all rural Mexicans now lived and worked on these large, privately owned haciendas by 1910."[5] *La Chingada* strikes again and again and again. While the majority of the modern republics around the world were establishing democracies in the 20th century, Mexico was going backwards.

Porfirio Díaz was the main reason Mexico was going backwards. Like Juárez he was from Oaxaca but unlike Juárez he was a military man. Díaz was born to a Mixtec mother and a Criollo father, thus he was Mestizo. He was a national military hero who led the successful campaign against the French in Puebla in 1862. At the time, the battle of Puebla appeared to be decisive enough to free Mexico from the French onslaught. The French recovered, however, and in 1863 occupied Mexico City and put Maximilian on the throne. Nevertheless, Porfirio Díaz was a Mexican National hero. The battle of Puebla was won on May 5, 1862, and *Cinco de Mayo* is still celebrated as a national holiday.

Díaz was elected president in 1876, after two unsuccessful military coups against Juárez. In typical Mexican fashion his revolts were preceded by elaborate plans and declarations. The ironic thing about Díaz' Plan de La Noria, his proclamations against the Juárez government of 1871, and his Plan de Tuxtepec in 1876, was that it supported single presidential terms. Juárez was the first president to bring any stability to Mexican politics since the War of Independence dispelled the Spanish. Díaz, on two occasions, instigated armed revolts against Juárez over the concept of presidential term limits. He lost each time, but what is so ironic is that he eventually became the dictator of Mexico for almost forty years. In 1876, fifty-five years since the War of Independence from Spain, Mexico had seen seventy-five presidential changes. Although elections were defined and mandated in the various constitutions, prior to Juárez, the Mexican's idea of an election was basically: form a group of dissenters, draft a plan, organize a rebellion, force the incumbent from office, and assume the presidency. It was an equation that was applied time and time again. Juárez had brought a new level of stability to the presidency and ironically Díaz initially opposed Mexico's new found continuity. But after taking over the helm, his ideas on term limits changed radically.

I equate Benito Juárez Juarez with Abraham Lincoln. Porfirio Díaz, on the other hand, was Mexico's Joseph Stalin. Certainly Díaz did not shove ten million people in the hole as Stalin would later do, but he was sinisterly ruthless. Political opponents were assassinated in the cities while the expanded Rurales ran shod over the masses in the countryside. Editorial comment in the press was at first curtailed then later not permitted at all. Critics were jailed for years then disappeared never to be seen again. He relied on election fraud to gain the presidency for his second consecutive term. He then amended the constitution to assure himself of an unlimited time in power. Hugo Chavez followed suit in Venezuela, in January of 2009.

When Díaz took the presidency, as usual, Mexico was in a big mess. The foreign debt was high and was not being retired. Internal infrastructure was fifty to seventy-five years behind other developing countries. The U.S., for example, had 30,000 miles of railroad track which crisscrossed the country. Mexico had a 400 mile track from Mexico City to Veracruz. The ports, on both coasts, were dilapidated and in many cases almost unusable. The roads were unsafe as banditos roamed freely throughout the countryside. The Rurales of Juárez had their hands full safeguarding the shipments of silver and gold from the mines to the capital. Díaz realized that Mexico's chaos was the antithesis of modernization. Mexico would only be able to advance if strict order were imposed on the citizens. He decided that the democratic gains of the Reformist Period were dispensable. In other words, he was prepared to negate the gains which had been realized in human suffrage, individual rights, democracy, freedom of speech, and social integration for modernization. He also quadrupled the size of the Rurales, who became his personal terror squad, elite guard, or the muscle of his repressive regime.

So just when the Mexicans began to think that things could get no worse, that the democratic advances under Juárez' stewardship would usher in a new age, Díaz entered the stage. And it got worse. Historians try to judge Díaz by balancing the positive effects of modernization against the degradation of society during the Porfiriato, as his dictatorship is known in Mexico. The means to the ends were so unbalanced; however, that history portrays Díaz as a tyrant who did more evil than good for Mexico. During his regime, the wealthy Mexican families solidified their complete control of the country. The Mexican peasants who did own land in the countryside, approximately four to five million people, lost virtually everything they owned. The very wealthy became the super-wealthy. Imagine five million people losing the rights to their millions of acres of communal land and ownership being assumed by a thousand or fewer families. In the state of Chihuahua, Don Luis Terrazas became the Carlos Slim of the late 19th century. After Díaz changed the land laws, "Terrazas owned some fifty haciendas and smaller ranches totaling a fantastic seven million acres; Don Luis was the largest hacendado (hacienda owner) in Mexico and perhaps in all of Latin America; his holdings were eight times the size of the legendary King Ranch in Texas. He owned 500,000 head of cattle, 250,000 sheep, 25,000 horses, and 5,000 mules." "Don Luis also owned textile mills, granaries, railroads, telephone companies, candle factories, sugar mills, meat packing plants, and several Chihuahua mines. "6

The general population, in contrast, suffered tremendously. The workers in these huge haciendas had few or no human rights. They continued to be born, work, and die on the hacienda without having the opportunity of education or land ownership. The workers were basically indentured servants as they had to buy their food and clothing from the hacienda stores. They were, therefore, constantly in debt to the owners who charged exorbitant prices and interest rates. Díaz' implemented a new law which forbade any indebted worker from travel or work on another hacienda. Protestors or chronic complainers were often sequestered and sold as slaves to work and die in the sugarcane fields of Tabasco or Veracruz. The poor Mestizos and Mexicans who lived in the slums of the large cities had a horrible existence as well. They suffered from malnutrition even worse than the workers in the countryside. The workers in the mines suffered even worse conditions as they died faster than they could be replaced. It was a terrible situation that deteriorated by the decade. "Many persons, including the old liberals, honestly thought the Díaz regime was preparing the country for the transition from the feudal past to the modern world. In reality, however, the regime was the heir of colonial feudalism…" "The past returned, decked out in the trappings of progress, science and republican laws, but with a complete lack of fecundity. It could produce nothing except rebellion."[7]

It is very easy to romanticize about the concept of social revolution. The renowned book by Anita Brenner, The Wind That Swept Mexico, which describes the revolution, is so powerful because of the one hundred and eighty-four photographs that accompany her text. The photographs of Pancho Villa, Emiliano Zapata, Venustiano Carranza, and Álvaro Obregón, the four revolutionary leaders who were responsible for overthrowing Díaz and giving Mexico another chance at democracy, give me goose bumps. Emiliano Zapata in his all black, silver-studded, charro (Mexican cowboy) outfit, with his distinctive moustache and piercing black eyes seems to embody the spirit of revolution. Viva Mexico! Viva Zapata! The photographs of the twelve-year old Mexican boys with their bandoliers, rifles, and pistols are extraordinary! They are dressed as if they are in a movie with large sombreros, charro outfits, and dead serious expressions. But the Mexican revolution was not a movie. The shots of the trains, train stations, train attacks, exploded train tracks, train wrecks, armies on the move in trains, trains with explosives headed towards heavily fortressed walls, and revolutionary families living in trains, cooking and dancing on top of trains, sleeping in swinging hammocks under trains, horses jumping out of trains, just knock me out! So much of the fighting simply followed the railways. The masses of brave men in their rural garb are very moving as well. The shots of the Mexican countryside with blue-agave fields, blooming magueys, the picture of the erupting volcano, Mt. Colima in 1910, and a beautiful shot of the passing Comet Halley also in 1910 paint a romantic, emotional revolution. These two cosmic events were seen as signs of the inevitability of the revolution by many. I am caught up in the emotionalism as I view the old photographs in Brenner's book. The young men look very heroic. The passion caught in the eyes of the women who followed their men into battle is riveting. Then I look closer and see the photos of decapitated corpses, handsome soldiers lined up in front of firing squads, listless bodies hanging from gallows and trees along roadsides. The photographs of Álvaro Obregón after his right arm was blown off by a cannon and Zapata's ghoulish face as his dead body was passed among the soldiers who had tricked and ambushed him, now posing for souvenir photos, and suddenly the romanticism fades. I see the fields scattered with more corpses than grazing cattle and the piles of bodies in the main square of Mexico City. I realize how costly this romantic revolution became. The ten years of fighting left more than one million Mexicans dead.

The revolution was as chaotic as was Mexico. Very little was planned. Porfirio Díaz was re-elected for the eighth time in October 1910. The election, of course, was fraudulent as eighty-five percent of the population was illiterate. Díaz was eighty years old but was not ready to step down. The Strong Man, as he was known, was still issuing his infamous decrees. The perspective of Porfirio Diaz was simple, " ...in a land where not even fifteen per cent could read, how absurd to spend money on open elections! How visionary among a people more than ninety per cent mixed breed, dominantly Indian (indigenous), racially inferior! The conquerors (conquistadors) had indeed made a mistake (which was) influenced by religious sentimentalisms in allowing the creatures to live and propagate. They should have been handled as the indigenous masses were in the United States (genocide). It was now Mexico's misfortune to try to progress with such a burden upon it: more than three-fourths of the population nearly pure Indian (Mexican), practically subhuman, degenerate, apathetic, irresponsible, lazy, treacherous, superstitious, destined to be a slave race. Such beings could never perform, surely could not claim, participation in the acts of government. Let them work, and keep the peace. For them (I give) the standard, pan y palo -- Bread and Club. The government must be an aristocracy, an aristocracy of brains, technicians, wise and upright elders, scientists."8 By 1910, ninety-five percent of the country's wealth was held by three percent of the population. The majority of that was actually held by less than one percent of the population. The state of affairs was so terrible, the racial and color dominance so severe, the living conditions of the vast majority so intolerable, that a revolution spawned spontaneously.

It all started when Francisco Madero unwittingly united the intelligentsia against the *Porfiriato* when he released his book, The Succession of the Presidency in 1910. A curious political atmosphere had begun to engulf the country. In 1909, Díaz told an American reporter, in an exclusive interview, that he had plans of ending the dictatorship. He suggested that Mexico was once again ready to experiment with democracy. This was, of course, pabulum that he was feeding the American press and public. During his forty year dictatorship he had invited the Americans, British, and Germans into the country to develop the natural resources and construct the national infrastructure. As a result foreigners owned, in whole or part, the majority of the railroads, ports, mines, steel mills, oil wells, and had invested in real estate, agriculture, and ranching. Over the decades Díaz had been keen to portray the proper international image of Mexico in the press. Now, he made a serious blunder. The Strong Man, the tyrant, the Fidel Castro, the Joseph Stalin, made a big mistake. He had no intentions of abdicating his political power. Madero and others, however, quickly set in motion an electoral machine which anticipated democratic elections. Díaz dealt with them as if they were traitors. He issued orders for his Rurales to apprehend and shoot on the spot any citizen advocating changes to the presidency. As a result Madero and the political intelligentsia fled to Texas. At the same time armed rebellions broke out all over the country. These rebels were not the intelligentsia. They were the children of *La Chingada* and they were tired of the *Porfiriato*.

Although rebellion broke out all over the republic, there were four focal points that everything gravitated towards in the beginning. Pancho Villa emerged as the leader of the northwest quadrant. He was a rascal from way-back. It is rumored that his blood was Yaqui, a northern indigenous group of Mexicans famous for their warring capabilities. His real name was Doroteo Arango. He took the alias, Pancho Villa, to avoid persecution from the Rurales decades before the revolution ignited. In reality, he was a Yaqui-Yori Mestizo. He was a mixed-breed Mexicano, a Yaqui-Yori. Niño Cochise, the grandson of the famous Mescalero Apache Cochise, crossed paths with Villa a number of times in the eighties and nineties in northern Mexico. Villa was a cattle rustler and bounty hunter. The Apaches had a reputation which was worse than any other indigenous group in the U.S. or Mexico They roamed back and forth between northern Mexico and Colorado in an attempt to stay a few steps ahead of the U.S. cavalry and the Mexican Rurales. They were the most brutal, savage, independent, and unyielding group of barbarians that the U.S. government had ever encountered. Also, they were the last nomadic group to be rounded up and put on a reservation. So, it is interesting to note Niño Cochise's comments about the Yaqui-Yoris and Pancho Villa in his biography, The First Hundred Years of Niño Cochise. "It has been said that the Apache is the most cruel when dealing with his enemies, but I say they are amateurs compared with Yaqui-Yori."[9] Niño Cochise was describing an encounter with Villa, and a group of Yaqui-Yori bounty hunters who were espousing the wisdom of taking the heads of their victims back to the authorities in order to secure their pay. In the mountains it was much easier than hauling back the entire body! That was before the turn of the century. Pancho Villa! The famous Pancho Villa! Viva Villa! Long live Villa! Pancho Villa and a small group of cattle rustlers with the financial backing of the Madero family became the foundation for the northwest Mexican army for the rebellion.

To the northeast, Venustiano Carranza, funded and led his group of rebels. He was a successful cattle baron with holdings in Tamaulipas, Coahuila, and Tampico on the gulf coast. He was aligned with Texas businessmen but hated the Americans in general. He was diametrically opposed to the concessions that

Díaz had been giving foreigners in order to develop Mexico's resources and infrastructure for the past forty years. The ten years of the Juárez democratic experiment had made an impact on Carranza. His hot button was foreign intervention in Mexico. He believed in democracy. He believed in Mexico for the Mexicans (the rich Mexicans anyway). There were many reasons for being opposed to Diaz' past relations with foreigners. In many areas, Díaz had given away the store, the warehouse, the workers, the profit, the whole enchilada. The Guggenheims and other American businessmen controlled the entire northwest mining business. Various British companies owned the oil rigs in the gulf. Díaz had even enacted laws which protected foreigners from prosecution and due process in Mexico. American, British, and German investors were exempt from civil and criminal prosecution on any level. Carranza was a nationalist and wanted to minimize foreign influence in Mexico. His money, friends, and influence funded the northeast revolutionary army.

Surprisingly, another front, also in northwest was led by a stubborn mechanic from Sonora, Álvaro Obregón. Many of his followers were Yaquis, the blood kinsman of Pancho Villa. His troops were stalwarts to the last man and never retreated in battle. Obregón was a socialist. He was a unique Mexican in the Sonora Desert. He valued the input of his lieutenants and often won battles by listening to their advice.

Emiliano Zapata, Emiliano Zapata! Viva Zapata! I have to write it with exclamation marks. Everyone knows about Emiliano Zapata. Marlon Brando played Emiliano Zapata in the movie, <u>Viva Zapata</u>. John Steinbeck wrote the biography and the screenplay for the movie. As an American what more do you need to say? If you are portrayed in a Hollywood film by Marlon Brando, wow! Well, Zapata was special. He was an early 20th century Mexican super-hero. But he was not interested in Mexico. He was interested in his home state of Morelos. Actually he only cared for Morelos in the sense that it supported his real agenda. His real agenda was liberation for his family and fellow campesinos (farmers and ranchers) around Anenecuilco where he was born. His friends said the only thing he really fought for was his ranch. His zealous fight for his home and ranch catapulted him into history. He fought for his ranch, his home. He fought for his family. He fought for his neighbors, his pueblo. He fought for his freedom. He had been sequestered at a young age into the military and yearned for freedom. His motto was simple, land and liberty. He was interested in nothing else. One reason Zapata was a hero is because he was the only leader who really knew why he was fighting, refused to lose focus of his goals, and stalwartly stayed true to the end. His passionate followers, with him as their general, constituted the southern army of the revolution.

The beginning of the fighting was a sort of spontaneous combustion affair. Madero was organizing and sending money from Texas, to Villa and Obregón. Carranza managed his own funds and Zapata seemed to fight without funds at all. The Strong Man, Porfirio Díaz, after trying to initially quell the rebellion, sensed defeat and followed traditional Mexican wisdom. He grabbed as much money as he could and went to Europe. Madero, the intellectual and funder of the revolution was elected president in the first quasi-democratic elections that Mexico had seen since the days of Juárez. Mexico once again embraced a quasi-democracy for fourteen months. The ex-generals of Díaz regrouped, gained power, and shot Madero. A temporary government filled the void but quickly fell to the onslaught of the re-energized rebels. Carranza with his troops entered the capital first, declared victory, and terminated the revolution. It was all over. He assumed the presidency and ordered the dissolution of all revolutionary activity. What a joke! This is so very characteristic, historically, of any Mexican who has had the opportunity to seize power in the name of democratic ideals. They immediately declare a dictatorship and dissolve their agreements with all their political cohorts who do not want to participate in their dictatorship. Carranza, a liberal, free-market, democratic, nationalist converted to a want-to-be dictator overnight. Power corrupts. Carranza was corrupted in twenty-four hours. Obregón aligned with Carranza, Zapata aligned with Villa and the real civil war started anew. This was crazy! This was Mexico! But the revolution started without rational planning, without rational goals, why should the outcome be rational. What could have ended in an eighteen month revolution turned into a ten year bloodbath. More than 1.5 million people died needlessly. They were all led to their deaths by colorful heroes of the revolution.

Mexico had these wonderfully heroic and colorful revolutionary leaders in Zapata, Villa, Carranza, and Obregón. And what happened? They could not get along. They could not decide how best to define Mexico. They all wanted different things. They all wanted a different Mexico. This is the story of Mexico. At every major crossroads in Mexican history, time and time again, the Mexican character proved unable to save the Republic. The Mexican continued to be too egocentric to put the nation before the individual. The Mexicans were too divided to coalesce. There was no shared vision of a democratic nation. They were still too insecure and greedy to put down their pistols and rifles. The result of the Mexican Revolution, therefore, did not alter the social or economic landscape. This war would be no exception. Every respected, revered revolutionary leader was eventually murdered, ambushed, or shot in front of a firing squad. There were no exceptions. Villa was the last to go. It was disgraceful, the entire affair. It almost completely destroyed the country. And very little was accomplished. The only thing that ended with the Mexican Revolution was the dictatorship of Porfirio Díaz. Between 1.5 and 2 million people lay dead (almost 15% of the total population) and Porfirio Díaz with his looted millions was exiled in Europe. It was a high price to pay for a failed attempt to change the social fabric of the country.

The price was: the death of almost 2 million Mexicans and destruction of the majority of the infrastructure that had been built in the last forty years of the Díaz dictatorship. More than thirty percent of the educational infrastructure was destroyed. The mining industry was almost completely eradicated with bombings and intentional flooding. Railway lines were smashed, bridges blown, and engines destroyed. Agriculture was so devastated that fifty percent of the population was estimated to be malnourished. Tens of millions of people had become displaced refugees. The infant mortality rate was staggering. There were two million fewer Mexicans in 1920 than in 1910. The decade produced an amazing negative growth result of almost ten percent!

It was a civil war like no other. The revolution was extremely chaotic. At first federal troops fought rebel troops. Then rebel troops became federal troops and fought their prior allies. The rebels fought rebels. There were so many crossovers of allegiances and alliances that no one could keep up with whom were fighting who. The general population suffered more than the combatants. Early on, civilians were shot in an attempt to teach loyalty or allegiance. Later on, entire villages were murdered in front of firing squads at the whims of small-minded tyrants. After ten years of chaos perhaps the entire population had become so barbarous that mass death was the only thing that would assuage the hatred at the end of a battle. It became so common for the soldiers to rape and pillage that the women and children began travelling with the soldiers. This was common among federal as well as rebel forces. The scholars of Mexican history suspect that two or three civilians were killed in cold blood for every soldier that was killed on the battlefield.

There was not an army for the north fighting against an army from the south as in the U.S. Civil War. It was all-out mayhem. It was reminiscent of the Pre-Columbian wars of central Mexico, savage, bloody. Mutilation became common. Beheadings and genital dismemberments were the rage. The Mexicans once again proved that without order, without the control of a strong fist, a Strong Man, such as Díaz, the population would go berserk. The participants, outside the intelligentsia, scarcely knew why the battles were being fought. And the intelligentsia was not controlling the war. No one was controlling the war on a national level. In the end, the fight, more than anything else, ended up being about land.

Carranza, the new dictator, convened a congress in 1917, in an attempt to solidify his position as dictator and end the chaos. He did not succeed on either count.

The Constitution of 1917 was written, approved, and Carranza was elected as the new president with a limited four year term. Oddly, something extraordinary came from the Constitutional Convention of 1917. The liberals and democrats prevailed in writing a document which defined a democratic state. Except for the fact that Carranza would be president for the next four years it was a huge step in the right direction for Mexico. The Constitution was a return to the concepts of Benito Juárez and secularism, in other words, a real democracy. Carranza, however, continued in power as a dictator and the civil war and brutal fighting persisted for another four years. The civilian fatalities during this period were even more horrendous than they had been previously. Although Carranza had convened the congress which wrote the Constitution of 1917, he did not follow its guidelines. A coup, not surprisingly, engulfed the capital; Carranza fled for his life and was murdered on the road to Veracruz. Again, it was impossible for Mexico to realize a peaceful transition from one government to another.

The revolutionary commander, Álvaro Obregón, assumed the presidency after Carranza's murder. The popular leader from Morelos, Emiliano Zapata, had been tricked and murdered. A plan was launched to placate Pancho Villa by awarding him a large hacienda in the north. Finally the civil war began to wind down. As there was very little central command or agreement on either side even this took a few years to happen. But after a dozen years of carnage the fighting mostly stopped. Octavio Paz later commented on the debacle, "...it (the revolutionary movement) was incapable of creating a vital order that would be at once a world view and the basis of a really just and free society. The Revolution has not succeeded in changing our country into a community or even in offering any hope in doing so".[10]

And then, as security and peace seemed to be at hand, another rebellion started. Obregon's government was attacked by an alliance of new power seekers. This rebellion lasted well into 1924, cost another ten thousand Mexicans their lives, and proved once again that Mexico had not yet evolved to the point of being able to transition from barbarism into civility. It seems that it makes little difference what is written in a Mexican constitution and even less importance who agrees to support it. The Mexican Republic always plays second fiddle to any group which is powerful enough to arm a rebellion. And that is still true today in the form of armed drug lords. They have the money, power, and will to administer their business and make their profits as they wish. The Calderón government launched a war against the drug cartels in 2006, but the indicators suggest that the narco-rebels are completely beyond the control or influence of the federal government. As the body counts were tallied in September of 2008, Mexico edged out Iraq to become the most violent country on the globe. The numbers that are coming in daily in November 2008, as I write this chapter remind me of the way casualties were reported in Vietnam in the late sixties. Everyday there are another fifteen, twenty, or fifty dead corpses found throughout the Republic. No state is immune. And, the horrendous practice of beheading and mutilation continues to track Mexico's violent past from Aztec times through the revolutionary period and into the 21st century.

Being in the 21st century I continue to be shocked at the small amount of coverage that is produced by the American press relative to the size of the problem in Mexico. More Mexicans have been killed in the drug war in Mexico in 2007 and 2008 than American soldiers have been killed in Iraq and Afghanistan in almost seven years. The monthly magazines run an occasional piece when they can get gruesome pictures of decapitated bodies and running street fights. The national evening news broadcasts also cover the most heinous activity such as the current trend of cutting out tongues of tortured victims. A few of the more affected border-city daily newspapers, the Los Angeles Times and the El Paso Times, for example, dedicate an ongoing section which covers the war. So does the San Diego Union Tribune. But, mostly, the American press seem not to realize or be prepared to report the seriousness of what is happening in Mexico on a routine basis. The paramilitary group, The Zetas, which hire as mercenaries for various drug cartels (and perhaps the federal government as well), for example, declared on October 6, 2008, that they were the true army and police enforcers in Mexico. This was one day after the daily body count was forty-eight which is becoming a very common occurrence. These daily body counts may certainly substantiate the claims of The Zetas and the ineffectiveness of Calderón's attempts to win the war. Unfortunately, the American press, to my knowledge did not even cover the story. And this is so important in lieu of the fact that Mexico was declared the most dangerous country in the hemisphere and 2nd in the world behind Iraq for journalists by the Inter American Press Association in Miami, Florida on July 21, 2008. On October 9, 2008, two more journalists were murdered. One was a reporter covering the carnage in Ciudad Juárez, and the other, Miguel Villagómez, editor and publisher of The News of Michoacán. Unlike the American press, both were scrutinizing the continuing violence which has engulfed the country.

The American press was scrutinizing the revolutionary events in Mexico in 1924, however, when the last large rebellion that resulted in ten thousand more deaths was put down by Álvaro Obregón. Presidents Warren G. Harding and his successor Calvin Coolidge definitely had their eyes on the events unfolding in Mexico. Oil was the reason. U.S. and British oilmen controlled seventy-five percent of Mexican oil production and were at a risk of losing it all to a nationalization movement. Politically Mexico was drifting to the left. Obregón won re-election but before he could take office was assassinated and the dictator-like Plutarco Calles took charge of the government. This worked out very well for the American oilmen. It was the same old cycle in Mexican politics. The country had drifted a little towards the left so it was time for the emergence of a new Strong Man. Calles was that man. He basically strong-armed the executive branch for a decade. He founded the PNR political party which later became the PRI. The PRI ruled Mexico for the next seventy years without interruption until the election of Vicente Fox in 2000. "Calles was the most strong-willed president since Díaz. He had an abiding faith in his own political instinct and, over his years in office, became increasingly domineering." "...Calles was untormented by scruple when treating with his enemies. As the years passed he became less and less tolerant, more openly dictatorial, and relied heavily on the army to dispatch his foes. Deviation from presidential fiat was not tolerated during the Calles years. Political prisoners began filling the jails, and an alarming number committed suicide. That the excesses were gross cannot be denied."11 As can be imagined, yet another rebellion surfaced. This time the rebels united under the banner of the Church. The fighting lasted for three years and thousands more were killed. The state destroyed churches. The rebellious Catholics burned schools. The abuses on both sides were in sync with the never-ending revolutionary atrocities. Eventually, with the assistance of the American ambassador, a truce was called and an agreement reached. This intervention secured the American oilmen a fair shake in legal battles with the

Mexican government until 1938, when they were nationalized by Lázaro Cárdenas.

Lázaro Cárdenas created a government controlled oil company, Petróleos Mexicanos, (PEMEX) from the holdings of the nationalized American and British oil companies. It is a blatant example of governmental theft. Seventeen American and British oil companies, with Mexican subsidiaries valued at 200 million and 250 million dollars, respectively, were grabbed by Cárdenas. Years later a Mexican court awarded the two companies 24 million dollars in a settlement which, by the way, was never paid in full. PEMEX produced 1.3 billion barrels of oil in 2007, generating an approximate market value of 110 billion dollars. This is what is commonly referred to as Montezuma's revenge! Well, we use that phrase for another discomfort as well.

Lázaro Cárdenas was the last of the militaristic revolutionaries to rule Mexico. He was president from 1934 to 1940. During his presidency the last of the rebellions was squashed. Cárdenas was from a small town in rural Michoacán. Early in the revolution he and one friend started an armed rebellion which grew into a small fighting force in their rural community. Eventually his guerilla troop joined Obregón in the revolutionary wars. Cárdenas' presidency saw a turning point in Mexican politics. The revolution ended. Industrialization began. Corruption followed. Many scholars characterize this period as the beginning of Mexican political corruption. But that is because they forget to remember the situation before the Revolution or perhaps because the revolution was so long (thirty years) that they forgot how corrupt Mexico was before the revolution. The country was in disarray for thirty years and the historical, imbedded system of corruption and accommodation was not so dominant during that period.

There is no doubt among historians that corruption became a national institution with Mexico's new found road towards industrialization. "This period...is most perplexing. If it were possible to know what had taken hold of the leadership of Mexico in those debased and clouded years, it would illuminate much of Mexican history. Here was a group of new men, most of whom had come from the ranks of the revolution and had risked their lives in a hundred battles for the redemption of the people from poverty and serfdom.....and yet, at the first opportunity, each fell an easy victim to pelf and power....Perhaps their difficulty lay in the fact that they had come to power suddenly and without preparation, either morally, psychologically, politically, or even administratively.....This new world was filled with a thousand temptations they had not dreamed of..... Here, at no price at all, just for a nod, all their hearts desired was offered them in return for a favor, a signature, a gesture, a word." 12 This would be the new definition of Mexico in the 20th century, institutionalized corruption.

Post-revolutionary Mexico was a march into industrialization and corruption. It would be a mirror image of what had existed in the Aztec Empire, then the Colonial Period, and eventually the Porfirio Dictatorship. It was the same equation that had existed before the revolution. A small percentage of wealthy individuals leveraged control of the entire country. Calles' party, the PRI, became the political arm of the wealthy. Once again Mexico's masses would be shackled with all the ills that accompany tyranny. The old wealth under the old regimes was land. The new wealth was industrialization (and land). There was no balance between economic growth and social justice. Political diversity was not tolerated. The one-party system became firmly established. The PRI nominated and elected every president from Calles (1924) through Zedillo (2000). The PRI was basically another dictatorship with a new face at the helm every six years. Embezzlement, fraud, bribery, personal gain from public funds was the unofficial but real party line. The PRI became the head of state, the government, the dictatorship.

Institutionalized corruption reassumed a face that had been seen in Mexico throughout its history but it became even more proficient. The concept and practice of governmental corruption spread from the federal, to the state, and down to the municipal level. Vicente Fox, elected in 2000, became the first non-PRI president since Calles was elected in 1924 (the PRI was established in 1929). Ninety-nine percent of the federal senators from 1929 to 2000, were elected from the PRI. Every state governor was handpicked by the PRI until Ernesto Ruffo was seated in Baja California in 1989. The first non-PRI mayor of Mexico City, in sixty-eight years was elected in 1997. In others words, the federal party, the PRI, became pervasive, omnipotent, and eternal. Throughout the reign of the PRI, opposition parties were allowed to exist but never to win or seat a candidate in office. Even in unusual and remote regions such as Tijuana and Mexicali elections were routinely annulled if PRI candidates were not elected. Political violence and intimidation were habitually practiced in Oaxaca and Chiapas in the rural south. The PRI completely dominated Mexico and Mexican politics until the beginning of the 21st century. PRI or governmental corruption was ubiquitous.

This corruption completely infiltrated Mexican society from the president to the peon. The political payoff or bribe was emulated throughout the business environment as well. As industrialization became a part of Mexican life, the cost of bribes in order to do business became part of the Mexican culture. Bribery became so common as to exist at all levels. It became a part of doing business, an acceptable way of living life. The pinch, the bite, the mordida, is so common that it is not seen in Mexico as an evil (although the current PAN government is trying to change this). From the simplest personal interactions to the most sophisticated business deals, it is still the accepted way of accommodating the flow of commerce and the mundane day to day human activities in Mexico. If a traffic cop, for example, pulls me over for speeding or more likely approaches me for illegally parking or detects an expired vehicle registration sticker he is tasked with writing me a ticket or taking me to the station to pay a fine. In my hometown, in Mexico, the traffic cops are tasked with removing the car's license plate which can later be retrieved after the fine is paid. The traffic cop is not paid a reasonable wage for his services and therefore is typically looking for an opportunity to increase his income. It is not just a big city occurrence. My experience living in Mexico for the last ten years has been the same as it was in Mexico City in the nineties. The traffic cop will slowly begin removing the screws from the license plate or begin an engaging and casual conversation with the offender. He begins to look for the appropriate opportunity in which to initiate the illegal transaction. He prefers to get paid a bribe versus writing a ticket. He is not moralistic about it. He wants to get a payoff for not taking the license plates. He is offering you a service and wants to get paid for it. The typical Mexican (and gringo ex-patriot too for that matter) prefers to pay the bribe versus the hassle of going through the Mexican bureaucracy and paying a fine. The Mexican bureaucracy, at any level, is so inefficient and such a waste of time that virtually everyone prefers the corrupt system of the *mordida* (bribe). I can remember arguing its merits many times when I lived in Mexico City. The system is so entrenched in Mexico City, that many of the traffic cops pay a commission in order to patrol certain neighborhoods. Many traffic cops must even purchase their own uniforms out of their meager salaries. They are forced to apply the system of bribery. There tends not to be a lot of administrative overhead in enforcing traffic laws. It is mostly managed on the street between the traffic cop and the offender. How is that for efficiency? But in the long run, corruption does not work. It breeds contempt and hatred.

The small bribe to a traffic cop of twenty dollars becomes a larger bribe of thousands, tens of thousands, and millions of dollars to do business. I had been coming to Mexico for decades and had paid the occasional twenty or thirty dollar bribe on many occasions. But, when I first came to work in Mexico City in 1991, I learned how the bribe system is applied exponentially in business. It is the way business is done in Mexico! There is no getting around it. If you want to do business in Mexico, you learn to pay bribes and follow a corrupt system of accounting.

The Mexican accountant's first priority when advising a foreign client is to explain the system of book keeping. Two sets of books are required. One, official set, is used for reporting and paying taxes and also to have for review with the Mexican IRS in case of an audit. This official set of books typically states a company's revenue at thirty to fifty percent of what it actually is. The other set of books which records actual business levels is kept in secret and used for making rational business decisions. A cash account is kept in ready for the eventuality of an audit. On average foreign firms are audited once every three years. The cash, of course, is in reserve in order to bribe the auditor into accepting the false set of books. Chances are very high that if the auditor is happy with the bribe he will show up again in three years for the next audit. And it all continues very smoothly. On the other hand, the auditors can be extremely penal and assess exorbitant fines if they so choose. No one wants to get caught in the incessant audit with the Mexican IRS. It, like the legal system, is often referred to as a revolving door. The problem with this particular revolving door is finding the exit.

The Mexican businessman plays by a similar set of rules as do foreigners. Only there is one big exception. He and his family have been playing this game for decades, generations. Corporations try to avoid income tax altogether. That translates into an even more corrupt setup with even fewer taxes being paid. The big loser is the Mexican citizenry. The result of this corrupt tax system is obvious. There is only a paltry amount of money available for infrastructure. Mexico has grown with its population of 110 million people into the 15th largest economy in the world. Mexico's per capita tax collection, as a percentage of GDP, bounce between 15% and 17% per year as compared with a 28% rate in the U.S. Almost five percent of that came from PEMEX in 2007, the national oil company. It looks like PEMEX will contribute seven per cent in 2008. It is easy to understand that the 10% to 12% of tax collected as a percentage of GDP does not pay for very many new schools or roads. As a consequence the roads are dilapidated and the educational system is inadequate and non-competitive worldwide.

This centuries old acceptance of corruption is the primary reason Mexico is currently in the throes of a national drug war and economic crisis. Felipe Calderón, sworn in as President in December of 2006, also swore to launch a war against corruption, drugs, and violence. This war is in full-tilt gear and its outcome is uncertain.

The lessons that can be drawn from Mexican history lend credence to this uncertainty. The PRI continued its legacy of corruption throughout the seventies, eighties, and nineties. Finally, it all collapsed for the dinosaurian PRI. The peso devalued in 1982, shortly after President José López Portillo had purchased a two million dollar mansion in Acapulco for his mistress. Then his successor, Miguel de la Madrid allowed inflation to run rampant at historical rates of 150% to 200% for years, as he personally became extremely wealthy. He passed the mantel to the chameleon, Carlos Salinas de Gortari, who enchanted the country for four years with promises of financial reform only to eventually, under mafia influence, erode the value of the entire Mexican stock exchange and cause the worse peso devaluation in Mexico's history in 1994, three weeks after he left office and went into hiding in Europe where he had secretly stashed tens of millions of dollars. His successor, Ernesto Zedillo, had no choice but to play the Mexican version of Mikhail Gorbachev, and dismantle his own party. So, as Mexico entered the 21st century, the PRI, had finally corrupted itself out of power. For the first time in seventy years, a semblance of a multi-party political system emerged. Vicente Fox, of the PAN party was elected as president.

Vicente Fox with much fanfare took office in December of 2000, just one month before George W. Bush succeeded Bill Clinton in the U.S. As usual the expectations were high for change in Mexico. Fox was aggressive in his first two years in office, established a very amiable relationship with Bush, and seemed to be a genuinely new type of Mexican politician. Not having majority support in Congress, however, he was unable to pass legislation. The government was virtually gridlocked during his entire administration and he was unable to bring any of his promised reforms to reality. He and Bush, who initially agreed on the importance of immigration reform could never find enough common ground or the support in their respective legislatures to pass their programs. According to the press their biggest accomplishment was a number of reciprocal visits to each others' cattle ranches. Both loved black cowboy hats, boots, and a cowboy image. Fox eventually discovered that Bush was in reality a windshield cowboy and was too timid to even go for a horse ride at his ranch. In his autobiography he referred to Bush derogatorily as being cocky and completely unprepared to be president of the U.S. The defining issue of the final years of Fox's presidency was the perennial teacher's strike in the city of Oaxaca in June of 2006, which turned into a six month civil uprising.

Financed with money from Venezuelan Hugo Chavez to the PRD, Mexico's socialist party, and the lack of a presidential response by Fox, the civil uprising turned violent and riotous.

Manuel López Obrador, the PRD candidate, a Chavez cohort, orchestrated the entire affair as a campaign vehicle. The beautiful capital city of Oaxaca was occupied by the teachers who had aligned with a group of miners, student activists, PRD supporters, and Chavez instigators who had illegally entered the country from Guatemala. It was an interesting standoff. Obrador was running against Fox's successor and current President Felipe Calderón. The coalition occupied the city, expelled the city government, denounced the tyrannical administration of the sitting PRI governor of the state, Ulises Ruiz, announced their support for PRD candidate Obrador, and demanded negotiations. President Fox, fearing political ramifications against Calderón and his party the PAN, did nothing for months. The inner city was barricaded, looted, and historical buildings were burned. It was a big mess.

The explosive nature of the uprising helped Obrador solidify his position in an already close race with Calderón. The vote on July 2, 2006, was extremely close. The press reported Calderón as winner with a scant 250,000 vote lead (nationwide). Obrador cried fraud and demanded a recount. It was reminiscent of the Gore/Bush election in 2000. The Federal Electoral Institute reviewed the facts, ordered a recount for eleven per cent of the fraudulent appearing precincts and on September 5, 2006, declared Felipe Calderón president of Mexico. Unlike Al Gore, Obrador denounced the results, the legitimacy of the Federal Electoral Institute, and declared himself the President of Mexico. Mexico, once again, became a sovereign with two heads of state. A precedent was not being set, it just had not happened since the turbulent years of the revolution when the Mexicans for ten years could never agree on who was president or which government was legitimate. Those years were extremely violent and millions of Mexicans died in a ten year civil war. And now, a similar scenario exists.

Felipe Calderón is the president of Mexico but Manuel López Obrador and 49.75% of the population (according to the 2006 election) do not recognize his legitimacy. The mayor of Mexico City, the capital, does not recognize his presidency. The entire country has erupted into a violent war, second only to Iraq in its monthly casualties. Criminality has exploded on all fronts from bank robberies to kidnappings, murder, extortion, and weekly executions. Mexico's experiment in multi-party democracy is at serious risk. Historically, a strong man has emerged during the Republic's times of chaos and uncertainty and used the military to restore order. Calderón, in typical sequence, has called out more than fifty thousand federal troops, and twenty thousand federal police in an attempt to quell the violence and end the chaos. His plan is not being successful. The army and police ranks are rife with corrupt officers. Many of the professional soldiers have left the force and have formed a professional mercenary corps, The Zetas, who hire out to the drug cartels and/or political radicals to assassinate competitors, army and police officers who have integrity, federal and local prosecutors, judges, city mayors who are aligned with Calderón, and even the journalists, editors, and publishers who are reporting on the situation. In September of 2008, The Zetas started a new front of violence by lobbing grenades into a crowd of innocent citizens who were celebrating Mexico's day of independence. Mexico has entered the 21st century in chaos. The fabric of its democratic system is at risk. Its relations with the U.S. are at an all time low. Its economy is failing in the world economic crisis and its uneducated, poor masses are reverting to their savage, barbarous behavior of the past. All indicators suggest that there is a fifty/fifty chance as to whether or not Mexico is headed for another bloody civil war.

200 Years of Mutual Disrespect

T here are a thousand reasons why Mexicans, in general, dislike their northern neighbors. And do not be mistaken, Mexicans, in general, do not like the citizens of the United States of America or its government. There are just as many reasons that Americans use in support of their distrust and disparaging attitude towards their southern neighbors as well. The simplest, most direct explanation of Mexican dislike for Americans is one of success versus failure. The European immigrants that conquered, settled, and formed the United States of America created a successful democratic nation. With all of its problems it is still a democratic, free nation where human beings have the opportunity to live freely and strive to accomplish their goals and dreams. Mexico, on the other hand, held its first, free, democratic election in the year 2000. That was just a few short years ago. The Europeans (the Spaniards), in Mexico, did not create a successful democratic nation. The Mexicans, like human beings everywhere, want freedom, democracy, and opportunity. But, the greedy, wealthy, elite, upper two per cent of Mexican society has kept the Mexican citizenry in bondage for a thousand years. Whether the brutal Aztec war lords, or ruthless Spanish over lords, or corrupt Mexican politicians, or heartless, wealthy business owners, the results have always been the same. The Mexicans have been kept poor, uneducated, and have been exploited. When they look north, they look at their neighbors with contempt, jealousy, and desire.

The Europeans to the north in the U.S. fought for independence and created a new democratic nation. The Mexicans fought for independence yet failed to create a new democratic nation. Octavio Paz, Mexican author and Nobel Prize winner, compares the results of the two unambiguously, "But in North America (U.S.) those ideas (to change the social fabric and create democracy) were expressed by groups who proposed a basic transformation of the country in accordance with a new political philosophy. What is more, they did not intend to exchange one state of affairs for another, but instead -- and the difference is radical -- to create a new nation. In effect, the United States is a novelty in the history of the nineteenth century, a society that grew and expanded naturally. Among ourselves (Mexicans), on the other hand, the ruling classes consolidated themselves, once Independence was achieved, as heirs of the old Spanish order. They broke with Spain but they proved incapable of creating a modern society."1 This is the crux of it. The Mexicans have been incapable of creating a modern society. That is the root cause of the hatred the Mexicans have for the gringos. It is simple. The Mexican culture, society, and state is bordering on failure. The Mexicans know this. It is no secret. They hate the gringo because the gringo was successful at creating a modern, functioning, civilized society and they were not.

The tangible reasons that substantiate and fortify the Mexican's dislike for the gringos go back to the Spanish hatred of the Anglo-Saxon. The Anglo-Saxon and Spanish racial and cultural dislike for each other started in the 14th century. The Spanish invasion and attempt to conquer Portugal was thwarted by a superior Portuguese army which was fortified by British troops. Two hundred years later the invincible Spanish Armada was sunk in 1588 by the English, during the Anglo-Spanish War which lasted from 1585 to 1604. The English and Spanish again fought a war in the 17th century from 1654 to 1660. The British, once again, sunk the Spanish fleet in the Caribbean and took control of the island of Jamaica as war spoil. During this Anglo-Spanish War, participating troops from New Spain (Mexico) were soundly defeated by the British. Other British spoils included the Mediterranean islands of Menorca, Majorca, and the southern tip of Spain, the Rock of Gibraltar. The Rock, of course, is still a British territory, still claimed by the Spanish, and continues to be a contentious dispute between both countries. This is just about the most southern tip of Europe and was historically known as one of the Pillars of Hercules. As Americans we have constantly seen the depiction of the Rock of Gibraltar as the symbol or logo of economic stability. It has always been a strategic location for guarding the mouth of the Mediterranean Sea.

It is one of those strange, politically, out of place parcels of land. It is like Guantanamo in Cuba. Guantanamo belongs to the Americans but it is on the island of Cuba. That is strange. Gibraltar is just as strange. It is the southern tip of the Iberian Peninsula and clearly should be part of Spain. But the British captured it in 1704, and they have no intentions of giving it back. I was there for the first time in 1982. As I was travelling west along the Costa del Sol, I wanted to visit the famous Rock. Unfortunately, the Spaniards had closed the land border in 1969, and the road was blocked by gates and Spanish troops. It felt as though the Gibraltarians were under siege. I learned that my only option for visiting the Rock was to arrive by ship or plane. Since I was planning to cross the straits and visit Morocco, I decided to enter Gibraltar on my way back from Africa. I arrived in Africa at Ceuta only to discover that I was still in Spain. This was too funny! Ceuta is a small Spanish territory on the northern tip of Morocco. It is actually just a municipality of twenty-eight square kilometers. It clearly should be part of Morocco but it belongs to Spain. So when I arrived in Africa, I was still in Spain. The Spanish have no more intentions of giving Ceuta back to the Moroccans, than the English have of relinquishing control of Gibraltar to Spain. I was able to cross into Morocco from Ceuta and had a fabulous time touring North Africa.

The Spanish initiated the next war against the Brits in 1779 in attempt to repatriate Gibraltar and the Balearic islands. The result was a split decision in 1783. Spain regained control of Menorca and Majorca but the British kept Gibraltar. The Rock makes an almost impenetrable stronghold, being practically impossible to conquer. The final Anglo-Spanish War was fought between 1796 and 1808. The Battle of Trafalgar in 1805 was Admiral Lord Nelson's famous victory over the combined naval fleets of both France and Spain. With this victory, the British would dominate the Atlantic Ocean and Mediterranean Sea for the next hundred years. The Spanish still remember this defeat with great disdain. It was the second time in which a superior, Spanish fleet, which was considered invincible, was destroyed by the English.

The Anglo-Spanish Wars basically ended in the beginning of the 19th century just as Mexico began its War for Independence against Spain. Mexico became an independent country with its first president, Guadalupe Victoria, taking office in 1824. The Spanish had not lost their hatred of the Anglo-Saxons who had defeated them in five major wars over the past four hundred and fifty years. The Anglo-Saxons, just as vehemently, disliked their arch enemies the Spanish. With four hundred and fifty years of intense political, social, religious, and economic competition, coupled with five major wars, hundreds of thousands of casualties, the British and Spanish had established a relationship of cultural and racial hatred. What had become the United States of America was an extension of England. What had become the United States of Mexico was an extension of Spain. All of the suspicions, historical hatred, and insecurities had crossed the Atlantic and manifested in the so-called New World. In other words, instead of two new countries, two new peoples, two new cultures, which came into being almost simultaneously, having a clean slate with which to begin commerce, neighborly, and political relations, the opposite was true. The cultural, racial bigotry which had been spawned in 1384, and had grown over the subsequent four and half centuries between the Spanish and the English was now simply transferred to the Americas.

Problems between the United States of Mexico and the United States of America began almost immediately after Mexico's first president took office in 1824. Prior to that, in 1819, the U.S. president, James Monroe, signed a boundary agreement with Spain. The agreement, known as the Transcontinental Treaty of 1819, set the borders between the Texas Territories which belonged to Mexico, with the Louisiana Territories which belonged to the U.S. The border was designated along the Sabine, Red, and Arkansas Rivers and then followed the 42nd parallel to the Pacific Ocean. The Sabine River is the current state border between Texas and Louisiana. James Monroe recognized Mexico's new nationhood, president, and these boundaries in 1824. From the Mexican perspective, this act of national and border recognition by Monroe would be one of the last gestures of friendship to be extended from the north for many decades to come.

In 1824 Mexico was about twice as large, in square miles, as the organized portions of the U.S. (total of the states and organized territories). The current U.S. states of Texas, New Mexico, Arizona, California, Kansas, Colorado, Utah, and Wyoming (in all or part) were part of Mexico. During the next twenty-four years, via wars, independence movements, and improbable land sales, Mexico lost all of this territory to the U.S., accounting for approximately sixty percent of Mexico's total sovereign land. This loss would be equivalent to the U.S. losing all of its current day states west of the Mississippi, for example. Many Americans who do not know Mexican-U.S. history have the idea that the Mexican-American War was about settling the small land dispute in Texas over the southwestern border between the U.S. and Mexico. That was part of the conflict, but in reality, at the end of the war in 1848, the U.S. suddenly possessed sixty per cent of Mexico. Most Mexicans believe that the gringos, one way or another, stole that portion of Mexico. They think it was an unjustifiable, illegal theft.

This so-called theft started soon after Monroe recognized Mexico's sovereignty. The first big issue between Mexico and the U.S. was Texas. In reality, the issue was between Mexico and its citizens in the state which was known as Coahuila and Texas. This area is often referred to as a territory of Mexico but, the state of Coahuila and Texas, was one of the original nineteen states that were defined and organized under Mexico's Constitution of 1824. Texas was an appendage or county of the state of Coahuila. The Mexican government issued land grants to American immigrants in an attempt to develop Texas beginning in 1823. By 1835, more than thirty thousand Americans had immigrated to the Texas portion of Coahuila and Texas and had become Mexican citizens. The new arrivals, in the Texas appendage of the state, outnumbered the indigenous Mexican population in that section by four to one. This population, however, represented a small portion of the entire state and was therefore ill-represented in the faraway state capital of Saltillo. As the Texas citizenry and Mexican government drifted farther and farther apart, American immigration was legally terminated. During this same period the Mexican federal government was having an extremely difficult time in defining itself as a new nation. Fifteen different presidents were seated in Mexico City between 1824 and 1834. The infamous Antonio López de Santa Anna took office for the third time in 1834, annulled the Constitution of 1824, and became Mexico's new dictator. The Texans, both American immigrants and indigenous Mexicans, decided to form a government, declare independence, and become The Republic of Texas. The short four month war for Texas' independence followed. The dictator Santa Anna, leading his own troops, was defeated and Texas became an independent nation in April of 1836.

This would be the first of many humiliating losses to be suffered by the Mexicans at the hands of the Americans (Texans). It would also be the first of many large losses of Mexican land to the gringos. A number of interesting things came out of the Texas War for Independence. First, the hatred between the Mexicans and the Americans became solidified in reality. The Mexican-Spanish had contempt for the American-British and vice versa for centuries. That was just natural, historical baggage. Now, the Mexicans, trying to find a national identity, had found a neighborly enemy in Texas and the U.S. Second, a precedent was established. Land that had been controlled by the Spanish, in New Spain, that was now under Mexican control was vulnerable to being taken by the U.S. Third, Santa Anna's massacre of 257 Texan soldiers at the Alamo and the subsequent execution of 365 Texan soldiers (who had surrendered under a white flag) via firing squads in Goliad, solidified Texan and U.S. hatred of the Mexicans. These two black events still linger in the hearts and probably the subconscious minds of most Americans and all Texans. These dastardly, despicable acts of the cowardly Santa Anna are taught each year to Texas school children. The shouts of "Remember the Alamo!" and "Remember Goliad!" that were yelled by the victorious Texan soldiers at the Battle of San Jacinto where Santa Anna was eventually defeated, captured, and disgraced are still very much a part of the anti-Mexican lore in Texas.

When I was a kid I learned the Texas version of history. In the sixth grade when Texas history was taught, I lived in Pasadena, a Houston suburb, just ten miles from the San Jacinto

Battleground where the Texans defeated Santa Anna and gained their independence. There is a placard at the battleground that commemorates the event. It states that eight hundred Texans surprised, surrounded, and captured six thousand Mexicans in an hour and a half. Furthermore, it insinuates (or maybe we got it at school) that the lazy, no good, tequila-drinking, siesta-taking force of six thousand Mexicans were no match for the brave, stalwart Texans. As a matter of fact, probably three or four hundred Texans would have been more than sufficient to defeat the lazy Mexicans who were caught undressed, drunk, napping, and cavorting with their prostitutes in the middle of the afternoon. The prevalent Texas lore was not kind to the Mexicans. Their leader, Antonio López de Santa Anna, tipped off to the attack, changed clothes with a common infantryman and ran along with two thousand others back towards Mexico. Two days later, however, he was exposed, caught, shackled and brought to General Sam Houston's camp. Initially, lore has it, he acted like a peasant. The great Santa Anna, who had been the President of Mexico three times, and now was playing the part of the wartime general, who was safeguarding the Republic, was dressed as a common soldier, trying to convince Sam Houston that he was nothing more than a common soldier. It did not work.

Finally, Santa Anna signed two treaties with the Texans. The first was an agreement to withdraw the Mexican troops south of the Rio Grande River and cease all hostilities. The second treaty recognized Texas' independence and sovereignty. Then Santa Anna, upon his return to Mexico City, declared the treaties invalid. This entire affair established the basis for future relationships between the U.S. and Mexico. The Mexicans became, in the eyes of the Americans and Texans, a people capable of blatant massacre, ruthless and cowardly execution, and furthermore, a people incapable of eliciting trust, and void of ethics, or honor. The Texans had won the war, signed the treaties, and upheld their end of the agreement by releasing all their prisoners as well as Santa Anna, only to discover that the Mexicans completely disavowed the agreements. Mexico would soon pay a high price for their immoral character and subsequent actions.

The immorality, on the other hand, as taught in Mexican

history is one of a greedy land grab. History as taught in Mexico seems to ignore the fact that one of the founders of the Republic of Texas and its first vice president was Lorenzo de Zavala. He had been the chairman of Mexico's Constitutional Congress which had written Mexico's Constitution of 1824. He was actually the first person to sign the Constitution of The United States of Mexico. He was a democrat. He knew that there was little chance that the rich Mexican elite would ever agree to establish a democratic country. A free, independent Texas was the best hope for the establishment of a democratic nation in the ruins of New Spain. He sought out freedom, democracy, and became known as a traitor instead.

So, the first large land grab by the gringos was Texas. The Texans declared and won independence from Mexico in 1836 and with the recognition by the U.S. in 1837 defined their new Republic as being all the lands between the Sabine River in the east, the Nueces River to the west, the Red River to the north, and the Gulf of Mexico to the south, approximately half the size of the current state. It was approximately 135,000 square miles or almost as large as New York, Ohio, and Pennsylvania combined. The Mexicans, of course, were incensed, not in agreement but unable to mount a military campaign with which to repatriate Texas.

The bonds between the fledgling Republic of Texas and the U.S. grew stronger and in 1845, President John Tyler agreed to annex it as the 28th state of the union. The Mexican response was to recall their ambassador from the U.S. and begin preparing for war. President Tyler decided to get greedy and extend the borders of the new state of Texas even further to the south to the Rio Grande River. He sent General Zachary Taylor west across the Nueces River to attack the Mexican troops stationed north of the Rio Grande River and then characterized it as an aggressive attack on the part of the Mexicans against the U.S. He had convinced Congress and his war cabinet that the land between the Rio Grande and Nueces Rivers was actually part of Texas and therefore should be protected. It was a contrived land grab that the unorganized and ill prepared Mexicans could not prevent.

The Mexican-American War followed. It started in May of 1846 and the final battle at Chapultepec Palace was fought in September of 1847 in Mexico City. The Mexican version of this war is very different when compared to the American version. The Americans did not spend a lot of time justifying the war but instead hid behind the concept of Manifest Destiny. This was sufficient for most Americans. The U.S. was determined to expand its boundaries to the west coast as quickly as possible and the Mexican War was the perfect pretense. The Mexicans, on the other hand, refer to the war as a U.S. invasion. It is not seen in Mexico as the Mexican-American War but as the U.S. invasion, occupation, and illegal land steal of 1847. The result of the War, of course, continued to cement the feelings of hatred and mistrust between the two nations.

The most horrible and egregious acts perpetrated by the victorious Americans are still disdained by the Mexicans. For example, the story of General Winfield Scott's bombardment of the coastal town of Veracruz on his march to the capital was unnecessary and brutal. His ground forces surrounded the city, closed all of its exits of escape and then his naval brigade lobbed more than six thousand seven hundred bombs into the civilian center for more than forty-eight hours. More than one thousand fifteen hundred Mexicans were killed. Many were women and children. Historians believe Scott and his troops had revenge of the Alamo and Goliad on their minds. The Mexican version of history treats the attacks as a sinisterly cruel and cowardly event. The Americans were prepared, funded, and organized. They planned and actuated a multipronged offensive which sent more than 75,000 troops south towards Mexico and westward towards California. The first prong, under General Kearney marched into Santa Fe (New Mexico) unopposed after making a deal (bribe) with the Mexican Governor Armijo to abdicate. The second thrust, lead by Naval Commodore John Sloat who was in charge of the Pacific Squadron attacked at the Monterey Peninsula, captured San Francisco, and secured California with the help of Captain John Fremont's Bear Flag revolt. A group of Missouri militiamen led by General Alexander Doniphan formed the third offensive and defeated the northwest Mexican army at Chihuahua. Their unsavory behavior during the occupation is still bitterly remembered by the citizens of Chihuahua. The infamous general, Santa Anna, once again raised an army and confronted the fourth

prong of the American attack led by General Zachary Taylor just
after the fall of Monterey. The fighting was intense, fatalities
were heavy in the Mexican ranks, and Santa Anna decided to fall
back on Mexico City. In true Mexican fashion, upon his return,
he displayed a captured canon, an American flag, a few rifles, and
declared that he had defeated the invaders. A few weeks later,
however, General Scott's army demolished Veracruz and marched
on the capital. His campaign was bitterly and valiantly opposed
but the Americans eventually captured the capital. The last battle
was fought at the military academy located at Chapultepec Palace
in Mexico City. The young cadets of the military academy fought
bravely alongside the others soldiers. One brave, stalwart, patriot
of seventeen wrapped himself in a Mexican Flag and jumped from
a turret to his death in a final defiant, helpless gesture. He became
a national hero and the symbol of everything that was evil and
wrong in this imperialistic invasion of a defenseless Mexico. The
story turned into a national folktale. The facts have been rearranged
to depict the entire battle for Chapultepec Palace as one between
a seasoned, mature American military division of thousands of
men against a small group of thirteen and fourteen year old junior
cadets. The American barbarians, of course, slaughtered the young
cadets to the last except for the hero who wrapped himself in the
flag of patriotism and committed himself to God. It makes a good
story and breeds a lot hatred and resentment against the gringos.
Six of the Niños Héroes (Boy Heroes) are remembered by name
on the monument that was later built to commemorate their valiant
efforts on the hill at Chapultepec Palace.

The Mexicans were eventually forced to surrender and cede
half of their country to the U.S. This was the second large land
grab by the gringos in less than ten years. First, the Mexicans lost
the eastern half of the current state of Texas. This time they lost
the western half of Texas, the vast California and New Mexico
territories, and much more as they formally signed the Treaty
of Guadalupe Hidalgo in 1848. "The war reinforced the worst
stereotypes that each country held about each other, and these
stereotypes in turn contributed to the development of deep-seated
prejudices. United States historians rationalized, justified, and even
commended the decision to wage the war as well as the prosecution

of it. On grounds ranging from regenerating a backward people to preordained destiny..." "Mexican historians, too, stereotyped and distorted. Not content with a vigorous condemnation of the United States government, they pinned the responsibility on the American people and the congenital defects of their Anglo-Saxon heritage. It is almost axiomatic that wars nurture the development of xenophobia..." "This particular war yielded its own particular variety -- a virulent, almost pathological, Yankeephobia. The fears and hatred of the United States run deep..."2 The Mexicans began to blame the U.S. for all of their shortcomings. This tradition continues very strongly today. The love-hate relationship that the Mexicans had with the Spanish was now completely transferred to the Americans. When General Scott and his green-coated troops marched from Mexico City towards the new border that had been forced on the dispirited, beaten, down-trodden, disenfranchised, humiliated, and helpless Mexicans, they coined the new term, *Green Go!* They had been thoroughly defeated, occupied for months, robbed, financially bankrupted, and forced to cede their motherland to the gringos. Surely, they hoped to never see their hated neighbors again.

The biggest reason that the Americans were able to so handily defeat the Mexicans was that the Mexicans were their own worst enemy. The Mexican-American War or American invasion of Mexico, whichever name, was not a war fought between two stable and competitive national governments. The Mexican government, economy, culture, and people were still in disarray from the War of Independence from Spain. They could not get it together. Their concept of nationhood was not defined in a cogent way that could be agreed upon by the citizenry or the leaders. When the U.S declared war on May of 1846, the very young twenty- two year old republic had already seated thirty-three different presidents. Mexico had thirty- three presidents in twenty two years! That is astounding! Mexico was so volatile and politically unstable it is amazing that the Americans did not annex the entire country. Certainly, after the war, the defeated Mexicans could have done little to preserve their sovereignty. At the beginning of the war, the Mexican army upon receiving their orders to march to the border of Texas, and protect the country, instead, immediately overthrew

President Paredes. Eight different presidents tried to bring unity to the country during the short seventeen month war. The political disarray, as much as anything, caused the military defeat. Many Americans, at the end of the Mexican-American War, urged President Polk to annex Mexico just as he had annexed Texas. Polk, who had orchestrated the invasion which resulted in the deaths of more than fifty thousand Mexicans, was content to take half the country and leave the disorganized, desperate Mexicans to their own devices. He had no intention of assuming the large costs which would be needed to rebuild Mexico's infrastructure. As a last insult, he authorized the filing of private claims by American citizens against the Mexican government. So, although the war was over, the demands of the U.S. against Mexico continued.

This trend of losing the motherland to the gringos would continue as well. Five years later, acting as president for the eleventh time, Santa Anna agreed to sell the remaining part of New Mexico and all of southern Arizona to the Americans. For a paltry ten million dollars, the Gadsden Purchase transferred another thirty thousand square miles of Mexico to the U.S. In a short period of time, from 1836 to 1853, Mexico had suddenly lost sixty per cent of their country to their northern neighbor. The citizenry hated it then, they lament it now. There are millions of Mexican citizens, both in Mexico and in the U.S., as well as millions of Chicanos (Mexican Americans) who openly discuss the dream of repatriating all of that lost territory. Many believe that continued illegal immigration and super-high birth rates among immigrants will eventually accomplish the goal of repatriation. Perhaps, they are right.

Another momentous event that took place in January of 1848, just months after the fall of Mexico City, was the discovery of gold at Sutter's Mill in California. The California Gold Rush, which was the impetus of western U.S. migration and settlement, the springboard for the development of one of the world's most virulent, cultural forces, made thousands of millionaires and billionaires, and should have happened in Mexico not the U.S. Most Mexicans believe the riches of California were stolen from them. Many Mexican historians equate the California Gold Rush to the Spaniard's stealing the Aztec gold and silver in the 16th century. All of the great things that have happened in California should have been part of Mexico's history. Many Mexicans believe that they were robbed of the wealth, culture and influence that has emanated from California. Their consolation has been the ability to illegally sneak across the border and keep the lawns cut and the houses clean of the gringos who stole California. There is not a lot of happiness or satisfaction with the fact that they were cheated-out of California. If ranked as an independent country, California's 1.7 trillion dollars of GDP would make it the eighth largest economy in the world. Mexico's GDP barely reached 800 million in the same year of 2006. California's economy is twice as large as Mexico's. Whether it is Hollywood, the Redwoods, San Francisco Bay, the Silicon Valley, all of the tons of gold, the world's 8th largest GDP, or just the life-style, California, The Land of Milk and Honey, was carelessly lost by the Mexicans. Or as the Mexicans see it, stolen by the gringos!

Mexico's world-wide reputation by the middle of the 19th century was very negative.   The government was unstable and therefore any continuity of political purpose, direction, or advancement was almost impossible. The government had reneged on its foreign debt and was unable to acquire international funding for development projects. The country was recognized internationally as being backwards, corrupt, and lacking any respect for the rule of law. Nationally, lawlessness had practically become an institution. Travelling foreigners as well as nationals were attacked and robbed on a routine basis. Marauding cattle rustlers and bandits crossed the new international border of the Rio Grande into Texas for decades after the Mexican-American War was fought. This was the period in which the infamous Mexican bandit was born. Another international and negative perception was the ubiquitous poverty throughout the country. Mexico City, in particular, had come to be known as a city of beggars, lepers, prostitutes, and criminals. In the world view Mexicans began to be stereotyped as lazy, uneducated, lawless, ungovernable and backwards. This ungovernableness and lack of respect for law continues to characterize Mexicans into the 21st century as once again Mexico has become so lawless that foreigners fear to travel freely in the country. By 2006 most western governments issued travel advisories to their citizens warning them of the serious dangers that could be encountered if they travelled or vacationed in Mexico. The image of Mexico that had emerged after fifty years of sovereignty from Spain was not a pretty one. The country was in a financial and cultural crisis.

Finally a strong leader, a dictator, Porfirio Díaz took control of Mexico's destiny. He realized that foreign investment, engineering, and management, was desperately needed if Mexico, were to advance past its brutal and failed past. He first strengthened the internal military and police apparatus to introduce order and control. He then invited in the foreigners. The British and American investors heartened by Díaz' militaristic control began investing in Mexican infrastructure such as railroads, oil and gas, as well as the mining industry. The federal government also contracted with foreign firms to build the much needed infrastructure of roads, bridges, railroads, and utilities. Billions of dollars that could have gone to local contractors and business went to foreign companies and investors. In order to reestablish political ties with the U.S. government, Díaz also agreed to pay four million dollars to satisfy claims that had been made by private American citizens. The Mexican press reported the agreement as a fabrication by the Americans in order to once again bamboozle their southern neighbors. One outcome of this event was that Díaz began to restrict the freedom of the press to report on his policies. Much to the dismay of most Mexicans, the American investment swelled to almost two billion dollars by the end of Díaz's dictatorship. The British and German investment and participation was also very large.

The results were very positive in the mining, agricultural, ranching, oil, and gas industries. The majority of the profits of these revitalized and expanded industries, however, went to foreign firms and corrupt Díaz politicians and cronies. The country's infrastructure was hugely expanded under the Díaz dictatorship but once again the monetary beneficiaries were Díaz and his foreigner cohorts. The foreigners invested, engineered, designed, built, managed, and demanded the profits and control in return. A Díaz policy was put into effect which made Americans, Brits, and Germans into super citizens. "Cases (legal) involving a foreigner against a Mexican were decided according to the principle that the foreigner must be right, unless word came from Don Porfirio Díaz, exceptionally, to discover otherwise. In the remotest places judges understood the fine points of these usages, and could interpret skillfully the precepts taught by the U. S. State Department, that Americans were guests and must be spared the judicial annoyances unavoidable to Mexicans; that every American living and working in Mexico....and every company that had American money in it (Mexico)--had the right to this extraterritorial immunity."3 They were, in effect, beyond incrimination. These foreigners who had invested in time, money, or effort in building Mexico's industry and infrastructure were granted a special status that was not available to ordinary Mexicans. This was a point that was not forgotten during the Mexican Revolution (civil war) of 1910-1920. It is just another reason why the Mexicans hate the gringos. When Calles became president after the Revolution, he not only annulled this special super citizen status, but also vowed that Mexico would never again allow another nation to create a privileged status for its citizens inside Mexico.

Relations between the two governments improved during the Díaz regime. Relations between the citizenry of the two countries, however, deteriorated even more. Mexicans continued to distrust the motives of the Americans. It was obvious that the Americans were exploiting Mexico's natural resources on the one hand while being paid very handsomely for constructing their infrastructure on the other. It was the best of all worlds for the American investors. They were reaping huge profits in all the major industries of the 19th century, being paid very well to construct Mexico's outdated infrastructure, and making profits in the banking sector by loaning the money needed for the infrastructure. Most Mexicans began to view the Americans and other foreign investors as the new colonial rulers of Mexico.

The American management of Mexican industry and construction during this period was quite brutal. The Mexican workers had few rights and died by the thousands in the mines in northern Mexico. The oil fields in the Gulf of Mexico were just as bad. Mexican workers, typically poor performers, were considered biologically inferior by the foreigners and therefore paid subpar wages. Those workers who participated in the labor strikes which began after the turn of the century were dealt with severely. "The first signs of unrest came through labor unrest. In 1906, at Colonel William Green's Cananea Consolidated Copper Company, Mexican workers struck over unfair wages and conditions. Arizona Rangers were invited into Mexico and given power by Mexican officials to suppress the workers. Díaz' was willing to give foreigners power over Mexicans. A second strike at the Rio Blanco textile mills, in 1907, resulted in Federal troops firing point blank into a crowd of striking workers, killing over a hundred men, women, and children."4 It was obvious that Díaz was unwilling or unable to defend Mexico's sovereignty. American Rangers and federal troops were able to cross the border and impose American discipline and constraint on Mexican workers. If deadly force was needed to suppress an uprising at a mine or manufacturing facility it was used.

American intervention is probably what is needed now in order to stop the violent drug wars and chaos that are engulfing the country. Calderon does not want to invite the American soldiers or DEA agents into Mexico but it may very well be his last resort for winning the war against the superior drug forces which have the advantage militarily.

The abusive techniques which were used at the mines and in other industries contributed to the start of the Mexican Revolution of 1910. The hatred that erupted against the corrupt Díaz regime spilled onto American soil. Many Mexicans wanted revenge against the gringos. The first incident occurred in 1916, when a train with fifteen American mining engineers was derailed adjacent to El Paso by Pancho Villa. The innocent and unarmed engineers were murdered, stripped, mutilated, and their bodies put on display. In March of 1916, Pancho Villa and five hundred men invaded the town of Columbus, New Mexico. Their battle cry as they burned and looted the town was "Death to the Gringos!" Once again innocent American civilians, this time eighteen, were murdered. Prior to Osama Bin Laden, Pancho Villa was the only foreigner who ever conducted a successful military invasion on U.S. soil against the U.S. and escaped unharmed. Unfortunately it is once again happening up and down the border as drug soldiers kill and kidnap American citizens in Texas, New Mexico, Arizona, and California.

The Americans did not sit on the sidelines as an uninterested bystander during Mexico's ten years of revolution. They tried to influence the outcome and protect American investors. After President Madero was assassinated in 1913, Woodrow Wilson refused to acknowledge his successor, Victoriano Huerta, and sent American troops into Veracruz on the gulf coast. They were there, of course, to protect the interests of the American and British oil companies. The American invasion was barely confronted as the Mexican garrison withdrew and left a small contingent of naval cadets to protect the city. The Mexicans had unsuccessfully tried this tactic fifty years before at Chapultepec. It seems to be an ongoing Mexican trait. When the fighting gets desperate or defeat is imminent, the trained and mature Mexican soldiers retreat and leave teenage cadets to suffer the consequences, armed only with slogans of patriotism and love of the motherland. This time the American warships pounded the naval academy, killed fifteen cadets, and took control of the city. The only surprising event is that the Mexicans did not declare another national holiday for the deaths of their brave teenaged cadets. Maybe, this habitual propensity to put teenagers in harm's way explains why so many of the decapitated drug soldiers turning up dead in the streets of Juárez and Tijuana are teenagers. The American troops occupied Veracruz from April through November of 1914.

At the other end of the country, General Pershing was ordered to invade Mexico with orders to destroy the revolutionary army of Pancho Villa. The results were predictable on both sides and led to continued hatred and folktales of success and bravery on both sides. The Pershing brigade of twelve thousand soldiers occupied Mexico for a full year without every engaging in a single battle. One regiment lead by the famous WWII General George S. Patton, *Old Blood and Guts*, attacked and subdued a Mexican regiment that was actually fighting against Pancho Villa in their civil war. It was a mistake and its only accomplishment was to further infuriate both sides of the civil war and create even more anti-Americanism. A mini-industry sprang up in the small towns which housed the twelve thousand soldiers. The liquor and prostitution businesses soared. In the small town of Colonia Dublán, General Pershing had a large group of prostitutes sequestered and housed in order to service the soldiers. Prophylactics were issued to the soldiers and venereal disease was minimized. Basically, twelve thousand soldiers meandered among the northern Mexican towns in the state of Chihuahua looking for Pancho Villa during the day and relaxed with tequila and a senorita in the evening. As had been the case during the French occupancy fifty years before, many blue-eyed, blond-haired offspring were left behind. In the case of the French debauchery, hundreds of thousands of Mexicans were impregnated with Anglo-Saxon genetics. The scale was not so large with Pershing's invasion force of twelve thousand but Mexico's hatred of an American occupying force was no less intense than that of the Iraqi's of today. Pancho Villa was never captured; attacks and raids continued inside American territory, and President Wilson finally ordered the activation and deployment of one hundred and ten thousand troops along the border. Both countries were on the brink of war but with Wilson's securing of the southern border suddenly the Mexican raids stopped and an all-out invasion was averted. The Americans withdrew from Mexico, in early 1917, Pershing claimed success if not victory, and Pancho Villa did the same.

Historically, a secure border between the U.S. and Mexico seems to bode well for both Americans and Mexicans. Tensions eased, not escalated, when Wilson sent the one hundred and ten thousand troops to the border in 1917. Mexicans stopped raiding border towns and ranches because they were afraid of being caught or killed. Mexican encounters with hostile American troops inside Mexican territory ceased. Pershing's troops withdrew and Mexico regained her sovereignty. Today the border is not secure; tension, danger, and criminality flourish. It is always easy for cultures to look back at history with a whimsical, romantic perspective and consider characters like Pancho Villa as something less severe and dangerous than they were. But the reality of the early 20th century along the border was a reality of open-ended lawlessness, raids, murders, bank robberies, cattle rustling, looting and destruction. When Wilson sent in the troops in 1917, he brought security to a lawless region. This same region once again has fallen under the control of lawless criminals. President Wilson solved the problem by securing the border between Mexico and the U.S. Obviously, it is time for the two governments to secure our common borders again. The sooner Janet Napolitano can convince Barack Obama of this reality the better!

The Mexican Revolution continued as the U.S. joined its allies against Germany in WWI in June of 1917. Although Mexico declared to be neutral, the U.S. and Mexico chose to continue with their relationship of mistrust and suspicion. Germany tried to recruit Mexico into joining in their effort to defeat the American allies. The Mexicans were promised the return of all their lost lands of Texas, New Mexico, Arizona, and California as an inducement. An official communication between the German Foreign Minister and the German Ambassador to Mexico was intercepted by the British and shared with the Americans in January of 1917. "We intend to begin on the 1st of February unrestricted submarine warfare. We shall endeavor in spite of this to keep the United States of America neutral. In the event of this not succeeding, we make Mexico a proposal of alliance on the following basis: make war together, make peace together, generous financial support and an understanding on our part that Mexico is to re-conquer the lost territory in Texas, New Mexico and Arizona. The settlement in detail is left to you. You will inform the President (of Mexico) of the above most secretly as soon as the outbreak of war with the United States of America is certain and add the suggestion that he should, on his own initiative, invite Japan to immediate adherence and at the same time mediate between Japan and ourselves. Please call the President's attention to the fact that the ruthless employment of

our submarines now offers the prospect of compelling England in a few months to make peace. signed, Zimmermann."5 The American government leaked the document to the press and the Mexicans became vilified as supporters of the Germans and were quickly portrayed as a threat to American national security. Furthermore, scholars believe the Zimmermann message convinced Woodrow Wilson to declare war against Germany. The American newspapers, covering the story, left no room for doubt that their southern neighbors, whom were never trusted anyway, were secretly planning to attack and repatriate the four southwestern U.S. states. This event also convinced Wilson of the necessity of having secure southern borders.

World War I ended as did the Mexican Revolution only to find the two countries with more of a strained relationship than ever. The Mexican Constitution of 1917 was enacted which legalized the nationalization of all foreign oil companies. The U.S. president, Warren Harding, refused to recognize the newly sworn-in Mexican president, Álvaro Obregón unless American oil interest was guaranteed. After three years of hateful negotiations an agreement was reached which allowed Americans to retain ownership of all oil wells that were drilled prior to the 1917 Constitution. Interestingly, the oilman William F. Buckley played a pivotal role in convincing Harding not to recognize Obregón as president without a guarantee for American interests.

Post-revolutionary Mexico saw even more growth of Anti-American sentiment than had existed before the Revolution. The Mexican press began blaming the Americans for all the economic ills that were being suffered in Mexico as a result of ten years of civil war. They even took exception with the citizens of The United States of America use of the term Americans. If only the founding fathers could have come up with another name that would have been more fair. Mexico is, of course, The United States of Mexico, so it is fair enough that their citizens be called Mexicans. But, how do the gringos come off assuming the name of Americans. Everyone who lives in the western hemisphere has a rightful claim to that name. Brazilians, Mexicans, and Chileans have as much claim to that name as the Americans. But during the twenties and thirties it became fashionable and then common to refer to the Americans simply as gringos. Although the term had been around for decades the press began using the term gringo on a routine basis after the Civil War (1910-1920) and for decades was the prominent, derogatory description used when referring to American citizens. Today, seventy years later it is not even considered a derogatory term unless used with an adjective such as pinche (fucking) in front of it, which is very common. This expression, pinche gringos (fucking Americans), defines the current, prevalent Mexican sentiment towards Americans that is found throughout Mexico.

Currently, the more common name used by Mexicans who live in the U.S. and by Chicanos is gabacho. Many consider the term gringo to be old-fashioned and antiquated. Mexican racists like to be hip and use terms like Bolillo, which is a Mexican bread made of bleached or white flour. Gustavo Arrellano, author of the popular OC Weekly column, in Orange County, California, Ask a Mexican advises against using the term gringo. He writes that it is completely outdated. It may be outdated for Orange County Chicanos to use the term gringo but it is obvious that Arrellano's Mexico is really southern California and his Ask a Mexican should really be entitled Ask a Chicano. His witty and all-knowing commentaries consistently reveal a Chicano mindset that has spent very little time in Mexico. But his columns are witty, intelligent, and often reveal many of the underlying hatreds that exist between Gabachos and Chicanos. He suggests that the term gringo did not even originate in Mexico but that etymologist attribute the word to be a bastardization of the Greek word griego (Spanish for Greek). Yet, he offers no etymological proof of this assertion and cynically advises racists to at least stay current with their slang as they badger each other.

The Mexican revolution was supposed to be about social and economic changes but real liberal change did not take place in Mexico until Lázaro Cárdenas came to office in 1934. He was an anomaly in Mexican politics and it did not bode well for the Americans. He is famous for his land redistribution programs for the poor. He gave fifty million square acres of land to the poor, indigenous, disenfranchised, rural Mexicans. Most of the land, of course, was of marginal quality and unsuitable for agriculture. But, more importantly, he nationalized the holdings of the seventeen largest oil companies in 1938. Nationalize, in this case, is synonymous with steal. The multinational companies, mostly American based, had spent billions of investment dollars in Mexico, beginning in the late 19th century. The oil companies were expelled from Mexico. Decades of investment and billions of dollars was lost with one stroke of Lázaro Cárdenas' pen. Ten years later, the International Arbitration court awarded the seventeen firms a mere twenty-four million dollars in compensation. They lost their entire investment in Mexico, drilling platforms, equipment, storage facilities, and millions of barrels of stored oil. The ironic and expected consequence was the immediate deterioration of Mexico's oil industry. Production had reached a peak of 190 million barrels under foreign management which quickly dropped to less than 20 million barrels under Mexican control. Each year on the 18th of March, Nationalization Day, the President gives a speech boasting of Mexico's fortuitous oil industry. In reality, it took Mexico forty years to recover from the destruction that resulted from its nationalization program. In the mid 1970's, Mexico finally began to produce large levels of oil again.

Mexico's oil grab had severe consequences throughout Mexican industry and banking. The U.S., Great Britain, and the Netherlands boycotted Mexican exports until WWII. They also strangled foreign investment into Mexico, for decades. Mexico, once again, became perceived as a huge risk for banking and investing worldwide. The popular and much ballyhooed oil grab was not necessarily an advantageous move on the part of Cárdenas. Mexico would have fared much better if his government would have negotiated a co-ownership program with the likes of Shell, Standard, and Sinclair oil companies.

Today Mexico is still suffering from undercapitalization in their oil industry. The majority of the profits from oil production are going into the government coffers and very little is being reinvested in infrastructure or exploration. Mexico had the good fortune of discovering the Cantarell Field in 1976, which reached production of 2.2 million barrels of oil per day in 2003. This made it the 2nd highest producing field in the world. The original field was estimated to contain 35 billion barrels of oil. In comparison, the largest U.S. Gulf of Mexico field contains one billion barrels and produces 250,000 barrels per day. But new technology is required to extract the huge reserves from beneath the Gulf and Mexico has neither the technology nor the investment in which to proceed. When Cárdenas nationalized the oil fields in 1938, he amended the constitution to preclude foreign ownership or investment in Mexican natural resources. Therefore, Mexico is currently in a self-strangling situation. They have huge oil reserves but lack the money and technology for developing them. Their constitution prohibits them from bringing outside firms such as

BP (British Petroleum), who constantly tries to negotiate a deal, in order to develop the existing fields and explore new, deeper fields. In October of 2008, President Calderón, in an attempt to acquire the political support for foreign participation was only able to pass a weak bill which will allow foreign companies into Mexico to maintain existing infrastructure. In other words, oil platform and storage maintenance companies will be given contracts to maintain the current infrastructure that PEMEX has allowed to become outdated and nonfunctional. This will be little more than a band aid applied to a patient who is bleeding to death.

The reason the Mexican Congress will not give Calderón support on the issue of foreign investment in the oil industry is part political and part historical. When Cárdenas nationalized the oil companies in 1938, he was making a statement about Mexican sovereignty and foreign intervention. Whether or not he was aware of the catastrophic affect his program would have on oil production is unknown. He was very aware, however, that his actions were a repudiation of imperialistic domination of Mexico by foreigners. He portrayed it that way as well as did the press. It was a defiant act against the Americans (and others). Consequently, he established the Nationalization Day as a commemorative gesture so Mexicans would never forget to snub their noses at foreign involvement in interior Mexican affairs. Calderón won the presidential election of 2006, against Manuel López Obrador with less than one percent of the popular vote. Obrador campaigned against changing the constitution in order to allow foreign investment in the energy industry. The short-sided Mexican Congress agreed with his socialistic platforms. This is unfortunate for Mexico and the United States, as oil production has fallen every year since 2004. Mexico currently supplies the U.S. with sixteen per cent of its oil, being their 3rd largest supplier. At 2008 prices that amounts to more than ten per cent of Mexico's annual GDP. A full forty per cent of Mexico's national budget is paid through petroleum sales. Experts predict, as Mexico's internal demand for oil increases and its continued output decreases, by 2014, a short few years from now, Mexico will no longer have excess oil to export. This calamity will be momentous!

Cardenas' nationalization of American oil companies in

1938, continued to fuel the hatred between the two countries. The Mexican oil industry suffered initial losses of production but eventually recovered and became an important revenue generator for the country. For once Mexicans could gleefully thumb their noses at their rich American neighbors. The Americans became even more convinced of the irascible and unpredictable nature of their southern neighbor. Americans began to develop a more sophisticated understanding of the cultural differences that exist between Mexicans and Americans. The Americans were beginning to understand how little meaning the rule of law has in Mexico. Since the early twenties Mexican oilmen such as William F. Buckley had persuaded Presidents Wilson, Harding, and Coolidge of the importance of protecting American investment in Mexico. But Franklin Roosevelt, distracted by WWII, instructed his foreign minister to settle the oil nationalization issue in favor of Mexico in 1941. This marked the first time in the history of American-Mexican relations that the U.S. government failed to come to the aid of American citizens who had been victimized by the Mexican government. This was quite a contrast from the 130 million dollars President Wilson spent trying to track down Pancho Villa's marauding murderers a few decades earlier.

As both countries contemplated the inevitable Second World War Mexico again decided to announce neutrality. The aggressive attacks on shipping in the Gulf of Mexico by the Germans, however, convinced Mexican President Manuel Camacho to support the Allies against the Axis powers. He was afraid that the Japanese had plans to use Mexico as an invasion front against the U.S. After Camacho's announcement in support of the allies, the Mexican press criticized his decision. The U.S. was Mexico's sworn enemy and it was embarrassing to now be supporting them in war. The shrewd Camacho, however, saw the obvious advantages in supporting the allies. First, he had no intentions of joining in the war effort or even of supplying military support. Second, he knew there would be a greater opportunity to sell Mexican products to the Allies than to the Germans or Japanese if he could convince the U.S. to end the oil and trade embargo which was put in place after Mexico had nationalized the oil industry in 1938. By the middle of 1942, the Americans had secured the shipping lanes in the Gulf of Mexico and there was no longer a major concern of losing freighters which began sailing between Veracruz, Texas, and Florida, or the East Coast. The only two Mexican freighters sunk during the war were in the Gulf prior to that. Third, he had already begun negotiating a multi-million dollar labor deal with FDR. This would eventually result in the export of approximately 500,000 Mexican workers to the U.S. This was the beginning of the historical worker-immigrant (legal or illegal) relationship between Mexico and the U.S. Fourth, he had full intentions of allowing private Mexican businesses to continue to operate and contract with the Axis powers. As a matter of fact, Italy had become its largest customer for exported oil.

The Americans, obviously, were very suspicious of Camacho's motives. In the United States there were fears that Axis secret agents were operating in Mexico. J. Edgar Hoover produced a stream of reports purporting to see Axis agents in many quarters. Hoover entertained fears of the Mexican Right cooperating with Germany. In one report he stated that a revolution led by General Almazán and most of the army officers of the Mexican Army was likely to break out at any moment with the purpose of keeping petroleum from reaching the Allies or even obtaining that resource for the Axis powers. The U.S.'s top crime fighter passed along undigested rumors from businessmen operating in Mexico. Hoover reported the alarming news that not only was a new revolution brewing in Mexico, but that the Mexican Army was about to attack the British Empire in British Honduras. This confidential source also indicated that information had previously been obtained that there was a large concentration of Mexican troops on the British Honduran border and it had been suggested that this was synchronized with the German attack on Scandinavia. President Roosevelt was sufficiently concerned about the possibility of a German-Mexican rapprochement to call a joint session of Congress in May, 1940. At the conference he warned that, in the event of a war, Mexico might fall under German influence. As he reminded his listeners, "Tampico is only 2 1/4 hours away [by air] from Saint Louis, Kansas City and Omaha."6

President Camacho was shrewd enough to use the circumstances of World War II in order to negotiate an advantageous deal for

Mexico. He convinced FDR to lift the trade sanctions, settle the oil nationalization issue, and open the U.S. borders to migrant workers. Over the next four years more than 500,000 Mexican laborers would immigrate to the U.S. This deal would establish a symbiotic relationship between American producers and Mexican laborers. What started as a migrant worker program, evolved into a more permanent mass immigration. Unfortunately, the 21st century result has been the relocation of approximately fifteen or twenty million illegal Mexicans into the U.S. Many historians characterize the Mexican-U.S. relationship during World War II as a partnership of allies. Most Americans, who were still stateside or abroad risking their lives for freedom and liberty in Europe, saw it quite differently. The Mexican government used the impending war in order to manipulate FDR. His idea was to invite Mexican workers into the U.S. for a finite period in order to meet the country's labor requirements. He emphasized the concept of migrant workers not unabashed illegal immigration. His plan even had a caveat which withheld ten per cent of all the wages of migrant workers. This money was sent to the Mexican government with the agreement that it would be paid to the migrants upon return to their homeland. It was intended as an incentive to insure that the workers returned to Mexico. However, two predictable things happened. One, many migrants took this opportunity to illegally immigrate. They never returned to Mexico, to receive their ten per cent withholdings. And two, the corrupt Mexican government never implemented a repayment plan. They just kept the money which experts estimate to be thirty to fifty million dollars. Finally in 2005, as a result of a lawsuit filed in Chicago, the Fox administration in Mexico agreed to settle with the former migrants. The vast majority or their descendants are living in California. They had until January of 2009, to apply for a one-time payment of three thousand and five hundred dollars from the Mexican government.

In retrospect the migrant worker program of 1942-1946, appears to be a failure in many ways. It fanned the hatred between the citizenry of both countries. The farmers who used the Mexican laborers despised their complacency in World War II. Although it is true that a small group of Mexican pilots trained in the Navy Air Corps and fought for a brief period in the Pacific, this hardly constitutes the definition of participation in World War II. Most Americans had sons who were fighting and dying in Europe yet the Mexicans were content to sit on the sidelines and even migrate in order to take their jobs. The American farmers were happy to have Mexican laborers but the entire affair did little to enamor the Mexicans to the American public. The Mexican migrant worker, on the other hand, hated the discrimination that existed in the U.S. Most were underpaid or stiffed completely, and treated as inferiors. It was customary, upon entry into the U.S. , for example, for the customs officials to strip and dust the workers with DDT. New nicknames such as beaners and tortillas were commonly used to refer to Mexicans. This period is also credited with the rise of anti-Mexican racial jokes such as the popular: Do you know what you get when you cross an Indian with a buffalo? In the end, neither government enforced the agreement of repatriation. The Mexican government stole thirty or fifty million dollars which rightfully belonged to the workers. And perhaps worst of all, it firmly established the precedent of a second-class citizenry in the U.S. in regard to Mexican workers.

Chronologically, the next political issue that festered between the U.S. and Mexico started in 1959, when Fidel Castro's revolution took control of Cuba. Mexico recognized Castro's government, voted against expelling Cuba from the Organization of American States, and continued to have normal relations with the Cubans on all fronts. The past fifty years have seen Mexico stubbornly refuse to succumb to Washington's pressure against Cuba. As a result there has also been decades of resentment between the Mexicans and Cuban-Americans. For the first time in forty years, however, relations between Mexico and Cuba turned for the worst when Vicente Fox, in an attempt to win points with President George Bush, recalled the Mexican ambassador from Havana and expelled the Cuban ambassador from Mexico City, basically breaking diplomatic ties between the two countries. The action was supposedly taken in response to human rights abuses being suffered by the Cuban population (as if that were something new). Prior to that action, Mexico and Cuba had maintained friendly and often anti-American relations. Since 1959 there has been a Mexican-Cuban understanding that Cuba would not export communism to

Mexico and in return receive favorable political support against the U.S. In late 2004 Fox and Bush's relationship soured and once again, the current president, Calderon has reestablished relations with Havana. The Mexican government has even turned a blind eye to the tens of thousands of illegal Cuban immigrants who pass through Mexico each year on their way to the U.S. In 2007, for example, more than eleven thousand illegal Cuban immigrants were arrested crossing the Mexican-U.S. border. And guess what pisses off the Mexicans about this new phenomenon, all eleven thousand Cubans were given visas by the U.S. government after they were apprehended.

The Mexican-American-Cuban issue has been a problem between the U.S. and Mexico for almost five decades and is growing in intensity. Perhaps Barack Obama will do the right thing and terminate the ridiculous trade embargo the U.S. has against Cuba, convince Raul Castro to end human rights abuses, and normalize relations between the two nations. The Mexicans are a perennial voice against the U.S. trade embargo in the United Nations which isolates Cuba. In October 2008 the U.N. voted for the 17th consecutive year to condemn the American embargo against Cuba. Mexico is not alone in its support of this issue as the vote was 185-3 against the U.S. But, the Mexican-American-Cuban problem has intensified as Mexican drug smugglers have turned their attention in the Caribbean to smuggling Cubans into the U.S. Bush's intensified embargo has caused more scarcity within Cuba thereby causing thousands to illegally seek refuge in the U.S. In response, the drug smugglers have widened their operations, using Mexico's Caribbean islands as drop-off points for the Cubans. It has created a horrific situation as tens of thousands of Cubans have become vulnerable to extortion, brutality, kidnapping, and rape once they reach the mainland of Mexico. This new smuggling route is a problem for the U.S. and a new business opportunity for the Mexican drug cartels.

As the U.S. and Mexico have entered into the 21st century, problems of hatred, suspicion and cultural incompatibility have increased. The majority of the ongoing problems result from illegal immigration, drug importation, NAFTA, increased kidnapping in the U.S. by Mexican nationals, and a myriad of cultural differences. Immigration and drug issues deserve separate chapters unto themselves but NAFTA and a number of ongoing cultural differences will be discussed here.

NAFTA, the North American Free Trade Agreement, between Mexico, the U.S., and Canada, was signed in 1993, by Carlos Salinas, George H. W. Bush, and Brian Mulroney. Its impact prior to implementation was unknown but now after fourteen years its impact is obvious. The Big Sucking Sound from the south that Ross Perot talked about during the 1993 presidential campaign can be heard very clearly in every state of the U.S. Experts continually review the impact of NAFTA in order to understand its positive and negative consequences. The winners appear to be the owners and stock holders of multinational companies that were able to move their operations from the U.S. to Mexico, and the losers appear to be the U.S factory workers. The average pay for a worker in a U.S. factory based in Mexico is approximately $20.00 per day. The American worker, prior to NAFTA, was making approximately $130.00 per day for the same work. These are estimates and vary from industry to industry but are not extremes. It is easy to see that many firms made the easy decision to move factories to Mexico in order to take advantage of the inexpensive labor. The estimate of job loss in the U.S. varies. NAFTA went into effect in 1994. The U.S. Department of Labor reported that by the end of 2001, more than 507,000 applications for lost-job benefits as a direct result of factories relocating to Mexico had been received. The Economic Policy Institute estimates that loss of jobs in the U.S. was probably closer to 900,000 in this same eight year period which can be attributed to NAFTA. The Mexican Labor Department attributes the creation of 1.3 million new Maquiladora (border factories in Mexico) workers during this same time period. This math is easy to follow. The U.S. lost almost one million factory jobs, attributable to NAFTA, and Mexico gained 1.3 million jobs as a result of NAFTA.

Another simple measurement of NAFTA's impact is seen in the balance of trade statistics between Mexico and the U.S. since NAFTA was implemented. In 1992, two years prior to NAFTA, the U.S was running a 5.4 billion dollar trade surplus with Mexico, according to the U.S. Census Department's official statistics. By

2007, the U.S. had a 74.6 billion dollar trade deficit with Mexico. The trade imbalance happened immediately and has increased dramatically every year since NAFTA's implementation. In 1994, the first year of implementation, the surplus for the U.S. dropped from 5.4 billion to 1.4 billion. In 1995 it had changed from being a surplus to an amazing 15.8 billion dollar deficit. Five years later by the year 2000, the deficit had reached almost 25 billion dollars. In 2005, another five years, saw another doubling to 50 billion dollars. And the 2007 year ended with an astounding fifty per cent increase in just two years to almost 75 billion dollars. The total trade deficit with Mexico for the U.S. during this period is a staggering 440 billion dollars. Couple that with a million lost jobs and it becomes very easy to hear that Big Sucking Sound coming from the south that Ross Perot was talking about in 1992.

There is another negative impact to the U.S. as a result of NAFTA. The poor, uneducated masses that emigrate from rural southern Mexico to work in the Maquiladora sweat shops are more than happy to illegally enter the U.S. in search of work within months after arriving at the border. The Maquiladoras are a huge magnet for attracting the uneducated, poor masses that are willing to work for meager wages. When the U.S. goes into a recession or its maquiladoras factories experience layoffs, these workers head north and join the tens of millions of illegal Mexicans who are already in the States. Although it cannot be numerically substantiated, it is a well known fact that the hundreds of thousands of Mexican workers that head north with the idea of finding work in a Maquiladora have an eventual plan for illegally migrating to the U.S. NAFTA has turned into a giant magnet sucking money southwards and workers northward.

Mexico's fortune with NAFTA was so successful that President Zedillo negotiated the Mexico-European Union Free Trade Agreement in 2000, hoping to further take advantage of Mexico's underpaid work force. It is called the Mexico-EFTA and opens the Mexican markets to the European Union the same as does NAFTA for American and Canadian companies and trade. The idea of an exclusive, open trade agreement between the U.S. Mexico, and Canada has instead become an exploitation of poor Mexican labor at the expense of skilled American and Canadian workers. One of the few American beneficiaries turns out to be businesses and manufacturing suppliers located along the border in Texas. This industry has grown to a multibillion dollar industry and counts President Bush, former governor of Texas, as one of its most ardent supporters. While U.S. industry has suffered almost half a trillion dollar loss in its trade balance with Mexico since the initiation of NAFTA a few rich Texans have gotten even richer. President Barack Obama campaigned with an agenda to change or renegotiate NAFTA citing the well-documented loss of one million American jobs. He will be wise to secure the southern border with Mexico while he renegotiates or strengthens NAFTA.

Without going into all the cultural idiosyncrasies which keep the two cultures separated it is interesting to note some of the current events, thoughts, phenomena, methods of living, preconceptions, and misconceptions that exist. And not in any particular order but worth mentioning would be Mexicans dislike of: George Bush, control of the world's international institutions such as World Trade Organization, United Nations, World Bank, International Monetary Fund, Jim Gilchrist and his border Minuteman Project which terrorizes and puts the fear of vigilantism into illegal immigrants, U.S. drug consumption which fuels Mexico's drug war and culture, the fact that American economic problems are always amplified in Mexico, the U.S. occupation of Iraq and Afghanistan, Guantanamo occupation in general and GITMO in specific, U.S. egoism, the 500,000 U.S. troops that are stationed in countries around the world, the dumping of criminals (illegal immigrant Mexicans) at the Mexican border, dropping the atom bomb, gringo expatriates who refuse to learn Spanish and Mexican culture, the fact that every Mexican military uprising or revolution was planned on American soil, past American slavery, African-American racism and oppression, American cold-hearted, non-family oriented values, pure capitalism without a socialistic bent, U.S.'s near-extermination of its indigenous population, America's respect for the rule of law, Dick Cheney, U.S. soccer team eliminating Mexico from the World Cup in 2002 and dominating them ever since, their own President Vicente Fox who characterized Mexicans as being willing to do America's work that even Blacks refuse to do, the movie A Day without a Mexican, worker exploitation in the U.S., the new border fence, U.S. support and manipulation of dictators like Pinochet, Marcos, the Shah of Iran, and Saddam Hussein, the Americanization of Mexico, U.S oil companies stealing offshore, deep-sea oil, American imperialism, The U.S. Department of Homeland Security, CBP, ICE, FBI, CIA, U.S. selling and allowing gun smuggling to the drug cartels, U.S. water usage (stealing) in the southwest, impartial coverage of Lorena Ochoa, Olympic joke, "Why does Mexico always do so poorly in the Olympics? Anyone who can jump, run, or swim has already left the country.", American tap water, Lou Dobbs obsession with illegal immigration, cold weather, or as one Mexican once summed it up "I hate America for being a hypocritical, white supremacist, capitalistic patriarchy".

Gringos, on the other hand, despise Mexico for: a judicial system which in practice lacks a 6th amendment, the lack of respect for rule of law, NAFTA, banditos, Mexican students demonstrating at California schools and showing disrespect for the American flag and value system, LBJ giving back the Chamizal territory to Mexico, how ninety-five per cent of the population can be Catholic in an anti-clerical state, bullfighting, Mexico permitting central Americans and Cubans to cross Mexico in order to illegally enter the U.S., holding of dual citizenship, coyotes (smugglers), Mexican soccer fans chanting "Osama bin Laden" at American soccer players, the fact that Mexicans gleefully call Guatemalans "Mexico's Mexicans", corrupt politicians, policemen, and army personnel, illegal Mexicans using the U.S. welfare and health systems, illegal immigration, open sewers, graffiti, Geraldo Rivera's scurrilous and inaccurate characterization of the percentage of illegal immigrants that are criminals, creation of Mexifornia, drug smuggling, kidnapping, laziness, the yearly May 1st boycott of American businesses, Mexico's poor quality of workmanship, Absolut Vodka commercials in Mexico which include California and Texas inside a redrawn Mexican map, all the Hondurans and Salvadorans from Mexico, the secret plan for repatriating the southwest U.S. , election fraud, Pancho Villa, shooting rafters along the Rio Grande River at Big Bend National Park, infectious leprosy, Montezuma's revenge, Pocho (Spanish-English hybrid language), Mexican's basic lack of honesty and integrity, Albert Gonzalez, nationalization of American properties along Mexican beaches, Makesicko City (nickname for Mexico City), Mexican crime wave in 2008 in Atlanta, Houston, Laredo, and Phoenix, wetbacks, cocaine, marijuana, meth, marrying gringas (American girls) in order to get a green card, Mexican criminality within the U.S., illegal workers sending twenty-six billion dollars back to Mexico every year, Mexican street gangs, illegal Mexicans receiving in-state tuition at California universities while out-of-state U.S. students get shafted, Mexicanization of the southwest U.S., pervasive corruption, identity fraud, identity theft, employment fraud, and especially Mexico's hypocritical hatred of a country that allows twenty per cent of its population to occupy, work in, use its social services, emulate its culture, and prosper as if they were American citizens at any given time in the U.S.

VII

Mexamerica

How Many Illegal Mexicans are there Anyway?
The United States of America is very often referred to as a nation that was built and populated by immigrants. Americans are proud to be called a nation of immigrants, because that is exactly what it is. Except for the indigenous Americans that were either obliterated or relegated to reservations, this is recognized as a good thing. The fact that the U.S. has historically been a fantastic democracy argues well for its scores of ethnicities. American citizens are immigrants from around the world. They are, however, legal immigrants and their descendents. And, of course, there are millions who immigrated illegally and were later afforded amnesty and became American citizens. Unfortunately, there are also a very large number of illegal immigrants living in the U.S. And not surprisingly, there is a significant difference between the impact that legal and illegal immigration has had and continues to have on American culture. This fact is an important reality. By the 20th century the nation was established and uninhibited immigration became not only untenable but also undesirable. Prior to 1929, millions of European, Asian, and African immigrants arrived, settled, and defined the United States of America. Illegal immigration, per se, was not an issue, as immigration was basically wide open. In 1929 a new immigration law went into effect which had been passed in 1924. It established new quotas on overall immigration levels, defined percentages of immigration by country, established educational and skill prerequisites for immigration, and required legal documentation which would be generated from the country of origin of immigrants. From 1929 until 1965, U.S. immigration laws were, more or less, enforced

and legal immigration continued to have a positive impact on American culture. Illegal immigration existed, but because of its small size had a negligible negative impact on the entire culture.

Since 1965 illegal immigration levels have changed drastically. The U.S. Congress passed the Immigration Act of 1965 which raised the ceiling on legal immigration and in essence opened the door to illegal immigration. Poor, destitute Latinos saw the change in immigration law as an open invitation to illegal immigration. Five years later, more than 10 million immigrants had literally swarmed into the U.S. One million or ten percent of this new wave of immigration was legal. The other 9 million were illegal. By 1970 the U.S. population had reached 200 million. In a short five year period since the passage of the 1965 Immigration Act U.S. demographics changed drastically. Five percent of the U.S. population was now made up of foreign-born immigrants. This was the beginning of an ever upward spiraling trend that has not subsided into the 21st century. Since the passage of the Immigration Act of 1965 ratios between legal and illegal immigration have flip-flopped. There are probably nine illegal immigrants entering the country each year for every legal entrant. The federal government lost control of immigration after the passage of the 1965 Immigration Act and have yet to regain control of it.

It is difficult to obtain an accurate count on illegal immigrants as they cross the border without acquiring legal documentation and are, of course, uncounted. After decades of studying immigration, however, many professional and governmental organizations publish statistics which estimate undocumented immigrants, their trends, whereabouts, lifestyles, political persuasions, criminal behavior, and more. Political think tanks, lobbyists, and activists, among others, publish statistics on illegal immigrants in order to persuade the government and citizens to respond in certain ways. Therefore, estimates of illegal immigration tend to be very diverse. Some conservative groups with websites such as the Right Side News seem to publish estimates that are exaggerated on the high side while other more liberal groups like the PEW Hispanic Center publish estimates that appear to be deflated and understate reality. Many of these groups, however, publish the data that is reported by the various branches of the Department of Homeland Security (DHS) as well as U.S. Census Bureau. DHS is a cabinet-level department and its current Secretary, Janet Napolitano, who has been on the job since January of 2009, reports to the President. The previous Secretary of DHS was Michael Chertoff. The two agencies within the DHS that have the most direct impact on immigration are the U.S. Customs and Border Protection(CBP) and the U.S. Immigration and Customs Enforcement (ICE). Other DHS departments such as the Coast Guard, the Citizen and Immigration Services, and the Transportation Security Administration also play pivotal roles in the enforcement of U.S. immigration laws. Certainly CBP and ICE along with the Coast Guard are the frontline enforcers of American immigration law.

The burgeoning problem of illegal immigration, in sheer numbers, has exploded even more since 1970, growing fifteen or thirty times in size. Conservative estimates suggest that 15 million illegal immigrants were living in the U.S. in 2008, although the most recent (January 2007) official DHS estimate was 11.8 million. Many other immigration experts believe the number is 30 million or higher. It is probably somewhere between those two estimates. Although DHS statistics in general are respected by immigration experts, their overall estimates of total illegal immigration is commonly recognized as being understated. This is because of the methodology used by DHS for obtaining their estimates. They use a method which backs into or deduces their estimate on illegal immigrants as opposed to being a numerical counting process. Here is how it works. They start with the U.S Census number or estimate of total foreign-born residents who reside within the U.S. They then subtract, from that total, the number of legal foreign-born residents who reside within the U.S. The resulting number is what they use for estimating the total number of illegal immigrants. The problem with this methodology lies within the parameters of the U.S. Census Bureau's actual survey. When they are taking their census they do not ask foreign-born residents for proof of citizenship. The respondents, therefore, may or may not answer the census accurately. The results are obvious. The U.S. Census estimates of foreign-born residents are inaccurate. They are unsure as to how many foreign-born residents are living in the U.S. The DHS recognizes this inaccuracy, but unfortunately continues to use the U.S. Census numbers in order to estimate the number of illegal immigrants who are living in the U.S.

One estimate range that most experts seem to agree upon is the percentage of illegal immigrants that come from Mexico. The number is somewhere between sixty and eighty percent of the total. That means that if 15 million illegal immigrants live in the U.S., in 2008, somewhere between 9 and 12 million are Mexican citizens. And if there are actually 25 million illegal immigrants in the U.S., in 2008, the math works out to 15 or 20 million illegal Mexicans. A Mexican CONAPO (National Population Counsel) official suggested that the total number, counting offspring which are born in the U.S., is probably closer to 32 million. Whatever the actual number is for Mexicans, authorities believe another fifteen per cent of the illegal immigrants are other Latinos who immigrate through Mexico from Central and South America. The numbers are staggering. On the humorous side it reminds me of the joke: After successfully sneaking into the U.S., two Arab terrorists are having an espresso at a sidewalk café in California, when one says to the other in Arabic, "Well, we made it." His compatriot quickly admonishes him, "Hey don't blow our cover, speak in Spanish, we are in the United States!" Both governments, Mexico and the U.S., believe the yearly immigration of Mexicans who are not apprehended by ICE or CBP and do not have legal documentation is greater than 750,000. The Interior Department of Mexico, in CONAPO's most recent report, forecast the number of immigrants coming to the U.S., to be between 500,000 and 750,000 per year for the next fifty years. In other words, they estimate an additional 25 to 40 million illegal Mexicans will be living in the U.S. by the middle of the 21st century. If the U.S government does not get control of its southern border many experts believe the number of additional illegal Mexicans crossing into the U.S. will be 50 million by 2150! Estimates, guesses, and deductions from trends can go out the roof. The immigration numbers since 1965 and more importantly since 1995 obviously indicate the fact that a large portion of the Mexican population is illegally immigrating to the U.S.

Most demographers believe one out of every five to seven

Mexican workers live in the U.S. Mexico's total work-force is estimated at 80 million. Approximately 12 to 15 million of them work and live in New York, Los Angeles, Houston, Atlanta, and throughout the U.S. The Department of Homeland Security officially reports that more than ten per cent of the total Mexican citizenry live in the U.S. That number does not include the five to seven million American-born dependents of Mexican citizens, who, according to Mexican law, hold dual citizenship. The DHS officially reports that fifteen per cent or more of Mexico's total labor force is illegally employed in the U.S. Many experts think it is actually 20 percent. Prior to 1965 there were an estimated 500,000 illegal immigrants living in the U.S. In 2008 estimates suggest that there were more than 15 million (conservative estimate) illegal immigrant Mexicans living in the U.S. That is a net (less those millions that returned to Mexico) of approximately 400,000 immigrants a year crossing into the U.S., from Mexico, for thirty-eight consecutive years and staying. Since 2000, the average net has been higher than 500,000 illegal Mexicans per year, not total immigration, just Mexican illegal immigration. That equals almost 42,000 per month or about 1,500 per day every day of the year during that period. That is quite an operation! It would take twelve sold-out and fully-loaded Boeing 737's flying from Mexico City, to say Chicago, Houston, and Los Angeles, every single day, three-hundred and sixty-five days of the year, to transfer that many immigrants. Or if they came by chartered bus, it would take thirty buses crossing into San Diego, Tucson, and El Paso every single day of the year. But that is only part of the total picture of the actual onslaught we are seeing of illegal immigration from Mexico. In 2008, ending in September, the CBP had captured and returned 723,825 illegal Mexicans, and their associates at ICE had removed another 349,041 to Mexico. Thus, the total of these three figures, 500,000 or more illegal immigrants who avoided detection, plus 723,825 caught by the CBP, plus the 349,041 removed by ICE is a grand total of 1,572,866. That is more than 4,300 illegal immigrants per day. More than one million were caught and returned and approximately 500,000 eluded capture. Or in other words, it would take thirty-five Boeing 737s by air or eighty-six chartered buses to move 4,300 illegal immigrants into the U.S. per day. That would be enough business to start a new low-cost airline from Mexico to the U.S., with enough dedicated passengers to make it easily viable.

This large, mass-immigration has broadly changed the demographics of the United States racially and culturally. Fifty-one per cent of the total population growth in the U.S. during the last decade has come from the Hispanic minority. Hispanic, of course, includes Mexican American citizens, Latino American citizens, and all Latino or Hispanic immigrants both legal and illegal. Any child born in the U.S. is an American citizen regardless of the legal immigration status of their parents. Thus, all so-called anchor babies, children of either an illegal immigrant mother or father, are legal American citizens. The current American population by race according to the U.S Census Bureau is:

Population of the United States by Race and Hispanic/ Latino Origin, Census 2000 and July 1, 2005[1]

Race and Hispanic/ Latino origin	July 1, 2005, population1	Percent of population	Census 2000, population	Percent of population
Total Population	296,410,404	100.0%	281,421,906	100.0%
Single race				
White	237,854,954	80.2	211,460,626	75.1
Black or African American	37,909,341	12.8	34,658,190	12.3
American Indian and Alaska Native	2,863,001	1.0	2,475,956	0.9
Asian	12,687,472	4.3	10,242,998	3.6
Native Hawaiian & other Pacific Islander	516,612	0.2	398,835	0.1
Two or more races	4,579,024	1.5	6,826,228	2.4
Some other race	n.a.	n.a.	15,359,073	5.5
Hispanic or Latino	42,687,224	14.4	35,305,818	12.5

U.S. Census Bureau Population Estimates, May 10, 2006

Somewhere between 15 and 25 of the 43 million Hispanic or Latino population is illegal or 36 to 60 percent of the total. The ambiguity of numbers illustrates how out of control illegal immigration actually is. The exact number will only be known when the DHS can secure the national borders and the U.S. Census Bureau adopts a different attitude towards counting American residents.

Who are they, Where do they come from, Where do they go, and What do they do?

The PEW Hispanic Center believes that 85 percent of all Mexican immigrants residing in the U.S. are illegal or as PEW likes to designate undocumented. This terminology has become the politically correct method of referring to immigrants who enter the country illegally without visas. It sounds sort of nice, undocumented worker, as if everything were in order except one little thing, the undocumented worker did not apply for or receive approval to enter the United States of America. He or she is, therefore, technically a criminal. It is a felony to enter the U.S., and practically every other country in the world without approval and documentation. The immediate downside of this situation, besides the illegality, is that the typical, poor, uneducated Mexican, who illegally crosses the border, suddenly realizes that he is a criminal. He knows that he has broken the U.S. immigration law and is subject to arrest, prosecution, and internment. This act, like any other act of criminality, changes the perspective of the immigrants. Even if the immigrant had a belief in the rule of law before he illegally sneaked across the border, he compromised his belief system with his illegal immigration. He now knows that he is living illegally. He must develop the senses and awareness of a criminal, constantly on the watch for police or immigration officials. He must seek out other criminals in order to live, to rent, and to eat. He enters a new life which is based on criminality and deception. He typically assumes an alias, and begins a quest to obtain illegal and false identification. Without documentation he cannot find work or cash an employment check after he has done so. At every step of the way he must rely on other illegal immigrants who have developed a subculture of criminality. The so-called coyotes or people smugglers, the owners and managers of the safe-houses along the route, the transport drivers, the identity thieves, the slum landlords, the employers who accept fraudulent documentation, and even the scurrilous, deceptive tax filers are all part of the criminal atmosphere that exists, supports, and feeds off the illegal immigrant.

How many laws has the typical illegal immigrant actually broken by the time he finds his first illegal employment in the U.S.? It is interesting just to imagine a typical scenario of an arriving illegal immigrant. How many laws will he break before his first day on the job? He has illegally crossed the border without permission and without documentation. (that is two broken laws). He probably paid a smuggler to bring him across the border to a safe house. He must be guilty of conspiracy to immigrate without proper documentation (that is a third violation). Is it illegal to knowingly hide from immigration officials and to cross state lines in illegal, often stolen vehicles in order to consummate a plan which calls for illegal employment? (That would be at least four or five more counts of breaking federal law depending on the circumstances). And then to seek out and buy fraudulent documentation such as a driver's license or a social security card would be the sixth and seventh broken law. Then to use the fraudulent documents to falsely acquire employment would be the eighth offense. Then the filing of false tax documents as has happened in Greely, Colorado (and all over the country) in the fall of 2008, where 1300 warrants have been filed against illegal immigrants who received more than 2.6 million dollars in illegal tax returns, would be the ninth offense, etc. etc. etc. The illegal crossing of the border is not a one-time, innocuous event in which the only negative fallout from this act is that suddenly the U.S. has one more undocumented worker. Quite the contrary is true. The crossing of the border illegally is just the first step of an immersion into the world of illegality, the criminal industry that is associated with it, and the probable destruction of any reasonable value system the immigrant may have had back in Mexico. The illegal immigrant begins to learn this behavior and becomes desensitized to the danger and wrongness of breaking the law. He lives and breathes the life of a criminal, constantly aware of his insufferable position as a second-class citizen, with second-class rights, sub-par pay, intolerable discrimination, and an uncertain future.

Who would leave their home and family for that type of existence? This type of existence is not the American dream and the millions of Mexicans who illegally immigrate are not looking for that dream or to further build a nation that was built by immigrants. They are poor, uneducated, peasants and inner-city dwellers who come to the U.S. because they have no more options in Mexico. The majority are males who leave a wife and children behind in hopes of sending money back home from the north. The American dream is not part of their outlook on life. They come from all thirty-one states and the federal district. How many come from which states is unknown, however, some assumptions on state of origin can be made by tracking the remittances of money that are sent back home to their families. Citizens in six states, according to the Federal Reserve Bank of Dallas, perennially receive more than fifty percent of all remittances. The six states in order of remittances received are: Michoacán, Jalisco, Guanajuato, State of Mexico, Puebla, and Veracruz. Three of these six have large, rural, poor populations while the other three are home to the country's three largest cities: Mexico City, Guadalajara, and Puebla. The U.S. Census Bureau believes that 60 percent of all illegal immigrants arrive illegally, and the other forty per cent enter with legal visas but have planned in advance not to return to Mexico. They therefore become illegal immigrants as soon as their visas expire. Unfortunately there is very little reliable information on exactly who these illegal immigrants are, which states they came from, what their educational background, marital status, family information, financial standing, political persuasion, religious affiliation, or criminal background may be.

Experts and demographers make the best educated guesses, assumptions, and estimates they can but in reality there is more that is not known about these millions of immigrants than is actually known. Most, probably eighty percent, are males. Historically, very few Mexican women illegally emigrated to the U.S., as a percentage of the total, although this has changed to some extent in the last decade. During the past decade there has also been a shift of more immigrants (including the female shift) coming from the poor slums of the large inner-cities of Mexico. Whether the immigrants come from rural, small towns, and ranches, or from large, failed, inner-city slums, it is obvious that the vast majority are ill-educated and untrained. The Mexican education system is one of the worst in the world and in the poor areas of Mexico (rural or inner-city) it is almost nonexistent. "In Mexico, education inequality is large even by Latin American standards: the average person in the poorest fifth of the population has 3.5 years of schooling, compared with 11.6 years for the average person in the richest fifth (this is not withstanding the differences in the quality of education received)."2 The illegal Mexicans that are entering the U.S. are coming from this poorest fifth. Whether from the slum or from the countryside these immigrants have less than an elementary school education. They did not drop out of high school. They never even reached middle school because they did not earn the prerequisite of finishing elementary school. In an interesting parallel, Abu Ismail, the only surviving terrorist from the November 2008 Mumbai, India, atrocity that killed two hundred innocent people is a nineteen year-old peasant with a third-grade education from a rural Pakistani town in the Punjab where marijuana is grown to make hashish. There is a spigot at the bottom of the societal barrel in Mexico, just as in Pakistan, and it is directly connected to the U.S. border. The immigrant PhD. recipients who are driving taxis in San Francisco because they cannot legally practice their profession are not from Mexico. The evidence suggests that the vast majority of the Mexicans that are immigrating to the U.S. are less educated and less qualified than the Okies and Razorbacks that were immigrating to California during the Great Depression four generations ago. The Mexican government, who supports illegal immigration to the U.S., produced and distributed a guide in January of 2005, which instructs immigrants how to enter the U.S. illegally and live there without being arrested. The guide was produced in comic-book form with elementary level vocabulary so it could be easily understood by the uneducated migrants. They are poor, malnourished, and desperate. As recent as 1990, the International Society of Public Health reported that 40 per cent of all Mexicans still suffered from malnutrition. The poor Mexican who has only the bleak chance of producing a living for his family on fifty dollars a week is perhaps the perfect candidate for qualifying for the Statue of Liberty's beckoning: "Give me your tired, your poor, Your huddled masses yearning to breathe free, The wretched refuse or your teeming shore. Send these, the homeless, tempest-tossed, to me: I lift my lamp beside the golden door."3

The problem, of course, is that the U.S. of the 21st century is not legally, socially, culturally, or economically prepared to receive 500,000 or more illegal immigrants each year decade after decade from Mexico. The U.S. is a democracy built upon the rule of law and illegal immigration does not qualify as acceptable behavior under the rule of law. The Immigration Act of 1929 set standards by which the tired, poor, masses would be allowed to immigrate and integrate into the American culture and that standard is not met when fourteen year-old, homeless, Mexicans swim across the Rio Grande for an opportunity to steal cars out of Laredo parking garages in order to make enough money to buy fraudulent documents and transportation to Chicago; that is not the fulfillment of the American dream!

Respect for the rule of law is an important concept in the U.S., but not in Mexico. People, world-over, learn respect for the rule of law through enforcement and fear of paying the consequences if they are caught. In Mexico, there is very little enforcement of the law. During the last ten years I spent in Mexico, 1999-2008, I lived in a vibrant city of one hundred and twenty thousand people. Something as simple as driving, for example, was chaotic as there is no respect for the rule of law. Speed limits there are completely, 100 percent, ignored. Why are they ignored? There are no traffic cops enforcing the law. Drivers routinely, not occasionally, drive in both directions on one way streets. No one gets upset as it is accepted to break the law without suffering negative consequences. You literally can drive wherever you choose. There is complete tolerance for lawlessness. It is considered rude to honk at someone who is breaking a traffic law. Everyone has the right to drive the way they please. There is universal agreement in Mexico that every person has the right to drive however he chooses without being bothered by anyone else. As a matter of fact, the concept of not interfering in someone else's affairs applies to all things, not just driving. The concept of communal responsibility for upholding the law does not exist. Adults will never be caught correcting, instructing, or scolding someone else's child. Ninety percent of the transit police in my city of one hundred and twenty thousand are on foot. Their tool kit consists of a screw driver and a wrench. Their task is to monitor illegal parking, which they rarely do, as it is an enormous and unpopular task. No one pays attention to legal or illegal parking. It is o.k. to park wherever you want, night or day. If they decide to enforce the law against a parking violator they remove the vehicle's license plates. That assumes, of course, that there are plates to be removed. The violator must go to city hall and pay a small ticket in order to retrieve his plates. Most drivers who have had their plates removed simply drive without plates. No one cares. There is no fleet of police or transit cops who are tasked with pulling over violators and enforcing the law. The whole concept of driving in Mexico is a microcosm of the Mexicans approach to law, order, and the concept of a structured society. In other words, the law is not very important. It is not respected and it is hardly ever enforced. The culture has developed a complete lack of respect for the rule of law.

There is a legal requirement, for example, to acquire a driver's license in order to operate a motor vehicle. Many people, in the smaller cities, towns, and countryside, simply disregard that requirement. They drive without a license. Children, who have access to cars, start driving as early as they physically can (assuming the parents permit it and have a vehicle). It is common to see twelve year olds, who have had absolutely no driver's education, meandering down the middle of a street in an old dilapidated pickup truck. They do not have a clue as to what is proper or improper when it comes to driving. Their fathers and grandfathers learned to drive in the same manner. It is chaotic, dangerous, and leads to thousands of accidents, amputees, and deaths every day. In my town, a driver must take an exam in order to receive a license. The exam does not have to be passed in order to receive a license, only taken. It is such a joke! The exams are never reviewed or graded, they are only filed. The Mexicans drive like they walk. Since there is no driver education programs, most drivers have very little knowledge of the laws which prevail on the roads and highways. The concept of right of way is whoever gets there first. The concept of lanes is ludicrous in Mexico. Space is what is important. Driving a car is no different than walking. Space is space. People drive exactly like they walk. There is no concept of a reserved space that has been designated by painted lines on the road. Once in Mexico City, in 1993, in order to alleviate traffic congestion on the interior loop on the north side of the city, five lanes were painted in the space where four had been painted previously. Newspapers actually covered the story as if it were a serious attempt to address the traffic issue. To the drivers in Mexico City, it was a joke as they never paid attention to the painted four lanes, so why should a fifth lane make any difference. The space was the same and it, of course, had no affect on the traffic. The funniest and most absurd consequence of the plan was that the original four lanes were not removed from the loop. The result looked like a thoroughfare for motorcycles with about eight lanes. So, whoever gets to an open space first has the right to that space, regardless as to where the lines are painted on the road. And that applies for pedestrians who prefer to walk in the road. A pedestrian has the right to the road the same as a car. It is just space and it is available for everyone. Larger cities in Mexico, are more modern, of course, and traffic cops are somewhat more attentive to applying the law. But, typically, city cops who actually pull over violators prefer a bribe as opposed to writing a ticket.

The 500,000 to 750,000 or more Illegal Mexicans that come from these small towns and inner-cities and elude the CBP and ICE each year disperse throughout the U.S. They do not arrive in 737s or chartered buses but overland to the four border states of California, Arizona, New Mexico, and Texas. They arrive in buses, hitching rides with truck drivers, in organized smuggling caravans, and walking. Drive from central Mexico to the border and you will see them walking and hitching their way along every northerly route from the Pacific to the Gulf of Mexico. You can see them loaded into pickup trucks and be completely astounded at how many actually can fit into a single pickup. It is reminiscent of John Steinbeck's book, The Grapes of Wrath. I think of the scene in the adapted movie version with Henry Fonda when the Joads family rolls into the gas station on their way to California.

They stop and buy one dollar's worth of gas. They are all piled on top of each other, hungry, desperate, and broke. Mrs. Joad, the old grandmother, is dead and hidden under a blanket in order to avoid the authorities. As they pull out of the station one attendant asks the other, "How can anybody live like that?" These are the millions that are illegally invading the U.S. and starting to quickly become twenty-five percent of the American population. But they are not the Joads. They are from a completely different cultural fabric. The six corresponding border states of Mexico, from west to east are Baja California North, Sonora, Chihuahua, Coahuila, Nuevo León, and Tamaulipas. These ten border-states which had a population of less than 16 million in 1940, have grown to more than 91 million in 2008. That is almost twenty-five per cent of the total population of both countries combined. Prior to 1990, the illegal immigrant Mexicans were predominantly living in California, Texas, Illinois, New York, and a few other states. But, since the peso devaluation of 1994, coupled with the burgeoning U.S. economy of the nineties, not only has the immigration accelerated but the geographic dispersal has also intensified.

Recent studies show illegal immigrant Mexican populations in every state of the union including Alaska. California and Texas each have more than two million illegal Mexicans. New York, Illinois, and Florida each have close to or more than one million. There are more than 250,000 residing in: Arizona, Georgia, North Carolina, Colorado, Washington, and Virginia. States with more than 150,000 illegal Mexicans include: Oregon, Nevada, Wisconsin, Michigan, Ohio, Pennsylvania, and Tennessee. These numbers are based on estimates but are generally accepted to be accurate by state governments, the federal government, and professional demographers. That means that at least eighteen states are home, permanent or temporary, to more than 150,000 illegal Mexicans each. It is now acceptable for illegal Mexicans to work openly in many states where it was strictly taboo ten and twenty years ago. Texans and Californians have never had a problem with Mexicans working illegally in their states. Quite the contrary actually as Texans and Californians have always promoted the so-called wetback labor force. But now the entire nation seems to have embraced the second-class Mexican worker from coast to coast.

The industries most affected by illegal immigrants are the construction, manufacturing, and hotel/restaurant industries. Although no one knows the exact breakdown by industry most experts use the following numbers when discussing illegal immigration participation in the work place:

ESTIMATES FOR 2009
ILLEGAL IMMIGRANTS PARTICIPATION IN THE
WORKFORCE

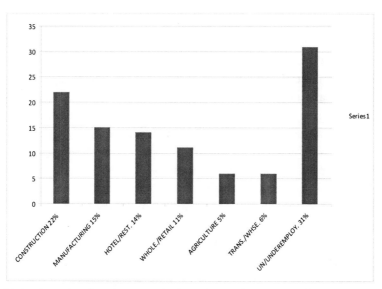

Note: Levels of *undocumented workers* who are employed cleaning homes and tending lawns is unknown but probably account for 6% of the illegal workforce.

The exact number of illegal Mexicans working in the U.S. is unknown but it can be estimated using a few calculations and assumptions. Assume that there are 15 million illegal Mexicans living in the U.S. in 2008. The PEW Institute believes that the unemployment rate among foreign-born residents is approximately twenty-six percent. Unemployment and underemployment coupled together is probably around 31% in the spring of 2009. That is more than hree times higher than the staggering national average which just topped a thirty year high. If that number is applied to the illegal Mexican population of 15 million it yields some 10.35 million workers. That also means that there are almost 5 million unemployed or underemployed illegal Mexicans. Verification of these numbers is impossible. The PEW Hispanic Center reports that 25 percent of all agriculture work is being done by illegal immigrants, who are also filling 30 percent of the hotel and food industry positions. They estimate that 14 percent of the nation's construction jobs are held by illegal immigrants. It is probably higher than that as illegal immigrants now dominate the fields of masonry, concrete, insulation, carpentry, sheetrock, roofing, flooring, painting, landscaping, and general-labor construction. Ten years ago, illegal Mexicans performed the entry level construction jobs. They now have moved solidly into the subcontracting business owning the equipment and tools necessary to land contracts (signed or otherwise, legal or otherwise). Illegal laborers are no longer working for *gringo* bosses. They are working for illegal subcontractors who arrived in the states ten and fifteen years ago. Integration with upward mobility in the construction industry is one of the few success stories among the *undocumented worker* community. In this case it is very positive for both countries. The U.S. needs construction workers at all levels and there is opportunity for advancement even for *undocumented workers*. Any new immigration legislation should address this *win-win* situation.

Whereas the construction boom of the nineties and the years since the turn of the century have offered the enterprising immigrant the opportunity to advance his economic standing by becoming a subcontractor or skilled worker in the construction industry, the vast majority of the illegal workers still toil in entry level positions in the other industries. They still make less than their legal counterparts, have fewer benefits, and are generally treated as second-class citizens. The vast majority are also not paying taxes, except at the retail level, which is not insignificant. The workers that are paying employment taxes have acquired illegal social security numbers and operate under the federal radar and even collect tax return refunds on the illegal taxes they paid during the year. The Mexican workers have become ubiquitous, north to south, east to west, and are considered by many Americans to be indispensable. This was both tragically and comically illustrated in the 2004 cinematic satire, A Day Without A Mexican. This movie demonstrates vividly how unchecked illegal immigration is leading the American culture into a future of apathetic, irresponsible, incompetents who must rely on a subculture for their daily needs and nourishments.

Remittances or Money Laundering?
The Mexican government actively began promoting illegal immigration and organized remittances, money sent back to Mexico by immigrant workers, after Mexico's financial crisis of 1994. President Bill Clinton arranged forty billion dollars worth of loans from the U.S., and international banking community to bail out Mexico; President Zedillo agreed to use petrol dollars and envisioned remittance increases in order to pay back the loans. He accomplished his goals. The more remittances that come into Mexico, of course, impact the amount of taxes collected by the federal government. The billions of dollars also go directly into the Mexican economy. Prior to the 1994 financial crisis, Mexicans were immigrating to the U.S. at a rate of approximately 300,000 per year. Some years had seen higher immigration and it has always been a mixture of legal and illegal movement. In the decade from 1980 to 1990, remittances had gradually grown from one billion a year to more than two billion a year. Suddenly immigration began to spike and remittances followed suit. By the turn of the century, immigration had jumped to more than 500,000 a year and remittances were becoming one of the strongest parts of the Mexican economy, generating more than 10 billion U.S. dollars a year. Six years later it would exceed 26 billion.

Zedillo's vision of exporting millions of illiterate Mexican workers to the U.S. had become a reality. The Yale educated economist and president of Mexico wasted no time in sending Mexican bankers north to negotiate more formal routes for sending the money back to Mexico. Deals were structured between lending institutions and the two governments which recognized newly created Mexican identification cards, lowered rates for money transfers, and thousands of additional destination and point of origin access locations. In other words, the two governments, the banking industry, and money transfer companies revolutionized their approach to sending and receiving money from the U.S. to Mexico. The average cost of sending one thousand dollars to Mexico went from one hundred dollars to ten dollars. In 1994, the Bank of Mexico, responsible for reporting on remittance totals, tallied less than 100,000 transactions nationwide. By 2006, the aggressive immigration and remittance thrust pushed the yearly number of remittances higher than 8.5 million transactions. Remittance dollars grew from 2 billion to almost 26 billion U.S. dollars by 2006. Depending on the tax range and how the recipients spend the money, it generates somewhere between 1.5 and 3 billion dollars in new taxes for the federal government of Mexico annually.

The result in Mexico is both tragic and sad. More than 12 percent and perhaps 15 percent of the Mexican population is illegally living and working in the U.S. in order to support their families and government back in Mexico. The poor Mexican family has become splintered and dysfunctional. Their government which has become content to export its workers instead of developing its economy is even more dysfunctional than the Mexican family. The export of Mexican labor has become the second largest source of foreign income behind oil (not counting the illegal drug industry). It is now 20 percent larger than Mexico's total foreign investment and twice as large as Mexico's annual tourist industry which generated 12 billion dollars in 2006, compared with 26 billion in remittances for the same period. It is not a sustainable industry yet Mexico has become increasingly dependent on its revenue. Mexican laborers have sent home more than 200 billion dollars in the last fifteen years. It is easy to understand the reasons why Vicente Fox and now Felipe Calderón are pressuring the American government to continue with the clandestine arrangement that allows 25 to 30 billion dollars a year to be transferred from the American to the Mexican economy. Felipe Calderón, in his state of the union address in 2007, had the audacity to accuse, "On behalf of the Mexican Government, I again strongly protest the unilateral measures taken by the United States Congress and Government, measures that are making the persecution and humiliating treatment of *undocumented Mexican workers* worse. Finally, I have said that Mexico does not end at the border, that wherever there is a Mexican, Mexico is there."[4] This speech was in response to the U.S. Congress voting to support the DHS in enforcing American laws as they reviewed illegal employer hiring practices. How can one sovereign government protest the legitimacy of its neighboring, sovereign government of taking *unilateral measures* on issues of internal domestic affairs? The U.S.'s decision of enforcing or not enforcing its own internal employment requirements is hardly open to Mexico's bilateral participation. But what is open to question is the transfer of billions of dollars which has been earned illegally. Is this money laundering? Was it legal for the Bush and Fox administrations to revise the remittance infrastructure in order to more easily facilitate the transfer of billions of dollars which are illegally earned? More than 11 million illegal Mexicans who acquire work after securing fraudulent documentation are then sending more than 26 billion dollars out of the country each year. It is plain and simple illegal money laundering. Both governments are complicit and encourage the activity.

Consider what 26 billion dollars would do for the American economy each year. The Big-three auto makers asked Congress for 25 billion dollars in loans to bridge their financial situation in the fall of 2008. Twenty-five billion dollars would purchase more than 1,500,000 automobiles. The same amount would purchase 15 million computers. Now consider what 200 billion dollars would have done for the American economy in the past ten years. That amount or more was sent to Mexico by illegal workers. Fifteen million additional automobiles could have been sold along with 150 million additional computers. That money, those cars sales, and computer sales went to Mexico, not the U.S. Mexico has become one of the fastest growing auto and computer markets in the western hemisphere crossing the one million mark in new cars sold in 2005. The majority were Japanese models. In the same period that the immigration and remittance numbers were skyrocketing, so was Mexico's auto industry. Sales of new cars jumped from two hundred thousand in 1994, to 1.2 million in 2006. Mexico's two largest producers are Nissan and Volkswagen. As the U.S. struggles with the worst financial crisis in eighty years it is time to realize the negative drain that the *Giant Sucking*

Sound from Mexico is having on the American economy. The U.S. employment level has reached 8.1% in February of 2009 and will be in double digits by the end of the year. Yet the national government refuses to secure the southern border, continues to allow millions of illegal workers to garner the wages of unemployed Americans, and send the same wages out of the American economy by the tens of billions to Mexico.

Crime, Fear, and How Geraldo got it Wrong

In March 2008, Geraldo Rivera, in an attempt to champion the virtues of Latino immigration to the U.S. released an anti-fear-mongering book entitled, HISPanic Why Americans Fear Hispanics in the U.S. Being the son of a Latino immigrant from Puerto Rico and a Jewish mother from New York, Rivera epitomizes the success that a Latino immigrant (or their children) can have after legally immigrating to the U.S. After completing law school, Rivera, established a thirty-year successful career as a television journalist. His book is interesting but completely sidesteps the immigration problem that exists in the U.S. in the 21st century. Rivera focuses on legal immigration and would have his readers believe that there is no difference between legal and illegal immigrants in the U.S. or their impact on the U.S. culture. Or at least he would have them believe that the consequences of illegal immigration are negligible. This is where he is completely off track. He writes about the merits of legal immigration and correctly demonstrates how well legal Hispanic immigrants assimilate into American culture. He also explores Hispanic criminality and correctly deduces that legal Hispanic immigrants are no more prone to criminality than are native born American citizens. They do not appear to have any more of a propensity for crime than do native born Americans, but, he does not critically evaluate the illegal Hispanic immigrant or their propensities for crime. His book makes a grandiose appeal to minimize the thousands of problems that exist as a result of illegal immigration because legal immigration is a success. It is an argument that is invalid.

Any scholar who studies the relationship between Mexico and the U.S. understands the important symbiotic bonds that exist between the two cultures. History shows us that legal Mexican immigrants become valuable members of U.S. society and culture. As well as assimilating into American culture, legal Mexican immigrants also add the wonderful flavors of the Mexican culture to the U.S. Legal Mexican immigration is a necessary and viable part of the relationship that exists between the U.S. and Mexico. Illegal immigration, on the other hand, is a scourge that is damaging both cultures tremendously. Rivera not only fails to recognize the huge difference between illegal and legal immigration but does not seem to understand that America's negative response to illegal immigration is not fear. It is a desire to maintain its level of education, values, and integrity. If Rivera would take the time to understand the tremendous differences between legal and illegal immigration he would understand why Americans want their government to retake control of the southern border with Mexico. Americans are not afraid of Mexicans (I know his book is about Hispanics not just Mexicans) but are starting to realize that the millions of illiterate, unskilled, un-assimilating and illegal Mexican immigrants are having a deleterious effect on our their entire culture, infrastructure, and way of life.

Immigrating Mexicans can be correctly categorized as follows: legal, illegal, and legal that become illegal (visa overstays). The difference is not a just a legal definition. Semantics is not the problem. The legal immigrant has the privilege, authority, and respect of the American legal system and theoretically the respect and support of society. Citizens of a country built on immigration have the natural inclination to respect and appreciate legal immigration. The legal immigrant, whether Mexican, Puerto Rican, or Martian, has the right to be in the U.S. He is authorized to come and go, enroll in school, work, be part of society, and fully participate in life. Illegal immigrants, in contrast, do not have authorization to even be in the country. They enter the country illegally and immediately fall into a life that by definition is a criminal life. They do not have the respect or support of their neighbors. They do not have the opportunity to live free, unencumbered lives. They must instead live a shadowy existence, hiding from authorities, acquiring illegal, fraudulent documentation, apart from their families, and are afraid to openly communicate or travel. They have little chance of developing into meaningful, content, fulfilled human beings. The legal immigrant who overstays his visa and becomes an illegal immigrant falls into the same dismal situation as his countrymen who entered illegally.

Generally speaking, successful Mexican immigration has reached approximately one million per year. By successful, I mean that those who illegally avoid the authorities plus those that legally obtain visas or work permits. Of course, there are another 800,000 to 1.2 million who are caught at the border or corralled and sent back from the interior each year. Prior to the intense interdiction and enforcement policies of 2007 and 2008, the ratio of illegal versus legal immigration was approximately at a three to one ratio (9 to 1 if apprehended and repatriated illegals are included in the count). In other words, for every legal Mexican immigrant there were approximately three illegal immigrants entering the country. The trend of late 2007 and early 2008 showed the relationship dropped to almost a 2 to 1 ratio. This is attributable to expanded border interdiction (a recent phenomenon), more aggressive interior immigration, and work-place enforcement, and the financial recession which has been in full swing since December of 2007. Therefore, successful illegal entries have dropped from approximately 750,000 (or 1 million) in 2006, to perhaps 500,000 in 2008. The number of overstays is not known as the DHS tracking system is inadequate. The Pew Hispanic Center attributes at least 45 percent of all residual illegal immigrants as being visa or work permit overstays. If their estimate is accurate, it confirms that some eight to fifteen million Mexicans consciously chose to break American immigration law even after being legally allowed to enter the country as visitors or temporary workers. This, of course, highlights the problem that would exist with a future temporary worker program. Janet Napolitano, Barack Obama's newly appointed Secretary of DHS, is in favor of a newly structured work-visitor program. But she knows it will not work until the DHS can introduce a professional, state-of-the-art, tracking, and identification system. This obviously should be part of the hoped for comprehensive immigration plan which was promised during the 2008 Presidential Campaign by Obama.

Another part of the illegal immigration reality that Geraldo

Rivera misrepresented in his current book is the relationship between non-immigration crime and illegal immigrant-based crime. Rivera states that the crime rate among Hispanic immigrants and average American citizens are the same. His numbers are wrong but more importantly, the big difference in crime rates becomes obvious when legal immigrant activity is segregated from illegal immigrant activity. For example, in an ICE report of October 23, 2008, which detailed the past twelve months the following was stated. "Overall, the number of illegal aliens repatriated by ICE jumped 20 percent in the latest fiscal year, which ended September 30, 2008, to 349,041." But what is staggering about the report is, "Notably, one third of the illegal aliens removed from the United States last year were foreign nationals who had prior criminal convictions in addition to being in the country illegally."5 In other words, more than 115,000 of the 350,000 illegal immigrants that were deported had also been arrested, charged, tried, and convicted of criminal acts inside the U.S. Of the 350,000 that were deported it is not known or was not reported by the ICE how many had been arrested or charged and not yet convicted. I wonder how many had outstanding warrants. I wonder how many committed crimes and were never caught or charged. It is staggering to realize that one third of those deported had already been convicted of criminal activity, not suspected but convicted. I do not think there is a better barometer than the ICE report for understanding the extent of the illegal immigrant's involvement in crime.

As incredulously high as the numbers are, the ICE report is not comprehensive. Two problems persist. One, ICE's lack of sufficient manpower, budget, and the fact that they have only recently gotten serious about entering local and state jails are well known facts. Also, many law enforcement agencies are allowing tens of thousands of convicted criminals to return to the streets as opposed to being deported. Second, hundreds of cities and even some states are purposely refusing to cooperate with ICE's effort and new program to identify and help deport convicted illegal immigrants. ICE, of course, has prioritized the deportation of illegal immigrants who commit more serious crimes as opposed to those who are simply breaking federal immigration laws. But they are focused on both. A recent study, sponsored by the

Houston Chronicle and released in November of 2008, revealed the basic problems facing ICE even when they are working with a cooperative agency such as the Houston Police Department and the Harris County Jail. The study found, consistent with other major metropolitan studies throughout the nation, that ICE is woefully understaffed and overwhelmed in its current efforts to identify and deport convicted criminals who are admitted illegal immigrants. During the period of the eight month study from July 2007 to February 2008, more than 75 percent of all known illegal immigrants were released to the street after serving their sentences in the Harris County jail. Less than 25 percent were deported by ICE. The other 75 percent were never identified to ICE as illegal immigrants. Furthermore, an astounding eleven percent had been convicted three or more times prior to the study and had never been identified to ICE much less deported. ICE agents and other authorities believe that somewhere between 750,000 and 1,000,000 illegal immigrants are convicted annually of crimes around the nation. Congress and ICE both agree that only ten to fifteen percent of the total numbers of illegal immigrants that are committing crimes are being identified to ICE for deportation.

It is an intolerable situation which unfortunately is widely known throughout Mexico. Criminals are migrating north by the tens of thousands as they have discovered the ease of illegal immigration and the U.S.'s inability to identify and deal with them. Mexico's drug cartels and organized criminals have become transnational and no longer recognize the border as a constraint to their illegal activity. Mexico, once only a migratory route for cocaine on its way northward, is increasingly gaining control of production in Colombia and Bolivia to the south. Northward, the drug cartels have successfully gained control of the distribution and retail channels for not only cocaine but marijuana newly-expanding methamphetamine markets. The Mexican cartels are no longer content to take their cut of the cocaine business as they smuggle it to the U.S. They plan to dominate the industry growth/ production through consumption. Their recent successes have convinced them to also enter the heroine industry. The millions of illegal immigrants that enter the U.S. are often, easy victims, future clients, and in many cases eventual employees for the drug cartels.

Many immigrating Mexicans use *coyotes* (people smugglers) in order to enter the U.S. as the CBP continues to make it more difficult to illegally enter the country. As the CBP has grown in size and focus under Secretary Chertoff's directions, the cost of smuggling has escalated. Smugglers who charged five hundred dollars in 2000 are now, in 2008, commanding twenty-five hundred to five thousand dollars for their services. Since many illegal immigrants do not have the cash to pay in advance, a network of indebtedness and obligation has arisen and is becoming more prevalent as the prices increase. The *coyotes* who smuggle people are often part of the same network which is smuggling illegal drugs. The illegal immigrants who cannot pay in advance are frequently, therefore, employed into the ranks of the drug network as *burros* (donkeys) for smuggling marijuana, meth, and cocaine or as distributors or enforcers once they are safely located in Houston, Chicago, Atlanta, or wherever. Unfortunately, thousands turn to the drug industry for their permanent employment. These destitute immigrants are the perfect target to be easily victimized by the drug cartels.

The illegal immigrants, whether in San Antonio, Los Angeles, or Baton Rouge become part of an illegal network once they arrive in their new homes. The new arrivals, via the smugglers, are put in touch with their accomplices in the inner cities of America. Typically, housing, illegal documentation, and even work contacts are available. There is a cost, of course for everything, and the new arrivals become beholden to the network, the thugs. In millions of cases the hard-working immigrants are able to quickly acquire independence and assimilate into the Latino neighborhoods and become otherwise law-abiding individuals (illegal immigration, identity theft, document and employer fraud aside). The majority has familial or village ties from back home and are less vulnerable targets for organized crime. Millions of others, however, become part of the more treacherous network of immigrant criminality whether within the network of organized crime or just in the world of criminality. Women who cannot find or do not want to find domestic work turn to prostitution, nude dancing, or other crime. Many men join the smuggling circuit which is actively going north and south. People and drugs are smuggled to the north while guns, cars, and money are smuggled southward. It is now even becoming popular to smuggle kidnapped victims into Mexico, from the U.S. Others turn to the criminal life of armed robbery, car theft, drug distribution, kidnapping, gambling, and whatever proves profitable. The allure of the gang lifestyle attracts many of the younger immigrants especially in the larger cities such as Los Angeles, San Francisco, and San Diego. Here, the larger gang memberships often reach twenty or thirty thousand or more. Some of the more notorious gangs recruit and operate on a national basis, and have been brutalizing and terrorizing American citizens for decades. The 18th Street Gang, of southern California, which numbers more than twenty thousand is estimated by local authorities to be predominantly (65 percent or more) illegal immigrants.

One interesting aspect of illegal Mexican immigration is the ease by which many are lured into or assimilate into the ranks of organized crime. Part of this ease is relative to the marijuana scene in Mexico. Smoking marijuana in Mexico, for example, is very common but not excessive. Cultivation, on the other hand, is astronomical as Mexico is the number one cultivator and exporter of marijuana in the world. The U.N.'s latest report of 2008, estimated Mexico's 2006 production at 7,400 metric tons or approximately 20 percent of the world's total. It is cultivated in every Mexican state that has the appropriate soil and climate conditions. Mexicans, therefore, are very familiar with and accustomed to marijuana use and the marijuana export industry. Thousands of small Mexican towns, villages, and rural communities rely on marijuana as their agricultural livelihood. It is the same concept as the rural Afghanistan peasant who is raising poppies for the Taliban. Marijuana export to the U.S. generates 25 to 30 billion U.S. dollars annually in Mexico. The marijuana industry (excluding cocaine and methamphetamines) is as large as the annual remittance industry which exceeded 26 million dollars in 2007. This is obviously a very important part of the Mexican economy. The point being, Mexicans are very accustomed to marijuana being an acceptable and necessary part of their culture. Without the money generated from marijuana sales in the U.S.

millions of poor Mexicans would be suffering an even greater calamity than that which currently exists. Therefore, it is easy and comfortable for millions of illegal immigrant Mexicans to participate in the distribution, sale, and use of the drug once they are in the U.S. There is not a difficult line to cross from being a poor, illiterate Mexican peasant or inner-city dweller, to then becoming an illegal immigrant, and then to participate in the distribution and sale of marijuana or other drugs.

Another obvious downside to illegal immigration, and relevant to the subject of marijuana, is drug use. There are no accurate studies which correlate marijuana use to illegal immigration but it is easy to understand the norm of human behavior. The vast majority of Mexicans who illegally immigrate to the U.S. are from small, rural areas, in the states where marijuana is cultivated or from the inner-city slums where drug use is rampant. Without doubt, large percentages of these illegal immigrants are drug users, definitely marijuana users. So when they come to the States and make ten times more money than they made in Mexico, are in contact with the criminal scene, marijuana is easy to get and very popular, voilà, an instant market for the narcotic traffickers. If there are 30 million illegal immigrants in the U.S. and 50 percent use marijuana that is a market of 15 million people. If only 30 percent of this subculture uses marijuana it is a market of ten million people. Mexico is not only exporting its drugs to the U.S. but is also exporting a market of its own citizens to buy the drugs. What a setup! And I was not including the cocaine and meth trade which are being dominated by the Mexican cartels as well. Historically, Mexicans have not been large consumers of these two drugs, but unfortunately that has been changing in the last five years. As a matter of fact, as both the Mexican and American governments have become keener to prosecute the illegal distribution of drugs from and through Mexico to the U.S., the cartels have begun marketing fiercely to the young Mexican population. This bodes badly for both the U.S. and Mexico, as crime rates in Mexico are beginning to approximate that of the U.S. If the trend continues, as most experts agree, Mexican crime will continue to soar and the U.S. will continue to see higher levels of illegal immigrant (hard) criminals entering the country.

But, according to Geraldo Rivera, crime among illegal immigrants is nothing which should cause concern to the fragile, freaked-out, uptight, and fearful *gringos*. While promoting his book, Rivera accused the Lou Dobbs evening news program (Lou Dobbs Tonight) and a guest on the Bill O'Reilly's (O'Reilly Factor) show of fear-mongering and making claims against illegal immigrants without having substantiated statistics with which to prove their points. He then, misquoted numbers from the Government Accountability Office (GAO) report of 2005. He writes that, according to the GAO, there are never more than fifty-five thousand illegal immigrants incarcerated in the U.S. at any given time. He concludes, therefore, that ninety-seven percent of those incarcerated must be U.S. citizens. The report, however, completely disputes his numbers and conclusions. The 2005 GAO report states, "The percentage of all federal prisoners who are criminal aliens (illegal and legal immigrants) has remained the same over the last 3 years (2002-2004)—about 27 percent."[6] Twenty-seven percent of the total federal prison population in the U.S. is composed of illegal immigrants. The GAO reports the actual numbers that represent illegal immigrants who were incarcerated at all levels. Out of 178,512 federal prisoners, 48,708 in 2004 (the 27 percent) were illegal immigrants. At the state level, which they did not quote the total, 74,000 were illegal immigrants and at the local or county level there were an additional 147,000 illegal immigrants of an unquoted total by the GAO. These were all year-end totals and not accumulated numbers or *passed around inmates* as Geraldo Rivera tried to argue. According to federal officials, at any given time, there are approximately 300,000 illegal immigrants inside federal, state, and local jails. The estimated annual cost by the GAO report, to the various federal and local governments, is approximately 1.5 billion U.S. dollars. Furthermore, not included in these numbers were the illegal immigrant criminals that were arrested and deported by ICE during the same period. In 2008, for example, ICE arrested 34,155 of these types of illegal immigrants. Their charter which started in 2003 states, "ICE's Fugitive Operations Teams give top priority to cases involving aliens who pose a threat to national security and community safety, including members of transnational street gangs, child sex offenders, and aliens with prior convictions for violent crimes." 7

The facts are black and white. Illegal immigrants turn to crime in high numbers and with an amazing ease. It is arguable that the rate is at least three times as high as in the general population (excluding the illegal immigration activity). It is getting worse instead of better but the efforts of the DHS over the past few years is starting to have an impact on illegal immigration, work-place enforcement, deportation of hard criminals, and the view in Mexico that the U.S. will forever be a safe haven for criminals and illegal immigrants. But it is only a beginning and without a firm commitment from the new Obama administration it will not continue.

Sanctuary Cities, States, and the Fed

The symbiotic relationship that has strengthened between Americans and Mexican immigrants over the last ten or fifteen years has existed for decades in Texas, California, and a few other states. Various industries have become dependent on immigrant workers, legal or illegal. Unfortunately, the federal government has not responded with an adequate immigration or foreign worker program which addresses this need. Employers have historically broken the law and hired illegal as well as legal immigrants as needed. In decades past, employers enjoyed the advantage of paying illegal workers a wage which was below the minimum amount required by law. Those days are long past as supply and demand during the nineties elevated the average wage for illegal workers far beyond the minimum level. The minimum rate required by the federal government to be paid to hourly workers has been fairly static over the past decades. In the eighties it was $3.35 before rising to $4.25 for the first half of the nineties. Then for ten years it was static again at $5.15 before changing in 2007, to $5.85. In 2008, it adjusted to $6.55. The common rate demanded by and paid to common day laborers at municipal pickup zones throughout the southern U.S. is in the range $8.00 to $10.00 per hour. Day laborers on the west coast and in northern states often demand even more. In the construction industry, where approximately 22 percent of the illegal immigrants find employment, skilled trades pay rates which can top $20.00 per hour. By the way, the 2008 minimum wage in Mexico is fifty-seven pesos or about $5.00 a day. The Mexican national average as reported in June 2008 was three times that amount at two hundred and twenty pesos or approximately $15.00 a day. The ambitious, hard-working immigrants who learn a construction trade are able to earn a fair, equitable income. Even though the illegal immigrant continues to be a second-class citizen, his wage level now far exceeds the minimum requirement. The argument that American industry is paying the illegal immigrants a wage which is below the federal minimum is no longer valid. It is still true, however, that the total compensation package earned by American citizens and legal immigrants far exceeds that which is paid to illegal immigrant workers.

The argument that American industry needs foreign workers is valid. The reality that Mexico has the available, unemployed man-power just across the border is obvious. But instead of having a logical foreign worker program we have chaos. The natural demand of the capitalistic system pulls the Mexican worker to the U.S. The disastrous failed state of Mexico pushes the worker to the north. The inadequate federal response to the situation exasperates citizens on both sides of the border. Many cities and some states have openly defied the federal immigration laws and declared their territory as safe havens for the illegal immigrants. They have issued orders to their law enforcement departments which forbid direct communications with the CBP and ICE. They outlaw the sharing of immigration status with federal officials. In many cities they forbid local police to even question detained suspects on the subject of immigration status. Convicted felons, who are illegal immigrants, are released on the streets in lieu of being deported. To understate it quite succinctly, it is a big mess.

On no other issue are the federal and state governments at such odds. The federal government is spending billions trying to control the influx of illegal immigrants, while many state governments are publicly sending the message to Mexico that it is o.k. to send millions of workers illegally across the border and into their states. The sanctuary concept is capsulated as follows, "Despite a 1996 federal law, the Illegal Immigration Reform and Immigrant Responsibility Act (IIRIRA) that requires local governments to cooperate with Department of Homeland Security's Immigration and Customs Enforcement (ICE), many large urban cities (and some small) have adopted so-called "sanctuary policies." Generally, sanctuary policies instruct city employees not to notify the federal government of the presence of illegal aliens living in their communities. The policies also end the distinction between legal and illegal immigration--so illegal aliens often benefit from city services too."8 The Congressional Research Service, an important investigative arm of Congress, officially lists fifteen states with more than thirty major cities which have official sanctuary policies in opposition to federal law.

The negative fallout from municipal sanctuary policies is, of course, unintended. City councilmen, supervisors, and overseers pass laws to facilitate or legitimize the lifestyle and protect the civil rights of illegal immigrants. They do this primarily to allure workers to their cities. The trade-off, however, of protecting hardened criminals is not worth it. Municipalities want to protect illegal immigrants from immigration enforcement. That in itself can be argued as being just, reasonable, and warranted under the circumstances of capitalistic supply and demand, antiquated foreign-worker legislation, and humanitarian concerns. What is completely unjustifiable, however, is the inadvertent protection of habitual criminals. And unfortunately, that is one of the manifestations of sanctuary policies. In cases from California to Maine, Florida to Washington, violent criminals, illegal immigrants, who have been released on the streets instead of being transferred to the ICE for deportation have robbed, brutalized, raped, and murdered innocent Americans on thousands of occasions. It is unconscionable, intolerable, and misguided to have such programs which undermine the rule of law and invite anarchy. Unless we forget, the four pilot terrorists who perpetuated the gruesome September 11, 2001, heartless murders of 3,500 innocent human beings were illegal immigrants who had over-stayed their visas and acquired driver's licenses and flying lessons in the sanctuary cities of San Diego and Miami.

Border Fences and the Berlin Wall

The U.S. is building a wall between Mexico and the United States. Where is Ronald Reagan? "Mr. Gorbachev, tear down this wall". In 1961, the German Democratic Republic built a wall to prevent their citizens from exiting into democratic, western Berlin which was controlled by the Americans. Twenty-six years later the American President implored the Soviet leader to tear down the horrendous symbol of tyranny and repression, the Berlin Wall. On October 26, 2006, President George Bush signed the Secure Fence Act of 2006 (SFA). In response many critics are referring to the fence that is being built under the SFA as the 21st century Berlin or Mexico Wall. The Germans built a wall in an attempt to keep disgruntled, noncommunist citizens from escaping to a free democratic country. The concept of the SFA, however, is conceptually very different, practically the opposite. The SFA is not intended to keep anyone inside the U.S. but specifically designed to keep illegal immigrants and drug smugglers out of the U.S. It is not designed to keep legal immigrants out of the U.S. It is not designed to keep legal visitors out of the U.S. Approximately 750,000 legal immigrants enter the U.S. each year. In 2005, more than 1 million legal immigrants were granted permanent resident status in the U.S. The seven hundred mile fence which is being built under the SFA will not affect this legal immigration activity. On the contrary, it is intended to help CBP officers secure the border with Mexico.

The border between Mexico and the U.S. is one thousand nine hundred and fifty-two miles long. The scope of the SFA does not intend to build fences and walls along this nearly two thousand mile border. It does, however, focus on those areas which are easily crossed and are currently blatantly used to smuggle more than 500,000 illegal immigrants and hundreds of billions of dollars of marijuana, cocaine, and methamphetamines. The intent of the SFA is to fortify DHS's efforts to regain control of the border. Securing the border is widely recognized as one of the first steps which are needed in order to create a new, comprehensive immigration policy. And more importantly, it is absolutely essential in battling the import of illegal drugs.

The first meaningful U.S. border fence was constructed in San Diego in 1992. It is fourteen miles long and runs from the Otay Border crossing to the Pacific Ocean. Illegal immigrant apprehension dropped from 202,000 in 1992, to 9,000 in 1994, in the San Diego sector after completion of the wall. The natural response, of course, was obvious. Smugglers moved eastward and developed new routes in Arizona, New Mexico, and Texas. But the lesson learned by the DHS, in retrospect, was important. Strategic fencing can have an immense impact on smuggling. The seven hundred miles which have been defined for fencing under the SFA strategically defines 90 per cent of the most porous and actively used areas by smugglers. The vast majority of the other 1200 miles of border falls into one of two categories. One, the natural terrain is so severe that high-volume smuggling is difficult and detectable. Two, the adjacent desert terrain, remoteness, and inaccessibility of populated areas, also, make high-volume smuggling untenable. The unfenced areas will not be immune from smuggling but the high-volume of smuggling can be controlled more easily with the construction of the 700 mile fence.

It appears that the controversy created by the passing of the SFA in 2006, has left an inaccurate impression among many Americans of exactly what this 700 mile fence will actually be. Even Janet Napolitano, the new Secretary of Homeland Security, was critical in 2006, when the SFA was passed, suggesting that if a fifty foot fence were built that the smugglers would simply bring fifty-one foot ladders to the border. That mentality suggests a misunderstanding of the SFA strategy that many Americans must have. In reality, the fence is nothing at all similar to the Berlin Wall which was built in 1961. The seven hundred mile fence designed by DHS experts consists of 370 miles of pedestrian fencing which is of three types depending on the specific application. It could be steel pickets set in concrete, steel rails and posts with a wire mesh at the top, or a concrete wall with a steel mesh at the top. The other 330 miles are one or the other of two types of vehicle fencing. One type is the traditional vehicle bollards that are commonly seen around government buildings. The other is a Normandy Beach-style fence of crisscrossed steel beams. The traffic fences are, of course, constructed in the more remote, wide open desert areas. The pedestrian fences are being constructed in urban areas such as Laredo and El Paso where illegal immigrants currently need only to cross a street and blend into the indigenous population. The SFA and DHS strategy is to make certain that most high-travelled, high-volume areas are very difficult to cross. This program is being coupled with two other Boeing partnership projects which will build high-tech monitoring and surveillance towers. It is impossible to completely secure a 2,000 mile border which has rugged, mountainous terrain in many areas. But it is not impossible to severely crimp the unbridled smuggling of drugs and people which is currently overwhelming the DHS. The DHS is not tasked with fixing a small leak in a dam. It is trying to stop an all-out inundation. Hopefully, Janet Napolitano has reevaluated her earlier perspective on the fifty-one foot ladder. She is the only border governor to use the National Guard in attempt to secure the borders in Arizona. She understands the border issues and has received a healthy endorsement from outgoing Secretary Chertoff. It will be interesting to see if she is tough enough for the job of securing the border.

Many critics claim that the wall is a black hole which is gobbling up American tax dollars with a budget of approximately 1 billion dollars. Security funding at the border has gone from 4.6 billion in 2001 to 10.4 billion in 2006. This is a modest investment relative to the astronomical cost we are suffering as a result of drug smuggling. Others argue that somehow it will be a hindrance to free trade. But how can the potential eradication of millions of dollars of contraband hurt free, legal trade? Many on the Mexican side argue that the local economy of their towns will be adversely affected. Once again, it is hard to see how these arguments support anything but the illegal smuggling activity that takes place along the border. I am reminded of the poem by Robert Frost, "Mending Wall". Although Frost does not seem to be one hundred percent convinced of his wise neighbor's argument he is reminded that "good fences make good neighbors".

Economic Crisis---Call the Doctor

There is an old economic saying in Mexico that goes something like this. When the U.S. gets a head cold, Mexico gets the flu. If the U.S. gets the flu then Mexico will catch pneumonia. If the U.S. catches pneumonia it is time for Mexico to start digging a grave. Unfortunately, on December 1, 2008, the U.S. was diagnosed as having very serious influenza flu, a recession to be exact. According to the National Bureau of Economic Research which has the responsibility of officially designating the beginning and end of recessions, the U.S. economy actually sneaked into recessionary territory in December of 2007. Officials do not have accurate barometers for forecasting the depth and length of this recession but it seems that every economist, conservative or liberal, believes that this is the worst economic downturn the world has seen since the Great Depression of the 1930's. Call the doctor, or maybe the undertaker.

The impact this economic turmoil is having on illegal Mexicans in the U.S. as well as their countrymen back home is devastating. The jobs that are performed by the majority of illegal workers are the most fragile in times of economic uncertainty. Seventy percent of all illegal workers are in industries which have already been seriously affected by the economic downturn. These industries, construction, manufacturing, hotel/restaurant, and wholesale/retail trade, are expected to continue tumbling downwards for the foreseeable future. In construction alone more than one million illegal immigrants had lost their jobs by the end of 2008 and another 2 million are at risk in 2009. The Mexican government began reporting record numbers of returning citizens in August of 2008. Since January of 2008 they believe approximately 500,000 workers have returned to Mexico as a direct result of the economic crisis. Each year in December thousands of Mexicans return to spend the holidays with their families and then sneak back across the border in January. Many believe that in 2009 there will be very few reasons for risking the cost and danger of illegally reentering the U.S.

In October of 2008, the unemployment level in the U.S. crept to 6.5 percent a rate not seen for fifteen years. That equates to 10.1 million unemployed workers as reported by the U.S. Department of Labor (DOL). At the end of the first quarter of 2009 it had soared to 8.5 percent. Many economists are speculating that the number will reach a level between 10 and 13 percent by the middle of 2009, or in real numbers somewhere between 16 and 20 million unemployed workers. It is interesting to note that the DOL issues a disclaimer in each of their monthly reports regarding illegal or undocumented, foreign-born workers. Once again, the federal surveyors do no ask those being surveyed whether or not they are legal or illegal workers. The DOL reports, however, make monthly and yearly estimates of the percentage of foreign-born workers that are in the workplace. The October 2008 report, for example, estimates that 47.7 per cent of the net increase of the total U.S. labor force between 2000 and 2007 were foreign-born workers. That is an eye-popping statistic to come from the federal government! It is also interesting to note the difference that is reported between the employment losses and the unemployment increases. For example, in October of 2008, overall U.S. unemployment increased by 603,000 to reach the aforementioned 10.1 million level of 6.5 per cent. For the same period, employment fell by 240,000 jobs, a loss of 1.2 million jobs for the first ten months of 2008. The DOL does not report the breakdown of unemployment increases or employment declines relative to the illegal work force but it is reasonable to assume that if 47.7 per cent of the net increase in labor during the last eight years was from the pool of foreign-born workers (illegal or otherwise) that there are currently millions of illegal immigrants wandering the streets of the U.S. trying to decide what in the hell to do. The illegal immigrant workers are at the bottom of the labor chain. They are the most vulnerable to lose their jobs, have the least amount of infrastructure to fall back on in hard times, and in many cases will not be covered by federal or state unemployment programs.

As bleak as the near-term outlook may be for many Americans it is even worse for the millions of undocumented, illegal immigrant Mexicans. Another unpleasant reality for the illegal Mexican is the decline of the peso relative to the U.S. dollar. In late August of 2008 the exchange rate was 9.75 pesos to the dollar. In early December it was 13.75 to the dollar. In three months the peso lost forty per cent of its value against the dollar. Call the doctor. Call the undertaker! Furthermore, with the U.S. being Mexico's largest trading partner, as orders for manufactured goods are declining, especially in the automotive industry, massive layoffs are rampant in Monterrey and Saltillo. The once skyrocketing trade imbalance between the two countries did an about face in September and declined twenty-five percent from the previous month, down more than 1 billion dollars. The current economic crisis seems to spell near-term doom for Mexico. Trade with the U.S. has begun to trend downwards. The peso lost 40 per cent of its value in late 2008 and early 2009. In the first three months of 2009 remittances were down by 20 percent and forecast to drop even more drastically. The big-three American car producers are cancelling orders from little Detroit (Saltillo, Mexico). Orders for manufactured goods are down at maquiladoras, hundreds of thousands of illegal workers are returning to Mexico and in need of work. The price of oil has dropped below fifty dollars a barrel. The DHS is both interdicting and returning illegal immigrants at unprecedented rates as well as shutting down illegal entry into the U.S. The tourist industry is floundering with sudden reporting world-wide of the violence associated with Mexico's drug war. Rightly or wrongly, the swine-flu pandemic is being blamed on Mexico. Foreign expatriates are leaving by the thousands. Incoming dollars from the drug trade is declining, crime is burgeoning, and President Calderón is begging President Obama not to renegotiate NAFTA. It does not take a genius to add all of this together and realize the importance of securing our southern border.

This near-term doom and the world economic crisis will perhaps squeeze the illegal immigrants more than anyone else in the U.S. They are losing their jobs at unprecedented rates, yet back home the conditions are even worse. The economic plight of millions of illegal immigrants hit the press in October, when conservative radios and newspapers reported a supposed quote from a Housing and Urban Development (HUD) official which stated that illegal immigrants held five million bad or foreclosed mortgages. The source was variously quoted as being from an anonymous ICE agent or a HUD official. HUD officially debunked the story and admitted it had no idea how many bad loans were in the hands of illegal immigrants. The concept of bad loans in the hands of illegal immigrants should be shocking. It is even startling to hear HUD actually acknowledge the reality of what has illegally transpired with credit and mortgages in the last few years. Beginning in 2006, Bank of America initiated a new credit card program in California which allowed illegal immigrants to acquire credit cards without a social security number. Wachovia quickly followed suit. They began accepting the Mexican issued Matricula Consular as valid identification and a U.S. government issued Individual Tax Identification Number (ITIN) in lieu of a social security number. Wells Fargo in only two and a half years, for example, has opened more than 500,000 accounts based on Matricula Consular identification cards. Other mortgage companies saw their success and quickly began offering mortgages which accepted the same flimsy identification. Both the Matricula Consular card and the ITIN are easy to obtain and certainly should not be acceptable documentation for generating mortgage loans. But the lure of selling millions of homes to illegal immigrants was so great that many mortgage companies and banks relaxed their normal lending practices and jumped on the gravy train. The majority of these so-called ITIN mortgages were given, of course, to low-income illegal immigrants with insufficient credit histories. Requirements for down payments were often dropped, tax returns were not required, and unrealistic adjustable- rate mortgages allowed otherwise unqualified buyers to generate loans. These were some of the notorious and disastrous sub-prime loans. They were packaged as mortgage-backed securities and sold to unaware investors. And now thousands of illegal immigrants, no one knows how many, are walking away from their responsibilities and Wachovia, Bank of America, and others are either bankrupt or are being bailed out of the situation by the rest of us.

The shoddy mortgages generated by greedy lenders who were anxious to grab the business of unqualified illegal immigrants did not cause the economic crisis. But It certainly contributed to it. The interesting point to be drawn from this disaster is obvious. It reminds me of the European rush to multiculturalism that has caused so many problems in France, England, and Norway, to name only a few. An unrealistic set of standards was applied to mortgage lending in order to generate more business under the guise of multiculturalism. Or perhaps more accurately, it was veiled under the concept of being fair to the Hispanic community. The National Council of La Raza (NCLR), Latino civil rights and advocacy group, actively counseled illegal immigrants on how best to secure these types of loans. Give NCLR kudos for effort but zeroes for championing a failed and disastrous concept.

Generating mortgages for individuals who are ill-qualified and unable to maintenance them, regardless of reason, is folly. But the lending establishment was buffered by a set of double standards which was encouraged in a gold-rush atmosphere where suddenly millions of potential illegal immigrants appeared on the mortgage radar screen. Mortgage companies even avidly advertised the fact that income tax returns and immigration papers were not required as qualifications for obtaining a loan. And now the NCLR, among others, are referring to the illegal immigrants who are walking away from their loans, as victims. I just wonder how many gringos can generate a mortgage without a social security number or verifiable identification, a questionable work-history, no down payment, and at a rate which exceeds the standard payment-to-income ratio.

What will happen to the tens of thousands of illegal immigrants who lose their homes to foreclosure? What will happen to the millions of Americans who lose their homes to foreclosure during this recession/depression atmosphere? The future is bleak and uncertain for both but it is reasonable to assume that the illegal immigrants have fewer infrastructure support systems from which to rely. They have fewer options, fewer safety nets. This entire debacle evidences the dangers of double standards, the suspension of the rule of law, and the resulting consequences. And in this case it starts with illegal immigration. Complacency about illegal immigration is where it begins. In this case, loans which were contrived using unethical lending practices and abnormal standards are not yielding profits to the lenders but instead millions of dollars in foreclosures and untold numbers of families without homes. Will the federal government decide to finally deal with immigration reform? Will the illegal Mexican community ever decide to follow the rule of law? In reality, signing up for a flimsy, fabricated, poorly-structured mortgage loan is no different to an illegal immigrant than acquiring a fraudulent identification card in order to get a job.

Population Growth and Immigration – Oops!

There is an astounding correlation between immigration and population growth in the United States. The best place to get population statistics is the United States Census Bureau (USCB).

As crazy as it is, the USCB still does not ask whether or not anyone is a legal or illegal citizen or immigrant in their surveys. It is acceptable to ask if someone is Hispanic, Black, Asian, Native, or White. But, it is totally unacceptable to ask about anyone's immigration status. It is the old and acceptable adage, I suppose, that less information is best. Or, is it that the U.S. government does not want to insult foreigners who do not respect immigration laws. Perhaps they would get mad and go back home! Or at least get legal permission to immigrate to the U.S. In any event, the official census numbers do not differentiate between legal and illegal Hispanic immigrants or any other ethnicity for that matter. It is really funny! The USCB asks individuals whether or not they are Hispanic, White, etc. If the respondent answers affirmative to being of Hispanic origin they are then queried as to whether their origins are Mexican, Puerto Rican, Honduran, Cuban, Guatemalan, Colombian, Spanish, etc., etc. The Census Bureau then reports this information very professionally and categorically. What a joke! The surveyors of the USCB play this funny little charade. They want to show a breakdown in their census report by nation or historical ethnic origin but they refuse to ask the question of immigration legality. So, the census reports show a breakdown by foreign country but it puts citizens, legal immigrants, and illegal immigrants in the same bucket. We have a national census bureau which is being funded by U.S. citizens that is too delicate to ask the question of immigration status.

One argument suggests that the USCB would not be able to adequately verify the validity of the response to questions of immigration status. How would they know if a person were a legal or illegal immigrant? This argument is no more or no less valid for the question of ethnicity. How does a surveyor verify if a respondent is from Colombia or Mexico? Does he tell by the color of the skin? Or, is it by the infliction of the accent? Hondurans are darker than Spaniards, right? And, of course, Chileans talk faster than Guatemalans! Or is it simply obvious because of information taken from a particular application? Surveys and estimates are done by the USCB with the assistance of the Federal State Cooperative Program for Population Estimates (FSCPE). Neither department has the capacity or scope which would be required to investigate the validity of information which is taken from personal surveys, administrative records, federal and state agencies, tax records, or Medicare and vital statistics records. They take the surveys, collect the data, analyze the data, and make intelligent estimates regarding most aspects of population in the U.S. They accept the validity of the information they collect at face value. They do not investigate its validity. So the stark, blaring question remains: Why does not the USCB and the FSCPE report on illegal immigration into the United States? It is vital information that is needed for making legislative decisions yet the USCB has not been given this task by Congress.

As of December 04, 2008, the USCB estimates the total U.S. population at 305,808,435. The total number of people identified as being of Hispanic origin is approximately 46 million. It is important to understand that the U.S. Office of Management and Budget (OMB) instructed the USCB in how to appropriately deal with race and ethnicity in the case of Hispanic origins. Hispanic origin is not a race. Hispanics come in various colors and should not be confused as being a race. The OMB, for example, instructs the USCB to report on the number of Black Hispanics and non-Black Hispanics. It can be confusing but not particularly important as far as I am concerned. I am only interested, in this section, on focusing on illegal Mexican immigration and how it is affecting population growth. Since the USCB does not differentiate between legal and illegal immigration, it is hard to understand the exact impact illegal immigration is having on population. It is obvious, however, and reasonable, to draw a few conclusions using the USBC's estimates of the Hispanic population. First, their estimate of 42 million American Hispanics includes citizens as well as legal and illegal immigrants. Assume, for purposes of determining trends and making an easy, reasonable analysis, that fifty per cent of that total are illegal immigrants. Some experts think the number is 15 million while others believe that it is 30 million. I am going to use 21 million for this analysis. Furthermore, assume that the demographic makeup of the vast majority of the Hispanic, illegal immigrant population is not very different than that of the illegal Mexican immigrant population. In other words, assume that they are poor, unskilled, and uneducated. To begin with, approximately sixty-five or seventy percent of this pool of 21 million are from Mexico, and are poor and uneducated. I am not vouching for or trying to characterize the other immigrants. I am interested in portraying, in a reasonable manner, the probable trends regarding illegal immigrants and population growth.

Now, look at the total U.S. population and the forecasted growth over the next fifty years. There are two things which are very alarming about unbridled immigration. One is the negative impact that will result from overwhelming numbers of immigrants if trends are allowed to continue at the current rate. The second is about the quality, integrity, and preparedness of the immigrating individuals. The numbers alone are staggering! According to the USCB and the Center for Immigration Studies, findings show that the current level of net immigration (1.25 million a year) will add 105 million to the nation's population by 2060. While immigration makes the population larger, it has a small effect on the aging of society.

Among the findings[9]:

- Currently, 1.6 million legal and illegal immigrants settle in the country each year; 350,000 immigrants leave each year, resulting in net immigration of 1.25 million.
- If immigration continues at current levels, the nation's population will increase from 301 million today to 468 million in 2060 — a 167 million (56 percent) increase. Immigrants plus their descendents will account for 105 million (63 percent) of the increase.
- The total projected growth of 167 million is equal to the combined populations of Great Britain, France, and Spain. The 105 million from immigration by itself is equal to 13 additional New York Cities.
- If the annual level of net immigration was reduced to 300,000, future immigration would add 25 million people to the population by 2060, 80 million fewer than the current level of immigration would add.
- The above projection follows exactly the Census Bureau's assumptions about future birth and death rates, including a decline in the birth rate for Hispanics, who comprise the largest share of immigrants.

These numbers do not need a lot of interpretation or comment. The U.S. immigration levels rose from a yearly average of 178,000 prior to the 1965 Immigration Reform Act to an out-of-control and unsustainable level of 1.2 million in 2006. The deleterious effects to the nation will be incredible and irreversible if the current immigration levels are continued. Every aspect of life will be degraded, from education to the environment, due to the sheer numbers of people. If, for example, 40 percent of our rivers and lakes are unusable for swimming (which they are) in 2008, what will the result be in 2060 with 468 million people? Will the U.S. be like Mexico where 90 percent of the rivers and lakes are polluted and can no longer be used? Coupled with the overall numbers is the troublesome aspect of demographics. If 63 percent of the population growth comes from immigration and their descendents and 75 percent of these immigrants are from the ranks of the poor, uneducated and unskilled, what will our social fabric become by the year 2060? The scenario does not look good unless we change our immigration habits.

To summarize, the argument against continued unsustainable immigration, need not be about race, color, or nationality. It needs to be about smart immigration. It needs, most importantly, to be about numbers but it also needs to be about quality. Congress should limit the number of immigrants to no more than 300,000 per year and requirements for basic education (high school level) and/or skill sets should be mandatory. We do not need 300,000 additional welfare recipients immigrating into the U.S. every year. And we do not need our pool of 15 to 20 million poor, uneducated, and unskilled illegal population to grow to 40, 50, or 60 million strong. But that is exactly what will happen if yearly levels continue to net 900,000 to 1.2 million new immigrants or if illegal Mexican immigration is allowed to continue at rates of 500,000 to 800,000 a year as it is today. Forty percent of Mexico's population of 109 million is living below the poverty line as defined by the Mexican government. If we continue on the same path that we are currently on, all 44 million or their children will be living in the United States by 2060. But what is even worse, for Mexico, is that with their current birth rate of 20 per 1000, the population will more than double in the next fifty years. If that trend continues, more than 100 million Mexicans will be living below the poverty line in 2060. Immigration to the U.S. (legal or illegal) is not the solution to Mexico's 21st century population or poverty ills.

Other Things Americans Should Know About Illegal Mexican Immigrants

What are the chances that Congress will give the 8 to 12 million Mexican illegal immigrants that are currently in the U.S. amnesty? The general consensus is that it is a coin toss. Obama has a tendency to be pro-amnesty but with the economic crisis at hand he will be looking for alternatives. With unemployment levels at 8.1 percent as of February 2009 and forecast to approach double digits by year's end amnesty for illegal Mexican workers is not very popular. A comprehensive immigration act will probably not be passed either, as some type of amnesty would be part of it. A more likely scenario is a *wait and see* approach by Obama and the Congress. There are a few dynamics in play which make this quite attractive. One, illegal Mexicans are leaving by the hundreds of thousands for two reasons: there are very few job opportunities as a result of the economic recession and the DHS is beginning to enforce immigration law. Many legislators want to see the impact of a couple of years of *enforcement attrition*. Second, American sentiment against illegal immigration is at an all time high and continuing to grow. Some surveys show that Americans are against immigration legal or illegal, in general, by as much as 70 percent. Americans, overwhelmingly, have become pro-immigrant but anti-immigration in their views. In other words, Americans relish the concept of immigration and typically like and support the immigrants that they know personally but are against the continued practice of unsustainable immigration in theory. Third, the DHS is controlling illegal immigration with more efficiency than in years past. The southern border is not secure but it has become harder for illegal immigrants to enter the U.S. There is still a long way to go on this front but the DHS is definitely taking steps in the right direction. It will be interesting to see if Janet Napolitano's stewardship will continue along the same direction as Chertoff's.

What is the Federal E-Verify program and is it working?

"E-Verify (formerly the Basic Pilot/Employment Eligibility Verification Program) is an online system operated jointly by the Department of Homeland Security and the Social Security Administration (SSA). Participating employers can check the work status of new hires online by comparing information from an employee's I-9 form against SSA and Department of Homeland Security databases. More than 87,000 employers are enrolled in the program, with over 6.5 million queries run so far in fiscal year 2008. E-Verify are free and voluntary, and are the best means available for determining employment eligibility of new hires and the validity of their Social Security numbers."10 The system was tested in the spring of 2008, and in January of 2009, all federal contractors and subcontractors were scheduled to mandatorily use the system in order to obtain a federal contract. The Obama administration, however, put the system into abeyance until May or the summer of 2009. Most of the initial problems have been resolved and more than one thousand new employers are being qualified on the system each week. It is the best tool available to employers for identifying identification fraud. The Obama administration which is committed to creating 2.5 million new jobs will have the responsibility of using and policing the system. If Obama's New Deal creates jobs for illegal immigrants at the expense of U.S. citizens the proverbial shit should hit the fan.

What is the current policy and path to deportation for illegal immigrants? The two departments of the DHS that are the most active in deporting illegal immigrants are the CBP and the ICE. The CBP is guarding the border and make the majority of their apprehensions within a few miles of Mexico. Historically, they would repatriate Mexican illegal immigrants as soon as possible. Non-Mexicans would be jailed in a CBP lockup or a local jail and be processed through the courts. This policy/process had two serious problems. Most Mexicans who were immediately repatriated simply went looking for another route to illegally enter the country. Non-Mexicans were typically released after appearing in court and given a future date on which to return and be tried for illegal entry. Well, the non-Mexicans would simply grab a bus for Chicago or wherever and blow off their court dates. Because of this double standard, many Mexicans began claiming their nationality as Honduran, Salvadoran, or anything besides Mexican. Since the forming of the DHS, and especially since Chertoff took the helm, things have changed drastically. Beginning in 2006, most detainees have automatically been held for fifteen days before being processed. The Federal government passed new legislation in 2006 which put some serious teeth into the reentry infraction. There are now serious consequences for reentry offenders. The policy has evolved into a misdemeanor/felony setup. First-time offenders are fingerprinted, photographed, cataloged into the system, given fifteen days in lockup and then repatriated. Basically, the offense is treated as a misdemeanor. Reentry offenders are jailed, charged with a felony, processed through the courts and given prison terms of up to thirty years. The courts, of course, are actually applying prison terms of 6 months to two years in most cases. And in many cases, the sentences are suspended and the offenders are repatriated to their country of origin. But, repeat offenders are more often being given stiff sentences and this new policy is one of the reasons illegal immigration is starting, for the first time decades, to trend downwards. The CBP, regardless of the new policies, still apprehended 1.02 million offenders in 2008. I want to repeat that number. The CBP, the old Border Patrol Agency, apprehended 1.02 million people in 2008, who tried unsuccessfully to cross the border. That equates to 2,800 people a day, every day, 365 days of the year. Ninety-five percent of those apprehensions were along the southern border with Mexico. The U.S southern border with Mexico is 1,952 miles long. Imagine 2,800 lines of foreigners stretched along the southern horizon from Brownsville, Texas, to San Diego, California spaced 3/4 of a mile apart. Each day one individual steps to the front of the line, illegally crosses the border, is apprehended, and is sent back to Mexico or incarcerated. That is the scope of the apprehension activity by the CBP.

The ICE, on the other hand, apprehends offenders all across the country not just at the borders. Their strategy and focus is quite different than that of their associates at CBP. ICE is the U.S. Immigration and Customs Enforcement. Starting in 2006 after Michael Chertoff took control their focus finally began zooming in on enforcement. ICE and CBP are, of course, organized under

DHS's mandate and report to the Secretary of the DHS. ICE, under Chertoff's stewardship, has modernized, and become more focused on their self-defined mission to enforce immigration, primarily through their Office of Detention and Removal (DRO). They have placed a priority on pursuing and deporting dangerous criminal immigrants. To do this, they have partnered with many local and state authorities and are implementing criminal identification programs throughout the nation. The goal is to have a comprehensive network which will identify all illegal immigrants which are incarcerated for criminal activity or have outstanding criminal warrants. The current program is focused on deporting non-violent criminals early (which saves local governments money); deporting violent criminals upon completion of their sentences, using border-state officials as deporting agents, and consequently deportations (removals) are skyrocketing. The ICE reports that removals or deportations grew from 116,460 in 2002 to 349,041 in 2008. According to the ICE "notably, one third of the illegal immigrants removed from the U.S. in 2008 were foreign nationals who had prior criminal convictions in addition to being in the country illegally". [11]

Another ICE initiative is focusing on so-called immigration fugitive cases. They have established almost 100 fugitive operation teams over the last three years to address this issue. Slowly but surely they are beginning to make headway in this area which has been ignored for decades. As the number of teams comes onboard, the number of arrests and deportations increase. The teams are dispersed in most states and are working with local authorities in an attempt to track down and deport or incarcerate all illegal immigrants who have outstanding criminal warrants. The task is enormous, but fortunately, has finally been undertaken seriously. "The ICE reports that 1,900 cases were filed in 2003 and has grown to 33,997 cases in 2008." [12]

These illegal immigrants have outstanding warrants for criminal activity. As impressive as the chart appears it only shows the uptick in results, it does not define the scope of the problem. At the end of fiscal year 2008, there were still outstanding (criminal) warrants for 560,000 illegal immigrants. It seems obvious that the number of ICE Fugitive Operation Teams needs to be increased by four or five-fold in order to adequately find, prosecute, and deport the community of more than 560,000 known illegal immigrant criminals in a reasonable timeframe. By the way, The U.S. Attorney General's Office reports that illegal immigration cases are the number one offense on their dockets.

Do Mexican Immigrants assimilate into American culture at the same rate and with similar results as other immigrants? Unfortunately, the easy and obvious answer is no. And, it is an emphatic no! The reasons are not terribly difficult to understand. Most Mexicans arrive with less money, less education, fewer skills (including language), and in comparison to other nationalities are prone to be illegal at a one hundred to one ratio. That translates into a very, non-competitive disadvantage. Another disadvantage Mexican immigrants have is within their own subculture. They must compete against the other approximately 15 million or more illegal Mexicans who are vying for the same jobs and opportunities. Their own culture slows their assimilation. Studies show that the rate of assimilation, for Mexicans, has been much slower in the 21st century than it was in the 20th century. However, the slower rates of assimilation began with the huge increases in immigration from Mexico, which began after 1965, and followed immigration trends throughout the century. In other words, as the illegal Mexican population has grown, their ability to assimilate has decreased drastically. Jacob Vigdor, Professor of Public Policy Studies and Economics at Duke University, published a comprehensive study, "Measuring Immigration Assimilation in the United States" [13] in May of 2008. He found Mexico, to be at the bottom of the list for all immigrating countries. In almost every measureable category Mexico is not only at the bottom of the list but in most cases exponentially behind all other cultures. Some additional and startling facts in his study found, for example, that Mexican adolescents are imprisoned at rates approximately 80 percent greater than immigrant adolescents generally. He also found great disparity between historical assimilation rates and successes when comparing Italians to Mexicans. The Italian, Irish, and European immigrants who immigrated into the U.S. successfully assimilated. Large percentages, however, of the Mexican immigrants are not fitting into the modern, American culture. They are remaining monolingual, poor, second-class, illegal immigrants. And, unfortunately, so are large percentages of their offspring.

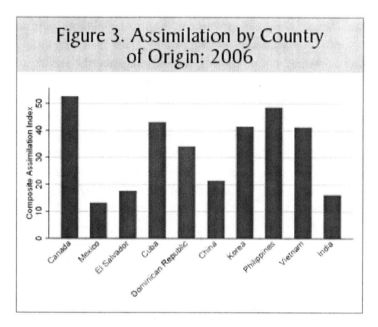

Figure 3. Assimilation by Country of Origin: 2006

Recent Mexican, anti-American demonstrations, in California and elsewhere, highlight how millions of Mexicans not only do not assimilate well but do not even desire to assimilate. In Montebello, California, for example, high school students flew an upside-down American flag under a Mexican national flag as they demonstrated against American immigration laws. They marched and shouted, 'Viva Mexico! Down with the Gabachos (Americans)'; the vast majority were American-born children of illegal Mexican immigrants. They were demonstrating against the same culture that has nourished and provided them with an education. In Los Angeles and San Francisco, it is common to hear state senators such as Joe Baca and house representatives like Fabian Núñez rally their immigrant supporters in an attempt to take control of the civil war against what they like to refer to as the white community. Baca tells his followers that the agenda is all about increasing reproduction (Hispanic) and winning the war against the whites through attrition. He is not bashful about characterizing white-Chicano relations as a civil war which will eventually be won in the bedroom. He knows that the whites are not having babies one-tenth as fast as Mexicans are illegally immigrating. Núñez exhorts all Hispanics to participate in the Aztlán National movement, Latino revolution, Chicano nationalism, or whatever; as long as they understand that through immigration and perseverance they will displace the whites and repatriate California and the southwestern U.S. into Latino hands. It is not an argument for assimilation. It is an argument which anticipates, right or wrong, the Mexicanization of much of the U.S. The Aztlán platform basically envisions everything west of the Mississippi as being part of some never-existent, mythical, indigenous Latino nation. Their more radical associates such as professors José Angel Gutiérrez, of the University of Texas at Arlington, and Armando Navarro, of the University of California at Riverside, overtly advocate a Latino uprising. Gutiérrez negates the fact that millions of illegal Mexican immigrants are even illegal. He suggests that anyone who has a single drop of pre-Columbian blood has the right to traverse the continent from Alaska to Tierra del Fuego as they please without respect for sovereign immigration laws. Navarro puts the entire immigration argument in military terms. He claims that the Latinos have the infantry, the artillery, and the ammunition to win the war. As he sees it, they currently lack organization and strong leaders. He envisions himself as a 21st century general. He wants to be the next Pancho Villa or Che Guevara it appears. Neither general assimilated into their respective cultures with any success during their failed careers and eventual violent deaths.

Is the U.S. Government enforcing immigration law in the workplace? Without a single doubt, the answer is NO. The ICE publishes frequent reports which point to the importance of attacking the magnet of illegal employment which causes and supports illegal immigration. In reality it is doing very little to curtail illegal hiring practices. In 2008, ICE arrested 1,100 individuals tied to worksite investigations. Of those, 135 were business owners or managers. Stop the presses! Read all about it! It is a scoop! There are somewhere between 10 and 15 million or more illegal workers in the U.S and the ICE was only able to find 1,100 guilty employer-type people. Of those, only 135 were business owners or managers. I guess it is a tough job. Bush at least had Bin-Laden cornered in a cave in Pakistan a few years ago but employers of illegal immigrants are tough to find. It is an almost impossible task. The official policy is to focus on only egregious business owners and managers (that is actually on the ICE webpage). I guess they do not have the time or manpower to look for just ordinary law breakers, just the egregious ones. For some reason, I do not think that the law was written to only prosecute egregious employers of illegal immigrants. In any event, the only positive step they have made, on this front, is the introduction of the new E-Verify system. At least that is better than an empty cave.

What does it mean to the American political system if 15 or 20 million or more illegal immigrants are given amnesty sometime soon? Or even 10 million? Many analysts believe that the Latino voting bloc grew from 5 million in 2000, to somewhere between 10 and 12 million in 2008. It also appears that they supported Barrack Obama and other democratic candidates by a 70 to 30 percent margin (more or less) over the Republicans. Hispanics made up approximately 9 percent of the total electorate nationwide as determined by exit polls and surveys. Demographers believe that there were a minimum of 46 million Hispanics in the U.S. in 2008. That is 25 percent of the total population. Of those, approximately 11 million voted in 2008. The 46 million estimates include all Hispanics, legal or otherwise. Let us suppose that 15 million of those 46 million did not vote because they are illegal immigrants and cannot vote. That means that of the 31 (hypothetical) million legal Hispanics approximately 36 percent voted. If 10 million illegal Hispanic immigrants are given amnesty in 2009, how would it affect the national election? It would mean that 3.6 million additional Hispanic voters would enter the process. If they vote the same way their fellow Hispanics voted in 2008, the Democratic Party can count on an additional 2.5 million voters nationwide. If 15 million Hispanics are given amnesty the Democratic Party can count on an additional 3.75 million voters and if 20 million Hispanics are given amnesty there will be an additional 5 million Democratic voters. Just to put those numbers in perspective, Obama won the 2008 election by 8 million votes and it is considered an overwhelming victory. Hispanics are in a large part credited with his victories in the swing states of Indiana, Virginia, Florida, Colorado, and New Mexico. All of these states have large illegal immigrant populations and with an amnesty would presumably become permanently painted blue. Unless politics change drastically, any large amnesty will most likely insure democratic domination in American politics for decades to come. This scenario, by the way, completely ignores any change that will be caused by continued immigration. It is a fact that after every amnesty program illegal immigration levels have soared.

Does anybody know what the cost of social welfare for illegal immigrants is to the nation? There are many opinions on this subject yet not a lot of hard data. It is another one of those difficult subjects to understand because of the nature of the beast. Reliable information on both sides of the equation is unsubstantiated because, of course, millions of workers live in a shadowy state of existence. In other words, the government is not sure exactly how much money is being collected through taxes on illegal immigrants. They also are not exactly positive how many social services are being used by illegal immigrants. The experts at the Center for Immigration Studies calculated the total cost in 2002 and reported a net 10 billion dollar deficit at the national level. Their study found that illegal immigrants received more than 26 billion in benefits while they paid approximately 16 billion in taxes. Another study, completed by the Federation for American Immigration Reform (FAIR), concluded that the cost in 2004 was more than 10.5 billion dollars just to the state of California. The PEW Hispanic Center completed a study in 2006, which reports on the public's attitude towards welfare being collected by illegal immigrants. By a two-thirds majority Americans believe illegal immigrants should not receive any social services from the government. They further state that more than two-thirds of Americans support the 1982 Supreme Court ruling which obliged public schools to educate youngsters regardless of their immigration status. Americans, do not want to pick up the tab for poor, uneducated, illegal immigrants but certainly are willing to educate their children. They understand that lack of education is a huge part of the immigration problem. Another way to understand how illegal immigration impacts welfare is by examining poverty, education, and teenage child-birthing. There is a lot of substantial data available for all three. All are indicators of whether or not illegal immigrants are burdens or boosts to society.

Mexican immigrants, in particular, are poorly educated. More than half, probably 75 percent have no more than a third grade education. The USCB numbers show that the amount spent by government through welfare programs is seven times as high for families headed by high school dropouts as compared to those headed by college graduates. The chart below illustrates the reality. [14]

U.S. WELFARE SPENDING PER FAMILY BY EDUCATION LEVEL (HEADS OF HOUSEHOLDS)

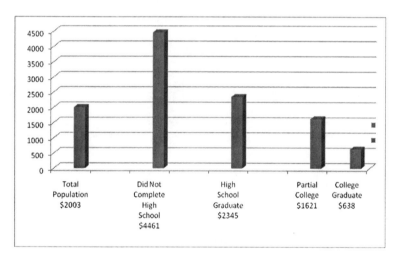

Source: United States Census Bureau

It is hard to calculate the burden on society caused by out-of-wedlock births but the birth rate among Hispanic immigrants is four times higher than Asians and non-Hispanic immigrants. Black immigrants have a very large out-of-wedlock birth percentage as well. Since 80 percent of all illegal immigrants are Hispanic and their out-of-wedlock birth rate is 42.3 percent it is easy to deduce that they are a burden on the welfare system. It is not quantitative but obvious. It is learned, cultural behavior that they bring from Mexico and Latin America. Mexico is a country of babies having babies. The standing joke in Mexico that sadly illustrates this point: "You know what the definition of a Mexican Virgin is? A really ugly thirteen year-old". The kids pass this joke around at about that age. I took an informal survey among my young Mexican friends recently. They believe that 95 percent of first-time births, in my home in Mexico, are out-of-wedlock. My questions were unscientific but the responses were revealing. The chart below shows the USCB numbers for out-of-wedlock births among first generation immigrant parents in the U.S. [15]

OUT-OF-WEDLOCK BIRTHS

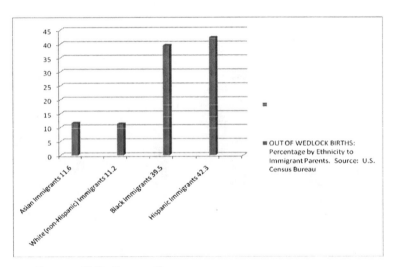

Source: U.S. Census Bureau

The same deductions can be made from studying the numbers of teen mother birth rates. Fifty percent of all Hispanic births are to teen-aged mothers of seventeen years or less; reference the chart below.[16] It does not take a rocket scientist to surmise that a culture which half the population has been born to teen-aged, out-of-wedlock mothers will turn to welfare if it is available. And it is available in the U.S. As the welfare program has decreased poverty over the last forty-five years, the immigration policy has increased it. Poor, uneducated, unskilled, illegal immigrants have a high probability of entering the ranks of poverty as well as the ranks of those receiving welfare. Poorly educated immigrants impose large costs on U.S. taxpayers. Any taxes they pay are greatly outweighed by the costs of the social welfare benefits they consume. The National Academy of Sciences has estimated that the average immigrant without a high school degree will impose a net cost of nearly $100,000 on U.S. taxpayers over the course of his or her life. This cost is in excess of any taxes paid and does not include the cost of educating the immigrant's children. The following chart from the annual National Vital Statistics Report illustrates the relationship between ethnicity and teen birth rates. The numbers are amazing. In Mexico it is referred to as *kids having kids*.

TEEN BIRTH RATES

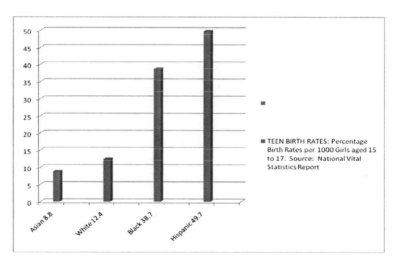

Source: U.S. National Vital Statistics Report

The data, various studies, and report after report all support the fact that illegal immigrants who are poor, uneducated, and unskilled are a burden to the welfare system, the economy, and American culture. The illegal immigrant community is somewhere between 25 and 31 percent unemployed or underemployed. And they naturally gravitate to the welfare system. The astute, free-market economist Milton Friedman correctly noted that it, "is just obvious that you can't have free immigration and a welfare state". It appears that we have both. What is the price tag of welfare for 10 million illegal immigrants? What is the price tag for 15 or 20 million? If the National Academy of Sciences is correct, the cost will be one trillion dollars for 10 million illegal immigrants..

What in the hell happened to Mexifornia (California)?

The same thing happened in California that happened in most of Western Europe in the last thirty years. Californians became convinced that multiculturalism was more valid, more important, and more politically correct than the concept of just maintaining a normal, decent place to live and raise children. They lost their bearings, their gyroscope. California is everything that the rest of the nation becomes. California is the nation's compass. It often predicts the national trends twenty or thirty years before they happen. Almost every cultural trend that starts in California becomes popular in the rest of the nation. Everything that identifies America as America does not start in California but everything that starts in California eventually is tried in the rest of the nation. California trends may catch on or they may be discarded but typically they catch on. California and, of course, New York are the avant-garde centers of cultural America. The most recent USCB census shows New York to be the ever-changing, multicultural, amalgam of America. Harlem, for example, recently had a 30 percent increase of white inhabitants. But California has become a failed welfare state. California is no longer a melting pot of international ideas. California has become tainted. California has lost its luster. It has become too populated with backward, unprepared immigrants and the impact has devastated many communities. It is sad. The immigrants are not prepared for the responsibility of being Californians. There are now almost 40 million Californians and it is one big mess. California has changed from a multicultural springboard of life to a downwardly spiraling Mexican barrio.

California itself is like a mirrored reflection of its population or perhaps the reverse is more accurate. Among international economies, California's ranks 7th with more than a trillion dollars of GDP, yet its government is so tasked by welfare that Governor Schwarzenegger is begging the federal government for a bailout. His state government is bankrupt. Mt. Whitney, at 14,495 is only one hundred miles from Death Valley which at 280 feet below sea level are the highest and lowest points in the continental U.S. Comparably, billionaires live in multi-million dollar mansions in Beverly Hills just a few miles from the squalor of the East L.A. barrios (slums). California's population doubled from 20 million in 1975, to almost 40 million in 2008 as millions of illegal immigrants pouring over the border from Mexico shouting the state motto, Eureka (translated from the Greek – I have found it). The U.S. Bureau of Citizenship and Immigration (USBCI) believe that 32 percent of all illegal immigrants in the U.S. have chosen California as their new residence. That means that somewhere between 4.5 and 5 million illegal immigrants reside in California. "California's addiction to cheap illegal alien labor is bankrupting the state and posing enormous burdens on the state's shrinking middle class tax base," stated Dan Stein, President of FAIR. "Most Californians, who have seen their taxes increase while public services deteriorate, already know the impact that mass illegal immigration is having on their communities, but even they may be shocked when they learn just how much of a drain illegal immigration has become."[17] The 2008 California state budget deficit, 11.2 billion, is equal to the amount most experts believe is being spent on illegal immigrants. Schwarzenegger, unsure of the deficit, has asked the federal government for 26 billion just in case. In January of 2009 the budget deficit for the upcoming 18 months was estimated at a staggering 41 billion dollars. The state is in a financial crisis which will engulf the citizens of California for decades to come.

Not only have the results been disastrous at the state level but small towns throughout the state, like Selma, which is the home and backdrop of Victor Hanson's book, Mexifornia, have become mired in poverty, crime, and the onslaught of Mexicanization. He warns "For those of you who live outside of California, far away from Mexico, and sigh that the problem is ours, not yours: be careful." "Wherever you live, if you want your dirty work done cheaply, by someone else, you will welcome illegal aliens, as we did. And if you become puzzled later over how to deal with the consequent problems of assimilation, you will also look to California and follow what we have done, slowly walking the path that leads to Mexisota, Utexico, Mexizona or even Mexichusetts---a place that is not quite Mexico and not quite America either.[18] Will the U.S. become another Mexifornia, but on a national level? Will the country with the world's largest GDP soon go begging for a bailout because of overstrained social services caused by unsustainable immigration? Will America become Mexamerica? It is our responsibility to decide.

A little more than a thousand years ago the central valley of Mexico flourished with one of the most astounding cultures that have ever populated planet earth. They faced the same conundrum that we face today. For six hundred years this culture lived in relative peace. Archaeologists refer to it as a Golden Age. Their understanding, manipulation, and control of agriculture freed their minds to wander, envision, dream, invent, question, explore, and develop their culture. We can only guess as to the limits that their abstract thinking soared. They mastered astronomy with complete understanding of not only the solar system but the milky-way galaxy. Architecture and art intermingled as it always does in great cultures. The great pyramids that were built by the Mexican cultures were not envisioned, designed, and built by the murderous, sacrificial Aztecs but by the education-loving Teotihuacanos and others. Their architects were artists as well as builders who designed the great Meso-American cities with an appreciation of visual textures, layout, and composition. Their art-sculpted buildings copied, in stylistic form, the organic life that was their domain and the celestial ceiling that they observed in the clear skies above the Sierra Madre Mountains. Beautiful sculptures of loving, embracing couples still remind of us of their tender caring society. Mathematicians devised the zero-based system used for calculating 500 hundred years before the Arabs introduced it to Europe in the 13th century. This same precise understanding of mathematics produced the most accurate calendar ever devised by man. Government perhaps performed at a level which has still never been replicated. We are uncertain of the specific governing principles that prevailed but it is obvious that the leadership was not only dedicated to a sense of order and progress but also maintained an atmosphere of peace and tranquility. But as always the darker-side of humanity reared its ugly head.

Many scholars believe that at the beginning of the end of the Golden Age of Mexico poor, uneducated, unskilled, peoples from the northwest regions were allowed to immigrate into the central valley and the heart of the great cities. The Teotihuacanos could afford the luxury of a second-class citizenry who could do their dirty jobs, those things which must be done in order to sustain a first-world culture. These were the Aztecs and they came by the millions. The fate of the Teotihuacanos still eludes us but we know that after some period (perhaps as much as 200 years) of continual immigration which was followed by a large Genghis Khan-style invasion the Aztecs usurped control of the entire central valley of Mexico. The Teotihuacanos disappeared. The laborers, maids, nannies, gardeners, and their millions of descendents became Mexico. If the Teotihuacanos architecture were not so extraordinary and had not persevered we would probably not even know of their 600 years of cultural development.

Cultures evolve, grow, flourish, decline and are lost in time. History teaches many lessons. Did the Aztecs drift into the central valley of Mexico intent on being its new masters? No, they were poor, uneducated humans willing to do the work that needed to be done. The work that it seemed no one else wanted to do. Did the Teotihuacanos suspect that their housemaids and gardeners would usurp control of their culture and displace their entire existence as they had previously known it? No, they did not suspect the consequences. Now, one thousand years later history is trying to repeat itself. This time the Aztecs have slowly drifted northward. At first it was slow; they migrated by the hundreds and thousands. Now they are arriving by the millions. Their offspring have become so ubiquitous and prolific that they now represent more than half of the total growth of the American culture. Is America ready to repeat the history of Meso-America? Will Americans be content to watch their culture continue to be degraded as millions of uneducated masses dilute its value? There is still time to change, to reverse the trend of unsustainable immigration. There is time to change immigration law and upgrade the requirements on immigrants. The American culture is worth saving. But we must change before it is too late. We must embrace immigration change or America will go the way of Teotihuacán.

VIII

Kidnapping Capital of the World

The most valued prize in pre-Columbian Mexico was a palpitating heart that had just been extracted from the open chest of a sacrificial victim who laid stretched taut, hands and feet bound tightly, on the altar to *Huichilobos*, god of blood. The *priest*, an expert at rending open the human chest, would hold the palpitating heart high above his head as he invoked the blessings of *Huichilobos*. He would then bite deep into the heart, sucking the warm blood into his mouth as it streamed down his cheeks and chest. His waist-long hair, encrusted with the blood of prior victims, dripped with the fresh sacrament. The heart would be shared with the other priests and Aztec hierarchy that had ascended the sacrificial platforms. The bound victim, just losing consciousness, would then have his head severed with a jagged blade which was chipped from a piece of flint. The severed head, impaled on a six foot pole would be raised skyward so as to be displayed to the hungry masses waiting at the base of the pyramid. The corpse, untied, shoved off the steep-angled pyramidal wall, bounded and bounced, headless to the outstretched hands of the carnivorous masses. Arms and legs were quickly dismembered and eaten, being passed around until only the white, fleshless bones remained. Hernán Cortés and his Spaniards conquistadors watched this brutal cannibalistic orgy night after night as they lay siege to Tenochtitlán in 1520.

Most experts agree that by the time the European and Mesoamerican cultures collided in the 16th century somewhere between 100,000 and 250,000 humans were being sacrificed and eaten in Mexico on a yearly basis. The trading in human life had become the most important commerce of Mexico. The alliances that were maintained by the hundreds of city-states were structured in a way to promote an endless flow of live humanity from region to region. The currency of this economy was the warrior. Humans were not bought and sold. They were stolen, captured, sequestered. It was a diametric culture in a strange sense. The primary goal of the city-states was to perpetuate the commerce of human flesh. To achieve this goal each city-state allied with various neighbors but also had to maintain an independence from other alliances. If they did not, there would be no pool of victims available for sacrifice. In other words, if the Aztecs, for example, had conquered all the various city-states and made them part of their empire, the availability of humans, in the close proximity would be extremely limited. Even the barbaric Aztecs did not want to eat their own family or neighbors. So, whereas the Aztecs were the dominant city-state in central Mexico, they did not have political control of all of the city-states. They had their alliances with various city-states and were arch enemies of the others. Economically, this system availed ample product (humans) to all the various groups.

The warring among the city-states was not about conquest. It was about commerce. In order to acquire sacrificial victims, the Aztecs, for example, would attack the Cempoalans. This was commerce in action. The battles were like stock trades on Wall Street. The successful traders were the warriors who returned with live human beings. These so-called warriors were, in essence, kidnappers. The goal of every battle was to sequester or grab as many humans as possible. The battles were never fought to secure land or riches, although gold, silver, precious stones, and armaments were prized and of course, were taken whenever possible. But the warriors were after live human beings. They were glorified kidnappers. They were the kings of kidnapping. It was a culture of kidnapping. It was a hemisphere of kidnapping! Mexico was the 16th century kidnapping capital of the world!

Five hundred years later Mexico has become the kidnapping capital of the world again. It surpassed Colombia in 2006 for having the most kidnappings, annually, of any country. Once again, it appears that the palpitating human heart has become a most valued prize in Mexico. The Mexican authorities who were completely unable to put an accurate count on kidnappings suspect the total in 2008 exceeded 10,000 victims. In September 2008, President

Calderón's National Security Council implemented legislation allocated 1.2 million dollars to each of the thirty-one Mexican states in order that they each establish a new, anti-kidnapping task force. This new thrust against kidnapping is very similar to the U.S. response to the 9/11 attacks when the Bush administration created the Homeland Security department. The situation is completely out of control, nationwide, so Calderón has established a federal response. The Mexico City Prosecutor's office reported a seventy-six per cent increase for the first six months of 2008 over 2007. And the scary part of this upward trend is that there are almost no convictions. The number that is quoted everywhere, of unsolved kidnappings, is 99%. There are investigators who have been on the job in Mexico City for ten years and have still not seen a single conviction in their specific districts. Only 1% of the abductors are being caught! Mexico City had more than 1,600 documented kidnappings in 2008, with another unknown amount, perhaps 2,000 that were unreported. As wealthy Mexicans exited by the thousands to the U.S., the numbers suggest that Phoenix may have become the city with the second highest reported kidnappings in the world. The weak U.S. border security is not deterring Mexican criminals from kidnapping wealthy Mexicans who move to the U.S. or U.S. citizens either.

Historically, Latin America has ranked as the most prolific kidnapping region of the world. In any region of the world where there is great disparity in wealth between the upper and lower classes, kidnapping is prominent. The rich are targets for the poor. Children of the wealthy are sequestered and demands must be paid in order to secure their return. Thus, the term kidnapping exists. In the U.S., kidnapping is sensational but not common. When I think of kidnapping, Charles Lindbergh Jr., George Weyerhaeuser, and Frank Sinatra Jr. come to mind. The Lindbergh kidnapping is often referred to as the *crime of the century*. It is interesting to note that the Lindbergh baby was kidnapped and murdered by an illegal immigrant, Bruno Hauptman. Famous, successful, wealthy people have always been the targets of kidnappers in the U.S. and around the world. Mexico is no exception. What has evolved in Mexico since the early nineties however, is very different than the high-profile, sensational kidnapping of the son of a successful industrialist or entertainer.

The world of kidnapping changed drastically in 1994 in Mexico. Prior to this, nationwide, fifty to one hundred kidnappings or sequestering were reported annually. This level or rate of kidnapping was consistent throughout the 20th century. It is interesting to note that kidnappings are not called kidnappings in Spanish or in Mexico. They are called sequesterings. The reason, it appears, is that historically in Mexico, children were not the primary victims of this crime. Adults have always been sequestered with more frequency than children in Mexico. Sequestering has always been more of a business than a desperate abduction of some innocent child. "In the US, the great majority of the kidnapping cases are solved," said Walter Farrer, the Mexico operations chief at the security firm Pinkerton and Burns International. "Here in Mexico, it has become a business, and as awful as it sounds, it is treated as a transaction."[1] The entire business atmosphere changed when Alfredo Harp Helú, then owner of Banamex, cousin of Carlos Slim, was sequestered in 1994. A new industry was born. Alfredo Harp Helú was held for three and a half months. His son, priest, and business associates made highly publicized television appearances pleading with his abductors to negotiate. The case and eventual payment of thirty million dollars was not only followed by the public but also by organized crime, thugs, want-to-be criminals, corrupt police officials, and politicians.

The following month, super-market magnate, Ángel Losada Moreno was abducted. Authorities suspect that the successful kidnappers of Helú were the culprits. The negotiations followed the same course as had those for Helú, but this time the stakes were upped to fifty million dollars. The ransom was paid, he was released, and the criminals have not looked back since. Journalists began to refer to kidnapping as the hottest Mexican *growth* industry of the decade. Industry or just plain crime, it has seen tremendous growth both in terms of overall abductions and in market segmentation. There are at least eight different types of kidnappings in Mexico: traditional, executive, political, express, foreign- expatriates, drug war or narco, U.S. abductions, and virtual. Each focuses on a different type of victim.

The *traditional* targets for kidnappers, all over the world, are those loved-ones of the super wealthy. The highly publicized abduction and much decried murder of fourteen year-old Fernando Martí in the summer of 2008, is a perfect example. It was preceded by the well-publicized sale of Alejandro Martí's (Fernando's father) chain of sporting good stores for 562 million dollars. This sale did not go unnoticed by the underworld in 2007. Although his millions provided his family with state of the art security, it did not deter the kidnappers. As is common in this type of scheme there seems to have been both insider accomplices and police participation. The traditional kidnappers are expert professionals and are often part of a kidnapping family such as The *Flower Gang*, a Mexico City gang, or *La Familia*, a Morelia, Michoacán gang. In many cases they are policemen, security guards, investigative agents, or former military personnel. They are savvy, typically acquire schedules and routes of intended victims, and use bogus police checkpoints, pullovers, or even fabricated documentation to achieve contact. Young Martí was apprehended at a fake AFI (Mexican FBI) checkpoint where the kidnappers were dressed impeccably as AFI agents. In this case the routes in all four directions had been blocked by their associates, supposedly dressed as police officers, and in bogus patrol cars. Now after months of investigation authorities believe that none of the kidnappers were faking their police involvement. Three police officers have been arrested and others implicated. The evidence and testimony of the bodyguard, who was originally reported killed, have implicated not only the police officers but also a former high ranking captain in the AFI itself. The twist, ironically, is that the AFI has the specific responsibility of investigating and solving kidnappings.

The most common response by families in these *traditional* abductions is to try and adhere with the demands of the abductors. An entire support industry of insurers, consultants, security, and even negotiators has bloomed since the mid-nineties. Fernando's kidnappers demanded the usual. Alejandro Martí complied. He hired an exclusive private negotiating firm, tried his best to meet the terms of the abductors, paid a two million dollar ransom and then, no doubt, almost died when communications ceased and his son was not returned. He followed the instructions, he paid the ransom, he kept quiet, and still his son did not return. Unfortunately, the odds were not in his favor. A very high percentage of the young, defenseless abductees are murdered and never returned. In this case, young Fernando's partially decomposed body was eventually found two months after the abduction in the trunk of a car. These types of violent, reprehensible acts are crimes against the entire family not just the victims. But not only are they increasing in frequency, the government is becoming less and less capable of incarcerating those that are responsible. It appears very likely that in the vast majority of *traditional* kidnappings that the police at one level or another are involved. Ninety-five per cent of all *traditional* kidnappings are never solved and no one is prosecuted.

Alejandro Martí went public after his son was not returned. He enlisted the support of politicians, newsmen, and his wealthy companions. The personnel tragedy became a national tragedy and ignited marches and demonstrations in Mexico City. But marches are of no consequence when the very institutions that are tasked with safeguarding the citizenry, investigating the crime, and bringing justice to society are actually preying on the innocent. Alfredo Harp Helú, a family friend and former kidnap victim, attended the funeral and later spoke of the impotence of law enforcement that has become part of Mexican life. Many talk of taking matters into their own hands. In other words, the idea of wealthy businessmen funding paramilitary organizations, arming, and empowering them with the mandate to wipe out the criminals is becoming a very real possibility. "Another business leader at the funeral who survived a kidnapping and asked not to be named asked a <u>TIME Magazine</u> reporter: "What are we to do? Get the Israelis as bodyguards? Somebody else was mentioning using American Special Forces, as they are being demobilized and are more serious. Do we have to have our own paramilitary forces? We have to be organized, as the government obviously is not. I am sending my family to the U.S."[2]

Many wealthy and upper income Mexicans have already immigrated (legally) to Phoenix, San Diego, Los Angeles, Chicago, Houston, Miami, and other Latino-cultured American cities in order to escape the onslaught of violence back home.

Legal immigration into the U.S. is easy for wealthy Mexicans. More than two thousand wealthy Tijuana families have immigrated to the San Diego area in the last three years. "So many upper-class Mexican families live in the Eastlake neighborhood and Bonita, an unincorporated community adjacent to Chula Vista, that residents say the area is becoming a gilded colony of Mexicans, where speaking English is optional and people can breathe easy cruising around in their Mercedes-Benzes and BMWs. I always say that Eastlake is the city with the highest standard of living in all of Mexico," joked Enrique Hernandez Pulido, a San Diego-based attorney with many Mexican émigré clients."[3] Those that can afford to leave are exiting by the thousands.

The first filter of discrimination that is used by U.S. immigration officials to determine immigration eligibility, of course, is economically based. Mexicans who can prove financial stability and a strong net worth can easily obtain a tourist visa, a student visa, a work visa, or make application for and receive legal resident or permanent immigration status. If you are poor it is not easy. Other upper class Mexicans who have not immigrated to escape the violence have turned to a new method of high-tech tracking in a desperate attempt to thwart the ubiquitous kidnappers. They are buying high-tech offerings from companies such as XEGA S.A. DE C.V. and VeriChip Corporation who have perfected satellite-based, global, tracking systems. With the insertion of an electronic chip the size of a grain of rice, under an arm pit or behind a knee, XEGA can track their clients anywhere in the world. At a cost of $4,000 for the implant and an annual fee of $2,200 per person many Mexicans are opting for this new, high-tech hope of security. Hopefully, the criminals will not be armed with chip sensing technology anytime soon or will not be able to purchase client lists from these corporations.

The second type of sequestering is the *executive kidnapping*. This really emerged in 1994, with the abductions of Alfredo Harp and Ángel Losada. It differs from the *traditional* method in a number of ways. The executives themselves are the victims and the negotiations often directly involve their participation. Tens of millions instead of millions are sought and typically the victims are released and almost never harmed. The professional, executive kidnappers have established a protocol. The victims know the protocol and are aware that there is a high probability that they will be released unharmed if they are able to secure the outlandish sum of funds that are demanded. This has almost evolved into a straightforward business transaction. Major European insurers offer expensive, large deductible policies and most of the larger, successful Mexican firms are covering their CEO's and other important executives. The catch-22 reality of kidnapping insurance, however, is scary. "The way it works is that the company takes out insurance with an insurance firm--Lloyds of London, AIG and Chubb are leaders in the field," explains Robillard, from Kroll. "If an employee has the misfortune to be kidnapped, the kidnappers contact the company demanding a ransom, and the company contacts the insurance firm who then negotiate with the abductors. The police aren't involved at any stage." But he has a word of warning to those thinking of taking out kidnapping insurance; executives must always remember that as soon as anyone is aware that an executive has insurance, he becomes a prime target. "I would go as far as to say you shouldn't even tell your spouse," he says. "Having kidnapping insurance may be a good way of making sure that, if you are abducted, you will return home safe and sound and in one piece. But, on the other hand, if it becomes known you have such insurance, you become an attractive proposition for any gang of kidnappers."4 Not surprisingly, fifty per cent of the world's insurance policies which cover executive kidnappings are written in Mexico.

It is difficult to know the true number of kidnappings that are occurring in Mexico. Most of the independent agencies that monitor crime in Mexico, believe the number will be between six and ten thousand in 2008. Of these, perhaps only twenty or thirty per cent will be reported. These same agencies believe the number of overall executive kidnappings is growing on a yearly basis but now represents only one in ten or even less of the total kidnappings. That number translates to somewhere between four and eight hundred executive victims. Since very few of the executive kidnappings ever go public, it is hard to estimate this criminal activity. I personally know two executives, both Mexicans that were kidnapped recently. One was actually kidnapped twice.

He was attending the wedding of his wife's best friend. He and his family were staying with the in-laws of the bride. While returning from a pre-wedding event they were mistaken for the bride and groom and kidnapped. His abductors soon realized their mistake but after seeing his business card decided to proceed anyway. His company paid the ransom, he was released unharmed, and the targeted couple was happily married. Unfortunately, six months later the kidnappers targeted my friend a second time. They had learned who he was, where he lived, where he worked, and more importantly they knew that his company would pay the ransom. Needless to say, my friend decided to change employers, sell his home in Mexico City, and relocate to New York for a few years after he was released the second time. He is now back in Mexico City living the dodgy life of a business executive hoping that the kidnappers have lost his scent.

I found the other kidnapping even more intriguing. An acquaintance of mine in Mexico City who was a young, aspiring, architect was forced off the road and yanked from his car one morning while taking his children to school. His father, who was very wealthy, entered into the normal negotiations, and hired a private European firm to manage the transaction. The amateur kidnappers were operating out of a remote farm house which was easily surrounded by the private security personnel who had triangulated the location using the signal from the abductor's cell phone. The kidnappers agreed to let the victim live if they were paid one million dollars and given a one hour advantage in which to make their escape. The father agreed to the terms, the money was paid, the kidnappers disappeared, and the young man returned home unharmed but scared. He moved to Phoenix for two years then returned to Mexico. Upon his return he quickly established his own firm with glamorous offices and hired five junior architects. His family was flabbergasted. He, so it appeared, had swindled his own father out of a million dollars. Luckily for both of my acquaintances they had not been sequestered by Daniel Arizmendi. He, his brother, and gang became notorious for their special trademarked kidnappings. Contrary to the other executive kidnappers, the Arizmendi gang introduced the feared tactic of ear dismembering in 1996. Daniel, the leader, would pare the victim's ear off with a pair of scissors in order to expedite the ransom process. It worked. His gang was attributed with more than eighty kidnappings and brutal disfigurations.

Another segment which is perhaps easier to quantify is the *political* sequestering. The southern states of Chiapas, Oaxaca, and the western states of Michoacán and Guerrero have historically seen disenfranchised peasants and unionists malcontents turn to kidnapping for political purposes. In the state of Guerrero, for example, Governor Figueroa was kidnapped in a sensational case that lasted for almost four months. A generation later, his grandson, and namesake was kidnapped for the same political reasons. The demands always involve property rights of indigenous Mexicans, civil rights, or workers rights. Another sensational kidnapping involved Lydia Cacho, a Yucatán based journalist and author who exposed a child pornography ring. Mario Marin, governor of Puebla, and friend of one of the individuals who was implicated in Cacho's reports, ordered state police from Puebla to kidnap Cacho. Things went badly for Cacho, but she escaped with her life and fled to the U.S. for security. It is also common for children or cousins of politicians to be sequestered just prior to elections in an attempt to affect the outcome. These usually are not reported to the police or by the press. But they are common. The outcome tends not to be fatal. It is seen as a cowardly act but on occasion it has proven effective. In overall numbers, less than 2 per cent of the total kidnappings in Mexico seem to be politically motivated.

The other persistent political kidnappings are perpetrated by radical organizations intent on the overthrow of the federal government. The most active group, the Popular Revolutionary Army (EPR), made up mostly of Oaxacans, Chiapans, and Mexico City Marxists have sequestered more than 90 individuals since 2000. They have collected millions of dollars in ransoms in order to finance their cause. This is the same radical, military group that bombed three natural gas pipelines in 2006 and 2007. There are a number of other Marxist and radical groups which operate independently from the EPR, who employ kidnapping and bombing tactics in an attempt to destabilize both state and federal governments. Most of their activity is in the southern and western states. These, of course, are the most remote, undeveloped, terrain-challenging states in Mexico. They are also the marijuana growing zones in Mexico.

I witnessed the drama of another type of political kidnapping in 2006 while living in Mexico. The business dealings between a retired American developer and a Mexican partner who were developing a beach-front condominium project in Puerto Vallarta turned sour. Both filed lawsuits against the other and the Mexican partner, from Guadalajara was jailed on charges of embezzlement and misuse of funds. He claimed that his American partner had bribed the judge who set bail at five million dollars. For eight months the incarcerated partner mounted an intensive newspaper and email campaign in efforts to secure his release but to no avail. Finally, a certain individual who had given a deposition in favor of the American partner was kidnapped while having dinner with his wife in Puerto Vallarta. She was thrown to the ground but witnessed the abductors as they bashed her husband's head with a mason's hammer. When he was released two months later, barely able to function, the American partner, who had relocated back to the U.S. was assured that masons' hammers were available on both sides of the Rio Grande River. The American partner returned to Mexico, dropped the charges, negotiated a deal with his former partner and got the hell out of town. The police did nothing. Perhaps they had been bribed. Once again, I saw how a retired gringo just about lost his life because he thought he would win, Mexican-style. It is interesting to see these law-abiding, foreign expatriates as they check not only their brains but also their morals at the border. It is amazing to see the large number of Americans who have spent (presumably) their lives abiding by American law change their perspective on lawful behavior after spending six months or a year in Mexico. They develop a casual disregard for the *rule of law*. They cheat on taxes, drive vehicles that have expired American registrations, bribe the local police, neglect to report earned income on rental properties and Mexican business income. They adopt the bribing, tipping, buying of services, which is otherwise known as corruption. It is ubiquitous in Mexico. In general, American expatriates engage in behavior that is not only illegal but unacceptable in the U.S. They become comfortable with the bribe, with the accepted tip for a favor; as if the *rule of law* and the respect for law were an American idiosyncrasy that they need not bother with in Mexico. This lack of respect for the *rule of law* which is common in Mexico has become a disease which seems to infect foreigners who decide to spend even a few months living in Mexico.

At the opposite end of the spectrum from *executive* kidnapping is the phenomenon of *express and ATM* kidnappings which account for probably 60 percent or more of the total kidnapping activity. Somewhere I heard *express* kidnappings referred to as *Applied Economics 101, Mexican-style*. The express and ATM methods are different but are often committed at the same time.

Express kidnappings are generally believed to have originated or become widely popular in Caracas, Venezuela, in 2001. The horrendous economic situation was blamed as the cause. It took very little time for this carcinogen to spread to the other Latin American countries. By 2005, Mexican and especially Mexico City criminals had perfected it to a science or a craft. It has become a new occupation in Mexico City. The methodology is simple, quick, and productive. The targets are middle-class Mexicans. Two or three cohorts or a mini-gang sequester their victims for a short period, typically one to forty-eight hours, and secure whatever cash can be paid in a hurry. The schemes are variable and commonly involve taxis. Taxis drivers are often directly involved or feign engine trouble in a remote or super-busy location and allow the criminals to grab the victims. Mafia networks run hundreds of mini-gangs in Mexico City, whom specialize in this activity. The concept is to grab someone quickly, get a quick payoff, and let the victim live. There is little necessity of infrastructure and the quick payoff is the key. Middle class victims and their families understand the scheme and are quick to make a payoff and end the confrontation. These typically are not brutal or savage encounters. The victims, of course, are robbed, and sometimes driven to ATM machines and forced to make withdrawals.

Thus, the so-called *ATM* kidnappings. It is another super popular sequestration scheme in the large cities such as Mexico City, Juárez, Tijuana, Guadalajara, Monterrey, and coastal tourist cities such as Cancun, Ixtapa, and Acapulco. Anyone with apparent wealth or middle-class means is a target. People are apprehended in taxis, at ATM machines, walking along sidewalks, anywhere. They are forced at gunpoint to reveal PIN numbers and are held captive while withdrawals are made. When the daily limit is exceeded the victims are typically released. It is very common for victims to be grabbed late at night, and then maximum withdrawals are made before and after midnight. With frequency, two people are grabbed and one is held hostage while the other is taken on a withdrawal spree. The vast majority of the *ATM* and *Express* kidnappings are not reported by the victims to the police. The assailants often threaten their victims with continued harassment if they report the occurrence. The victims take the threats seriously knowing that their assailants now have their names, phone numbers, and addresses. The general citizenry is aware of the web-like control the Mexican Mafias have on the large city streets, the complicity of the police forces, and therefore keep their mouths shut. It is a brutal system.

Another segment of kidnappings that is surging, but still in the infant stages, is the *foreigner-expatriate* sequestrations. Hundreds of thousands of Americans, Europeans, and Asians have been retiring to Mexico in the last two decades. A huge number of Californians, Texans, Canadians, East Coasters, and others choose to spend six months in Mexico, and six months back home. There are also the many expatriates working in multinational firms in the electronic, automotive, food, and tourist industries, just to name a few. As large numbers of foreigners relocate to Mexico, they are followed by the hordes of foreign real estate professionals as well. And more commonly we are seeing the arrival of younger, high-tech professionals who have the luxury to live anywhere in the world as they carry their offices in their laptops wherever they go. The retired expatriates and those that have the flexibility are choosing the garden spots of Mexico in which to relocate. Some of the most popular spots are up and down the Baja peninsula, along both the Pacific coast and the Sea of Cortés. Tropical, beautiful beach towns such as Mazatlán, Puerto Vallarta, Acapulco, and Zihuatanejo are located along its two thousand five hundred miles of Pacific coastline. Some of the smaller, undeveloped, beach towns are as pristine as they were before the arrival of Hernán Cortés, just fabulous! Other jewels are located inland in the mountains.

Cobble-stoned, colonial towns such as San Miguel de Allende are super popular because of their tranquility, livability, cost, and fantastic weather. The combination of six thousand, five hundred feet of altitude with a dry, mountain terrain located two hundred and fifty miles below the Tropic of Cancer yields a climate which is delightful year-round. Approximately ten thousand expatriates and retirees from around the world have relocated to San Miguel de Allende. More than one hundred thousand live in the surrounds of Guadalajara. The Mexican government believes there are a quarter of a million expatriates and foreign retirees living in Mexico. The vast majority are affluent if not very wealthy.

Their arrival in large numbers over the last ten years has not gone unnoticed. The criminals and kidnappers are beginning to realize what an easy target they present. The vast majority are wealthy, at ease, and unfamiliar with their surroundings. Ninety percent do not speak the language. According to Calderon's newly created Mexican Kidnapping Division they are the perfect target and are being grabbed in increasing numbers. This segment will probably grow faster in the next few years than any of the others. These expatriates present an easy target for robberies and burglaries as well as kidnapping. Until mid-2008 the forecasted numbers of retired baby boomers with aspirations of relocating to Mexico was literally in the millions. This, of course, was also being forecasted as a very positive growth potential for many Mexican towns and cities. But with the current epidemic in kidnappings, violent drug war, and world economic downturn these forecast are being drastically changed. Mexico is witnessing the beginning of both people and capital flight. Tourism in 2008 was down as much as seventy per cent in some areas. The kidnapping of tourist and expatriates as well as the daily violence is the reason. News travels fast. In San Miguel de Allende, where the second largest expatriate community lives, an estimated thirty percent or more of the perennial and full-time expatriates have returned home to the U.S. and Canada. Many are too fearful to return to Mexico and the real estate market is flooded with their unsold properties. Occupancy rates at hotels, bed and breakfasts, and luxury-home rentals were down more than sixty per cent in 2008 over 2006. The first quarter of 2009 showed the same downward trend. Fear which is fomented in part by brutal kidnappings is one of the reasons.

Baja California is suffering even more than San Miguel de Allende, Querétaro, and other mountain locations with more than two hundred reported kidnappings in the first six months of 2008. Remember, only 10 to 20 percent of all kidnappings are being reported. Of these two hundred, twenty-six are confirmed American citizens. More than fifty Americans were kidnapped in Baja California in 2007 and early 2008. The FBI is handling the investigations and of course, will not comment on the status of the cases other than to verify that the number of twenty-six for the first half of 2008 is accurate. It has become so dangerous in the Baja peninsula that the organizers of the world-famous Baja 1000 off-road race seriously considered cancelling the event. The one thousand mile race from Ensenada to La Paz has been held for forty-one consecutive years but is in jeopardy of being scrapped. One thousand miles of off-road security is impossible to insure under the current circumstances. The Baja kidnappers are organized, well-financed cells who are tracking the perennial movement of San Diego County residents who vacation, spend part of the year down south, or have businesses in Tijuana. Criminal headquarters and ransom houses are in Tijuana, Rosarita Beach, and Ensenada. The FBI, San Diego office, equates them to terrorist cells. They are typically structured with four groups, one for scouting, another makes the abduction, a third guards the victim, and the fourth handles the negotiations. A few random tourists have been kidnapped but the kidnappers are more focused on targets who return to the Baja routinely. The Americans are being identified, profiled, tracked, followed, and abducted. It is sophisticated and it works.

Another sophisticated and well organized form of kidnapping is the narco kidnappings. The reason this is a unique, identifiable, and new type of kidnapping is because the kidnappers are narco-traffickers who have turned to kidnapping. This activity is completely separate from the historical kidnapping scene that has grown so large in the last ten years. This is a new segment with completely different players. As would be expected, the majority of the activity is along the border with the U.S. Authorities believe that the successful prosecution of Calderón's drug-war is forcing narcotic traffickers to seek income from new sources. Kidnapping is a logical new market for these drug-thugs. "Corporate security experts estimate that drug gangs are now responsible for 30 to 50 kidnappings a day in Mexico and the ransoms often run to $300,000 if the victim is returned alive. They often hold several victims at a time." "The *Narco-kidnappers* are not looking for chump change," said Felix Batista, a Miami-based corporate-security and crisis-management consultant who's negotiated the releases of dozens of kidnapping victims throughout Mexico. It's a pretty darn good side business."[5] Unfortunately, these narcotic traffickers are turning to an array of other crimes as well, not only kidnapping. Crime rates in extortion and auto theft are up as much as 50 and 60 percent in the Mexican border cities of Tijuana and Juárez from 2006 to 2008. In another act of blatant disregard for the *rule of law*, twenty-seven peasants were abducted from a small village in the state of Sinaloa on November 11, 2008. Their families said they were kidnapped in order to work in the marijuana fields which are obscured in the regions coastal forests. When the incident was initially reported by the Mexican and American press the local police had neither apprehended the narco kidnappers nor located the victims. Later reports suggested that many of the kidnapped farm workers had escaped and wandered back home.

The other new phenomenon is taking place in the U.S. Mexicans kidnappers are increasingly grabbing American citizens and Mexican immigrants and smuggling them back to Mexico to be ransomed. This brazen activity is probably being carried out by the *narco kidnappers*. Almost never seen in the past, suddenly in 2007 and 2008, Americans are being kidnapped in southern California and Texas and taken to Mexico where they are held for ransom. It is a curious, surprising occurrence that is on the uptick. The assailants easily cross the border from the U.S. back into Mexico, as American agents literally have their backs turned. They are focused on incoming not outgoing traffic. The Mexican customs/border system is random, searching and scrutinizing perhaps one in twenty cars that cross the border headed south. The kidnappers obviously think that the risk of being caught as they cross the border is very low. Kidnappers are caught and prosecuted in the U.S. but not in Mexico. Eighty five per cent of the time, kidnappers are apprehended and prosecuted in the U.S. In Mexico it is the reverse. Eighty-five to ninety-five percent of the cases are never solved and the criminals are never apprehended. The small percentages of narcotic traffickers that are apprehended typically bribe their way out of prosecution. The Mexican government effectively prosecutes only one or two crimes out of every hundred that are committed. The U.S. border patrol is also behind the curve on this activity and has yet to make any serious attempt to modify their exit checkpoints along the border. In 2008 the FBI confirmed thirty abductions in southern California since late in 2007, and eleven more in Texas of American citizens. They suspect that the number of Mexican expatriates who have been abducted in these border regions and taken back to Mexico is three or four times higher than that of U.S. citizens. The skills, networks, logistics, and operational savvy that these transnational drug smugglers possess make the shift to international kidnapping an easy transition.

The tendency of narcotic traffickers to use kidnapping as a tool of intimidation is spreading north as well. In October, 2008, three Mexican nationals dressed as Las Vegas policeman kidnapped six year old Cole Puffinburger from his Las Vegas, Nevada home. His mother was gagged, tied, and left with a message for her father, Cole's grandfather, Fred Tinnemeyer, a Riverside, California drug-dealer. The police in Riverside, after arresting Tinnemeyer, uncovered the facts in the case. Tinnemeyer was hundreds of thousands of dollars in debt to his Mexican wholesale drug suppliers. In an attempt to recoup their money the drug traffickers sequestered his innocent grandson. This type of activity is common in Mexico, and unfortunately is spreading to the U.S. border-states and beyond. These thugs have absolutely no respect for international borders and are increasingly proving their willingness to illegally cross the U.S. border in order to maintain their brutal control of the drug trade. "U.S. drug czar John Walters said Friday (October 10, 2008) that Mexico's drug cartels are crossing the border to kidnap and kill inside the United States, and promised that an anti-drug aid package to help Mexico to fight the gangs will be ready soon." "Some of these groups not only engage in crime and violence in Mexico and along the border, but they come across and kidnap, murder and carry out assassinations inside the U.S.," Walters told reporters." "These groups do not respect the border."[6]

The other sequestering activity that is worth mentioning in association with the *narco kidnappers* is seen in the internecine warfare between the drug cartels. Gang members, cartel employees, drug soldiers, narcotic traffickers, mafia enforcers, hoodlums, and criminals, whatever name is appropriate, are grabbed by opposing combatants whenever possible. The captured are routinely tortured, mutilated, and then dumped in some public place. As the fighting has intensified among the cartels in 2007 and 2008, so has the brutality. The decapitated, tongue-less bodies that are turning up in Tijuana, Juárez, Merida, and elsewhere, accompanied with notes, were all kidnap victims. One of the most recent occurrences was a group of twenty-five men who had been kidnapped, executed with a bullet to the back of the head, and then dumped in La Marquesa, a nature park on the outskirts of Mexico City, in September of 2008. Their assailants were not interested in ransom but revenge and advantage. The authorities do not include these body counts in the upward spiraling numbers of kidnapping. But, they were kidnapped victims nonetheless.

The fear that has gripped the nation has spawned yet another type of kidnapping. It is the avant-garde, new craze in kidnapping criminality. Believe it or not, we have entered the age of *virtual* kidnapping. The populace is so fearful, there are so many opportunities, there is such little faith in the authorities, that a mere phone call can illicit the same results as an actual kidnapping. The activity associated with this new crime wave is staggering. "A new hot line set up to deal with the problem of kidnappings in which no one is actually kidnapped received more than 30,000 complaints from last December (2008) to the end of February 3, Joel Ortega, Mexico City's police chief, announced recently." "This reflects the fear in Mexican society, the collective psychosis about kidnapping," said one journalist, who succumbed to the crime herself. "If you think there's any chance that it's your child, you play along."[7] And thousands are playing along with the criminals. One report in Mexico City estimates that more than twenty million dollars was paid to virtual kidnappers in the first six months of 2008.

The targets and activity can be categorized along two fronts in this virtual kidnapping segment. One is the border. The U.S. Border Patrol has made it difficult enough for illegal aliens to cross the border that the majority are forced to use smugglers. The illicit trip to a safe haven in Texas or Arizona takes three to four days. The virtual kidnappers are using this as a window of opportunity in which to contact family members and extort ransom. In some cases the families are being extorted in Mexico, while others are being extorted in the states. The smugglers are participating in this virtual kidnapping activity or in many cases they are selling lists of names and phone numbers to those who practice virtual kidnapping. Immigrant smugglers are selling direct marketing lists to the virtual kidnappers. Information on Mexicans crossing the border seems to be in demand and available. Perhaps marketing lists are even somehow being generated out of the American embassy offices in Mexico City.

Drug cartel employees or drug-spies have been arrested working inside the American embassy as well as the Mexican anti-drug offices, so it is not far-fetched to believe that organized crime has the ability to acquire U.S. visa information. In August of 2008, a friend of mine moved from Mexico City to the U.S. As in the past, he acquired a one year visa for Maria, his son's nanny. It is quite easy for an American expatriate to sponsor and help obtain a visa for a Mexican national. He had done this before but found it particularly easy this time. It appears that the Bush administration decided in 2008, to make it easier for Mexicans to immigrate legally. The Consul in Mexico City practically rubber-stamped tens of thousands of applications. Anyway, shortly after he arrived in the States, he received a frantic phone call from Maria's father. He was freaked! Someone had placed a call to his workshop and convinced him that Maria had been kidnapped. The would-be extorters used the methodology that is common in this business. First, a woman (supposedly Maria) screamed, 'Papa, Papa!' into the phone. A husky male voice then insulted her father telling him all the brutal things he would do to Maria if he did not have the ransom by noon. Fortunately, Maria was not in the hands of kidnappers, but, wow! It was very interesting. Perhaps the virtual kidnappers somehow have access to visa and exit information at the U.S. Embassy in Mexico City, or someone who knew her plans in Mexico City made the call, or her father received a call in error. The caller gave him no specifics that would confirm that he really knew anything about Maria's trip to the north. No one is sure of the origin of the call. In any case it is just one more indication of the large volume of activity associated with this new craze

The second target for the *virtual* kidnappers seems to be any parent that can be reached by phone while a child is temporarily out of touch. Just recently, a group of more than a dozen Congressmen in Mexico City received threatening phone calls while they were in session. They were so alarmed that they cancelled the daily proceedings in order to investigate the situation only to find that the calls had been placed to their numerically sequential office phones. There seems to be no end to the schemes, lists, and absurdities surrounding this activity. The good news is that the kidnappings are not real. The bad news is that Mexico has deteriorated into such a state of lawlessness that even the suggestion that a child has been kidnapped, regardless of the parent's economic standing, is believable. The tens of thousands of virtual kidnappings are also not included in the official statistics on kidnapping.

Whatever the method, whatever the outcome, the thousands of kidnappings, coupled with its other problems are pushing Mexico towards failure. Mexican authorities are struggling to provide basic safety to its citizenry, foreign immigrants, and tourists. As a result, President Calderón has signed up for General Petraeus' surge strategy. He knows that in order to stop the kidnappings he must defeat the drug cartels, organized crime, and reestablish order throughout the republic. It is easy to draw a parallel between Calderón's strategy in Mexico with Bush's surge strategy in Iraq. Both programs started in January of 2007. Bush sent in an additional 20,000 army combat troops and 4,000 marines. Calderón likewise authorized 40,000 army combat troops and 5,000 federal police to be sent into the warring, border zones of Tijuana and Juárez as well as the mountains of Michoacán and Guerrero. After two years, many analysts believe Bush's strategy is beginning to reap rewards. On the other hand, Calderón's strategy has caused a tenfold increase in kidnappings and a violent surge in gang warfare. The response of organized crime was predictable in nature but not in numbers. This new, exploding trend in kidnapping was not.

Calderón's plan established anti-kidnapping departments in each of Mexico's thirty one states. General David Petraeus' goal in the Iraqi surge was to create independent zones (or states) that can govern themselves, defend themselves against lawlessness, sustain themselves by developing honest police units, and then guarantee the peace and security of the citizenry. Calderón has the same challenge. He must purge the police departments of corrupt officers, and create a climate in which officers will enforce the law and not turn to criminality. In September of 2008, more than one hundred and fifty thousand people marched in Mexico City demanding an immediate government response to this onslaught of kidnappings which were expected to reach 10,000 in 2008. Many carried banners that read, "Enough, we cannot take anymore!" The same marchers crowded the Mexico City main square in 2004, carrying banners that read "Enough, we cannot take anymore!" An estimated five thousand victims were kidnapped that year. Now it has doubled in four years. Calderón has implemented his strategic surge, but if it fails, Mexico will continue to be a lawless, failed state with the despicable title and reputation of **KIDNAPPING CAPITAL OF THE WORLD**.

IX

The Cancerous Violence of Mexico's Drug War
and Its Pandemic Spread to the U.S.

This is the part of the book where adults are advised to send the kids to bed or at least out of the room. The material that is about to be presented should be read with viewer discretion as it contains subject matter which should disturb you. It will illicit alarm, disdain, disgust, and outrage. I write this introduction in order to create the atmosphere that is normally associated with television documentaries on the starving, raped, abused millions in Darfur, the mutilated, hacked-to-death countless in Rwanda, or the genocide taking place in the Congo. This story of Mexico's drug war is that dark, that bleak, and in many ways more brutal. And it is just across the street, on the other side of the river, just there -- a few miles through the desert. As a matter of fact, the brutality has oozed across the border into some of our own cities and neighborhoods. For a non-militarized zone, the Mexican-American border as a result of the drug war has become one of the scariest, dangerous, and most heavily-armed regions in the world. The combined armed forces of the American CBP, ICE, FBI, DEA, Navy, Coast Guard, local police, state police, state national guard, private militias, and the Mexican Army, Navy, special drug police, preventative police, Mexican local and state police, armed cartel paramilitary groups, armed cartel, organized criminals, and thugs probably totals more than 250,000 armed personnel.

An all-out-drug war is waging in Mexico. Yes, there is/has been a war going on in Mexico for more than two years! As strange as it may be, a war is going on just across the southern U.S. border and it was not reported with much verve in the American press until the Spring of 2009. The American was just not interested. Mr. Independent, as he likes to be known, Lou Dobbs, however, has been an exception in the American press on this issue. His program stays focused on the dangers that are obviously associated with Mexico's drug war as well as illegal immigration. His right-wing attitude may not be palatable to many but his program has consistently been raising the issue of how very dangerous the situation in Mexicao has become over the past few years. There have been more Mexicans killed in the drug war in 2008, than all of the American soldiers that have been killed in Iraq and Afghanistan since those wars started. By year-end (2008), the total body count surpassed six thousand. That is in addition to the non-drug related homicides which will surpass 15,000 for the first time in Mexican history. Together, the two totals promise to push Mexico into the unenviable position of most violent deaths per-capita of any country on the planet. And yet, the U.S. press still reports the activity in a strangely benign manner. Perhaps the fear of retaliation is part of the reason as Mexico has been declared one of the world's most dangerous countries for journalists in 2008. Forty-five journalists have been killed since 2000, and countless others immigrated to the U.S. after receiving death threats. Mexican officials have scarcely investigated the intimidation and killing of journalists as they themselves are under constant threat of reprisals. Not a single suspect has been arrested in the murder investigation of a journalist in 2007 or 2008.

The war officially started in December of 2006, although the battles had been underway for years. Felipe Calderón, who took the presidential oath that month, immediately began mobilizing federal troops and special narcotics divisions in order to fight the drug cartels. By the end of 2008, more than 50,000 federal troops and five thousand drug police had been deployed. The violence that has manifested as a result is intense. The battle lines are obscure as fighting factions compete for billions of dollars of drug-industry money. As is typical in a third-world, corrupt culture the policing authorities are part of the internal drug trade. It is an understatement to say that the conflict is complicated. The U.S. is intimately involved for various reasons. For one, Mexico's drugs are, of course, being exported to the U.S. Although in the last five years Mexico's internal drug industry has sky-rocketed, the U.S. is Mexico's main retail market. The armaments which fuel the conflict, the AK-47s, AR-15s, the highly sought-after, Belgian, cop-killing pistol which shoots an armor-piercing rifle-sized bullet, are being sold along the Texas, California, and Arizona borders then smuggled into Mexico. And lastly, the U.S. government has funded Calderón's battle against drugs to the tune of 400 hundred million dollars via the Mérida Plan.

The major participants of the war are: the Mexican drug cartels, the paramilitary groups that have become their mercenaries, the local and state police (who are often members or business associates of the cartels), federal officials (who are often bribed by the cartels), legitimate businessmen (who launder the dirty money), 50,000 federal troops, President Felipe Calderón and his anti-drug team, the U.S. DHS, the Department of Alcohol, Tobacco, and Firearms (ATF) and the Drug Enforcement Agency (DEA), border city police departments, and other federal U.S. agencies. Not to mention American citizens and illegal immigrants who participate in the distribution and retailing of illicit drugs in the U.S. The DEA reported in March of 2009, that the Mexican drug cartels have operations in 230 cities inside the U.S. The drug war is not a well-defined struggle between the legal authorities and the drug cartels, the good guys versus the bad guys. It is a war that has many fronts and many faces. Any and all real or imaginary alliances take place. The battles are being fought over production, transportation routes (import and export), distribution, retail, money laundering, and security.

The Mexican drug cartels are an ever-morphing conglomeration of organized criminal gangs. Their main industry is the import of illicit drugs into the U.S. Twenty years ago Mexican drug cartels focused on growing and exporting marijuana to the U.S. Mexico is also the major transit country for Bolivian and Colombian cocaine that is smuggled into the U.S. After decades of success the Mexican cartels have expanded their business to include partial control of cocaine production in both Colombia and Bolivia. The Mexican cartels quickly moved into Colombia, after the demise of the Medellín and Cali Cartels during the nineties. They now control virtually all of the illegal importing and transportation of cocaine into Mexico, and its subsequent export to the U.S. They have also expanded, via gangs and illegal immigration networks, northward into the distribution and retailing of cocaine (and heroin) in the U.S. and Canada, as well as most of the other Latin American countries. Their marijuana production capabilities have spread from Mexico, to the U.S., as they are aggressively seizing control of both the distribution and retail channels for this drug as well. Their latest new-growth product is methamphetamine. Many of the sub-components are being imported from China, India, and other Asian countries and then cooked in Mexico. With this drug they are also determined to control the distribution and retail business in the U.S., as well as the production in Mexico. The new consumption trend among Mexican youth has also created a fairly new, fast-growing domestic market for all three drugs. As a naturally occurring add-on business the cartels are also controlling the arms smuggling activity between the U.S. and Mexico. Both Mexican and American authorities have also convicted cartel members for human trafficking, auto theft, and kidnapping.

True understanding of the size and depth of the drug cartels is impossible but the U.S. and Mexican drug enforcers have infiltrated many of the cartels, captured and interrogated cartel members, and pieced together a broad picture of their activities. The Mexican authorities are not as squeamish about torturing their captives as the Americans typically are. Dick Cheney's attitude towards torturing the bad guys is prevalent in Mexico. Human rights abuses are actually a matter of conflict between the two governments. There are at least nine identified major cartels in Mexico: Gulf, Sinaloa, Juárez, Tijuana, Valencia, Millenium, Oaxaca, Beltrán Brothers, and Colima. No doubt there are others. And no doubt by the time this book is published new alliances will have been negotiated and actuated. It is an ever changing scene that thrives on malleability and obscurity. As if straight out of a Mafia movie, the major cartels have formed two alliances or federations which are in opposition to each other. One, known only as *The Federation* consists of the Sinaloa, Juárez, and Valencia cartels. Their arch rivals are aligned under the banner of *The Gulf Federation* and include the Gulf, Tijuana, and Beltrán Brothers.

The alliances and definitions of the various cartels are constantly changing as members are captured, killed, or bribed into changing allegiances.

As the Mexican and American authorities combat the cartels, the violence escalates both between the authorities and the cartels as well as between the cartels and federations themselves. The pressure that is applied by the authorities often opens windows of opportunities for the federations or individual cartels. For example, when the Arellano brothers, founders of the Tijuana cartel, were recently caught and extradited to the U.S, their rivals in the Sinaloa cartel launched brutal attacks against the Gulf Federation sensing a weakness. Just like in the movies these blatant aggressions are countered with defensive, retaliatory killing sprees from the competition. In these cases the press often report on the discontent within the public over the government's inability to curb cartel violence. This is ironic; the government's direct confrontation with the cartels causes an escalation in violence. It is a complicated business. Mexican officials are corrupt and have participated with the cartels for decades in this industry. Policemen, soldiers, and feds are members of the cartels. Mayors are bribed in order to allow cartels to operate with impunity. Governors are paid to be informers of state police activity. Federal prosecutors become de facto consiglieri or advisors to the cartel leadership. Calderón's drug czar was arrested November 2008, for being on the payroll. Honest cops, soldiers, enforcers, and informants are being killed by the thousands. Those that the cartels cannot bribe are terrorized, threatened, or killed. If the cartels cannot get to a particular cop they will go after his family. Even families and individuals who have fled to the U.S., to escape violence have been tracked down and killed in the U.S. This violence respects no international boundaries.

The two federations probably control more than 80 percent of the illegal drug industry. The individual cartels continue to operate independently but in coordination with their federation associates. The Gulf Federation controls the Texas and California border-states of Mexico. The Federation cartels control the rest of the country, theoretically. It is more accurate to think of the federations as having a dominant influence in their respective zones. For example, the Juárez cartel has major organizations in twenty-one of the thirty-one Mexican states. Their associates in the Sinaloa cartel have major operations in seventeen Mexican states. The two dominant Gulf Federation members, the Tijuana and Gulf cartels, operate in fifteen and thirteen states respectively. Together they also have established organizations (known and cataloged by federal U.S. agencies) in more than forty-five cities across thirty states in the U.S. In most of the major drug-cities of Mexico, such as Mexico City, Juárez, Tijuana, Morelia, Matamoros, and Monterrey, multiple cartels have organizations in place competing for larger percentages of the business. This competition as well as the pressure being applied by Calderón to eradicate the drug industry drives the violence.

As the industry has grown into a 50 billion dollar a year (wholesale) endeavor, the cartels have developed a sub-industry of professional enforcers. I think back to the line in The Godfather movie when the Turk tells Robert Duvall that bloodshed is not what he wanted at all. The cost of blood is expensive he said. In Mexico blood is cheap. There is no prevailing concept of avoiding an all-out war among the cartels. It has become an all-out war, all the time, and the violence claimed more than 6,300 in 2008; another 1,000 lives have been lost in the first two months of 2009. The need for brutality has grown so large that the federations have established various paramilitary groups with which to administer the muscle. The concept is different than just having armed thugs on the payroll. These are paramilitary groups that have been trained in the latest techniques, outfitted with the most lethal hardware, and equipped with cutting-edge technology. Two of the most visible, active, and extensive are *Los Zetas*, hired by the Gulf Federation, and *Los Negros*, who work for The Federation. Make no mistake, the cartels have maintained their heavily armed cadres of armed thugs who brutalize and murder by the thousands. The paramilitary groups are focused on specific terror and turf battle operations. They are also skilled in coordinated assassinations and kidnappings.

The Zetas were formed in 1998, under the direction of Osiel Cárdenas, godfather of the Gulf cartel. He recruited Arturo Guzmán, a lieutenant in the Mexican Airborne Special Forces

Group (GAFE). GAFE is an elite special-forces arm of the Mexican Army. Their personnel are trained in state-of-the-art techniques. They are intelligent, motivated, highly-trained, killing machines. They are known as the best anti-drug commandoes in the Mexican special-forces. Cárdenas paid Guzmán to convince thirty of his companions to desert GAFE and form his personal body guard and elite assassination corp. As a result of the brutal, unorthodox methods employed by the Zetas (even for organized crime) Cárdenas' Gulf cartel rapidly grabbed market share and expanded its influence in more than thirteen states nationwide. The Zetas recruited more members from GAFE, ex-Kaibiles (the Guatemalan Army special-forces unit), and discontent Mexican military, local, state, and federal police. They established training bases in the dense jungles of the southern Mexican state of Chiapas. It is reported that training camps were also activated in Guerrero, Michoacán, and Oaxaca. The Zetas never had intentions of growing into a large force. It was always about elitism, quality, controlled missions and success. By 2003, their reputation had reached international attention as a result of their savage, brutal, and heinous decapitations and unworldly torture methods. They gained popularity with poor, malcontent, youngsters everywhere in Latin America. It has become widely popular for children to taunt bullies with threats of retaliation from their Zeta fathers. Many children have adopted Zeta nicknames which had been published in the press. Although there were probably never more than 500 members, their violent exploits began to be copied and employed by thugs everywhere. Many aspiring criminals now claim to be Zetas although they are not.

The popularity of the Zetas among youngsters reflects the strange obsession the Mexican culture has always had for the macabre, savage, brutal side of life. It is a holdover from their barbaric, Aztec past. Young criminals began to emulate what they perceived as Zeta behavior and seem to have lost all regard for the value of human life. Many experts believe the Zeta activity may have never been responsible for more than a few hundred brutal murders each year over the past decade. But their legacy and continuing presence has produced a drug-cartel culture that wantonly maims, tortures, and murders thousands each year. The common drug-thug from Culiacán, Sinaloa, may not be the elite, specialized, high-tech, savvy, Zeta special forces, super-hero, turned bad-ass enforcer for the drug cartels but he can still pump a competing drug distributor full of AR-15 armor-piercing bullets, then decapitate him, tie the severed head to its torso, chop-off his hands and bind them to his ankles, scrawl a message with a knife across his belly and prop the victim up against a tree next to a middle-school playground for all the teenagers to see. It does not take a Zeta to do that, just a thug emulating a trend. It is like wearing a baseball cap turned round backwards. Monkey see, monkey do. It is a horrendous trend that President Calderón says is threatening the very fabric of the Mexican state. Not since the Revolution of 1910 has Mexican sovereignty and democratic viability been so severely challenged.

In May of 2008, billboards (laser-produced, fiber posters) began appearing in Nuevo Laredo, with the intention of enticing police and military officers to desert and join the Zetas. The ads promised higher wages, family health care, signing bonuses, and good food. As a matter of fact some of the ads targeted the ramen noodle soup that is commonly served in military kitchens. The banners or ads were strung from overpasses along city streets. Many critics claim that the ads were the Zetas simply showing their middle finger to President Felipe Calderón. In any event, the ads (photos of the banners) were/are plastered across front page newspapers whenever they appear. They have become the drug cartels most effective method of communicating with the masses and the government. The public relations aspect of the ads was so great that an ongoing communication campaign using this technique has sprung-up in Michoacán, Sinaloa, Guerrero, Oaxaca, Querétaro, and the federal district. The drug cartels are using public relations or advertising tactic to threaten, claim victories, recruit personnel, and as is so often said in military circles these days to win hearts and minds.

Heriberto Lazcano, the current leader of the Zetas, prefers to win friends and influence enemies by defining new levels of barbarism. He spreads fear by murdering his victims in public, preferably in front of their young children. His most despicable habit may possibly be the feeding of some of his victims' beheaded torsos to his collection of exotic cats which he keeps at various hideouts. Not Persians or sweet little calicos but pumas, jaguars, and imported Bengal tigers and Serengeti lions. Although rumors which detailed these gruesome feedings surfaced in 2005, the authorities were never able or willing to successfully find any of his hidden ranches where the cats were kept. Then suddenly in the summer of 2008, a raid on a drug-mansion in Mexico City, turned up, among a group of narco-traffickers, tons of marijuana, kilos of cocaine, a virtual harem of young women, and a private cat collection with superb jaguars, pumas, and tigers. In the fall another beautiful home was busted in upscale Lomas in Mexico City. Tons of drugs, suitcases of millions of dollars of cash were found along with another private, big-cat collection.

The press reported the two stories with initial bewilderment. Evidently they were not aware of the rumors that had been on the streets for quite some time. They attributed the big-cat collections to opulence, excess of money. Others could see the tell-tale signs of Lazcano's involvement. When I first read of the initial bust and the cache of pumas and jaguars, I thought not only of the reports about Lazcano but also of Hernán Cortés' account of the Mexican capital of Tenochtitlán in 1523. Or was it his stalwart scribe Bernal Díaz's account? What they discovered after they re-conquered Tenochtitlán (Mexico City) was that the Aztecs kept a large zoo in the city which housed tens of pumas and jaguars. With further investigation they discovered that the Aztecs, after they had beheaded their victims, dismembered and eaten their legs and arms, would often feed the remaining torsos to their jaguars and pumas. The zoo was full of gnawed and pummeled human ribcages.

In the world of organized crime brutality has been met with brutality. In response to Cárdenas' forming of the Zetas, Shorty Guzman, godfather of the Sinaloa cartel, initiated The Federation's recruitment of two separate paramilitary groups, the Negros (the Black Ones) and the Pelones (the Baldies). Both groups received state-of-the-art armaments. They, like the Zetas, are better equipped and better trained than the Mexican army and police forces. Their mission was to attack, kill, kidnap, torture, and coerce the police in the Gulf strongholds in an attempt to change their allegiances. Although not formally trained as soldiers, these two groups have wreaked havoc, killed thousands, and made Shorty Guzman the most wanted criminal in Mexico. The U.S. Drug Enforcement Administration (DEA) has an outstanding offer of 5 million dollars for his capture. His tactics are gruesome but effective. Those police he cannot bribe are kidnapped, tortured, beheaded, and displayed in a public place with a personal note attached to their cadavers for other would-be-honest officers. Competing members of the Gulf Federation, on Guzman's orders, are tracked down in their homes, followed on vacations to the beautiful Pacific beach towns or high Sierra mountain resorts and gunned down like vermin. Wives, children, nannies, and friends are slaughtered along with the targeted victims in an attempt to spread as much fear as possible among his rivals. Once again, in the perverted Mexican sense of reality, Shorty Guzman is written about in the Mexican press as if he were nothing more than a modern-day, Mexican Robin Hood. The story of his 2001 prison escape has been romanticized hundreds of times in the press as he supposedly had time to: polish off a piece of ass (permitted in Mexican prisons), have a nice hot shower, and take a little nap before he slipped away in a laundry truck. He makes front page news as he frequently dines in famous eateries around the country. Famous Ranchero-style, superstar, musicians such as Los Tucanes de Tijuana and Los Tigres del Norte have recorded hits which not only romanticize his activity and lifestyle but pay tribute to his murderous ways. The words of a song about *El Chapo de Sinaloa*, for example, sarcastically criticizes the authorities for victimizing a corn farmer from Sinaloa, Shorty Guzman, just because he is an international businessman who successfully buys agricultural products from his Colombian friends and then distributes them throughout the U.S. and Europe. This aggrandizing music has become so popular in Mexico, that it is now considered a specific genre called *narco-corrido music* and its stars are routinely hired to play at events sponsored by the drug cartels. The point that this illustrates is simple. The drug industry, the cartels, the narco foot-soldiers, the drug growers, importers, shippers, money-laundering businesses, bribed authorities, extorted businesses, musicians, music companies, and so many, many more have become an acceptable and important part of the Mexican culture and economy. Mexico has embraced and accepted organized crime as part of their culture.

The problem of youth idolization of super-rich, narcotic traffickers has become an epidemic. In Tijuana and Juárez, the two most violent cities, outside of Mexico City, with over 840 and 1,800 drug murders in 2008, respectively (as wells as 17,000 car thefts and 1,650 car-jackings in Juárez in 2008) many Mexican kids have become desensitized to violence. The cartels learned years ago that their most fertile recruiting grounds were the areas where poor teenagers live. In an attempt to further degrade the moral fabric of Mexico, and thereby create fodder for the ranks of their foot soldiers the assassins began dumping bodies near elementary and middle schools in 2006. The disfigured bodies of hundreds of executed gang members have been systematically placed along routes to inner-city schools with attached notes glorifying the killers, the drug trade, and disrespecting the establishment. Young teenagers have not only become desensitized to the brutal violence but accustomed to it. They follow the stories of Shorty Guzman and the Zetas, the Negros, the Pelones in the press, in the rumor mill; they dance to the ballads, envision an escape from their pitiful existence and become easy recruits for the organized gangs. They are more than willing to illegally immigrate to the U.S., in order to work in a drug network. The fact that Shorty Guzman appears on the Forbes Magazine "Ten Most Wanted Fugitives" list in 2008, and its annual list of the world's richest people in March 2009, with an estimated fortune of 1 billion dollars, does not go unnoticed by his competition or the young punks in the barrios. The drug cartels have won the hearts and minds of the miserable misfits of Mexico. It is easy to recruit the millions of young kids who are destitute, whose fathers have split for the U.S., and left them in a dog-eat-dog world to fend for themselves. What other choices do they have?

Many choose the drug cartels because it not only has become acceptable but can be glamorous and very rewarding. That is what Laura Zúñiga Huizar thought. A natural beauty from Culiacán, Sinaloa, she was crowned Miss Sinaloa in the July 2008, Sinaloa beauty contest. It is not known whether she won the crown because of her beauty and talents or because her boyfriend, Ángel Orlando García Urquiza, is a lieutenant in the Juárez cartel. In any case, she travelled to La Paz, Bolivia, in November where she was subsequently crowned Miss Hispanic America. What a surprise! Bolivia is the second largest producer/exporter of cocaine in the world. Maybe her boyfriend Ángel, who accompanied her, was able to do a little business during the Miss Hispanic America contest. Maybe he even pulled a few strings or made a few deals which could not be refused in order to facilitate her winning of the crown. The happy couple returned to Mexico, but they were in for a big surprise. A few weeks later on December 22, their mini-caravan of two SUVs and seven thugs was searched at a routine checkpoint outside of Guadalajara. They apparently ran into a new group of police recruits who busted them in lieu of accepting the normal payoff. They were heavily armed with automatic rifles, pistols, more than 600 hundred rounds of ammunition, sixteen cell phones, and 53,000 U.S. greenbacks. Miss Sinaloa said they were headed for the airport and an eventual Christmas shopping spree in Bolivia and then Colombia. State beauty queen in July, Miss Hispanic America in November, and behind bars in December, Laura was not able to complete her holiday shopping. This is just one more example of how deeply entrenched the drug cartels are in Mexican life. And in the U.S., for once, the story was covered on all the national news programs. It seems that the Mexican drug war rates a little interest in the U.S. press if there is the scandal involved with the arrest of a beauty queen. Scandal, gossip, or sensation, those will get you on the evening news in the U.S. every day. After all, who cares about twenty-five headless cadavers found in a field in some god-forsaken field in the Yucatán?

Perhaps in response to the formation of the Negros and the Pelones, the Zetas moved into the southern state of Michoacán, and formed or organized a southern paramilitary group to do the dirty work of the Gulf Cartel. La Familia, as they are called, are now armed, trained, and pressing the battle for the Gulf Cartel in one of The Federation's strongholds. Morelia, Michoacán is the birthplace of President Felipe Calderón and also one of the largest marijuana producing zones in Mexico. In a brazen attempt of machismo, La Familia upped the stakes of engagement in

September of 2008. During the annual celebration of national independence, La Familia commandoes lobbed grenades into a crowd of more than 100,000 innocent civilians. Eight were killed and another 150 were evacuated to the hospital. The Gulf Cartel had decided to do more than show there middle finger to Felipe Calderón in public. The message was clear. The cartels had taken the battle to their enemies, to the police, to the military, and with frequency innocent civilians are killed. But now La Familia was announcing the Gulf Cartel's intentions of introducing terrorism in their fight against Calderón. The cartels kidnap innocent civilians for ransom and coercion which is certainly a form of terrorism, but lobbed grenades in a public square is something new in Mexico. It is a sign of the further deterioration of the rule of law. It indicates that the cartel leaders will fight this battle to the end if Calderón persists. Nothing is sacred. They have no qualms in murdering innocent civilians in order to win.

Calderón's response was very defiant. He immediately dispersed more federal troops to Michoacán and reaffirmed his commitment to destroying the illegal drug industry in Mexico. In response the cartels went on a three month killing spree that compares to nothing seen previously in this war. In a five-day period from December 12th through the 16th, sixty-two bodies were brought to the Juárez morgue causing the director to close the doors and initiate a waiting list program. All of the victims were the result of multiple gunshot wounds and stabbings. The entire state of Chihuahua, where Juárez is the largest border city, is in a state of war. In the state of Chihuahua, Calderón launched a counterattack dubbed *Operation Chihuahua Together*. He sent in additional troops to not only the border cities but to the drug growing and cocaine transporting areas in the Sierra Tarahumara Mountains. The Juárez cartel responded immediately. In these remote mountainous areas west of the capital of Juárez City, Chihuahua, marijuana and opium poppies are grown. There are also hidden airfields and warehouses where Colombian cocaine is shipped and stored on its way to the U.S. It is also the home to Mexico's most stunning natural landscape, the Copper Canyon.

The Copper Canyon at 6,136 feet deep compares to the Grand Canyon and is actually somewhat deeper. It is a spectacular place.

In 1985, I took the canyon train which climbs out of Chihuahua City, going westward into the Sierra Mountains. After traversing the various ridges along the rim of the canyon, stopping at a number of remote towns, it descends to the Pacific Ocean at Los Mochis which is across the Sea of Cortés from La Paz. What a trip that was! It is one of the most beautiful serene trips anywhere. Many visitors stay in one of the lodges at the small towns or along the rim and take fantastic hikes down into the river bottom which is more than a mile below the rim. The beauty, silence, and tranquility of the canyon disguise the danger that lies hidden in the remote mountains. Thinking back on that magical train ride, through some of the most incredibly brilliant terrain in the world, it is hard to believe what has become of the Sierra Tarahumara and the Copper Canyon surrounds.

On August 15, 2008, a group of young adults with their children gathered at an outdoor restaurant to dance and dine. The little town of Creel was even quieter than normal as the newly arrived troops who were participating in Operation Chihuahua Together had left the center of town to investigate a narcotics lead. Quietly, three black SUVs parked along the street adjacent to the party. Twelve men in ski masks armed with AR-15 automatic assault weapons opened fire on the crowd, brutally killing thirteen, including a one-year old baby. Within seconds it was over and the assassins, Zetas, exited as quietly as they had arrived. Strangely, there were no police, no soldiers, and no narcotics special-forces, only a transit policeman arrived on the scene. Most of the victims were family members of Carlos González, the mayor of Creel, who was repudiated to be playing both sides of the drug street. Some locals say he had decided to cooperate with the authorities in Operation Chihuahua Together. It is clear that the majority, if not all, of the bullet-ridden victims had nothing to do with the Gulf Cartel, the mayor's activities, or the government's thrust to stymie the drug business in Creel. They were young, innocent, Mexicans trying to enjoy a Saturday afternoon. They suffered the fate, the misfortune of being related to an official who had been corrupted by the drug trade and of living in a war zone that has been taken over by the drug thugs. I feel sympathy for the family, of course, but I also think of our treasured Grand Canyon, Yosemite, and

Grand Teton National Parks. Will they suffer the same fate as the Copper Canyon? Will their pristine atmosphere be destroyed the way the tranquility has been destroyed in the Sierra Tarahumara? The drug cartels are already cultivating marijuana in our national parks throughout the western and southern U.S. Do we await the same fate as those innocent merrymakers in Creel?

The impact the drug war in Mexico is having on the U.S., can be measured in many ways. The U.S. Justice Department estimates 25 billion dollars in cash from drug sales were smuggled out of the country (U.S.) in 2007. The 2008 number is estimated to be over 30 billion U.S. dollars. The amount of drug money that is laundered and leaves the country is unknown but various agencies including the DEA estimates that the amount of drug money laundered in the U.S. each year is in the hundreds of billions. The percentage of money laundered in the U.S. that makes its way back to Mexico, is unknown but it is considerable. It is another part of that *Giant Sucking Sound* going south again. How does that sound go: 30 billion in drug cash, 50 billion (estimate) in laundered money, 30 billion in remittances, and 75 billion NAFTA trade deficits. That is 185 billion dollars blowing south to Mexico each year. Remittances and legal trade are not part of the proceeds being generated from the drug war but Ross Perot was certainly right about that Giant Sucking Sound going south. The drug war is impacting the U.S. economy by hundreds of millions of dollars annually in addition to the impact the drug industry is having on the U.S. culture. The overall and specific impact the drug industry has on the U.S., is outside the scope of this chapter and this book.

The crime rates in American cities along the border are skyrocketing. Phoenix has become the second most likely place to be kidnapped next to Mexico City. That is because more than 350 wealthy Mexicans who fled their country for safety in Phoenix were kidnapped in 2008. Jan Brewer, the governor of Arizona who replaced Janet Napolitano, ordered an additional brigade of Arizona National Guard to the border in March 2009, as violence exploded both across the border and in Arizona border towns. She petitioned Robert Gates, Secretary of Defense, to either send in federal troops or at least to defray the cost of deploying Arizona National Guard in order to secure the border. Rick Perry, governor of Texas, is reported to be quickly following suit as he mobilizes the Texas National Guard. Neither governor wants a militarized border zone but see little alternative in fighting the quickly deteriorating situation in Mexico. Many border agents are fearful of a mass scale (millions) Mexican migration if order is not restored soon.

Another direct impact the war is having on the U.S. can also be seen in the money being allocated by the U.S. government to assist Mexico in its fight against the cartels. If properly managed this could be very positive but it is a very small investment relative to the size of the problem. The U.S. Counternarcotics Assistance Program to Mexico dropped from 34 to 27 million in 2008, in part due to the expected passage of the Mérida Initiative. In June of 2008, the Mérida Initiative which was negotiated between Bush and Calderón in March 2007 was finally signed into law. It is a three-year, 1.6 billion dollar plan which was scheduled to allocate 400 million dollars to Mexico in 2008. In comparison, Afghanistan's anti-narcotics program for 2008, of 1.02 billion was passed without a sixteen month battle in Congress.

It is also interesting to compare the Afghanistan opium industry to that of Mexico's drug industry. Afghanistan produced 90 percent of the world's opium in 2008, which was valued at approximately 1.5 billion dollars at the export level. The GAO believes that fifty percent or more of the opium is consumed in Afghanistan, and its five bordering countries of Iran, Pakistan, Tajikistan, Uzbekistan, and Turkmenistan. The majority of the other fifty percent is distributed to African, Asian, and European countries. The percentage that eventually arrives in the U.S. is so small that the GAO does not even estimate it in tonnage or dollar figures. In other words, the U.S. is spending approximately the same amount of money to fight the opium industry in Afghanistan, as it is the drug industry in Mexico; yet, Afghanistan's opium trade has almost no direct impact on the U.S. other than the fact that it funds the insurgency war in Afghanistan. The U.S. is chasing a 1.5 or 2 billion dollar opium industry in Afghanistan with 1.02 billion tax dollars. At the same time only 1.6 billion dollars over the next three years have been allocated to chase a 50 to 100 billion dollar a year drug industry in our own back yard in Mexico. Not only that, but the 400 million that is earmarked for Mexico will only be released on a conditional basis. For example, 119 million, the first installment was released in December 2008, a full five months after the law was signed into affect because the Mexican Army has been accused of human rights abuses. The 50,000 troops that Calderón has deployed in an attempt to bring law and order to an out-of-control drug zone occasionally bust down doors without search warrants, hold and forcibly interrogate Zeta assassins, and once in awhile screw-up and shoot an innocent citizen. So Congress and U.S. human rights groups denounce them as human rights abusers. If that is not the pot calling the kettle black, I do not know what is. Mexico is guilty of some of the same slip-ups as the U.S. has made in its prosecution of the Iraq and Afghanistan wars. But Mexico has done nothing that comes close to comparing with the abuses meted-out by the Americans at Abu Ghraib or GITMO. Yet, a ridiculous set of standards and values has been placed on Mexican soldiers and drug police who are in the firing line and are now losing thousands of men annually. Hello U.S. Congress, this is not a day-care center. Or as David Byrne would sing, "...this ain't no party; this ain't no fooling around...!" This is a real war!

Another way of measuring the war's impact on the U.S. is to look at the large border cities of El Paso-Juárez, Tijuana-San Diego, and Laredo-Nuevo Laredo. The worst of the three in terms of danger and negative impact upon its citizenry is El Paso-Juárez. These two border cities are in reality one huge concrete jungle. The El Paso part of the jungle is somewhat civilized because the local police, DEA, CBP, ICE, and Texas National Guard are well-equipped, trained, and dedicated to preventing all-out chaos. On January 5, 2009, as blood continued to run on the streets of Juárez, with more than twenty murders since New Year's Day, the city council of El Paso drafted a resolution which condemned the violence, defined the state of lawlessness, and besieged the new Obama government to immediately send more federal aide fearful that the rule of law is on the verge of being lost. The Juárez part of the jungle is already a lawless chaos. It is like Phenom Phen was in the spring of 1975, just prior to the takeover by the Khmer Rouge who eventually executed more than one million fellow Cambodians. In 2008, somewhere between 1800 and 2000

Mexicans were murdered in Juárez. That is fourteen times the homicide of Chicago, which was the 2008 murder capital of the U.S. In a city of approximately one million, homicide was the number-one killer exceeding the total of heart disease, diabetes, and cancer combined. There is enough firepower in Juárez to arm a medium-sized country. As unrealistic as it sounds, Mexican officials believe one to two thousand guns are smuggled into Mexico, from the U.S., every day. The criminals are better equipped, organized, and receive much more money than the Mexican army. Their cartel ranks are reinforced daily by the thousands of illegal immigrants that are repatriated by the CBP and ICE from the U.S. Remember, 33 percent of the illegal immigrants returned to the Mexican border cities by ICE in 2008, were convicted criminals. Approximately 150,000 hard-core criminals (not just immigration infringers) were returned to the border cities of Juárez, Tijuana, Matamoros, and a few others in 2008. These criminals are the foot soldiers of organized crime. During the same two-year period that President Calderón has sent 50,000 troops to the frontlines at the border, organized crime may have been reinforced by more than 150,000 from ICE repatriations. The numbers of criminals who have emigrated from the drug states to the border states to participate in the drug industry is unknown. But it is clearly recognized that the combined Mexican police and army forces are severely out gunned in every aspect of this war.

Juárez is a war zone. Following 2008's violence another 1000 people have been killed in the first two months of 2009. Its police department is a disaster of an organization. Calderón's national police commission dismissed seventy percent of its personnel in 2008, and replaced them with recruits from other states. Police commissioners, directors, captains, and lieutenants are assassinated and kidnapped with such frequency that scarcely anyone can be cajoled into taking leadership positions. The few men that remain on the job are bribed into being spies for the generals of organized crime. In November 2008, for example, Mexico's former anti-drug chief of the Specialized Investigation of Organized Crime department (SIEDO), Noé Ramírez Mandujano, was arrested on suspicion of passing information to and accepting more than 450,000 dollars from the Beltrán Leyva drug cartel. Anyone doing business in Juárez is subjected to extortion by the drug cartels. The criminals are not just smuggling drugs, they are running the city. Their mercenaries, the Zetas, murder or terrorize anyone that does not succumb to their extortion. Hundreds of police officers and army troops have been killed and beheaded. The Mexican newspaper reporters who had the guts to cover the violence have been killed, have gone into hiding in the U.S., are missing, or have agreed not to cover organized crime. Entire blocks of real estate which front the border with El Paso have been grabbed by the cartels and are used as fronts for tunnels. It is a more sophisticated system than that which exists along the Egyptian border in Gaza and is highlighted in the press. On this subject, it is interesting to compare Israel's response to Hamas' lobbing missiles into southern Israel with the U.S.'s response to a more treacherous threat from the Mexican drug cartels. The U.S. government and press are more fixated on the Israeli-Arab conflict than they are on the American-Mexican conflict. It is astounding to watch CNN's sensational coverage of the Hamas tunnel network on the Egyptian border and realize their lack of interest and coverage of the U.S. border. The amount of contraband and weapons which are smuggled into Gaza each year pales in comparison with the billions of dollars of illegal drugs, weapons, cash, and people that are smuggled over the Mexican-U.S. border each year. Yet, each day, the national press whips each other into a frenzy over the Palestinian issue, and turns a blind eye to the huge problem along the U.S. border. They spend millions of dollars with camera crews and reporters covering Hamas' tunnels into Gaza, but refuse to get serious about covering Mexico.

But why cover Mexico when the oil is in the Middle East? It is a no brainer. The U.S. must stay focused on protecting Israel, covering the Israel's political situation, and supporting Israel because they are the U.S.' only ally in the region where all the oil is located. Correct? Wrong! Mexico is the second largest producer of oil that is imported into the U.S. Canada takes the first place and Saudi Arabia is third. Of the top fifteen countries from which the U.S. imports oil or oil products, Iraq is the only other Middle Eastern country that makes the list. That is right. There are only two Middle Eastern countries are on the list of the U.S.' top fifteen oil producing partners. Mexico exports 1.5 million barrels of oil a day to the U.S., while Iraq exports only 400,000 barrels to the U.S. Yet, Mexico, the U.S.'s southern neighbor along a two thousand-mile border, second largest producer of American energy requirements, exporter of 50 billion dollars of illegal drugs, exporter of 15 million illegal immigrants, and a country on the brink of civil chaos and the U.S. government and the U.S. press stay focused on Hamas shooting missiles some 12 miles into a Israeli, desert communities. The American press as of January 2009, and prior to Obama's taking the oath, have prioritized his two most urgent missions as president. The first is to right the foundering economy and the second is to sort out the peace between the Palestinians and the Israelis. In addition to the press's short sightedness, the Obama transition team did not mentioned the war in Mexico, and its deleterious effects on the U.S., in a single public communication. It is as if the American government and the American press do not realize the gravity of the situation in Mexico. Finally in April of 2009 while this book was in the editorial stage, Obama and the press started focusing on Mexico.

Juárez is a war zone. The battles are being fought over the American illegal drug market, kidnapping, and organized crime in all of its ugly aspects. This is a real war with severe consequences in the United States, yet the national press seems uninterested in covering the story. The crime, the disrespect for rule of law, is saturating the border and infecting El Paso, San Diego, Laredo, all the border towns and cities. Having lost faith in the authorities attempt to restore safety, order, and law in Juárez, a group of citizens began circulating an email on the Eve of Christmas begging the narcotic traffickers, the lieutenants of organized crime, the mercenary Zetas, and the crime bosses to please give their beleaguered city two days of respite in which to worship and celebrate a few hours of peace. Unfortunately, on Christmas Eve, twelve more headless bodies were dumped on the route where the religious parade in Chilpancingo, Guerrero, was scheduled to pass. And in Juárez the bodies of two soldiers which had been decapitated were discovered with an accompanying note that warned Calderón that for every cartel member lost in the war ten soldiers or policemen would be executed and beheaded. The authorities removed the cadavers but the blood-stained streets were impossible to clean in anticipation of the passing of the parade of the Blessed Virgin.

What has happened in Juárez and Tijuana is unprecedented. The non-criminal citizenry are afraid to be on the streets at night, have lost trust in law-enforcement officials, and are trying to sellout and move to other Mexican cities or immigrate to the U.S. Life has become a surreal nightmare as headless bodies are deposited for view at elementary schools, ice coolers with heads arrive via express mail service at police headquarters, dismembered corpses in plastic bags litter the soccer fields, and daily gunfire is ubiquitous. Innocent school children, shoppers, and anyone on the streets are subject to random killing. Kidnapping has become so frequent that the authorities are no longer estimating the number of victims much less tracking down suspects. Anyone with a friend, family, or associate in the U.S. could possibly become a target. Decomposing bodies are routinely found in the 55-gallon barrels that are used for disposing of acid and toxic chemicals at the thousands of maquiladoras factories. Highway rest areas and city parks have become unusable dumping grounds of human carnage. In Juárez and Tijuana the battle has morphed from a turf-war between organized criminals to an onslaught against civilization and a drive to completely control the economy. Business and crime have become intertwined as the drug money has been washed or invested in every business imaginable. The El Paso Times newspaper's section, which covers the city of Juárez, is called "Bordering on Fear". The section of the Los Angeles Times that covers Tijuana is called "Mexico Under Siege". Both newspapers understand the danger of covering the Mexican drug war and keep their reporters sequestered north of the border.

The drug-war activity in the cities of Juárez and Tijuana, are currently not being covered in any meaningful way by the local Mexican press. Journalists have basically decided to cover the stories from long distance. Most now reside in their sister, American border-cities. In 2008, the local newspapers and television crews stopped sending their reporters and cameramen to the scenes of violent crime, locations of dumped bodies, or any story which may possibly be linked to organized crime. Reporters were marked by hit men and then either shot or kidnapped. As a result of the vicious and frequent violence against the press, Mexico has been designated by the International Committee to Protect Journalists as one of the most dangerous countries in the world to cover. The Mexican press is completely intimidated and fearful for their lives. The straight, local police officers, army personnel, and federal cops operate under the guise of ski masks, hoods, and bandanas in order to conceal their personal identities. It is that bad! I am not talking about undercover narcotic agents. Every single police authority along the border is in disguise. They are losing the battle against the bad guys and are deathly afraid of losing not only their lives but the lives of their families and friends.

And they have every right to be afraid as the drug cartels are armed to the hilt. The weapons are being smuggled across the border from the U.S. Mexican authorities state that 100 percent of the guns used by the cartels in this war originate in the U.S. Chances are good that this is a valid assessment. The U.S. ban on the sale of assault weapons to individual citizens was dropped in 2004. The result has seen a couple remarkable events. Belgium, Russian, and Chinese imports of inexpensive automatic weapons have soared. So has the trade and sale of these same weapons at gun shows all across the country, particularly in the border states of Texas and Arizona where more than 6700 registered arms retailers have surfaced since the 2004 ban on selling automatic weapons was terminated. That equates to more than one-third of all the guns in the entire country. The so-called wait period which is required for cursory identification and criminal checks in retail stores does not apply at gun shows. A front man for a cartel, for example, can legally buy hundreds of automatic weapons at a gun show on any given day. Eager gun show enthusiasts and traders have quickly recognized this demand for high-tech weaponry and have created a burgeoning industry. The transactions are in cash and few records are required or kept for future investigation or early warning of cartel involvement. El greedo strikes again! The arms race between the cartels is in full bloom and greedy gun sellers are willing to wear highly-tinted sunglasses so as not to recognize the danger.

Smuggling the guns into Mexico is easier than smuggling drugs into the U.S. First of all, the DHS does not have a funded and staffed program for outbound enforcement which stops the outflow of cash and arms from the U.S. They are so focused on securing the border, stopping drug and human trafficking, and stretching a thin budget that U.S. exit security is compromised. It is a matter of short-sighted priorities that is easy to understand. The ATF which has responsibility for combating gun smuggling was only allocated one percent of the 2008 U.S. anti-drug budget. Budget restraints and priorities notwithstanding, this important issue must be addressed sooner rather than later. The reverse, in a sense, is true for the Mexican authorities. The honest police and army personnel that are working for Calderón have their hands full (and more) trying to win the war. They are not focused on shipments coming into Mexico. It is easy to speculate that the vast majority of low-paid customs officials who have the responsibility of safeguarding Mexico's border are corrupt, work for the cartels, or are intimidated into not doing their job. Calderón consistently exhorts the Americans to control the smuggling of cash and arms from the American side as he knows he cannot accomplish this from his side of the border. To date the Americans are not addressing this issue in a meaningful way. Most probable and rational estimates suggest that 30 billion dollars and more than 100,000 arms illegally crossed the U.S. border into Mexico, in 2008. The equation, the setup is very simple. Retail drug sales are generating tens of billions of dollars in cash. The U.S., unlike Mexico, has attacked money laundering schemes and is making it more difficult for the money to be dispersed in the American economy. The cash must be smuggled out of the U.S., and back to Mexico. Highly armed, sophisticated, cartel personnel can, by de facto, control the Mexican side of the border with enough weaponry and violence. American gun sellers provide the weaponry. American drug users supply the cash, and voilà.

Many parallels can be drawn between George W. Bush's wars and Felipe Calderón war. Both Bush and Calderón were elected by the slimmest of margins amidst accusations of fraudulent vote counts. Both entered office beleaguered and quite shortly were in the middle of wars which could possibly be lost. Neither

Bush nor Calderón had a realistic exit strategy or victory plan. Neither president knew the scope of the war or the strength of their respective enemies. Both were and are stuck in disastrous situations. The current situation in Mexico is analogous to the pre-surge situation in Iraq in 2006. Calderón's critics are calling for an end to the war. They believe that the drug industry is tolerable. Some believe it is desirable. Calderón's effort is underfunded and understaffed. His counterparts programs in the various departments of the DHS are also under-budgeted and understaffed. The cartels have gained the upper hand in the two-year conflict. They now confidently and in broad daylight bomb newspaper offices, attack and bomb police headquarters and army intelligence centers, raid hospitals in order to finish-off their victims, and even attack federal offices of the Attorney General and state judges. They bombed the American Consulate in Monterrey in October of 2008. It is not a conventional war and most of the casualties have been among warring cartels but in the overall analysis of the war it is clear that the cartels are winning. The police are afraid to enforce the law. Attorneys are fearful of prosecuting. Judges refuse to adjudicate. The press has packed up and left town too fearful to continue covering the war. Clean businessmen are immigrating to the U.S., with their families. Many small towns in the mountainous war-zones have lost half of their populations as those residents who decided not to join the cartels have fled in fear for their lives. In any reasonable measure the cartels are winning. They have more funds, more troops, better equipment, and certainly have an insurgent's advantage (like the Taliban) of knowing the terrain, having the guerrilla-warfare experience, and having the support of the indigenous peoples who live in the battle zones. Furthermore, the world economic crisis is strengthening their hand. Drug use and retail sales also skyrocket in recessionary environments. As the unemployment rate hit 7.2 percent in December 2008, and heads for double digits in 2009, many of the unemployed citizens of the U.S., as well as illegal immigrants, will seek employment in the drug industry. It is a recessionary-proof industry. Mexico's economic downturn will likewise spur millions to turn to growing marijuana, smuggling, and the other nefarious organized-crime occupations. Calderón needs a surge of General Petraeus proportions on both sides of the border in order to win the war. Unfortunately, unlike the Americans in Iraq, he does not have the luxury of going home.

Note: Allegiances, alliances, murders, assassinations, arrests, and new manifestations or configurations of the drug cartels, their leaders and mercenaries happen with such frequency and rapidity that any report such as this chapter can be out of date or behind the curve in current information in the time period it takes to get printed.

The Best Response to a Chaotic Situation

One of the best things that could possibly happen to the U.S. would be the development of a strong, viable democracy in Mexico. It currently does not exist. Mexico is faltering on the edge of a precipice. It will soon be a failed state unless the U.S. changes its policies, laws, and relationships with Mexico. Mexico cannot succeed alone. The symbiotic relationship that exists between the two countries keeps Mexico from succeeding alone. Mexico thrives on the life-energy that it gets from the U.S. This energy is the lifeline of Mexico. This lifeline is like a huge conduit sucking energy and life out of the U.S. The energy flow is mostly one-directional with the one large exception being petroleum. Instead of choosing to be a good neighbor, an economic partner, a brother-in-arms in the advancement of life, Mexico has decided to prey on its neighbor, the U.S. It has decided to forsake the lawful and rational code which countries accept in order to live in harmony side by side. It has decided to prey upon its neighbor in lieu of establishing neighborly relations. Prior to Felipe Calderón's declared war on the drug cartels, it had decided that a 50 to 75 billion dollar drug industry is more important to Mexico than the millions of American lives, and Mexican lives, that are eventually destroyed by the use of dangerous drugs. Mexico is not the sleepy little banana republic of the sixties and seventies which exported marijuana to the U.S. Mexico has become *The Drug Cartel* (figuratively) for cocaine, methamphetamine, and heroine as well as marijuana. Mexico has taken control of the hard-core drug industry and ushered it into the 21st century. The Mexican criminals are quickly taking over the distribution and retail end of the business in over 230 cities of the U.S., in 2008 (versus 50 cities in 2006). Mexico's decades long argument that the U.S. must be responsible for controlling usage, sales, and distribution in the U.S. is no longer very applicable. The smugglers, distributors, pushers, and even many drug-users are now predominantly illegal Mexican immigrants. No one knows the exact demographic breakdown of the illegal drug industry and drug culture. That is the nature of the beast. But it is an undeniable fact that the unbridled influx of more than 15 million illegal Mexicans into the U.S. has also ignited an explosion of hard-core drug use and sophisticated drug distribution. The Mexicans are controlling and capitalizing on this scourge. They are using their profits to move into all arenas of organized crime including kidnapping, robbery, extortion, prostitution, human trafficking, and bribery. The scourge of the illegal drug industry, organized crime, and illegal immigration makes a lethal, slow-release plutonium weapon which is poisoning the American culture and Mexico's culture, for that matter. Make no mistake, a country or a culture which chooses to suck the life out of its neighbor instead of developing its own potential is worse than a scourge.

Felipe Calderón, president of Mexico, deserves tons of kudos for his two year campaign against the drug cartels. This is definitely a step in the right direction. Just keep your fingers crossed that he is sincere and that his war on drugs is not a smoke screen which is hiding a completely and different ulterior motive. Mexican presidents have historically robbed their country of billions while portraying the face of honesty and well-intentioned motives. Calderón appears to be sincere but so did Carlos Salinas de Gortari just a few years back. Calderón needs unbridled support from the Obama administration on this front. But, he also needs to be realistic and start cracking down on money laundering. As of March of 2009, despite all of his hard-hitting press conferences, he was still refusing to follow the money earned by the drug cartels. The billions of illegal dollars earned in the drug industry are invested (washed) in Mexico with complete impunity. Waging war against the foot soldiers of the drug cartels will never be successful unless it is coupled with a war against money laundering. For whatever reasons, Calderón refuses to prosecute the money laundering end of the business. Logic suggests that his fragile economy cannot survive without the estimated 50 to 75 billion dollars of yearly investment that comes from illegal drugs.

He also openly supports illegal immigration into the U.S. His government even publishes *how-to manuals* in comic book form for the illiterate peasants detailing methods for illegally crossing the border, obtaining fraudulent work papers, and networking with other illegal Mexicans who are already residing in the U.S. His government also chooses to encourage the practice of remittances which illegal immigrants send back 25 billion dollars to Mexico each year in lieu of respecting U.S. immigration law. Mexicans are illegally entering the U.S. and using fraudulent documents in order to secure work. When they send their illegally earned money back to Mexico, via wire transfers, they are in effect laundering illegal gains the same as the drug cartels. It is illogical and hypocritical to think that illegally earned money is suddenly legitimate because it was sent from the U.S. to Mexico via wire transfer.

Once again I must admit my mystification of the response to this situation in the U.S. As a nation we have become anesthetized to Mexico. We have also become bored. We have also developed such a superiority complex that we seem unable to recognize the true threats that exist. We have a national paralysis when it comes to analyzing the potential danger from Mexico. Historically, the U.S. dominated Mexico with military invasions, out and out stole (o.k. a few pennies were actually paid) one third of Mexico's land mass, and treated its citizenry as second-class humans. As a result of our centuries-long hateful relationship neither culture truly respects the other. But the Americans are not only drugged by the marijuana, cocaine, heroin, and methamphetamines but by their underestimating of the modern Mexican's capacity to turn to brutal crime in order to survive and reap the benefits of capitalism. We see the friendly, warm, little house keepers, nannies, gardeners, hard-working construction professionals, fastidious hotel maids, etc., etc. and we know who they are. They are good people. They are simple, hard-working, uneducated, often unskilled, meek, weak, mild, and anything but dangerous, right? I could get even more stereotypical and insulting but the point is simple. Many Americans continue to stereotype illegal Mexican immigrants in an unrealistic way. America's simplistic stereotyping keeps them from seeing what is more importantly wrong. What they are missing is the fact that perhaps twenty or thirty percent of the illegal Mexican immigrants that are in the U.S. participate in organized crime in one way or another. All the arrests, all the numbers, point to the reality that when all of the prostitutes, human traffickers, drug smugglers, arms smugglers, drug distributors, money launderers, kidnappers, robbers, mafia enforcers, drug users, plus violent criminals of assault, rape, murder, and others are totaled among the illegal population the percentages are in the twenty to thirty percentile range. At the end of 2008, ICE's Criminal Alien Program had completed filing repatriation documents for 164,296 illegal immigrant criminals who are currently incarcerated in U.S. prisons. That staggering number does not include all of the illegal immigrants that have been convicted of crimes and are in prison, but only those for which they have finished processing deportation paperwork in 2008. This is to insure that upon finishing their terms in prison they will automatically be returned to their home countries.

It is a reality that the poor, uneducated, illegal Mexican immigrants are turning to real crime in unprecedented numbers. The justification to turn to crime is so easy and basic for disenfranchised illegal immigrants. To begin with they recognize that they are already breaking American law just by being in the U.S. Illegal immigrants recognize that they are illegally working whether they choose carpentry or drug distribution. Their decision to turn to hard-core crime simply becomes a matter of assessing risk. Illegal immigrants who are apprehended repeatedly will eventually go to prison on immigration charges the same as cocaine dealers and prostitutes. For example, if Juan Valdez is illegally cleaning bathrooms at a hamburger joint for five bucks an hour his buddy José Jiménez can easily justify breaking into someone's house for the promise of thousands of dollars of goods. Both occupations are illegal. One is a little more risky than the other but the promise of higher rewards is enticing.

It seems obvious that the typical American and probably most politicians are not aware of the serious situation that exists in Mexico. The press does not cover the situation with the seriousness it deserves. Finally, as this book was headed to copyright in April of 2009, Mexico has become a hot issue in the press. And politicians who have ignored the situation are finally starting to get involved. But most are just now awakening to the seriousness of the problems. Barack Obama, for example, met with Felipe Calderón on January 12, 2009. It has become a historical habit for the incoming U.S. and Mexican presidents to meet for coffee prior to the president-elect being sworn into office. It is a photo opportunity of goodwill but the presidents also have the chance to address their upcoming plans. In this case a couple of poignant facts revealed themselves. One, for once in almost two years of being in the spotlight, Barack Obama appeared uneasy, uncomfortable. He obviously is not up to speed on Mexican-American relations. I mean the realities of drug smuggling and illegal immigration are not niceties that exist between the two governments. I think the only time Barack Obama is uneasy in a situation is when he does not have control of the facts. And he obviously does not have control of the facts. Second, the following day I searched the New York Times, the Washington Post, the International Herald Tribune, USA Today, the San Francisco Chronicle, and finally in the Latin American section of the Los Angeles Times, I found coverage of the meeting. I went on to scour eight or ten additional dailies around the country without finding coverage of the meeting. I then searched the Mexican daily newspapers. The meeting was covered on the front page of every single paper I searched.

In the press conference that followed their meeting, Barack Obama announced that the two countries would establish a cooperative group and task them with investigating NAFTA, immigration, and other issues. Barack Obama is very far behind the curve of reality in regard to Mexico. He seems to sense absolutely no urgency in delving into American-Mexican relations. As a matter of fact he quickly turned his attentions to the next installment of the TARP funds during the press conference. It was completely out of context with the meeting at hand and did nothing but illustrate his lack of familiarity with the situation. He should have reported that he had full intentions to immediately press Congress to release the remaining 300 million dollars of the Mérida Initiative funds that were promised for 2008 release. But he still does not get it. On January 21, 2009, the day after Obama was sworn into office the DHS webpage was updated with his immigration agenda. Although parts of the plan are very good he still is off-base on how best to address the issue of the existing 20 to 30 million illegal immigrants already in the U.S. His agenda, his plan for dealing with the 20 or 30 million illegal immigrants already in the U.S., as of January 21, 2009, is to "Bring People Out Of The Shadows: Support a system that allows undocumented immigrants who are in good standing to pay a fine, learn English, and go to the back of the line for the opportunity to become citizens."1 This is an out and out amnesty program. If enacted, it spells doom for the future relations between the U.S. and Mexico, as it will promote continued over-the-top levels of illegal immigration for decades.

The day following Obama's meeting with Calderón, on January 13, 2009, even more complacency and lack of focus was revealed on Capitol Hill during the first day of Hillary Clinton's confirmation hearing for the position of Secretary of State. Not a single Senator asked Clinton specifically about Mexico. They did not ask her about Latin America. As a matter of factual record she gave an extended opening statement which unfortunately demonstrates her and the incoming administration's lack of focus, awareness, urgency, and priority regarding Mexico. After her lengthy introduction the first subject on her agenda was terrorism and the Middle East. She clearly demonstrated the direction she intends to take the State Department as she said, "We must focus on Iraq, Pakistan, Afghanistan, and the security needs of Israel."2 Her statement consisted of approximately eighty paragraphs. After detailing her intentions of dealing with Al-Qaeda and the Taliban she discussed her concerns and future plans for solving problems in more than fifty countries and areas before briefly mentioning Mexico and Canada in the fifty-third paragraph. Astoundingly, the countries (or areas) that have more of her attention than Mexico include: Congo, Zimbabwe, Balkans, Sudan, Egypt, Jordan, Brazil, South Africa, Turkey, Gaza, and South Korea. These are just a few of the areas that she is so obviously ready to focus her attention before she has time to consider Mexico. Finally, she recognized that Canada and Mexico are the largest and third largest trading partners to the U.S., respectively, as well as our two largest suppliers of energy. And in her lavish expanse of three sentences (that was her entire text that dealt with Mexico and Canada together) she suggested that the U.S. must create a "deeper relationship" with Mexico in order to "address drug-trafficking and the challenges of the border".[3]

Contrary to the continuous chant of change, change, change from Obama, one of the first things he did upon taking office on January 21, 2009, was to fulfill his Secretary of State's prediction during her confirmation hearings that the new administration would focus on the security needs of Israel. One of his first acts, even before lunch, was to begin a series of calls to Israel's Prime Minister Ehud Olmert, Palestinian President Mahmoud Abbas, Jordanian King Abdullah, and Egyptian President Hosni Mubarak. His priorities are obvious and clear. The state of Israel's security, with the world's third most lethal military, is still more important to the president of the U.S. than the security of the U.S. This is not change. It is mindboggling! Israel can take care of itself against the threat of unsophisticated Hamas rockets. The U.S. does not have energy concerns that are at risk in Israel, Gaza, Jordan, or Egypt, yet President Obama spends his first morning in office preoccupied with Israeli security. In the afternoon he lectured his staff on conflict of interest and lobbying concerns. He issued an executive order which forbade near-term lobbying conflicts. Yet it appears that he spent his morning fulfilling his obligations to his Jewish campaign contributors. He certainly has his priorities and those of his Secretary of State, Hillary Clinton, prioritized. And, Israel is definitely one of the immediate beneficiaries. Sorry Barack, this is favoritism and hypocrisy not uninfluenced decision making which benefits the U.S.

The truth could not be more obvious or more staggering. Barack Obama and Hillary Clinton, two of the brightest, most capable politicians in Washington prior to the sensational press coverage in April of 2009 of Mexican drug-war violence and Obama's quick trip to Mexico did not appear to have a clue as to the gravity of our relationship with Mexico. They need to fully understand that its possible decline into a chaotic failed state will have a deleterious impact on the U.S. In January 2009 Barack Obama told Felipe Calderón that he thought it would be a good idea to put together a think tank in order to study the situation. Yet his knickers are in a wad over what to do about Hamas lobbing rockets into Israel, which have yet to kill more than a handful of Israelis. He immediately appointed George Mitchell as Special Middle East Envoy and put him on a plane for Israel. Obama and Clinton do not understand the risk of slow or no response to secure our southern border. An inadequate response has the potential to cause a problem greater than Iraq, Israel, or the entire Middle-East but in our own back yard.

This is not alarmism but recognition of a real risk. The Mexican government, for example, estimates that since 2004, more than 900,000 automatic weapons have been smuggled into Mexico making it the most highly armed country in Latin America. "More than 6,700 licensed gun dealers have set up shop within a short drive of the 2,000-mile border, from the gulf coast of Texas to San Diego, which amounts to more than three dealers for every mile of border territory. Law enforcement has come to call the region an *iron river of guns*."[4] Prior to the 21st century, the average Mexican citizen did not own or want a gun. That has changed drastically as hundreds of thousands are now part of the drug industry and support a robust arsenal of weapons. In addition, rural citizens in every state across the country have used remittance money sent from the U.S., to arm themselves against the drug gangs. Mexico has become a lethal tinderbox just waiting to ignite.

On the positive side, Barack Obama, in his inauguration speech, spoke of, "America's collective failure to make hard choices," and went on to assert that, "What is required of us now is a new era of responsibility -- a recognition, on the part of every American, that we have duties to ourselves, our nation and the world, duties that we do not grudgingly accept but rather seize gladly, firm in the knowledge that there is nothing so satisfying to the spirit, so defining of our character than giving our all to a difficult task. This is the price and the promise of citizenship."[5] Ideologically, according to these words, Obama is ready to get it. Although Obama and his team basically ignored the Mexico situation during the transition months after the election and prior to the inauguration, their perspective seems to be perfectly in-line with what is required in order to start solving the serious Mexican-American issues. Hillary Clinton declared that she would be the most prepared, best informed representative whether meeting with Russians or Europeans. Supposedly she has the same intentions regarding Mexico. As a matter of fact, her boss seems to be demanding that attitude of his entire staff and administration. Assuming that the Obama administration is ready for the challenge and the American public is ready to make the collective hard choices the Mexican-American relationship can be put in order.

Initially a few important recognitions must be made. Obama must be brought up to speed on Mexican-American relations, the current disastrous state of affairs in Mexico, the current impact it is having on the U.S., how important of a partner and neighbor Mexico is to the U.S., and the future consequences that are at risk if he does not act quickly. As of January 2009, it is obvious that he does not understand. Obama must recognize that his earlier rhetoric on how to solve the issue of the millions of illegal immigrants is 100 percent wrong. His idea of sending these millions of illegal immigrants to the so-called end of the line in order to apply for citizenship will not work and is not consistent with his inaugural remarks. He clearly defined what the price and the promise of citizenship is in his address. Obama must prioritize the entire theatre of Mexican-American relations as a top priority and mandate that it be addressed in the early months of his presidency. He must realize that this is more important than the security of Israel. Creating a think tank to study the situation which he suggested to Calderón in early January was obviously inadequate. The Obama administration must communicate to the public and the press its new concern and intended direction regarding Mexican-American relations and explain the consequences that would result by the potential failure of the Mexican state, our second largest provider of energy and third largest trading partner. Obama, as a result of the urgency of the situation, must recognize the legitimacy and need for structuring a comprehensive agreement or treaty with Mexico, which addresses all of the critical issues at hand between the two countries. This agreement or treaty would be negotiated independent of any other sovereign nation. It would define those things that must be accomplished in order to protect the U.S., and to preserve Mexico as a sovereign nation. It would be a win-win agreement for both nations. So, initially, Obama and his team must do the following: get focused and educated on the situation in Mexico, hit the reset button on past plans and hyperbole, prioritize and announce a new program, and negotiate an independent, comprehensive agreement or treaty with Mexico.

Many of the other *must-do's* belong to the citizenry as well as the government of the U.S. We *must* change our mindset regarding second-class citizens. We *must* realize the degrading consequences that our culture suffers when we allow more than 20 million uneducated, unskilled immigrants to illegally immigrate into the U.S. We *must* realize that the unbridled invasion of 1.5 to 2 million additional uneducated, unskilled illegal immigrants each year must stop immediately. We *must* make those collective hard choices not to create or continue to foster a second-class citizenry in order to have our dirty jobs or low-wage jobs done at a below market wage. We *must* take the responsibility for following the rule of law in our hiring practices. We *must* use good judgment to realize the high cost of greed and stop selling automatic weapons to criminals and their front men. We *must* discover how to stop our addiction to illegal drugs! We *must* demand that our government negotiate a new agreement with Mexico which solves the current dilemma.

The following section of this chapter covers the major issues that should be included in a new agreement between Mexico and the U.S. It is imperative to tie these issues together in order to have a comprehensive plan. Equitable tradeoffs between the two countries are plausible if all of these issues are on the table in one, comprehensive agreement. It is completely reasonable to assume that trade, foreign assistance, immigration, border control, and remittance issues can be negotiated as a stand-alone Mexican-American agreement which is independent of other countries. The U.S. can independently agree to immigration standards with Mexico that is different than those that exist or may be negotiated in the future with other countries. Historically, the U.S. immigration standards, for example, during the 30s, 40s, and 50s were slanted towards western Europeans and against other nations. In other words, a new immigration and comprehensive agreement with Mexico need not be predicated upon a U.S.-universal immigration reform act. Trade agreements vary widely from country to country as well as foreign assistance agreements. The Obama administration is justifiably arguing that extraordinary measures are needed to solve the economic crisis because the times are extraordinary. The same argument can be effectively used in dealing with the Mexican issues. It is certainly valid. The eventuality of Mexico becoming a failed state or the continuation of mass drug export to the U.S. coupled with millions of illegal immigrants flooding the U.S. justifies an immediate and unprecedented response by the U.S. government.

Border Security

The U.S. and Mexican governments must get serious about securing the border. Any current or future agreements between the two countries are worthless without a secure border. Fortunately, the DHS has made headway in the last two years in securing the U.S. side of the border, but it is only a few steps in the right direction. It is a good start but only a start. Congress has approved the building of seven hundred miles of a **border wall or fence** to assist agents in securing the border. Many people mistakenly equate this wall with something akin to the Berlin Wall which was built to keep people in, not out. The majority of the proposed U.S.-Mexico wall is a series of traffic barriers which try to cordon off vast areas of open desert which exist between the countries. Other parts of the wall are truly designed as impenetrable walls to keep out pedestrians. The argument that a twenty foot wall will only entice those wanting to cross to secure a twenty-one foot later is absurd. In all cases, for example, where the wall has been completed, both in the desert and in urban areas, illegal crossings are down by as much as 90 percent. It is absolutely impossible to secure a two thousand mile border against all illegal crossings. No one argues that point. The objective, however, is to make the illegal crossings and smugglings extremely difficult, time consuming, and costly for drug/contraband smugglers as well as human smugglers.

When the press talks about porous borders images of rugged mountain terrain along the Afghanistan border come to mind, a lawless land where armed Taliban ambush and kill frontline American soldiers then slip back into Pakistan undetected. The border between Mexico and the U.S. is very similar in many ways. The main characteristics that they share are porosity and danger. From the urban streets between El Paso and Ciudad Juárez, to the mountain passes along the Rio Grande River in Texas, to the vast expanses of the Sonoran and Chihuahuan Desert the two thousand miles of border is unsecure, porous, and dangerous. The opening scenes of the Academy Award-winning movie, No Country for Old Men, depict both the porosity of the rugged, rural border area and the brutal violence that so often occurs there. Unfortunately, there is not a lot of make believe in this movie. The urban border-areas are just as porous and even more violent as evidenced by the more than 1600 gruesome murders in Juárez in 2008. The new fence, wall, and traffic barriers will not stop all of the illegal activity but it will certainly slow it down and should therefore be continued. These border-crossing deterrents should be a perfect fit for Obama's stimulus package. When Obama met with state governors in January of 2009, and tallied their shovel ready projects a mere 135 billion of the 850 billion he was looking for was identified. The cost of the fence which is estimated in the tens of billions is a perfect fit. At the end of 2008, the first part of the project was approximately 70 percent complete. As Chertoff and company have designed and chosen a variety of fences, walls, barriers, and surveillance technologies, an amplification of the current program could easily be constructed or installed along the entire border region wherever it is applicable. This easily would fit into Obama's overall scope of the stimulus plan. It is infrastructure, shovel ready, would immediately create thousands of jobs, and the billions of dollars would go directly into the economy. Contractors and suppliers are ready to amplify the program immediately. It would also fit into his online, published agenda of better securing the border.

Another important element of securing the border has to be backwards looking or **outbound enforcement**. In other words, the U.S. must be responsible for scrutinizing, searching, and verifying the contents of vehicles which are exiting the U.S. on their way into Mexico. Mexico must assume the same responsibility for vehicles leaving Mexico and entering the U.S. The two countries need to enter into a new agreement on shared responsibility for contraband going in both directions. The Mexican and American governments must enter into a mutual agreement with mutual goals. It is the same war. It is the same problem. If Mexico and Felipe Calderón are sincerely interested in regaining control of their country, they will eagerly agree to enter into such a mutual agreement. The Mexican press constantly reports that Calderón will not enter into an agreement which even hints at some sort of sovereignty compromise with the U.S. He must surely realize that this argument has become nothing more than ridiculous hyperbole as he needs all the help he can muster. Obama cannot afford to be bashful about structuring new agreements with Mexico. He advocates international respect and cooperation. That is exactly what is needed between the two countries. Mexico and the U.S must turn a new page on trust, cooperation, shared intelligence, shared vigilance, and unabashed commitment to success against this dastardly anarchy that threatens Mexico, and wounds the U.S. It is no longer an option to standby as the drug cartels destroy the once burgeoning, newly emerging Mexican democracy. They are destroying the U.S. as well.

Increased levels of border security are imperative on both sides. In his sensational book, <u>Drug Wars, Narco Warfare in the 21st Century</u>, Gary Fleming accurately portrays the fragile state of the young Mexican democracy. He understands the urgency of properly **staffing** our border control agencies and suggests drawing upon returning war veterans from Iraq, as candidates for expanding our CBP forces. His book, unfortunately, failed to anticipate the urgent requirements in Afghanistan for U.S. servicemen. General Petraeus often characterizes the border between Afghanistan and Pakistan, as "drugs out, guns in" referring to the fact that smuggled opium pays for the armaments of the Taliban. The United Nations estimated that the 2008 opium export generated approximately 300 million dollars for the Taliban. And Petraeus with more than 30,000 troops is so outgunned that he has convinced Obama to immediately send 30,000 additional troops in order to secure the border. The Mexican drug industry in comparison is more than a 100 times larger, generating somewhere between 50 and 75 billion dollars a year. All of the combined forces of the DHS which include the CBP and ICE that are battling to secure the Mexican border total less than 19,000 agents. The Mexican-American border is 2,000 miles long in comparison with a 500 mile Afghanistan-Pakistan border. The American scope and approach to securing the Mexican-U.S. border is severely inadequate.

It is obvious that the manpower on the border must be significantly increased in order to stop the inflow of illegal drugs and illegal immigration which threatens to destroy the fabric of America. The numbers alone are overwhelming. It is impossible to know the exact quantities of illegal drugs being smuggled into the U.S. from Mexico each year but DEA officials believe that approximately 10,000 metric tons (22 million pounds) of marijuana, 1,000 metric tons of cocaine (2 million pounds), 8 billion dollars of methamphetamines, and 10 to 15 metric tons of heroin crossed the border in 2008. Add those to the 1.5 to 2 million illegal immigrants who successfully alluded the CBP or were caught and returned to Mexico, and the porosity of the border and the volume of illegal activity becomes obvious. Trying to stop this overwhelming level of smuggling with 19,000 agents is impossible. There are not enough agents, barriers to entry, or checkpoints. Authorities believe that they seize less than 10 percent of the drugs which are being smuggled into the U.S., and probably detain less than 25 percent of the illegal immigrants attempting to cross the border. In any reasonable measure, the program is a complete failure. Ninety percent of the drug cartels product is hitting Main Street America. And seven or eight of every ten uneducated, unemployed, wayward peasant and desperate barrio escapee are eluding the immigration authorities as they disperse throughout the cities of America looking for work.

The ICE and CBP are the two departments or agencies of the DHS which have primary responsibility for securing the national borders and enforcing immigration laws. Their published missions are as follows:

"U.S. Immigration and Customs Enforcement (ICE), an agency of the Department of Homeland Security, protects national security and upholds public safety by targeting criminal networks and terrorist organizations that seek to exploit vulnerabilities in our immigration system, in our financial networks, along our border, at federal facilities and elsewhere in order to do harm to the United

States. The end result is a safer, more secure America."6

"Department of Customs and Border Patrol (CBP). We are the guardians of our Nation's borders. We are America's frontline. We safeguard the American homeland at and beyond our borders. We protect the American public against terrorists and the instrument of terror. We steadfastly enforce the laws of the United States while fostering our Nation's economic security through lawful international trade and travel. We serve the American public with vigilance, integrity, and professionalism."7

The situation that exists is a sham to the American people and to the DHS. Both departments are sorely underfunded and understaffed. The success rate for apprehending illegal drug shipments is only 10 percent. The success rate of apprehending illegal immigrants is only 25 percent. With all the talk and hyperbole about terrorism, how can the DHS do anything but raise the red flag and scream for assistance along the Mexican border. DHS ranks should be quadrupled or increased even more if 19,000 agents are only intercepting 10 percent of the illegal drugs and 25 percent of the illegal immigrants crossing the border. Maybe we need 100,000 CBP and ICE agents along the border.

One place to look for new border agents may be in the ranks of the U.S. military. I am often surprised when I hear politicians, talking heads, and the press pontificating in flabbergasted terms when wondering how and where Obama will get an additional 30,000 troops to send to Afghanistan. They talk of how stretched and out of bandwidth the current military is. I do not understand the argument but I can count. As of May 2008, the official Pentagon numbers for the American military were as follows: "United States: American soldiers, sailors, airmen, and Marines make up over half of all the world's overseas troops, outnumbering all others(foreign soldiers) combined. With the world's only blue-water navy and largest basing network, America now stations 289,000 of its 1.3 million active-duty servicemen and servicewomen abroad. The largest deployment is in Iraq, now host to about 170,000 American servicemen and women. Next come Germany at 57,000, Japan at 33,000, Korea at 27,100, and Afghanistan at 26,700; the remainder are deployed in a long series of bases and training missions spanning 152 nations and territories. Another 92,000 naval personnel are at sea but stationed in the U.S."8 Why, in the 21st century, does the U.S have 120,000 troops defending the security of Germany, Japan, and South Korea, while the southern border with Mexico is being inadequately protected and secured with 19,000 agents? Should not the U.S. border be more important than the German border? It is time to abandon the mindset of the 20th century and deal with the realities of the 21st century. There are 1.3 million active-duty (not including reserves) servicemen of which 289,000 are stationed abroad. That means there are more than one million active servicemen that are not stationed abroad. The military should be redirected to either redeploy troops that are stationed abroad or to train and arm 50,000 of the support personnel that are in the states and send them to our southern border with Mexico.

Janet Napolitano, the new Secretary of DHS and former governor of Arizona, understands the situation perfectly well. She authorized the Arizona National Guard to the border with Mexico to support the ICE and CBP in 2006 and 2007. She also billed the federal government in order to compensate the state for doing the federal government's job of securing the border. Hopefully she will be the person who educates Obama and Clinton on the realities of our southern border. For all of Obama's multiculturalism, awareness, first-class education, and open-mindedness, his Washington, Boston, Chicago experience has given him very little knowledge of Latin America or Mexico. His Secretary of State, Hillary Clinton, despite a career of globetrotting also seems unaware of the seriousness of the Mexican situation. She, like Obama, spent her first day in office focused on Israel. She scoured the countryside in an attempt to find the appropriate representatives to appoint in order to safeguard Israel's security. Secretary Napolitano spent her first day reviewing the Mission of the DHS. I suspect she is focused on its implications regarding the southern border and is not preoccupied with Israel's security issues in the Gaza. I found it quite interesting that at her swearing-in ceremony as Secretary of DHS she was dressed in an attractive, olive-green business suit with a floral design that had a significant hint of army camouflage. I am not sure if it was accidental, subconscious, or if she was sending out a tough message to

American adversaries. I like to think that with her square jaw and shock of grey hair it was the latter. If she is as business focused and serious as she was characterized by her college, Governor Ed Rendell, as having no life other than her work, she should be excellent for the Department.

Securing the border is a complicated but achievable task. The mission is easy to define. **Create a border environment where 90 percent of the illegal drugs and immigrants are being apprehended instead of 10 percent.** In order to accomplish this task the DHS's fence program must be amplified and completed. The number of border agents or military personnel at the border must be drastically increased. Two types of personnel are required. One, trained inspectors for physically inspecting large quantities of cargo trailers, cars, trucks, and trains which are entering the U.S. NAFTA, unintentionally, became a windfall for the drug cartels. Prior to NAFTA the U.S. had a small positive trade surplus with Mexico. That has now turned into a 70 billion dollar trade deficit. That translates into a fluid conduit of drug smuggling containers and trailers. Many experts estimate that 60 to 80 percent of the illegal drugs enter the country via commercial freight carriers. The CBP reports that on an average day in 2008, 70,000 containers entered the U.S. by truck, rail, or ship. Another 331,000 privately owned vehicles entered each of the 365 days in 2008. Of these, less than ten percent are adequately searched or screened for illegal contraband. The reason is simple. CBP does not have the manpower or budget that it needs to more thoroughly search incoming freight. The drug cartels know this and use commercial carriers and private vehicles as their commercial freight lines. CBP needs the money to procure inspection compounds in every city along the border. In the larger cities like El Paso, Laredo, and San Diego, multiple compounds are needed. These would be akin to the freight forwarding compounds that are currently used by international shippers. The inspection compounds that the CBP currently use are inadequate to handle the volume. They are located at the points of crossing, are too small, too crowded, and inefficient. New compounds or yards should be located a few miles inland and staffed with thousands of new agents and high-tech screening equipment. The eventual cost of this service would be paid by the exporter of the goods. Remember, Mexico has a 74 billion dollar a year trade surplus with the U.S. If they want access to the U.S. markets they must assume the responsibility and cost of providing drug-free shipments. If anything, an expanded inspection program would put pressure on the shippers, freight-forwarders, and packers to exit the smuggling business.

Once again, these projects could be initially funded by Obama's stimulus package. They would create immediate employment, pump money into the economy, start squeezing-off the open conduit used by the drug cartels, and help safeguard the U.S. borders.

The second type of personnel which is needed at the border is armed, trained CBP and ICE agents. The border must be locked down. The current level of personnel is woefully inadequate. This can only be done with trained, armed, and experienced CBP and ICE agents, police officers, county sheriffs, and detectives. The current frontline personnel from San Diego, California, to Brownsville, Texas, are doing a tremendous job but are understaffed and underfunded. They need help. Their forces need to be doubled or tripled in order to defend their cities and eliminate the growing lawlessness that is spreading like a cancer. In Tucson and Phoenix, for example, more than 500 *home incursions* were reported in 2008. A home incursion is what local police refer to as a drug cartel attempt to collect money from a drug distributor or retailer who happens to be living in the U.S. The federal government must spearhead a national recruiting effort and find bilingual professionals who are willing to serve. Barack Obama is pushing the importance of patriotic service in the face of our economic crisis. He must use the same logic, argument, and marketing effort for recruiting an additional 20,000 or more border personnel.

The third type of personnel needed at the border is military personnel. The military needs to be brought in as backup to the CBP and ICE, to lock down and patrol the vast expanses of countryside, and to show the drug cartels that the United States of America has had enough. There is no better way to demonstrate America's will and determination to change the lawlessness that exists than by bringing in the military. The American press often report on America's intolerance of a militarized border with

Mexico. This is a myth which was started and promulgated by the press and is not consistent with what Americans want along the southwest border. Americans want secure borders and want to shutoff the conduit being used by the drug cartels. If U.S. citizens are prepared to spend the money and manpower to secure the border between North and South Korea why would they not be willing to do the same along the Mexican border? Why should the billions of dollars being pumped into the Germany economy in the support of 57,000 troops not be welcomed in the California, Arizona, New Mexico, and Texas cities and communities?

The U.S. Army needs to **establish a minimum of seven military installations** along the border. The idea is to put strategic bases in rural areas between the following large cities, south to north, between McAllen and Laredo, then Laredo and the Big Bend National Park, then another between the National Park and El Paso, Texas. Two would be established in New Mexico; one between El Paso and Columbus, and the other between Columbus and Douglas, Arizona. Another would be established between Douglas and Calexico, California, and the final installation would be between Calexico and San Diego, California. The system needs to be comprehensive and each base would have responsibility for a specific geographic area which would be connected to its neighboring base. The ICE and CBP have seen initial successes with the construction of the border fence but characterize the border as a large balloon. When they lock down one area it is like pushing on a balloon. The drug smuggling and illegal immigrants simply bulge to another area. The border must be secured from San Diego to Brownsville. These bases would be manned with two to three thousand soldiers each. The military units would be designed to be highly mobile and especially trained for interdiction purposes. Expensive firepower is not needed. Troops that are fast-moving and equipped with leading-edge surveillance and detection equipment are needed. They would need the latest high-tech equipment available in both ground and air transportation. Their objective would be twofold: stop the shipments of illegal drugs that use the cover of the vast, under-populated, rural areas between the large cities and to stop the influx of illegal immigration in the same rural areas. The bases would be equipped with temporary, immigration, detention facilities and transportation for rapid repatriation. They would also be equipped with smaller more secure jails for drug smugglers.

Again, the funding for this type of strategy falls in line with Barrack Obama's stimulus plan. These seven bases would be a wonderful Public Works Project which would employ tens of thousands of workers and pump billions into the economy. It is the right time to do it and the right thing to do.

The final part of a new Border Security Program must deal with contraband which exits the U.S. and enters Mexico. This would seem to be Mexico's problem but it is our problem as well. Specifically, we must **stop the flow of weapons and cash generated from the sale of drugs** into Mexico. The arms problem must be attacked at the source. The National Rifle Association, supporters of the Second Amendment, and everyone else must support special legislation which tightly regulates the sale of all armaments in a 150 mile zone along the Mexican border. At the end of 2008, there were more than 6,700 registered arms dealers between Brownsville and San Diego. They are the source of the hundreds of thousands of automatic weapons which are being smuggled into Mexico. Legislation must be put in place which stops this activity. It is an unusual situation and it requires a special approach. Prior to 2004, there was very little difference between a gun shop in Laredo, Texas, and Denver, Colorado. There were no more shops per capita in San Diego, than in Pittsburg, Pennsylvania. But that has all changed. The border zone has become a retail, military-complex. In five years, our neighbor, Mexico, has become the most heavily armed country in Latin America. And it is not their military that is so heavily armed. It is the tens of thousands of people who work in the drug industry. The 6,700 registered arms dealers in the border zone, legal Americans, are selling them their weapons. Our military would not let this situation exist along any battle zone anywhere in the world. This is a battle zone and special action must be taken to shutoff weapons sales which are eventually smuggled into Mexico.

The Mexican government believes that almost 1 million automatic weapons have been smuggled into their country since 2004. This amount of arms seems small compared to the estimated

250 million weapons that are estimated to be held by private American citizens. But in comparison to the one million machetes used to hack more than 1.5 million Tutsi and Hutu to death in Rwanda in 1998, it is significant. One million AK-47s in a chaotic third-world environment could quickly turn into one of the largest massacres the world has ever seen. Mexican authorities argue that the chaos has already begun as almost 7,000 victims were gunned down in 2008.

The obvious solution to the smuggling of cash and those arms which cannot be choked-off in the border zone is higher staffing in the CBP and ICE. The CBP does not have enough personnel to adequately search inbound vehicles, much less, outbound vehicles. Once sufficient levels of personnel are hired, an exit search program must be devised. The solution to exit security and interdiction is not difficult. CBP must develop a program and take responsibility for outbound as well as inbound traffic. But the federal government must give them the funding and personnel needed to achieve this task. They currently do not have the bandwidth or funds. As the border is secured or locked down a new immigration program must be put in place by the federal government.

Smart Immigration through Reform and Repatriation Program

A special piece of legislation that deals specifically and unilaterally with Mexican immigration reform should be written immediately. This can easily be defined in today's terms as **smart immigration**. If the U.S. secures its southern border with Mexico, and resolves the immigration problem with Mexico, the bulk of the immigration problem with all the other Latin American countries becomes minimized, almost nonexistent. Remember, 70 percent of *ALL* illegal immigrants who come to the U.S enter through Mexico. Obama wants to stimulate the economy by creating jobs that will solve some of the large national issues. He is focused on education, infrastructure, and renewable energy. It is a brilliant philosophy. Obama's job creation plan which addresses the current economic crisis should also include immigration reform which is coupled to a repatriation program with Mexico. This program will put unemployed Americans to work and begin solving the illegal immigration situation. This program can be seen as a variation of Obama's ill-thought-out pay a fine, learn English, go to the end of the line approach. But this program is well conceived and will work much better.

What is needed is a ten year plan that addresses both immigration and the status of the millions of illegal Mexicans that are already in the U.S. The first half of the plan which would span five years or perhaps a little longer addresses the current illegal immigration situation and couples it with a path towards citizenship. The second part of the plan establishes a new level and set of qualifications for future immigration. The second part of this plan is based on the lead of other western countries such as Ireland and Australia, who have recognized the need to set new standards for immigration as we move into the 21st century that are *sensitive to economic well being*. The plan will only be successful if it is conjoined with a secure border on both sides and recognition by the Mexican government that the plan is good for Mexico as well as the U.S. The U.S. certainly does not need Mexico's approval or agreement in order to establish a new immigration plan but the Mexican government's support would certainly be beneficial in actuating the plan. The third part of the plan is a new approach to the visa overstay situation. The fourth part is enforcement of current immigration law and denial (by law) of free social services and education to illegal immigrants. Here is how it would work and what its objectives would be.

Part One. The Five Year Plan: Path to Citizenship through Repatriation and Qualification. This plan makes some assumptions that are a little difficult to prove outright but are generally accepted by immigration experts. There are somewhere between 10 and 30 million illegal immigrants in the U.S. Probably 60 to 70 percent of them are Mexicans. More than 70 percent of all illegal immigrants enter the U.S. through Mexico (excluding visa overstays). Therefore, if the plan solves the problem of illegal Mexican immigration, establishes a reasonable path to citizenship for those that qualify, and establishes a new legal immigration policy for Mexicans then the largest part of the U.S.'s immigration debacle would be solved. Other plans and new approaches to Asian and African immigration need to be envisioned but if the Mexican situation is resolved; the Latin American situation is mostly solved. Individual or carte blanche legislation could deal with the rest of Latin America but the big problem would be solved. Part one of this Plan also assumes that the third part of this plan which deals with visa overstays is essential in dealing with the immigration issue as a whole.

This plan offers a path to citizenship for a maximum of 5 million illegal Mexican immigrants who entered the U.S. prior to January 1, 2008, and their immediate families. Those who illegally immigrated since the end of 2007 should theoretically have an easier time in rejoining their families and successfully repatriating to Mexico. They will not be able to participate in the plan. Part One of the plan is simple. Those illegal Mexican immigrants who will identify themselves, show proof that they entered and lived continuously in the U.S. prior to January 1, 2008, pay an application fee, and repatriate to Mexico for a period of 6 to 12 months will be eligible to legally reenter the U.S. on a legal work visa and make a subsequent application for permanent U.S. citizenship. In an overall concept or goal the first 500,000 applicants each year will be required to repatriate to Mexico for a minimum of 6 months or until which time they can meet reentry standards and the remaining applicants will be required to repatriate for one year or until they can meet the same standards and/or be processed in order of application. In other words, those who apply first will be processed first. It will be a first to come, first to return program. The actual priority of return would be based on a month by month application order. The first 50 percent of each month's participants would receive a 6 month repatriation bias and the second 50 percent would receive a 12 month repatriation schedule. This setup would encourage early participation. A bias will be shown to those illegal Mexican immigrants who have children who were born in the U.S. prior to January 1, 2008. These Mexicans will be put on the front of the list on a month by month basis. In other words, those that meet this special qualification will move ahead of all other applicants in any given month. Any convicted felon is ineligible for the program. Any Mexican who is apprehended trying to illegally enter the U.S. will be permanently ineligible to immigrate under the Second Part of the Plan. This plan will deal exclusively with illegal Mexican immigrants, but does not exclude other plans or schemes for non-Mexican illegal immigrants. The scope of this plan is restricted to the Mexican situation only. The Plan intends to deal with a maximum of 5 million Mexicans (plus their immediate families) but based on success rates could be expanded to include more individuals. The maximum number of reentering participants would be one million per calendar year (including immediate family members) for five years unless the program is extended or amplified. If a large percentage of the participants have spouses and children in Mexico, the reentry period will stretch beyond the five year goal. The number of exiting participants is only restricted by the availability to process immigrants through the exiting portion of the program. All 5 million participants could theoretically join the program and repatriate during the first year of the program.

All illegal Mexican immigrants who are married to U.S. citizens would have the option of taking their spouse and children to Mexico with them during their repatriation period. Illegal Mexican immigrants who are co-married would be encouraged to make application together and also to take their children with them during their repatriation period to Mexico. The centerpiece of the existing U.S. immigration program is extended family sponsorship. This would not be included in the new program. All children under but not including the age of eighteen would be eligible to return with their mothers and/or fathers if they meet the requirements of the program. All children under the age of eighteen must be proficient in English commensurate with their corresponding age for entering the public school system. In other words, a ten year-old must be proficient enough in English to enter and perform well at a fifth grade level. All spouses who were married prior to January 1, 2008, would also be eligible for reentry to the U.S. with their participating spouses. Once again they would also be required to speak English proficiently.

The actual numbers of legal immigrants that would reenter the U.S. under this program is unknown. But the current situation of having a shadow citizenry of millions of illegal Mexicans must be resolved. It must be a plan that is sustainable and tied to near-term (ten years) immigration levels. In other words, legal Mexican immigration will only be allowed under this program. If it takes ten years to solve the current situation, then there will be no more additional Mexican immigration outside of this plan for ten years. Both countries will support the concept of addressing the current disastrous situation before new immigration levels and standards are introduced. It also will be humane and address the issue of split families. It will also set requirements upon participants. It will be funded in part by the participants. This Plan is basically an offer to Mexico to allow one million Mexicans (and their immediate families) to legally immigrate to the U.S. for each of the next five or subsequent years. The participants must meet the requirements of the program. The participants have the sole responsibility of preparing themselves to reenter the U.S. under this program. It is a way of offering serious candidates a route to legal work, living, and citizenship. It is not an amnesty plan. If the Plan is successful it may be extended to include an even larger number than 5 million. During this period legal Mexican immigration outside of this plan would cease to exist.

All initial applicants will receive new legal documentation or identification. This identification will let them legally reside and travel in the U.S. during the process and repatriation period. The fee for the initial application to be registered, receive legal identification documents, and a probable reentry date would be set at three thousand dollars per individual. That is equivalent to the current market rate being charged by human smugglers all along the Mexican border. It is reasonable to consider a parallel between the amounts an illegal immigrant will pay an illegal smuggler and a legal government agency for the same service. The requirements for reentry into the U.S., and issuance of a legal work visa are: compliance with the new programs regulations for exit and reentry, proven proficiency in the English language, a high school diploma, its equivalent, or a proven proficiency in a skill or trade which is on an official government list. The DHS or Congress would determine on a yearly (or quarterly) basis, a list and quantity of skilled trades people which could be admitted under this program. The repatriation period in Mexico would in part give those who do not meet the requirements upon exit the opportunity to upgrade to the required level during their repatriation period. The reentry process would also require a fee of three thousand dollars per adult and one thousand and five hundred dollars for each child under the age of eighteen. This program will cost the U.S. tax payers billions of dollars. The benefit will be to the participant as well as the tax payer and the cost will therefore be shared by both. Remember, the current level of money being sent back to Mexico as remittances exceeds 25 billion dollars. Mexicans who choose to participate in this program have the capacity to share in its cost.

The DHS would establish a new department called the Department for Immigration and Repatriation. It would be independent of both ICE and CBP and have a completely different but complimentary mission. This would be to facilitate and manage the registration, application, identification, repatriation, scheduling, processing, reentry authorization, and tracking of all the applicants through the entire process. The goal would be to orderly assist all eligible and approved applicants achieve legal resident status and eventual opportunity to apply for U.S. citizenship. The responsibility of enforcing immigration and customs laws would, of course, remain the responsibility of ICE and CBP. The newly created department of Immigration and Repatriation would have an Assistant Secretary of Department as its head and report directly to the Secretary of Homeland Security, Janet Napolitano, the same as the Assistant Secretary of ICE and the Commissioner of CBP. The new department would, of course, be created with state of the art technological capabilities and would be tasked with sharing their database with both CBP and ICE.

Application offices would be established in all 50 state capitals, as well as additional twenty-five to fifty major cities where large illegal Mexican immigrant populations reside. These offices would have the responsibility of processing applications, issuing identification, and setting exit and reentry schedules. Exit and reentry offices would be established at all thirty-one ports of entry along the U.S. Mexican border. That would include six in California, six in Arizona, three in New Mexico, and sixteen in Texas. Additional exit and reentry offices would also be established at international U.S. airports in those major cities where large illegal Mexican immigrants reside such as Atlanta, Chicago, Los

Angeles, San Antonio, and Houston. Processing at these ports would, of course, be in the secured customs and immigration zones and require airline tickets for processing.

Part Two. New Immigration Levels and Standards. Most, modern 21st century cultures have come to the realization that foreign immigration is something that should benefit the host country and not solely the immigrant. In the U.S., unfortunately, due to the historical way in which the country was settled and has evolved, immigration is a sacred cow. Its defenders or promoters seem unwilling to dissect the cow and see the inherent ills that are associated with illegal immigration. They also seem to be unable to accept the valid argument that is so appropriately advanced in, The Immigration Solution, by Heather MacDonald, Victor Hanson, and Steven Malanga that tailoring an immigration policy around economic and educational criteria is not only being practiced world-wide but is essential in the U.S. If the U.S. continues on the immigration path that it has been on for the past fifteen or twenty years it will continue to experience a *dumbing-down* of its citizenry. It will also continue to see upward trends in criminality among immigrants. If the U.S does not rapidly change its immigration policy it stands the very high risk of becoming a hybrid 2nd-world type country. The 3rd world, uneducated, unskilled masses will drag down, not lift up, the U.S. in the 21st century. It is not a matter of race, color, ethnicity, or place of origin. It is a question of quality immigration. The old concept of inviting the masses to the shores of the U.S will not work in the 21st century.

As a matter of fact, part of the history of immigration to the U.S. seems to be widely misunderstood. For example, "...it's important to understand why previous generations of immigrants succeeded in America, how they helped the country grow, and how today's immigration differs." "A 1998 National Academy of Sciences study noted that the immigrant workers of that era (the early 20th century that arrived from Europe) generally met or exceeded the skills-levels of the native-born population, providing America's workforce with a powerful boost just when the country was metamorphosing from an agrarian into an industrial economy."[9] That is certainly not the case today as the average illegal Mexican immigrants has never even attended high school.

The U.S. infrastructure cannot feed, house, employ, educate, and prepare the tens of millions of illegal immigrants and their burgeoning families fast enough to insure America's advancement into the 21st century.

New immigration policy must be based on standards which appreciate education, skill, and experience. The needs of the U.S. must outweigh the needs of the countries that are exporting their workers. Situations like the one that exists with Mexico must be eliminated. A new relationship with Mexico must be established. What was once a positive, symbiotic relationship between Mexico and the U.S. has become a disaster as Mexico is becoming a welfare state of the U.S. Illegal Mexican workers have flooded almost every working-class industry in the U.S. and the effects are deleterious. An open, uncontrolled border which allows millions of illegal immigrants into the U.S. is not an immigration policy.

A new immigration policy should start by establishing a maximum number of immigrants that can be employed, absorbed, and assimilated into the U.S. each year without causing strain to the economy or social and education systems that exist. This maximum level is probably in the 200,000 to 300,000 level. Not just Mexican immigration but all immigration. And in periods of recession, depression, stagnation, economic crisis, or high-unemployment immigration should be temporarily put in abeyance. Immigration should not be a bargaining chip used to negotiate internationals deals or for manipulating foreign governments. The concept of allowing world-wide immigration to the U.S., in order to preserve a centuries-old concept of being the world's melting pot is no longer beneficial to the U.S., and should be abandoned. The U.S. is and will continue to be a mixed-race, multi-ethnic, cultural kaleidoscope of humanity. The die has been cast.

Next, national employment requirements should be matched with immigrant applications. In other words, employment sponsorship and/or government sanctioned categories of skills, trades, or employment requirements must be a prerequisite in the policy. The U.S. Department of Labor would be responsible for defining the levels of immigration that would be required in any given field. In all cases proof of the appropriate educational level and discipline and or skill would be a definite requirement. The

Australians, for example, have been doing this for a decade with great success. Studies show that the Australian model pulls the average wage earnings of both the immigrants and native-born workers upward. It is an overall benefit, not degradation to the economy and the country. In the U.S. the opposite is true. Because approximately 70 percent of illegal immigrants are poorly educated and trained their participation in the job market drives the level of wages downward for both the immigrants and native-born workers. Legal immigrant workers in the U.S., on the other hand, are more educated, have skills and more easily fit into higher paying positions which match with their abilities. Therefore, a two-pronged approach which ties specific applicants to specific sponsors on the one hand and allows a more general Department of Labor defined requirement on the other seems ideal.

Financial responsibility during the transition period would be the next part of the program. Immigrating applicants would be required to arrive with a minimum amount of liquid assets in order to adequately assimilate into their new environment. This is not a cruel and unusual punishment but a reasonable requirement. Americans who apply for expatriate or semi-permanent resident status in Mexico, for example, must demonstrate proof of $2,000 to $3,000 of monthly income in order to be approved. The idea of allowing desperate, broke, unskilled, and uneducated immigrants into the U.S. just does not make any sense. We have a sufficient abundance of unemployed, homeless Americans without the need to import foreigners of the same description. A standard minimum of five to ten thousand dollars or even more should be established prior to issuing immigration documents. If not, it is a sure recipe for an expanded welfare state and/or criminal state. As a matter of fact that is one of the largest problems that currently exist with the illegal immigration environment in the U.S. Studies show that U.S. immigrants are using welfare services at a rate twice as high as citizens. And in January of 2009, with unemployment at an astronomical level of 8.5 percent and underemployment actually pushing that number to 13 percent among citizens, the immigration unemployment and/or underemployed figure is estimated to be approaching 26 percent. ICE's annual report for the fiscal year ending in 2008 reported that almost 30 percent of the illegal Mexican immigrants repatriated during the year were convicted criminals. They clarified that they were not including immigration violations in this percentage. Thirty percent of the almost 350,000 repatriated Mexican immigrants were hard-core criminals. These realities must be factored into the equation when crafting new immigration legislation.

The final part of the new legislation would redefine the new immigrant's family sponsorship capabilities. The current definition is flawed and allows immigrants to basically invite and sponsor his/her extended family. This is, of course, irrational and undermines all the requirements set for immigration. Successful immigrants should only be allowed to sponsor their spouse and children under the age of eighteen.

As a final note on this section I want to emphasize the importance of differentiating between a smart, 21st century plan and the current open-ended immigration setup. The Obama administration, in its early days, is frequently using the terms smart administration, smart power, smart governing, etc. I want to encourage the use of the term **smart immigration**. With **smart immigration** the U.S., can proudly continue to boast of its historical and current characteristic of being a nation of immigrants. If, however, the U.S does not act quickly to enact **smart immigration** legislation and policy the consequences may very well be much worse than the current economic crisis.

Part Three. Fix Visa Overstay. The ICE reports that perhaps one third of the illegal immigrants in the U.S. today arrived on a legal tourist visa. It has become world-wide knowledge that the easiest way to immigrate to the U.S., is to go through the bureaucratic hassle of getting a visa, come to the U.S. legally, and then stay (forever). It is referred to as *Visa Overstays* and accounts for possibly 4 million illegal immigrants or more who are in the U.S. In Mexico, for example, it is very difficult for a peasant to convince the authorities at the border to give him a 30-day visa to vacation in Florida. A savvy, street punk, or anyone interested in defrauding the government, however, in Mexico City, who can present a fraudulent bank statement and utility bill (which is very simple in Mexico City) can easily acquire a tourist visa to visit Shamu and Sea World in San Antonio. In countries around the world, the U.S. Visa Express programs actually prioritize the needs of the applicant over the requirements of the U.S. Consulate. That is crazy but it is happening! In reality the U.S. consulates issuing tourist visas have become a customer service culture instead of a scrutinizing, filtering-type culture. There are millions of immigrants around the world who now recognize how easy it has become to acquire a tourist visa, arrive legally, and then stay in the U.S. In comparison to the dangers of sneaking across the border it has become a preferential method of illegally immigrating.

ICE is not budgeted, staffed adequately, or have the technical means to pursue the millions who intentionally use this method to allude authorities. Perhaps less than one percent of all Visa Overstay immigrants are pursued and eventually repatriated to their home countries. The common argument used against Visa Overstays since 9/11 focuses on terrorism. More than 30 percent of the terrorists involved in attacks inside the U.S. since the 1993 bombing of the World Trade Center (WTC), for example, were Visa Overstayers. The hijackers who destroyed the WTC in 2001 entered the U.S. on tourist visas. They, sadly enough, had applied for and been given visa extensions. The records show that fifteen of the nineteen involved hijackers did not actually qualify for a visa extension. They received visa extensions, however, under the prevailing mindset of *customer service* that existed at the State Department. Obviously that mindset has changed somewhat but still most of the steps that are needed to end illegal immigration through Visa Overstays have not been taken.

The entire visa-entry system is inadequate. For example, as noted by immigration expert Mark Krikorian, "The United States has no good way of knowing whether foreign visitors ever leave, rendering irrelevant the time limits imposed by immigration inspectors. The US-VISIT program is supposed to be an electronic check-in/check-out system for foreigners......but most Mexicans are exempt from being checked in when they arrive, and only a relative handful of people are checked out (when they leave)..... The result is that we still have little idea who is entering the country and almost no idea whether they have left."10 The best thing about this new program is that it requires the recording of biometrics, fingerprints and photographs, upon entry for all of those who fall under its auspices. The bad news is that it does not encapsulate 100 percent of those entering the country on tourist visas. As of January 19, 2009, the DHS under the US-VISIT program expanded the definition of who must submit for biometrics to include all non-citizens who have lawful permanent resident (LPR) status, a few other obscure categories, and anyone the CBP decides it wants to review a little closer at a secondary inspection station. These are all steps in the right direction but the system is still inadequate for two main reasons. It is not installed at all ports of entry nor does it require holders of tourist visas to participate.

The system needs to be comprehensive to the extent of registering 100 percent of entering tourist. Furthermore, the database needs to be shared with all state and local authorities. The reason is easy to understand. When Visa Overstayers come into contact with local police authorities whether it be a traffic violation or a criminal arrest it would be immediately apparent that they were in violation of federal immigration laws. Another requirement should be the deposit of a substantial sum of money in an escrow-type account which could be taken by the U.S., if Visa Overstayers did not leave the country and could not be located. This concept could easily be applied to only those countries with whom Visa Overstays proves to be a habit. The loopholes in our tourist visa programs must be changed in order to get the word out to the rest of the world that the U.S. is serious about legal immigration.

Part Four. Enforcement of Immigration Law and Denial of Social Services. It is impossible to have immigration laws that are respected by foreigners if they are not enforced. Immigration laws in the U.S. are not enforced. It has become completely acceptable for local and state governments to not only ignore national immigration law but to pass legislation which thumbs its nose at the federal authorities attempt to enforce immigration law. Cities across the nation have passed sanctuary laws which try to legitimize the presence of illegal immigrants. Businesses and individuals, of course, commonly ignore federal immigration and labor laws by hiring illegal immigrants. Business employers hide behind a thin veil of fraudulent identification or work papers and fake or stolen social security numbers that are presented by illegal workers. Individuals simply ignore the law under the time-proven reality that almost no one is ever prosecuted for hiring an illegal immigrant to mow the yard, clean the house, or care for the kiddies. It has become part of the American culture. It is acceptable. Pure and simple, American citizens have come to ignore the rule of law when it comes to getting a discount on labor. Individuals have agreed, subliminally, subconsciously, or consciously to ignore the big picture on immigration in order to get that dirty job done for a few measly bucks. It is a myopic, selfish decision which is causing tremendous damage to the American culture. Business owners and managers have made the decision out of necessity or greed to do the same thing. And then we try to justify this bad decision by looking out for the human rights needs of our accomplices in crime, the illegal workers.

From a humane perspective, a rational, reasonable, caring, perspective, the right thing to do is to allow illegal immigrants who work in the U.S. to participate in all of the social programs that are available to legal U.S. citizens. Illegal immigrants are decent human beings who deserve the same opportunities to use social services as anyone else. Or do they? In most cases they have not paid for them. So do they deserve to use social services which have been paid for by legal, tax- paying citizens? As altruistic as Americans tend to be, they cannot afford to pay for the social services and education of twenty or thirty million illegal immigrants who have not been participating in the tax-paying system which supports social benefits. The systems are going bankrupt. California is the best example. Its current budget deficit is forecasted at 45 billion dollars. Social services are the biggest reason. Illegal immigrants are the guilty culprit. Economically, the bottom-line is simple. The benefits that are realized by the U.S. middle-class of having an illegal, second-class citizenry available to do their low-paid jobs at a below-market value (at both the individual and business level) is heavily outweighed by the increased cost in social services, i.e., taxes.

Additional costs are seen in areas where illegal immigrants abuse systems, both private and public, such as hospitals. For example, in most states with large illegal immigrant populations what were once dedicated emergency (only) rooms have turned into immigrant hospitals. The illegal immigrants do not have health insurance yet know that most states require hospitals to treat all applicants who arrive at their emergency rooms. Therefore, the illegal immigrants have come to use the emergency facilities across the country as their hospitals. "The National Academy of Sciences has estimated that each immigrant without a high school degree will cost U.S. taxpayers, on average, $89,000 over the course of his or her lifetime. This is a net cost above the value of any taxes the immigrant will pay and does not include the cost of educating the immigrant's children, which U.S. taxpayers would also heavily subsidize."[11]

The majority of illegal Mexican immigrants do not have a high school degree. Most illegal Mexican immigrants never made it to intermediate school. The NAS study was focused on the cost of uneducated legal immigrants and certainly applies to illegal immigrants.

The most effective step in remedying this situation is to seriously enforce worksite compliance with federal law. ICE has established a social security identification program (E-Verify) which must be legislated to be mandatory across the nation. It is an online, easy-to-use system which verifies social security numbers. Employers must be forced to take the responsibility of screening employees for identification fraud. It can no longer be an option. The E-Verify program must become mandatory not optional. American employers must be tasked with policing their own workforce and prosecuted if they continue to hire illegal immigrants. It is as simple as that. With current unemployment levels approaching double digits there should be no excuses for employers not to hire American nationals or legal immigrants everywhere in the workplace.

As painful and inhumane as it is, cities and states must stop offering social services to illegal immigrants. Mexicans (and others) know that social services are readily available and make decisions to illegally immigrate in order to obtain them. The most bizarre abuse of this setup is along the border in Texas. In 2008, more than 50 gunshot victims stumbled across the border or were otherwise delivered to the emergency room at El Paso's city hospital. The majority were, of course, drug cartel foot-soldiers who were wounded in the line of duty, protecting drug-turf. A few others were Juárez police officers who preferred the treatment at the hospital in El Paso versus the one in Juárez. The cost to the hospital exceeded 1 million dollars. It and the cost of posting El Paso police officers in the rooms to guarantee security were passed along to the U.S. tax payer. The U.S. must adopt a perspective similar to that used in immigration policies in other economically advanced countries. Neither Ireland nor Australia, for example, allows illegal immigrants to participate in social programs. Australia, furthermore, requires legal immigrants to be in the country two years before they can begin receiving social benefits. It makes sense economically and it discourages immigration based on the ability to acquire free services.

Part Five. Establish a *real* Remittance Program. Mexicans are currently sending money back to Mexico via wire transfers, bank transfers, etc. at a 26 billion dollar clip per year. That estimate comes from the Mexican government. Remittances are the third largest industry in Mexico. Only the illegal drug and national oil industries are larger. Surprisingly remittance activity is barely regulated in either country. The Zedillo and Clinton administrations agreed to remove the onus from the American and Mexican banking systems from monitoring, tracking, or reporting this bi-country activity as a concession for lowering the rates they charge for this transfer activity. Both governments wanted to promote the remittance activity of illegal immigrants working in the U.S. The promotion worked very well as remittances grew from 1 billion to 26 billion in a decade. The Mexican government monitors the transfers that arrive via banks but the monies transferred via Western Union and other transfer companies that are sent to money houses, currency exchange houses, grocery stores, pharmacies, department stores, etc. are not being monitored or counted. The reason this activity needs to be reviewed and legislated anew is simple. It facilitates money laundering. Banks and money houses are not requiring Mexicans to meet any serious identification requirement before allowing them to send money back to Mexico. They are also not monitoring the quantity or frequency by which their transfer services are being used. Monies being earned illegally in the drug industry and illegally in legitimate commerce where fraudulent identification is used are being routinely sent to Mexico from the corner check cashing store, Western Union offices at the local grocery store, and increasingly popular money exchange houses. The only requirement for those wishing to transfer money is to fill out a form which asks for name and address of sender and receiver. No identification is required and none of the information is validated. These transfer companies happily charge their customers a hefty fee as well as use an exchange rate which is above market value for the transactions.

This industry needs to be reviewed and regulated with the objective of stopping the large amount of laundered money from crossing the U.S. border into Mexico. Legitimate workers who are making a legal living should have every opportunity to send their legally earned income back to Mexico or wherever. We need a system that requires valid identification, immigration status, and tax identification numbers. If a foreign visitor does not have a valid travel or work visa which corresponds to a legal passport he should not be able to routinely send thousands of dollars out of the country. It does not make sense for the U.S. to cater to the banking needs of millions of illegal immigrant workers and drug-industry launderers. Banks and exchange houses should not be allowed to make money on income that was illegally earned by illegal workers and drug smugglers.

Part Six. Suggestion for new Obama grass roots Employment Organization. Barrack Obama and his powerful campaign team have established a new foundation called Organizing for America. They have used the same grass roots organizing philosophy that elected Obama to create a foundation which is uniting political activity at the community level around the nation. It is modern, organized, and focused. This national organization is the perfect vehicle for addressing the unemployment crisis that exists in the U.S. Unemployment is at 8.5 percent or higher. When coupled with underemployment it is probably higher than 13 percent. Yet more than 10 million illegal immigrants are gamely employed throughout the nation. There can and should be a link between these two situations. Americans realize that the worst recession/depression since the 1930s has forced millions to reevaluate the work place and its opportunities. Americans need jobs.

The establishment of a new Corps of American Workers (CAW) could be established by Obama's Organizing for America foundation. Obama's foundation is already established, has millions of email-connected members, is community based, and a national organization. It is the perfect candidate for quickly establishing a new grass roots-based Corps of American Workers. The CAW's mission statement needs to be very simple. The purpose of the CAW would be to identify unemployed American workers who are ready for immediate employment and marry them with employers who are currently hiring illegal immigrants. The employers would terminate illegal immigrant workers as they are successfully supplied with legal American workers. The task would not be very difficult. In every small community, town, small city, and large metropolis illegal immigrants are illegally working. We all know who many of the employers and managers are. We see the illegal immigrant workers every single day. The employers, managers, owners are our friends and neighbors. They oversee the fast food chains, dry cleaners, grocery stores, restaurants, landscape companies, warehouses, etc., etc., etc.. We know who are in the kitchen making tacos, cooking hamburgers, and flipping pancakes. We know who are mowing the lawns and raking the leaves. We know are mending the hotel rooms and laundries. None of this is a mystery to any of us.

The envisioned methodology which would be used by CAW management would be simple. First, unemployed workers would be registered or enlisted into the ranks of the CAW. Second, employers who hire illegal immigrants would be contacted and given the opportunity to register and participate in the program without recrimination for past or current indiscretions of hiring illegal immigrants. This, in essence, would be an amnesty for the employers and would incent them to come clean on their illegal practices with impunity. Employers of illegal immigrants who are not willing to participate in the program would be subject to public disclosure of their hiring practices by the CAW.

Initial funding for CAW activity would come directly from the federal government in a manner similar to that of the public works programs of the 1930s. The workers however would be paid by the Taco or Pancake makers and not by the government. The workers would be charged a one-time fee for successful job placement which could be paid over an extended period of time. A $1000 fee, for example, would generate one billion dollars if one million American workers filled the ranks of only 10 percent of the positions currently held by illegal immigrant workers.

Obama consistently argues that extraordinary measures are justified during extraordinary times. This is definitely one of those extraordinary times. It is time to start displacing illegal immigrant workers with legal American workers. If Obama's foundation Organizing for America is not the proper vehicle then another similar organization, public or private, could easily tackle this task. The American worker and economy would both benefit. The illegal immigrant workers would have the opportunity to participate in Part One of this plan: path to citizenship through repatriation and qualification.

Conclusion:

The U.S. government has to reengage Mexico in a serious way and recognize the problems that exist on both sides of the border before it is too late. Fortunately, as a result of being bored with the economic recovery news or some other unknown phenomena, the press began covering the drug war and chaos in Mexico in March 2009. Finally, CNN sent in Michael Ware and Anderson Cooper to cover the situation. They are tardy and delinquent in their coverage but better late than never. I do not know which came first the chicken or the egg but on March 25, 2009, Hillary Clinton flew to Mexico to meet with Felipe Calderón as the American press was finally ablaze with the sensational-type reporting that Americans love. Suddenly reports are on every major television news program and in every major daily newspaper. Headlines are dramatically reporting the beheadings, torture, and thousands of killings as if it suddenly a plane crashed into the Hudson River yesterday. Their characterizations of what is going on are just as tardy and delinquent. The popular phrase that has been picked up and is being used is *spilling over*. The violence is starting to *spill over* into the U.S. they report. Or more popularly they report that the administration is worried that the violence may begin to *spill over* into the U.S. Where have these reporters and networks been the last two years? I only need to mention the 500+ home-incursions in Phoenix and Tucson in 2008 or the hundreds of kidnappings in the same two cities to make the point. It is hard to decipher who feeds off of whom. Is the government feeding off the press or is the press feeding off the government? Probably the feeding frenzies work in both directions. The press began covering the situation seriously in mid-March and on March 25th as the Secretary of State flew to Mexico; the President held a news conference and discussed Mexico's problems in a public forum for the first time since taking office. It was sad to see that he is still behind the curve on the situation but he is getting there. He announced in a very inadequate manner that arms and cash from the U.S. were "in part" fueling the drug wars in Mexico. What an understatement that is! The U.S. represents 95 percent of Mexico's market for drugs and 95 percent of the guns bought by the drug cartels come from the U.S. I can only conclude from Obama's statement that he is still not up to speed on reality in Mexico and the U.S. on this subject.

NAFTA must be re-evaluated by *ALL* participating partners and updated in a way that meets the requirements of the 21st century. The agreement must be strengthened in ways that benefit not only free-trade (theoretically) but all the participating players in reality. A stronger free-trade agreement or a modified NAFTA agreement is sorely needed.

Obama's administration must put the cards on the table. America's habitual drug use is the only reason the drug cartels exist. Although in the last five years the cartels have been developing their Mexican domestic market and diversifying in a few other countries. The American demand for drugs is the reason the cartels exist. The billions of dollars in profits afford the cartels the option to import the most modern and deadly weapons available in order to *out gun* the Mexican authorities. The 6300+ greedy, American arms-dealers along the border are sucking-up the profits from the sales of automatic weapons. For Obama to announce that the U.S. "in part" is fueling the situation is ludicrous. It is time for Obama to get educated on the situation and then fix it!

Secretary of State Hillary Clinton and Janet Napolitano are

starting to say the right things and take the right actions. It has
been announced that the U.S. will up its financial aid from 400
million (approved under the Mérida Initiative) to 700 million. That
is certainly a step in the right direction but actually allocating the
money to Mexico is the current dilemma. The money approved
under the Mérida Initiative has still not been released to Calderón
although Bush signed the bill in August of 2008. Obama must
do more than give press announcements that the monies will be
given to Mexico. His administration must really focus on fixing
the problems on both sides of the border. The year 2009 will be a
turning point for Mexican democracy. If the Obama administration
will adopt a set of plans which will secure the border, start
attacking the illegal drug culture, address immigration and trade,
and seriously engage the issue of how to deal with 15 to 30 million
illegal immigrants already in the U.S. then Mexico can be saved.
What goes hand-in-hand with this is the safeguarding of the quality
of life that exists in the U.S. If Mexico fails, the U.S. will suffer
hugely. If Mexico continues along the same path it is currently on,
the U.S. will lose in a big way. If the U.S. partners with Mexico
and seriously addresses these major Mexican-American problems
both countries can have a prosperous 21st century. The time has
long past for American inaction. I am hopeful that Obama's trip
to Mexico in April of 2009 will be the first of many steps which
will lead the U.S. and Mexico away from a failed policy of denial
of the problems that exist between the two nations and towards a
successful solution.

Glossary

Anchor babies are children born to illegal immigrant mothers or fathers within U.S. borders. The babies are legal American citizens and afford their illegal parents an advantage in immigrating. These children act as an anchor for the illegal immigrant parents and possibly other relatives who desire permanent U.S. residency.

Aztec is the name most commonly associated with the nomadic barbarians who invaded the central Valley of Mexico at the end of the first millennium and eventually dominated the entire region for five centuries. Modern Mexicans are their descendants either genetically or culturally in one way or another.

Aztlán is the Aztec mythical island of origin which was hypothetically located somewhere off the northwest coast of Mexico. It has been a rallying concept for Chicanos and illegal Mexican immigrants for decades who desire the return of lost Mexican lands to Mexico.

Barrio is a <u>Spanish</u> word meaning <u>district</u> or <u>neighborhood</u>. It has become synonymous with inner-city slums throughout the Latino world and the southwest U.S.

Bolillo, in Mexico, is a pejorative (racist) description of a white person. The person is described as a *little white bread roll.*

Calderón, Felipe Hinojosa. On December 1 2006, Felipe Calderón was sworn in as president of the United States of Mexico, for the 2006-2012 term.

Calles, Plutarco was president of Mexico from 1924 -1928 but de facto ruler until 1935. He was the founder of the party which eventually became the PRI, which ruled Mexico until the year 2000 as a one party system.

Campesinos are Mexican peasants or rural farmers and ranchers.

Carranza, Venustiano was one of the four revolutionary leaders of 1910. He eventually assumed the presidency, became a de facto dictator, and was assassinated.

(CBP) Customs and Border Protection is an agency of the United States Department of Homeland Security charged with regulating and facilitating international trade, collecting import duties, and enforcing U.S. trade laws. Its other primary mission is preventing terrorists and terrorist weapons from entering the United States. CBP is also responsible for apprehending individuals attempting to enter the United States illegally, stemming the flow of illegal drugs and other contraband.

Cempoalans were the people of the city of Cempoala, a city near the current city of Veracruz. The city was an important staging post in the conquest of Mexico, by Hernán Cortés. The Cempolans were dominated by the Aztecs, hated them, and aligned with the Spaniards in their eventual conquest of the Aztecs.

Chapultepec is a zone or Mexico City which has existed since pre-Columbian times. It has played an important role in Mexican history, most notably, as the site of the cadet defiance (**Los Niños Héroes**) of American invasion troops. Today it is a beautiful park and museum much akin to Central Park in New York City.

Charro is a Mexican cowboy.

Chiapas is the most southern state of Mexico bordering Guatemala. To the east Chiapas borders Guatemala, and to the south the Pacific Ocean.

Chicano is a <u>Mexican American,</u> a U.S.-born American of Mexican ancestry, versus a Mexican native living in the United States.

Chichén Itzá <u>is one the most beautiful Mayan archaeological ruins which is located in the</u> Yucatán <u>Peninsula.</u>

Chichimec is the term used to name the masses of barbaric nomads that invaded the central Valley of Mexico at the end of the first millennium of which the Aztecs were a part.

Chihuahua is the name of both a northern state in Mexico, and the name of the state's capital city. It is bordered to the north by the United States of America. Ciudad Juárez, also just known as Juárez, is in the state of Chihuahua. Juárez shares a border with <u>El Paso, Texas.</u>

Chilango is a <u>Mexican</u> <u>slang</u> word for a resident of <u>Mexico City</u> or someone from the city. It can have a negative connotation when used by someone who is not from Mexico City.

(La) Chingada, *the Fucked One*, is a Mexican concept made famous by Octavio Paz in his book, <u>The Labyrinth of Solitude.</u> Initially, La Chingada was the supreme rape, pillage, and desecration of the Mexican culture by the Spanish. Doña Marina, also known as La Malinche, is usually identified as being La Chingada. The Chingada concept has evolved beyond the Spanish conquest to mean, *being fucked over again.*

Chingar is the Spanish verb for fornication and is used in a thousand variations to explain everything including the Spanish Conquest of Mexico.

Chingón is a derivation of chingar and is used in many expressions in Mexico. It is commonly used to express the state of being *super cool* but can also mean the opposite.

Cholula is a city in the <u>Mexican state</u> of <u>Puebla</u>. It was, in many ways, the spiritual center of the central Valley of Mexico. Cholula was a contemporary city with **Teotihuacán. The Cholulans were stout allies with the Aztecs in their defense against the invading Spaniards in the 16th century. The great pyramid of Cholula of which only the base still exists is possibly the largest ever built by man.**

Cochise, Niño was the grandson of the famous American Apache Cochise of late 19th century fame. His Apaches were some of the last marauding groups to be sequestered on reservations by the American military. He went on to pursue a career in the travelling Wild West shows of the early 20th century.

Cortés de **Monroy y Pizarro, Hernán** was the Spanish conquistador who defeated and caused the fall of the Aztec empire.

Coyote, or people smuggler, is a person who is involved in (and paid for his/her services) the transportation of illegal immigrants across the U.S. and Mexico border.

Criollo (or Creole, in English) is a term derived from the <u>Spanish colonial</u> <u>caste</u> system in Mexico. It referred to a person born in the Spanish colonies of only Spanish (Iberian) ancestry. Criollos were offspring of a Spanish mother and Spanish father.

Cuauhtémoc was the last <u>Aztec</u> ruler of Tenochtitlán.

Culhuacán was the capital established by the Toltecs in the central Valley of Mexico after the demise of the **Teotihuacán** culture and prior to the Aztec's establishment of Tenochtitlán as their capital.

(DEA) Drug Enforcement Administration. The DEA is a <u>United States Department of Justice</u> <u>law enforcement agency</u> tasked with combating <u>drug smuggling and use within the U.S.</u> It also has sole responsibility for coordinating and pursuing U.S. drug investigations abroad.

Díaz del Castillo, Bernal was chief chronicler and an eyewitness to the conquest of Mexico, by the Spaniards under Hernán Cortés. The book that resulted from this journey was the, (The True History of) The Conquest of New Spain. Díaz was a lieutenant of Cortés and wrote his famous book when he became a sentimental octogenarian.

Díaz, Porfirio was Mexico's *Strong Man* **or dictator for four decades at the end of the 19ᵗʰ century and early 20ᵗʰ century. He championed the belief that after five centuries of European dominance that the indigenous Mexican was scarcely more than a mal- adjusted, uneducated brute who could not adapt to modern times.**

Doña Marina, also known as La Malinche, was a woman from the Mexican Gulf Coast, who played a key role in the Spanish conquest of Mexico, acting as interpreter, advisor, intermediary, and mistress to Hernán Cortés. Doña Marina gave birth to **Cortés** □ son, who is considered the first, symbolic Mestizo (a person of mixed European and indigenous American ancestry in Mexico). She is seen as a traitor by some and a heroine by others depending on perspective.

Ejidos are communal land holdings which were awarded to groups of indigenous Mexicans at various stages of Mexican history.

(La) Familia (The Family) is a drug trafficking cartel from the state of Michoacán.

(FBI) Federal Bureau of Investigation. The FBI is the primary agency in the United States Department of Justice serving as both a federal criminal investigative body and a domestic intelligence agency.

Fox, Vicente. Vicente Fox served as president of Mexico from 2000 to 2006. His election was historically significant because it was the first election of a president from an opposition party (breaking 70+ years of domination of the PRI). He was, in reality, the first democratically elected president of Mexico.

Gabacho is a pejorative term for an English-speaking, non-Hispanic.

Gallego(s) is a term used by Mexicans for Spaniards. Gallegos are from Galicia, a region of northwest Spain. In many parts of Spain the language is recognized as an official Spanish dialect.

"Giant (Big) Sucking Sound" was made famous by Ross Perot who spoke the phrase, "…there will be a giant sucking sound going south," during his 1992 U.S. Presidential debate with President George H.W. Bush and Gov. Bill Clinton. Perot was referring to the negative impact he felt NAFTA would have on employment and the U.S. economy as jobs transferred from the USA to Mexico. He hit the nail on the head.

Gringo is a Spanish word used in Mexico to denote people from the United States. Depending on the context, it may be pejorative.

Grito. The Grito de Dolores (Cry of Pain) was the battle cry of the Mexican War of Independence, first spoken on September 16, 1810, by Miguel Hidalgo y Costilla.

Güero is a Mexican term for a fair skinned or light, hair color person.

Hacendado is a landowner of a hacienda.

Hacienda is a large estate. It can also be the main dwelling of a large estate.

Huaraches are rubber-tire sandal produced in Mexico. It is also used as the name of a snack or market fast-food which is served on a fried tortilla. It is also another slang name for illegal Mexicans who live in the U.S.

Huichilobos or Huitzilopochtli (the Aztec spelling), was a god of war in <u>Aztec mythology</u> and the patron god of the city of Tenochtitlán. Huichilobos is the name used by Bernal Díaz in his book, <u>The Conquest of New Spain</u>.

(ICE) Immigration and Customs Enforcement is an investigative arm of the United States Department of Homeland Security (DHS), responsible for identifying, investigating, and dismantling vulnerabilities regarding the nation's border, economic, transportation, and infrastructure security.

Iztaccíhuatl (or Izta) is an active volcano and the third highest peak in Mexico.

Juárez, also known as Ciudad Juárez, is in the state of Chihuahua. The city shares a border with <u>El Paso, Texas</u>. It has become a *killing field* for the drug cartels since 2004.

Maquiladora. A maquiladora is a Mexican corporation, typically on the US-Mexico border, which legally allows a manufacturing company to foreign investment participation in the capital and in management (up to 100%); it entitles the company to special customs treatment, allowing duty free temporary import of machinery, equipment, parts and materials, and administrative equipment.

Matricula Consular de Alta Seguridad (MCAS) (Consular Matriculation of High Security) is an <u>identification card</u> issued by the <u>government of Mexico</u> through its <u>consulate offices</u> to Mexican nationals residing outside of Mexico regardless of their emigration status.

Maya. The Maya were a civilization acknowledged: for having the only fully developed <u>written language</u> of the <u>pre-Columbian</u> Americas, as well as its <u>art</u>, <u>architecture</u>, and mathematical and astronomical systems. The geographic area of the Maya civilization extended throughout the southern Mexican states of Chiapas, Tabasco, and the Yucatán Peninsula states of Quintana Roo, Campeche and Yucatán. The Maya area also extended throughout the northern Central American region, including the present-day nations of Guatemala, Belize, El Salvador and western Honduras.

Mérida Initiative (or **Mérida Plan**). **The plan is** between the U.S., Mexico, and the countries of Central America to combat the threats of drug trafficking, transnational crime, and terrorism in the Western Hemisphere. The U.S. agreed to release 400 million of the allocated 1.2 billion in funds in 2007 but no funds were released until early 2009. Obama has now prioritized its implementation.

Mestizo is a Spanish term that was used in the Spanish empire to refer to people of mixed European and Amerindian ancestry.

Mexica is probably the more appropriate indigenous name for the Aztec culture but is seldom used.

Michoacán is one of the 31 constituent states of Mexico. Its state capital is the city of Morelia.

Mitla is one of the fantastic Zapotec cities of Oaxaca which helped usher in the Golden Age of Mexico.

Mixtec (or Mixteca) are indigenous people inhabiting the Mexican states of Oaxaca, Guerrero and Puebla in a region known as La Mixteca.

Monte Albán was the capital of the Zapotec world and key in the development of Mexico's Golden Age. It and Mitla are wonderful archaeological sites in magical Oaxaca.

Montezuma II was the 9th ruler of Tenochtitlán. It was during Montezuma's reign that the Spanish Conquest began.

Mordida is the Spanish word for *a bite* but refers to the omnipresent bribe that exists in Mexico.

Morelia is the capital of the Mexican state of Michoacán.

Náhuatl is the language of the Aztec and is still spoken today.

(Ciudad) Nezahualcóyotl is the large, corrupt, disaster of a neighborhood / city in Mexico City which is governed by thugs. It has existed for at least five centuries as one of the worst barrios on planet earth.

Oaxaca is a southern state of Mexico and the capital city.

Obregón, Álvaro was one of the four revolutionary leaders of 1910 who later assumed the presidency and was assassinated.

PAN is the National Action Party of Mexico that unseated the PRI in 2000 with the election of Vicente Fox and subsequent election of Felipe Calderón, thereby establishing a true democracy for the first time in Mexican history.

Pátzcuaro is the beautiful city beside Lake Patzcuaro which was the home of the Tarascan culture.

PEMEX is the Mexican National Petroleum Company which controls 100% of oil production, distribution, and sales.

Pinche is used as an adjective to describe something as insignificant, lousy, miserable, or worthless. The crude translation of the adjective is *fucking worthless*.

Pocho (or *Spanglish* in English) is a language mix of Spanish and English words.

Popocatépetl, commonly referred to as *Popo*, is an active volcano and the second highest peak in Mexico.

Porfiriato refers to the four decade period under the dictatorship of Porfirio Díaz.

PRI (Partido Revolucionario Institucional) is the <u>Mexican political party</u> that wielded power in the country for more than 70 years.

Quetzalcoatl is the name of the **Teotihuacán** god which was later used by the Toltecs and their most influential leader who took the same name. Many Aztecs believed that Hernán **Cortés** was the reincarnation of the once powerful leader/god.

Rurales were the federal police who were originally organized to guard federal silver shipments from the mines to Mexico City and to maintain a federal presence in the rural countryside. They eventually became the apparatus by which the dictator Porfirio Díaz intimidated and controlled the masses.

Salinas de Gortari, Carlos was the president of Mexico from 1988 to 1994 and responsible for the catastrophic devaluation of the peso in 1994.

Slim Helú, Carlos. Carlos Slim, telecom baron, is one of the richest men in the world. Super billionaire Carlos Slim owns controlling interest of Telmex (fixed line **Teléfonos de México SA de CV.**) and **América Móvil** SAB de CV (a wireless telephone company).

Tarascans were the culture which lived in the current state of Michoacán and were arch enemies of the Aztecs.

Tenochtitlán was the Aztec capital, city-state located on an island in <u>Lake Texcoco</u>, in the <u>Valley of Mexico</u>. Today the ruins of Tenochtitlán are located in <u>Mexico City, Mexico</u>.

Teotihuacán is an archaeological site in the Valley of Mexico containing some of the largest <u>pyramidal structures</u> built in the <u>pre-Columbian</u> Americas.

Teotihuacanos were the people of **Teotihuacán.**

Tepotzotlán is a beautiful small mountain town in central Mexico located close to Curnevaca. It has recently become a haven for drug-cartel kingpins.

Tianguez is the traditional Mexican market which was originally based on bartering.

Tlaxcala, or Talascala which is the Spanish conquistadors' spelling, is one of the 31 states of Mexico, located to the east of Mexico City. Tlaxcalan or Talascalan are the people of the area / state.

Toltecs were people from the Valley of Mexico who ruled Mexico and Central America in the 10th-12th centuries, with their capital and religious center at Tula, northeast of Mexico City. After the fall of the Toltecs, the Aztecs took over much of their former territory, except for the regions regained by the Maya.

Trailero is a freightliner, truck driver.

Tula is the center established by the Toltec leader Quetzalcotl after he was banished from the capital of Culhuacán. The site today is known for its wonderful Toltec statues.

Tulum is the wonderfully preserved Mayan port city located on the Caribbean in Mexico's Yucatán Peninsula.

Uruapan is a city in the Mexican state of Michoacán. One of the major industries of Uruapan is avocado farming and packaging for export.

Villagomez, Miguel was the assassinated editor of The News of Michoacán.

Wetback is a derogatory word used for illegal aliens, primarily Mexicans, in the United States, who entered the U.S. by swimming or crossing a river (e.g. Texas and the Rio Grande River).

Yucatán is one of the 31 states of Mexico, located on the Yucatán Peninsula.

Zapotecs were an indigenous pre-Columbian civilization that lived in the Valley of Oaxaca. **Monte Albán was the capital of the Zapotec world and key in the development of Mexico's Golden Age. It and Mitla are wonderful archaeological sites in magical Oaxaca**

(Los) Zetas are paramilitary criminal gangs that operate as a hired army for the Mexican Gulf Cartel. Sometime around 2006 or earlier the Zetas actually began competing as an independent drug-cartel.

End Notes

Chapter II   The Collapse of the Golden Age of Mexico
1. Ellingwood, Ken. "Drug war bodies are piling up in Mexico". Los Angeles Times. 30 Aug.2008. <http://www.latimes. com/news/nationworld/world/la-fg-mexdrugs30-2008aug30,0,5217757.story>.
2. Fehrenbach, T.R. Fire & Blood, A History of Mexico. New York: Da Capo Press, Inc., 1995. pp. 28-29.
3. Ibid. p. 20.
4. Ibid. p. 31.
5. Meyer, Michael C., and Sherman, William L. The Course of Mexican History. New York: Oxford University Press, Inc., 1995. p. 15.
6. Fehrenbach, T.R. Fire & Blood, A History of Mexico. New York: Da Capo Press, Inc., 1995. p. 40.

Chapter III   Mexico's Collision with Europe
1. Díaz, Bernal. The Conquest of New Spain. London, England: Penguin Books Ltd., 1963. p. 37.
2. Ibid. p. 122.
3. Ibid. p. 183.
4. Ibid. p. 184.
5. Ibid. p. 184.
6. Fehrenbach, T.R. Fire & Blood, A History of Mexico. New York: Da Capo Press, Inc. 1995. p. 82.
7. Ibid. p. 85.
8. Ibid. p. 86.
9. Meyer, Michael C., and Sherman, William L. The Course of Mexican History. New York: Oxford University Press, Inc., 1995. p. 37.
10. Chandler, Tertius, and Fox, Gerald. Three Thousand Years of Urban Growth. U.S.: Academic Press Inc, 1974.
11. Díaz, Bernal. The Conquest of New Spain. London, England: Penguin Books Ltd. 1963. p. 236.
12. Ibid. p. 264.

13. Harner, Michael. "The Enigma of Aztec Sacrifice". LatinAmericanStudies.org. Apr. 1977. <http://www. latinamericanstudies.org/aztecs/sacrifice.htm>.

14. White, Matthew. "Selected Death Tolls for Wars, Massacres and Atrocities Before the 20th Century". 20 Jan. 2005. <http://users.erols.com/mwhite28/warstat0.htm>.

15. Díaz, Bernal. The Conquest of New Spain. London, England: Penguin Books Ltd. 1963. p. 387.

16. PAVÓN, Oliver A. "S.O.S. de Tijuana: El crimen organizado tiene secuestrada a la población a través del miedo e intimidación. La Crónica de Hoy. 10 Sept. 2008. <http://www.cronica.com.mx/nota.php?id_ nota=384136>.

Chapter IV   The New Mexican-European Hybrid

1. Meyer, Michael C., and Sherman, William L. The Course of Mexican History.   New York: Oxford University Press, Inc., 1995. p. 148.

2. Ibid. p.148.

3. Wilkinson, Tracy, "24 bodies found near Mexico City." Los Angeles Times. 14 Sept. 2008. <http://articles.latimes. com/2008/sep/14/world/fg-mexico14.>

4. Meyer, Michael C., and Sherman, William L. The Course of Mexican History. New York: Oxford University Press, Inc., 1995. p. 211.

5. Ibid, p. 211.

6. Paz, Octavio. The Labyrinth of Solitude, Life and Thought in Mexico. New York: Grove Press, Inc., 1961. p.86.

7. Ibid. p. 87.

8. Ibid. p. 78.

9. Ibid. p. 79.

10. Ibid. p. 81.

11. Ibid. p. 82

12. Ibid. p. 70.

13. Ibid. p. 70.

14. Ibid. p. 71.

15. Meyer, Michael C., and Sherman, William L. The Course of Mexican History. New York: Oxford University Press, Inc., 1995. p. 212.

16. Ibid. p.274.

17. Ellingwood, Ken. "Mexican officials blame organized crime for deadly blasts." Los Angeles Times. 17 Sept. 2008. <http://articles.latimes.com/2008/sep/17/world/fg-

mexattack17.>

18. Gibler, John. "Teacher Rebellion in Oaxaca." IN THESE
    TIMES. 21 Aug. 2006. <http://www.inthesetimes.com/
    article/discuss/2795/teacher_rebellion_in_Oaxaca/.>

19. Kroll, Luisa. Edited. "The World's Billionaires." Forbes.
    com. 5 Mar. 2008. <http://www.forbes.com/2008/03/05/
    richest-people-billionaires-billionaires08-cx_lk_
    0305billie_land.html.>

20. Meyer, Michael C., and Sherman, William L. The Course of
    Mexican History. New York: Oxford University Press,
    Inc., 1995. p. 322.

21. Ibid. p. 331.

22. Ibid. p. 332.

23. Sartorius, Carl. Mexico about 1850. Stuttgart: F.A.
    Brockhaus Komm, 1961. p. 69.

Chapter V   How Mexico Got to 21st Century

1. Cosío Villegas, Daniel. History of Modern Mexico. Mexico,
    1955-1972.

2. Ibid. p. 151.

3. Paz, Octavio. The Labyrinth of Solitude, Life and Thought in
    Mexico. New York: Grove Press, Inc., 1961. pp.128-129.

4. Ibid. p. 129.

5. Meyer, Michael C., and Sherman, William L. The Course of
    Mexican History. New York: Oxford University Press,
    Inc., 1995. p. 458.

6. Ibid. p. 459.

7. Paz, Octavio. The Labyrinth of Solitude, Life and Thought in
    Mexico. New York: Grove Press, Inc., 1961. p. 130

8. Brenner, Anita. The Wind That Swept Mexico. The History
    of the Mexican Revolution of 1910-1942. Photographs
    assembled by George R. Leighton. Austin: University of
    Texas Press, 2000. p. 10.

9. Cochise, Niño (Ciye) as told to Griffith, A. Kinney. The First
    Hundred Years of Niño Cochise. New York; Abelard-
    Schuman Limited. 1971. p. 228.

10. Paz, Octavio. The Labyrinth of Solitude, Life and Thought in
    Mexico. New York: Grove Press, Inc., 1961. p. 175.

11. Meyer, Michael C., and Sherman, William L. The Course
    of Mexican History. 5th edition. New York: Oxford
    University Press, Inc., 1995. p. 583.

12. Tannenbaum, Frank. Mexico: the Struggle for Peace and
    Bread. New York: Alfred A. Knopf. 1950. pp. 59-70.

Chapter VI   200 Years of Mutual Disrespect
1. Paz, Octavio. The Labyrinth of Solitude, Life and Thought in
    Mexico. New York: Grove Press, Inc., 1961. p. 121.
2. Meyer, Michael C., and Sherman, William L. The Course of
    Mexican History. New York: Oxford University Press,
    Inc., 1995. p. 352.
3. Bremer, Anita. The Wind That Swept Mexico. Austin, Texas:
    University of Texas Press. 2000. pp. 11-12.
4. Ratliff, Chris Michael. "20th Century Mexico." The Historical
    Text Archive. <http://historicaltextarchive.com/sections.
    php?op=viewarticle&artid=137>.
5. Zimmerman, Arthur. "The Zimmerman Note." WWI
    www. 1917. <http://wwi.lib.byu.edu/index.php/The_
    Zimmerman_Note>.
6. Niblo, Stephen R. "Allied Policy toward Germans, Italians
    and
Japanese in Mexico during World War II." Latin American
    Studies
Association, The Palmer House Hilton Hotel, Chicago, Illinois.
    24-26 Sept. 1998. <http://lasa.international.pitt.edu/
    LASA98/Niblo.pdf. 1998.> p.3.

Chapter VII   Mexamerica
1. United States. US Census Bureau. <http://www.census.gov/
    population/pop-profile/dynamic/RACEHO.pdf>.
2. McKensie, David and Papoport, Hillel. "Migration and
    Education Inequality in Rural Mexico." Inter-American
    Development Bank. November 2006. <http://www.
    iadb.org/INTAL/aplicaciones/uploads/publicaciones/
    i_INTALITD_WP_23_2006McKenzie_Rapoport.
    pdf. Institute for Integration of Latin America and the
    Caribbean>. p. 2.
3. Lazarus, Emma. "The New Colossus." 1883.
4. Myrick, Sue U.S. Rep. "Myrick Denounces Mexican
    President for Criticizing American Laws". 11 Sept.
    2007. <www.house.gov/hensarling/rsc/doc/ca_091707_
    myrickmexicanprez.doc>.
5. United States. U.S. Immigration and Customs Enforcement
    (ICE). "ICE multifaceted strategy leads to record
    enforcement results; Removals, criminal arrests,
    and worksite investigations soared in fiscal year
    2008." 23 Oct. 2008. <http://www.ice.gov/pi/nr/0810/

081023washington.htm>.

6.   United States. Government Accountability Office. Stana, Richard M. Director Homeland Security and Justice Issues. 7 Apr. 2005. "Information on Criminal Aliens Incarcerated in Federal and State Prisons and Local Jails". http://immigration.procon.org/sourcefiles/ InformationonCriminalAliensIncarceratedin FederalandStatePrisonsandLocalJails.pdf. p. 2.

7.   United States. U.S. Immigration and Customs Enforcement (ICE). "ICE Fugitive Operations Program". 19 Nov. 2008. <http://www.ice.gov/pi/news/factsheets/NFOP_ FS.htm>.

8.   Salvi, Steve. "Sanctuary Cities: What are they?" Revised 13 Apr. 2009. <http://www.ojjpac.org/sanctuary.asp>.

9.   Krikorian, Mark, Wattenberg, Ben, Camarota, Steven, and Beck, Roy. "100 Million More: Projecting the Impact of Immigration On the U.S. Population, 2007 to 2060." Aug 2007. Center of Immigration Studies. <http://www.cis. org/node/639>.

10. United States. Department of Homeland Security. "E-Verify". 20 Apr 2009. <http://www.dhs.gov/xprevprot/programs/ gc_1185221678150.shtm>.

11. United States. U.S. Immigration and Customs Enforcement. "Ice Multifaceted Strategy Leads to Record Enforcement." 23 Oct. 2008. <http://www.ice.gov/pi/ nr/0810/081023washington.htm>.

12. United States. U.S. Immigration and Customs Enforcement. "ICE Fugitive Operations Program." 19 Nov. 2008. <http://www.ice.gov/pi/news/factsheets/NFOP_FS.htm>.

13. Rector, Robert E. "Importing Poverty: Immigration and Poverty in the United States: A Book of Charts." 25 Oct. 2006. The Heritage Foundation. <http://www.heritage. org/research/immigration/sr9.cfm#_ftn9>.

14. Ibid.

15. Ibid.

16. Longley, Robert. "Illegal Immigration costs California Over Ten Billion Annually." Dec. 2004. About.com. <http:// usgovinfo.about.com/od/immigrationnaturalizatio/a/ caillegals.htm>.

17. Davis Hanson, Victor. Mexifornia, A State of Becoming. New York: Encounter Books. 2007. pp. xxii –xxiii.

Chapter VIII   Kidnapping Capital of the World

1.   Peters, Gretchen. "Kidnapping Thrives in Mexico." The Christian Science Monitor. 17 Sept. 2002. <http://www.csmonitor.com/2002/0917/p06s02-woam.html.>

2.   Mascarenas, Dolly. "No Help for Mexico's Kidnapping Surge." Times. com. 8 Aug. 2008. <http://www.time.com/time/world/article/0,8599,1830649,00.html>.

3.   Marosi, Richard. "U.S. Haven for Tijuana Elite." Los Angeles Times. 7 June 2008. <http://www.latimes.com/news/nationworld/world/la-me-haven,0,3041395.story.>.

4.   French, Jon M. 'Creating a corporate shield; Companies in Mexico are investing more to protect their main asset: the executive talent." 2005. The Free Library. <http://www.thefreelibrary.com/Creating+a+corporate+shield%3B+Companies+in+Mexico+are+investing+more...-a0142107433>.

5.   Ordonez, Franco. "Kidnappings soar in Mexico as drug gangs seek new income." McClatchy Newspapers. 22 Apr 2008. <http://www.mcclatchydc.com/226/story/34513.html>.

6.   Stevenson, Mark. "US official: Mexican cartels murder, kidnap in US." USA TODAY. 19 Oct. 2008. <http://www.usatoday.com/news/topstories/2008-10-19-1714053823_x.htm>.

7.   Lacey, Marc. "Exploiting Real Fears With 'Virtual Kidnappings'." The New York Times. 29 Apr. 2008. <http://www.nytimes.com/2008/04/29/world/americas/29mexico.html?hp>.

Chapter X   The Best Response to a Chaotic Situation

1.   Obama, Barack. "Immigration. Bring people out of the shadows". Organizing for America. 22 Apr 2009. www.barackobama.com/issues/immigration>.

2.   Rodham Clinton, Hillary Senator. "STATEMENT OF SENATOR HILLARY RODHAM CLINTON NOMINEE FOR SECRETARY OF STATE SENATE FOREIGN RELATIONS COMMITTEE." 13 Jan 2009. <http://foreign.senate.gov/testimony/2009/ClintonTestimony090113a.pdf>. p. 7.

3.   Ibid. p. 10.

4.   Serrano, Richard A. "Weapons Smuggled into Mexico Fuel Drug War." Los Angeles Times. 17 Aug. 2008. http://www.sfgate.com/cgi-bin/article.cgi?f=/c/a/2008/08/16/

MNIA128E0D.DTL.

5. Obama, Barack. "President Obama's Inaugural Address." America.gov. 20 Jan. 2009. <http://www.america.gov/st/usg-english/2009/January/20090120130302abretnuh0.2991602.html>.

6. United States. U.S. Immigration and Customs Enforcement (ICE). <http://www.ice.gov/ >.

7. United States. U.S. Department of Customs and Border Patrol (CBP). http://ww.cbp.gov/>.

8. Progressive Policy Institute (PPI). "Number of American Servicemen and Women Stationed Overseas: 289,000." 28 May 2008. <http://www.ppionline.org/ppi_ci.cfm?knlgAreaID=108&subsecID=900003&contentID=254647>.

9. McDonald, Heather; Davis Hanson, Victor; Malanga, Steven. The Immigration Solution, A Better Plan Than Today's. Chicago: Manhattan Institute. 2007. p. 171.

10. Krikorian, Mark. The New Case Against Immigration, Both Legal and Illegal. New York: Penguin Group (USA) Inc. 2008.

11. Rector, Robert E. "Importing Poverty: Immigration and Poverty in the United States: A Book of Charts." 25 Oct. 2006. The Heritage Foundation. <http://www.heritage.org/research/immigration/sr9.cfm#_ftn9>.

Bibliography

A Day Without a Mexican. Dir. Sergio Arau. Eye on The Ball Films, 2004.

ABCNews. <http://abcnews.go.com/>.

Apocalypse Now. Dir. Francis Ford Coppola. Zoetrope Studios, 1979.

Bawer, Bruce. While Europe Slept. How Radical Islam is Destroying the West from Within. New York: Broadway Books, 2006.

The Boston Globe. <http://www.boston.com/bostonglobe/>.

Brenner, Anita. The Wind That Swept Mexico. The History of the Mexican Revolution of 1910-1942. Photographs assembled by George R. Leighton. Austin: University of Texas Press, 2000.

Chandler, Tertius, and Fox, Gerald. Three Thousand Years of Urban Growth. U.S.: Academic Press Inc, 1974.

Cochise, Ciye "Niño" and Griffin, A. Kinney. The First Hundred Years of Niño Cochise. New York: Abelard-Schuman Limited, 1971.

Committee to Protect Journalists. <http://www.cpj.org/>.

Conrad, Joseph. Heart of Darkness. New York: Penguin, 1999.

Cortés, Hernán. Hernán Cortés: Letters from Mexico. Trans. Anthony Pagden. New Haven: Yale University Press, 1986.

Cosío Villegas, Daniel. History of Modern Mexico. Mexico, 1955-1972.

CNN.com. <http://www.cnn.com/>.

Excélsior. <http://www.excelsior.com.mx/>.

La Crónica de Hoy. <http://www.cronica.com.mx/>.

Diamond, Jared. Guns, Germs, and Steel. The Fates of Human Societies. New York: W. W. Norton and Company, 1999.

Díaz, Bernal. The Conquest of New Spain. Trans. J.M. Cohen. London, England: Penguin Books Ltd., 1963.

El Paso Times. <http://www.elpasotimes.com>

Ellingwood, Ken. "Drug war bodies are piling up in Mexico". Los
    Angeles Times. 30 Aug.2008. <http://www.latimes.com/news/
    nationworld/world/la-fg-mexdrugs30-2008aug30,0,5217757.
    story>.

Ellingwood, Ken. "Mexican officials blame organized crime for
    deadly blasts." Los Angeles Times. 17 Sept. 2008. <http://
    articles.latimes.com/2008/sep/17/world/fg-mexattack17>.

Fehrenbach, T. R. Fire and Blood. A History of Mexico. New York:
    Da Capo Press, 1995.

Fleming, Gary "Rusty". Drug Wars. Narco Warfare in the 21st Century.
    A Producers Journal. 2008.

Forbes.com.   < http://www.forbes.com/>.

French, Jon M. 'Creating a corporate shield; Companies in Mexico
    are investing more to protect their main asset: the executive
    talent." The Free Library. 2005.

<http://www.thefreelibrary.com/Creating+a+corporate+shield%3B+Co
    mpanies+in+Mexico+are+investing+more...-a0142107433>.

Frost, Robert. "Mending Wall." 1915.

Harner, Michael. "The Enigma of Aztec Sacrifice".
    LatinAmericanStudies.org. Apr. 1977. <http://www.
    latinamericanstudies.org/aztecs/sacrifice.htm>.

Gibler, John. "Teacher Rebellion in Oaxaca." IN THESE TIMES.
    21 Aug. 2006. <http://www.inthesetimes.com/article/
    discuss/2795/teacher_rebellion_in Oaxaca/>.

Hanson, Victor Davis. Mexifornia. A State of Becoming. New York:
    Encounter Books, 2007.

The Houston Chronicle. http://www.chron.com/>.

The Huffington Post. <http://www.huffingtonpost.com/.>

Information Please® Database, "Population of the United States by
    Race and Hispanic/Latino Origin, Census 2000 and July 1,
    2005". Pearson Education, Inc. <http://www.infoplease.com/
    ipa/A0762156.html>.

International Herald Tribune. < http://global.nytimes.com/?iht>.

La Jornada. <http://www.jornada.unam.mx/ultimas/>.

Krikorian, Mark, Wattenberg, Ben, Camarota, Steven, and Beck, Roy.
    "100 Million More: Projecting the Impact of Immigration On
    the U.S. Population, 2007 to 2060." Center of Immigration

Studies. Aug 2007. <http://www.cis.org/node/639>.

Krirkorian, Mark. The New Case Against Immigration. Both Legal
    and Illegal. New York: Sentinel, the Penguin Group, 2008.

Kroll, Luisa. Edited. "The World's Billionaires." Forbes.com. 5
    Mar. 2008. <http://www.forbes.com/2008/03/05/richest-
    people-billionaires-billionaires08-cx_lk_0305billie_land.
    html>.

Lacey, Marc. "Exploiting Real Fears With 'Virtual Kidnappings'."
    The New York Times. 29 Apr. 2008. <http://www.nytimes.
    com/2008/04/29/world/americas/29mexico.html?hp>.

Los Angeles Times. <http://www.latimes.com/>.

Lazarus, Emma. "The New Colossus." 1883

León-Portilla, Miguel. Aztec Thought and Culture. Trans. Jack Emory
    Davis. Norman: University of Oklahoma Press, 1963.

León-Portilla, Miguel. The Broken Spears. The Aztec Account of the
    Conquest of Mexico. Trans. J. Jorge Klor de Alva. Boston:
    Beacon Press, 1992.

Longley, Robert. "Illegal Immigration costs California Over Ten
    Billion Annually." Dec. 2004.

About.com. <http://usgovinfo.about.com/od/immigrationnaturalizatio/
    a/caillegals.htm>.

López de Gómara, Francisco. Cortés: The Life of the Conqueror of
    Mexico by His Secretary. Translated and edited by Lesley
    Byrd Simpson. Berkeley and Los Angeles: University of
    California Press, 1964.

MacDonald, Heather, Hanson, Victor Davis, and Malanga, Steven. The
    Immigration Solution. A Better Plan than Today's. Chicago:
    Ivan R. Dee, 2007.

Madero, Francisco Ignacio. The Presidential Succession in 1910. 1908.

Marosi, Richard. "U.S. Haven for Tijuana Elite." Los Angeles Times.
    7 June 2008. <http://www.latimes.com/news/nationworld/
    world/la-me-haven,0,3041395.story>.

Mascarenas, Dolly. "No Help for Mexico's Kidnapping Surge."
    Times.com. 8 Aug. 2008. <http://www.time.com/time/world/
    article/0,8599,1830649,00.html >.

McCaa, Robert. "Was the 16th century a demographic catastrophe for
    Mexico?" V Reunión Nacional de Investigación Demográfica
    en México,
    El Colegio de México, México, D.F. 5-9 June 1995. <http://
    www.hist.umn.edu/~rmccaa/noncuant/index0.htm>.

McDonald, Heather; Davis Hanson, Victor; Malanga, Steven. The

Immigration Solution, A Better Plan Than Today's. Chicago: Manhattan Institute. 2007.

McKensie, David and Papoport, Hillel. "Migration and Education Inequality in Rural Mexico." Inter-American Development Bank. November 2006. <http://www.iadb.org/INTAL/ aplicaciones/uploads/publicaciones/i_INTALITD_WP_23_ 2006_McKenzie_Rapoport.pdf. Institute for Integration of Latin America and the Caribbean>.

Meyer, Michael C., and Sherman, William L. The Course of Mexican History. New York: Oxford University Press, 1995.

Myrick, Sue U.S. Rep. "Myrick Denounces Mexican President for Criticizing American Laws". 11 Sept. 2007. <www.house. gov/hensarling/rsc/doc/ca_091707_myrickmexicanprez.doc>.

The New York Times. <http://global.nytimes.com/>.

Niblo, Stephen R. "Allied Policy toward Germans, Italians and Japanese in Mexico during World War II." Latin American Studies Association, The Palmer House Hilton Hotel, Chicago, Illinois. 24-26 Sept. 1998.

No Country for Old Men. Dir. Ethan Coen and Joel Coen. Paramount Vantage, 2007.

Obama, Barack. "Immigration. Bring people out of the shadows". Organizing for America. 22 Apr 2009. <www.barackobama. com/issues/immigration>.

Obama, Barack. "President Obama's Inaugural Address." America. gov. 20 Jan. 2009. <http://www.america.gov/st/usg-english/2009/January/20090120130302abretnuh0.2991602. html>.

OCWeekly. <http://www.ocweekly.com/.>

Ordonez, Franco. "Kidnappings soar in Mexico as drug gangs seek new income." McClatchy Newspapers. 22 Apr 2008. <http://www.mcclatchydc.com/226/story/34513.html>.

PAVÓN, Oliver A. "S.O.S. de Tijuana: El crimen organizado tiene secuestrada a la población a través del miedo e intimidación." La Crónica de Hoy. 10 Sept. 2008. <http://www.cronica.com. mx/nota.php?id_nota=384136>.

Paz, Octavio. The Labyrinth of Solitude. Life and Thought in Mexico. Trans. Lysander Kemp. New York: Grove Press, Inc., 1961.

Peters, Gretchen. "Kidnapping Thrives in Mexico." The Christian Science Monitor. 17 Sept. 2002. <http://www.csmonitor. com/2002/0917/p06s02-woam.html>.

PEW Hispanic Center. http://pewhispanic.org/

Progressive Policy Institute (PPI). "Number of American Servicemen
     and Women Stationed Overseas: 289,000." 28 May 2008.
     <http://www.ppionline.org/ppi_ci.cfm?knlgAreaID=108&subs
     ecID=900003&contentID=254647>.

Public Broadcasting Service (PBS). http://www.pbs.org/.

Ramos, Samuel. Profile of Man and Culture in Mexico. Trans. Peter
     G. Earle. Austin: University of Texas Press, 1962.

Ratliff, Chris Michael. "20th Century Mexico." The Historical Text
     Archive. <http://historicaltextarchive.com/sections.php?op=vi
     ewarticle&artid=137>.

Rector, Robert E. "Importing Poverty: Immigration and Poverty in the
     United States: A Book of Charts."

The Heritage Foundation. 25 Oct. 2006.

<http://www.heritage.org/research/immigration/sr9.cfm#_ftn9>.

REFORMA.COM. <http://www.reforma.com/>.

Right Side News. <http://www.rightsidenews.com/>.

Rodham Clinton, Hillary Senator. "STATEMENT OF SENATOR
     HILLARY RODHAM

CLINTON NOMINEE FOR SECRETARY OF STATE SENATE
     FOREIGN RELATIONS COMMITTEE."

13 Jan 2009. <http://foreign.senate.gov/testimony/2009/
     ClintonTestimony090113a.pdf>.

Rivera, Geraldo. Hispanic. Why Americans Fear Hispanics in the
     U.S. New York: Celebra, New American Library a division of
     Penguin Group USA, 2008.

San Francisco Chronicle. <http://www.sfgate.com/>.

Sartorius, Carl. Mexico about 1850. Stuttgart: F.A. Brockhaus Komm,
     1961.

Salvi, Steve. "Sanctuary Cities: What are they?" Revised 13 Apr. 2009.
     <http://www.ojjpac.org/sanctuary.asp>.

Serrano, Richard A. "Weapons Smuggled into Mexico Fuel Drug War."
     Los Angeles Times. 17 Aug. 2008. <http://www.sfgate.com/
     cgi-bin/article.cgi?f=/c/a/2008/08/16/MNIA128E0D.DTL>.

Stevenson, Mark. "US official: Mexican cartels murder, kidnap in US."
     USA TODAY. 19 Oct. 2008. <http://www.usatoday.com/
     news/topstories/2008-10-19-1714053823_x.htm>.

Talking Heads. "Life During Wartime." Fear of Music. Warner, 1979.

Tannenbaum, Frank. Mexico: the Struggle for Peace and Bread. New
     York: Alfred A. Knopf. 1950.

The Godfather. Dir. Francis Ford Coppola. Alfran Productions, 1972.

The Grapes of Wrath. Dir. John Ford. Twentieth Century-Fox Film
    Corporation, 1940.

Time.com. <http://www.time.com/time/>.

Tolkien, J. R. R. The Fellowship of the Ring, The Lord of the Rings,
    New York: Ballantine Books, 1994.

United States. Government Accountability Office. Stana, Richard M.
    Director Homeland Security and Justice Issues. 7 Apr. 2005.
    "Information on Criminal Aliens Incarcerated in Federal and
    State Prisons and Local Jails".   http://immigration.procon.
    org/sourcefiles/InformationonCriminalAliensIncarceratedin
    FederalandStatePrisonsandLocalJails.pdf.

United States. Department of Homeland Security. "E-Verify". 20
    Apr 2009. <http://www.dhs.gov/xprevprot/programs/gc_
    1185221678150.shtm>.

United States. U.S. Immigration and Customs Enforcement (ICE).
    "ICE Fugitive Operations Program". 19 Nov. 2008. <http://
    www.ice.gov/pi/news/factsheets/NFOP_FS.htm>.

United States. U.S. Immigration and Customs Enforcement (ICE).
    "ICE multifaceted strategy leads to record enforcement results;
    Removals, criminal arrests, and worksite investigations soared
    in fiscal year 2008." 23 Oct. 2008. <http://www.ice.gov/pi/
    nr/0810/081023washington.htm>.

United States. U.S. Immigration and Customs Enforcement. "ICE
    Fugitive Operations Program."   19 Nov. 2008.
    <http://www.ice.gov/pi/news/factsheets/NFOP_FS.htm>.

United States. CIA World Fact Book. <https://www.cia.gov/library/
    publications/the-world-factbook/>.

Union-Tribune. <http://www.signonsandiego.com/>.

EL UNIVERSAL.com.mx. <http://www.eluniversal.com.mx/noticias.
    html>.

USA TODAY. <http://www.usatoday.com/>.

La Voz de Michoacán. <http://www.vozdemichoacan.com.mx/>.

Vigdor, Jacob L. "Measuring Immigrant Assimilation in the United
    States." May 2008. Manhattan Institute for Policy Research.
    <http://www.manhattan-institute.org/html/cr_53.htm>.

Viva Zapata! Dir. Elia Kazan. Twentieth Century-Fox Film
    Corporation, 1952.

Wall Street Journal.   <http://online.wsj.com/home-page>.

The Washington Post.   <http://www.washingtonpost.com/>.

White, Matthew. "Selected Death Tolls for Wars, Massacres and Atrocities Before the 20th Century". 20 Jan. 2005. <http://users.erols.com/mwhite28/warstat0.htm>.

Wilkinson, Tracy, "24 bodies found near Mexico City." Los Angeles Times. 14 Sept. 2008. <http://articles.latimes.com/2008/sep/14/world/fg-mexico14>.

Zimmerman, Arthur. "The Zimmerman Note." WWI www. 1917. http://wwi.lib.byu.edu/index.php/The_Zimmerman_Note.

3816818

Made in the USA